Not Fit for Our Society

The publisher gratefully acknowledges the generous support of the Anne G. Lipow Endowment Fund for Social Justice and Human Rights of the University of California Press Foundation, which was established by Stephen M. Silberstein.

The publisher also gratefully acknowledges the generous support of William K. Coblentz as a member of the Literati Circle of the University of California Press Foundation.

Not Fit for Our Society

Nativism and Immigration

Peter Schrag

UNIVERSITY OF CALIFORNIA PRESS
Berkeley · Los Angeles · London

University of California Press, one of the most distinguished university presses in the United States, enriches lives around the world by advancing scholarship in the humanities, social sciences, and natural sciences. Its activities are supported by the UC Press Foundation and by philanthropic contributions from individuals and institutions. For more information, visit www.ucpress.edu.

University of California Press
Berkeley and Los Angeles, California

University of California Press, Ltd.
London, England

Library of Congress Cataloging-in-Publication Data

Schrag, Peter.
Not fit for our society : nativism and immigration / Peter Schrag.—1st ed.
p. cm.
Includes bibliographical references and index.
ISBN 978-0-520-25978-2 (cloth : alk. paper)
1. Emigration and immigration—Social aspects.
2. Emigration and immigration—Public opinion.
3. Emigration and immigration—Government policy.
4. Nativism. 5. Eugenics. I. Title.
JV6121.S35 2010
304.8—dc22 2009042976

Manufactured in the United States of America

19 18 17 16 15 14 13 12 11 10
10 9 8 7 6 5 4 3 2 1

This book is printed on Natures Book, which contains 50% postconsumer waste and meets the minimum requirements of ANSI/NISO Z39.48–1992 (R 1997) (*Permanence of Paper*).

For Ben and Yeung

Mrs. Hutchinson, the sentence of the court you hear is that you are banished from out of our jurisdiction as being a woman not fit for our society, and are to be imprisoned till the court shall send you away.

Governor John Winthrop at the examination of
Anne Hutchinson at the Court at Newton, 1637

Contents

Sources and Acknowledgments

This book originated in newspaper and magazine articles I'd been writing over more than fifteen years on the increasingly intense controversies about immigration and American immigration policy and the many issues related to them. In the course of that work I was often surprised that the great volume of material on the history of American immigration and its discontents, which is often so relevant to our contemporary debates, had been so consistently ignored in those debates—sometimes, it seemed, almost deliberately so. There is a vast amount of it, some going back to the earliest years of the Republic and in some cases to the colonial period—orders of colonial governors; the writings of Benjamin Franklin and Thomas Jefferson and the Declaration of Independence itself; records of congressional hearings and debates; papers and reports of the many groups that have sought to shape immigration policy; "scientific" studies and analyses on the various "races" coming to this country or hoping to come; magazine and newspaper articles; speeches of political leaders; broadsides issued by lobbies and political parties. In addition, there is a rich trove of secondary sources that sheds light not only on our history but on the ideas and organizations at the forefront of today's immigration fight.

I've drawn freely from it, most of it cited in the notes at the end of the book. What could not be fully credited or attributed without cluttering the story with an excess of footnotes and textual distractions are many of the hundreds of journals, magazine articles, cartoons, broadsides, photographs, and other documents I found so useful in the American Time Capsule and other collections of the Library of Congress; the voluminous material in the report of the U.S. Immigration Commission (the Dillingham Commission) and that of the National Commission on Law Observance and Enforcement (the Wickersham Commission); the reports of the House Committee on Immigration and Naturalization and other congressional documents; the historical statistics of the Census Bureau; the immigration documents of the Labor, Commerce, Justice and State departments and the Department of Homeland Security; the papers on eugenics and immigration policy in the Harry H. Laughlin collection of the Pickler Memorial Library at Truman State University in Kirksville, Missouri, and in the Open Collections Program on immigration at the Harvard University Library; the image archive of the Eugenics Movement; the archives of the Eugenics Record Office at the American Philosophical Society in Philadelphia; the Electronic Text Center of the University of Virginia Library; the Avalon Project at the Yale Law School; the California State Archives in Sacramento and the Oregon State Archives in Salem; the electronic archives of the *New York Times* dating back to the 1850s as well as the archives of CNN, the *Los Angeles Times,* and other publications and broadcasters of more recent vintage.

I also relied on more secondary sources—books and journal articles—than I can possibly credit or, in some cases, even recall. Among the most important: Ray Allen Billington's *Protestant Crusade 1800–1860: A Study of the Origins of American Nativism;* John Higham's *Strangers in a Strange Land: Patterns of American Nativism 1860–1925;* Henry Nash Smith's *Virgin Land: The American West as Symbol and Myth;* Vernon L. Parrington's *Main Currents in American Thought;* Oscar Handlin's *Uprooted;* Richard Alba and Victor Nee's *Remaking of the American Mainstream: Assimilation and Contemporary Immigration;* Richard Hofstadter's *Age of Reform: From Bryan to F.D.R.*; Matthew Frye Jacobson's *Whiteness of a Different Color: European Immigrants and the Alchemy of Race;* Richard Roediger's *Working toward Whiteness: How American's Immigrants Became White;* Dowell Myers's *Immigrants and Boomers: Forging a New Social Contract for the Future of America;* Mae M. Ngai's *Impossible Subjects: Illegal Aliens and the Making of Modern America;* Daniel J. Kevles's *In the Name of Eugenics: Genetics and the Uses of Human Heredity;* and Edwin Black's *War against the Weak: Eugenics and America's Campaign to Create a Master Race.*

I'm also grateful to many individuals and organizations—among them Steven Camorata of the Center for Immigration Studies; Douglas Rivlin of the National Immigration Forum; Angela Kelley of the Immigration Policy Center; Michael Fix of the Migration Policy Institute; Jeffrey Passel of the Pew Hispanic Center; Hans Johnson of the Public Policy Institute of California; Professor Belinda Reyes of San Francisco State University; Professor Dowell Myers of the University of Southern California; California state senator Gil Cedillo; James P. Smith of the Rand Corporation; Professor Jack Citrin, director of the Institute for Governmental Studies at the University of California at Berkeley; and Marian L. Smith of the Department of Homeland Security—for their help in research for this book and/or in my reporting on immigration issues over a period of many years. In the course of my research, I also realized again how much I owed to my own teachers of American history and literature, among them Professors Henry Steele Commager and Leo Marx, and to my late friend and Amherst colleague John William Ward.

Last, but far from least, I'm especially indebted to Professor David Hollinger of the University of California at Berkeley; my longtime friends and former *Sacramento Bee* colleagues Claire Cooper and Mark Paul, the latter now of the New America Foundation, for their sympathetic and very helpful reading of an early draft of this book; to Naomi Schneider, my editor at the University of California Press; and, as ever, to Patricia Ternahan for all of the above and a great deal more.

Introduction

It's long been said that America is a nation of immigrants. But for closely connected reasons, it's also been a nation of immigration restrictionists, among them some of the nation's most honored founders. Indeed it would be nearly impossible to imagine the first without the second. And since we were to be "a city upon a hill," a beacon of human perfection to the entire world, there were fundamental questions: Would America be able to refine all the imperfect material that landed on our shores, or would we have to determine what was not perfectible and shut it out? And what would happen when the once-unpopulated continent that badly required large numbers of settlers—unpopulated, that is, except for the Indians—began to fill up?

Our contemporary immigration battles, and particularly the ideas and proposals of latter-day nativists and immigration restrictionists, resonate with the arguments of more than two centuries of that history. Often, as most of us should know, the immigrants who were demeaned by one generation were the parents and grandparents of the successes of the next generation. Perhaps, not paradoxically, many of them, or their children and grandchildren, later joined those who attacked and disparaged the next arrivals, or would-be arrivals, with the same vehemence that had been leveled against them or their forebears

As a German-Jewish refugee from Hitler, I'm personally familiar with a slice of this story, having spent time on both sides of the nativist divide. In the late 1930s my parents and I were on the short end of the nation's immigration quotas. We narrowly escaped Nazi-occupied Europe in 1941 and arrived in the United States on a transit visa (to Mexico), later changed to a visitor's visa. We didn't formally immigrate until 1947. In the first years after our arrival, I and my friends in New York, several of us not yet citizens, endlessly lampooned people we called Japs, wops, and guineas; told jokes about fairies; assumed, often despite the protests of our anguished parents, that the Germany of our grandparents had always been a place of boors absolutely bereft of culture. In wartime especially, denial or rejection of one's heritage was the price one proudly paid for assimilation.

Most Americans have long forgotten—if they ever knew—the history of the sweeps and detention of immigrants of the early decades of the last century. Those sweeps were not terribly different from the heavy-handed federal, state and local raids of recent years to round up, deport, and too often imprison illegal immigrants, and sometimes legal residents and citizens along with them. But it's also well to remember that nativism, xenophobia, and racism are hardly uniquely American phenomena. What makes them significant in America is that they run almost directly counter to the nation's founding ideals. At least since the enshrinement of Enlightenment ideas of equality and inclusiveness in the founding documents of the new nation, to be a nativist in this country was to be in conflict with its fundamental tenets.

This book grew out of more than two decades of writing about immigration and the bitter battles that have been waged over immigration law and policies since the mid-1980s. It seeks to trace the complex history linking nearly three centuries of ideas, uncertainties, and conflicts about what America is, who belongs here, what the economy needs and doesn't need—who, indeed, is an American or is fit to be one—to our contemporary controversies and ambivalence about immigration and its many related questions. In that multigenerational process, nativism, always an essential element in what one writer described as "the nation's self-image of innocence and exceptionalism in a decadent world," has had a long and, one might say with only a touch of irony, an honorable history, going back to the very beginnings of British settlement.[1]

American exceptionalism echoes through colonial complaints about the estimated forty thousand British convicts sentenced to transportation who were arriving on American shores in the eighteenth century—"the dregs, the excrescence of England." All of the colonials, said Samuel Johnson, were "a race of convicts [who should] be content with anything we allow them short of hanging." In the same era came

Benjamin Franklin's warning (in 1751) that Pennsylvania was becoming "a Colony of Aliens, who will shortly be so numerous as to Germanize us instead of our Anglifying them and will never adopt our Language or Customs any more than they can acquire our Complexion."[2] Later, Jefferson worried about immigrants from foreign monarchies who "will infuse into American legislation their spirit, warp and bias its direction, and render it a heterogeneous, incoherent, distracted mass."[3]

Although already fading into obscurity, one of the most vocal and paradigmatic of latter-day immigration restrictionists, Colorado Republican Tom Tancredo, echoed much of that. Briefly a candidate for president in 2008 and, until shortly before his retirement from the House of Representatives that same year, leader of the Congressional Caucus on Immigration Reform—meaning immigrant exclusion—Tancredo liked to boast about his immigrant Sicilian grandfather. Tancredo forgot that his grandfather belonged to a generation widely regarded by the WASP establishment and many other Americans of the early 1900s, when he arrived, as genetically and culturally unassimilable—ill-educated, crime-prone, diseased. Yet Tancredo, like many of today's immigration restrictionists, echoed the same animosities. "What we're doing here in this immigration battle," he said in one of the Republican presidential debates in 2007, "is testing our willingness to actually hold together as a nation or split apart into a lot of Balkanized pieces"—not so different from Jefferson's "heterogeneous, incoherent, distracted mass."[4] Like other contemporary restrictionists, Tancredo's portrayal of Mexican immigrants was almost identical to the characterization of the Italians, Jews, and Slavs of a century before, and of the Irish and Germans before them, people not fit for our society.

If Franklin's and Jefferson's opinions turned out be of little practical consequence—Franklin later changed his mind; Jefferson in his purchase of Louisiana gobbled up a whole foreign (mostly French) culture—the nineteenth century provided an endless chain of more significant examples. Among them, Know-Nothingism and the anti-Irish, anti-Catholic virulence that swept much of the nation in the 1850s, waned briefly during and after the Civil War, and then flourished again for more than half a century after 1870: "No Irish Need Apply" (later, "No Wops Need Apply"), "Rum, Romanism, and Rebellion," and then "The Chinese Must Go" and, as the ethnic Japanese on the West Coast were interned after Pearl Harbor, "Japs Keep Moving." The magazine cartoonists' pirates coming off the immigrant ships in the 1880s and 1890s were labeled "disease," "socialism," and "Mafia." And always there was the shadow of the Vatican, looming to take over American democracy and, more ominously, seducing the nation's schoolchildren.

In almost every generation, nativists portrayed new immigrants as not fit to become real Americans: they were too infected by Catholicism, monarchism, anarchism, Islam, criminal tendencies, defective genes, mongrel bloodlines, or some other alien virus to become free men and women in our democratic society. Again and again, the new immigrants or their children and grandchildren proved them wrong. The list of great American scientists, engineers, writers, scholars, business and labor leaders, actors, and artists who were immigrants or their children, men and women on whom the nation's greatness largely depended, is legion. Now add to that the story of Barack Obama—who was not just the nation's first African American president, but also the first American president who was the son of a father who was not a citizen—and the argument becomes even less persuasive. Yet through each new wave of nativism and immigration restriction, the opponents of immigration, legal and illegal, tend to forget that history, just as Tancredo forgot that his Sicilian grandfather (who he says arrived as a "legal immigrant") came at a time when—with the exception of the Chinese, most of whom were categorically excluded beginning in 1882—there was no such thing as an illegal immigrant.

• • •

The list of factors contributing to the surge of anger, xenophobia, and imperial ambition in the two generations after 1880 is almost endless: the "closing" of the frontier and the western "safety-valve" in the 1890s;[5] industrial expansion and depression-driven cycles of economic fear; urban corruption and the rise of the big-city political machines. Mostly Democratic, they patronized new immigrants more interested in jobs, esteem, and protection—and were often more comfortable with their values of personal and clan loyalty than with the abstract WASP principles of good government and efficient management that fueled the Progressive movement and that most of the nation's respectable small-town middle class grew up with.

Many Progressives, as the historian Richard Hofstadter pointed out, joined moderate conservatives "in the cause of Americanizing the immigrant by acquainting him with English and giving him education and civic instruction." Still "the typical Progressive and the typical immigrant were immensely different, and the gulf between them was not usually bridged with much success in the Progressive era."[6] The Progressivism of academics like the sociologist John R. Commons and the influential labor economist Edward A. Ross, both close associates of Governor and later Senator Robert M. La Follette of Wisconsin, and the ethnic and cultural beliefs of nativism grew from the same roots: good government was an Anglo-Saxon legacy. Along with their confident sense of racial superiority came the heightening fear, bordering on panic in some circles, of our own immigrant-infected racial degeneration. It resounded through Ross's work, through Madison Grant's influential *Passing of the Great Race* (1916), through the writings of Alexander Graham Bell and countless others in the first decades of the twentieth century, and in the hearings and debates of Congress. In the face of the inferior, low-skill, low-wage but high-fecundity classes from southern and eastern Europe, demoralized Anglo-Saxons would bring fewer children into the world to face that new competition.[7] Grant's theme of racial extinction would later be picked up in books like Lothrop Stoddard's very successful *Rising Tide of Color* (1920) and would continue to echo through books like Richard Herrnstein and Charles Murray's *The Bell Curve,* published in 1994. To this day, these ideas are circulated (and promoted and defended) by the Virginia-based self-described "racialist" *American Renaissance* online magazine, which offers reprints of Stoddard's book for sale.[8]

But probably the most representative, and perhaps the most influential, voice for immigration restriction in the 1890s and the following decade was that of Representative (later Senator) Henry Cabot Lodge of Massachusetts, the paradigmatic Boston Brahmin, later leader of the isolationists who kept the United States out of the League of Nations in the 1920s. Lodge's articles and speeches warning of the perils of the rising tide of immigrants from southern and eastern Europe—many of them mere "birds of passage" who only came to make a little money and then return to the old country; many more bringing crime, disease, anarchism, and filth and competing with honest American workers—drove the debate and presaged many later arguments against immigration. By 1926, in congressional testimony about restricting Mexican immigration, Lodge's bird had become a pigeon—a "homer" who "like the pigeon . . . goes back to roost."[9] The late Harvard political scientist Samuel Huntington's restrictionist book, *Who Are We?* published in 2004, is shot through with Lodge-like fears.

There were countless reasons for the old patricians to be worried—and they weren't alone. The overcrowded tenements of the nation's big cities were incubators of disease and violence that put ever more burdens on schools, the police, charities, and social agencies. And so, in words and tones not so different from today's, members of Congress and other national leaders heard increasingly loud warnings about the social strains and dangers the immigrants imposed. Similarly, checking the rising political participation of the new urban immigrants and the power of the big-city machines that challenged the Anglo-Saxon establishment's authority—and in the view of a whole generation of muckraking reformers, corrupted democracy itself—was an obligation that the reformers were certain couldn't be escaped. The same fear had resonated through the Know-Nothings' nativist platforms of the 1850s, which, in calls for tighter voter requirements in elections, continues to run through conservative American politics.[10] As John Higham characterized him in his seminal study, *Strangers in the Land,* the nativist, "whether he was trembling at a Catholic menace to American liberty [or] fearing an invasion of pauper labor," believed "that some influence originating abroad threatened the very life of the nation from within."[11] Higham, writing in the early 1960s, could just as well have been writing now.

What's striking is how many immigration restrictionists came, and still come, from a Progressive or conservationist background. Madison Grant was a trustee of New York's American Museum of Natural History and active in the American Bison Society and the Save the Redwoods League. David Starr Jordan, the first president of Stanford, a respected ichthyologist and peace activist, along with a group of other leading scholars and clergymen, was deeply involved in the race betterment movement that aimed "To Create a New and Superior Race thru Euthenics, or Personal and Public Hygiene and Eugenics, or Race Hygiene . . . and create a race of HUMAN THOROUGHBREDS such as the world has never seen."[12] Like Hiram Johnson (the Progressive who became governor of California in 1910) and the McClatchy family (newspaper publishers in Sacramento and earnest backers of the initiative process, civil service, and municipal ownership of public utilities), many Progressives fiercely battled to forever exclude Asians from immigration and landownership. Why let Asiatics immigrate when the Constitution didn't allow them to be naturalized? "Of all the races ineligible to citizenship under our law," said V.S. McClatchy in Senate testimony in 1924, "the Japanese are the least assimilable and the most dangerous to this country."[13]

Again and again, as I hope this book will show, our history reflects the national ambivalence between the demand for more immigrants to do the nation's work and the backlash against them. Again and again, past debates presage our current immigration dilemmas. During and immediately after the Civil War, many of the states—trying to settle the prairies opened by the Homestead Act or to replace emancipated slaves with cheap labor—created immigration commissions, advertised abroad, and/or sent what were essentially recruiters. The states negotiated low fares with the steamship companies and railroads that brought newcomers, created information centers for new immigrants, and arranged for housing until the new people could get settled. But as backlash developed against what Americans began to regard as the problems they associated with thousands of newcomers in their communities, rules were tightened. As early as 1858, less than a decade after the discovery of gold, California passed an "act to prevent the further immigration of Chinese or Mongolians to this state."[14] Some states enacted legislation allowing for the interstate deportation of criminals, lunatics, and other social misfits to the states they'd come from. In 1901, Missouri prohibited the "importation of afflicted, indigent or vicious children." The states were in the immigration-management business in a big way. One hundred and fifty years later, they would be again.

Almost inevitably the stresses, violence, and insecurity brought by the shift from the agrarian economy and culture of the eighteenth and early nineteenth centuries to the industrial, urban nation that rapidly replaced them were deeply associated with the immigrants who helped build it and often became its most visible casualties. As industrialization, World War I, and the Russian Revolution drew the nation into a globalized world we didn't understand and that, in our founding, we thought we had forever put behind us, they brought yet another round of nationalism and xenophobia. With the war, Beethoven and Bach became composers non grata in American concert halls. States all through the Midwest stopped German-English bilingual education in the public schools. Americans were supposed to eat "liberty cabbage" instead of sauerkraut and their children suffered from "liberty measles." (Eighty years later, when Congress wanted to show the French what-for after they challenged the U.S. invasion of Iraq, the side dish of choice in the capital's restaurants became freedom fries).

Shortly after Armistice came the wave of labor unrest that brought the Red Scare of 1919 and Attorney General A. Mitchell Palmer's roundups and deportation of suspected anarchists and Bolsheviks, many of them immigrants. Although the Palmer Raids flamed out as quickly as they'd begun, the Depression a decade later would bring the widespread detention of Mexicans and other immigrants, not all of them illegal entrants, whose labor had been desperately wanted during the war and was now superfluous.

• • •

Just after the turn of the twentieth century, theories about the inferiority of the new arrivals also began to be reinforced by eugenic "science" that seemed to prove that virtually all the "new" immigrants—Slavs, Jews, Italians, Asians, Turks, Greeks—who arrived in the two generations after 1880 were intellectually, physically, and morally inferior. Henry H. Goddard, one of the American pioneers of intelligence testing, found that 40 percent of Ellis Island immigrants before World War I were feebleminded and that 60 percent of Jews there "classify as morons."[15] Meanwhile, the eminent psychologists who IQ-tested army recruits during the war, convinced that intelligence was a fixed quantity, concluded that the average mental age of young American men was thirteen, that a great many were "morons," and that those from Nordic stocks—Brits, Dutch, Canadians, Scandinavians, Scots—showed far higher intelligence than Jews, Poles, Greeks, and the very inferior immigrants, like Grandfather Tancredo, from southern Italy. "The intellectual superiority of our Nordic group over the Alpine, Mediterranean and negro groups" wrote Princeton psychologist Carl C. Brigham, who popularized the army data after the war, "has been demonstrated."[16] Only "negroes" were less intelligent than southern and eastern Europeans, a point made again by Columbia University psychologist Henry Garrett, former president of the American Psychological Association, when he cited the army test results in his testimony against school desegregation in one of the cases leading to the 1954 *Brown* decision.[17] Despite the growing volume of critical analyses debunking the racial theories and the shoddy science of the eugenicists, the miasma of racialism lived on.

But in the long chain connecting the country's historical nativism, the eugenic "science" of the 1920s and 1930s, and its shifting immigration restriction policies, past and present, it was Harry Laughlin who was far and away the most prominent single link, both between eugenics and immigration policy and between the nativist ideology in the immigration policies of the 1920s and the present. Laughlin, superintendent of the Eugenics Record Office (ERO) at Cold Spring Harbor, New York, from its founding in 1910 until 1939, was the author of such eugenic treatises as the *Report of the Committee to Study and to Report on the*

Best Practical Means to Cut Off the Defective Germ-Plasm in the American Population (1914).[18] Laughlin was a major promoter—call him the godfather—of eugenic sterilization in this country and the legitimization it gave racist sterilization in Nazi Germany, whose eugenic policies he lavishly praised. In 1921, Laughlin had also become the "expert eugen ics agent" and semiofficial scientific advisor to Representative Albert Johnson's House Committee on Immigration and Naturalization, which wrote the race-based national origins immigration laws of 1921 and 1924 that would be the basis of U.S. policy for the next forty years and, in some respects, well after.

It took Johnson's committee four years of fiddling to find the formula that would achieve the desired ethnic immigration makeup without blatantly confessing racism and thus (among other things) risking diplomatic difficulties and too obviously trampling on the nation's founding ideals. The number of immigrants from any particular country, excepting Asians, who were already excluded, and people from the Western Hemisphere (including Mexico) who were exempt from the new quotas, was capped, first, at 2 percent of a country's estimated share of the foreign-born, not in 1910 or 1920, the most recent censuses, but in 1890, when northern Europeans dominated the population of foreign-born. In 1924, the formula was changed to make it cosmetically more defensible, but the proportions were nearly the same as is if they'd been based on the 1890 numbers. Even when immigrants from favored nations didn't fill a given year's quota, the quotas for other countries would remain fixed. As late as 1965, John B. Trevor Jr., the patrician New York lawyer who was the son of the man who devised the national origins formula, would testify against repeal of the origins quotas, warning that "a conglomeration of racial and ethnic elements" would lead to "a serious culture decline."[19]

Laughlin spent his thirty-year career at the Eugenics Record Office reinforcing the belief, shared by legions of social reformers, Margaret Sanger among them, that "vicious protoplasm" had to be bred out of the native stock or, better yet, kept out of the country altogether.[20] In 1937, while still at the ERO, Laughlin also became the cofounder and first director of the Pioneer Fund, whose prime research interest has been—and continues to be—race and racial purity. Arthur Jensen, the Berkeley psychologist who caused an uproar in the late 1960s and early 1970s with work purporting to show that blacks were intellectually inferior, and thus would never benefit from better schools, got more than $1 million from the fund.[21] Stanford physicist William Shockley's

Foundation for Research and Education in Eugenics and Dysgenics got $188,000 in Pioneer funding. Murray and Herrnstein's *The Bell Curve*, which argued that group differences in IQ between blacks and whites were primarily genetic, and which included a sympathetic discussion of "dysgenic pressures" in contemporary America, some coming from inferior immigrants, relied heavily on the work of researchers funded, according to one estimate, with $3.5 million in Pioneer money.[22] The president of the fund in 2008 was J. Philippe Rushton, whose research purports to show a hierarchical order in the development of races, with Mongoloid (Asians) at the top, whites in the middle, and Negroid at the bottom, all of it accompanied by an inverse correlation between intelligence and the size of genitalia.

Through Laughlin and the Pioneer Fund particularly, the institutional, personal, and ideological links and parallels run almost directly from the eugenics and nativism of the first decades of the twentieth century to the present. Between the mid-1980s and the mid-1990s, the Pioneer Fund contributed roughly $1.5 million to the Federation for American Immigration Reform (FAIR), the organization started by the Michigan ophthalmologist John Tanton in 1979 that is probably the most influential immigration restriction organization in America today. FAIR, the Center for Immigration Studies, and its sister organizations have been essential sources of information for the radio and TV talkers, the bloggers and the politicians leading the immigration restriction campaign. They were also the primary generators of the millions of faxes and e-mails that were major elements in the defeat of the comprehensive immigration reform bill and the "shamnesty" of the Dream Act in 2007. In Congress, both were accomplished with the threat of filibusters and by putting the immigrant's face on inchoate economic and social anxieties—the flight of jobs overseas, the crisis in health care, the tightening housing market, the growing income gaps between the very rich and the middle class, and the shrinking return from rising productivity to labor.

We can't see the jobs that no longer exist or that were shipped overseas, but we can see the crowded schools and the Latinos waiting for day jobs in the parking lot at Home Depot. The descriptions of Mexicans taking jobs away from American workers, renting houses meant for small families, crowding them with twelve or fourteen people, and jamming their driveways with junk cars were often true but inevitably echoed the rhetoric of an earlier age. In 1900 also, "inferior" people were brought in as scabs, crowding tenements, bringing disease, crime, and anarchy (now become "terrorism"). The new arrivals of 2000, too, endangered the nation and lowered living standards to what Edward Ross a century ago called their own "pigsty mode of life."[23]

• • •

To anyone who's followed the latter-day arguments against immigration or the characterization of the hazards that immigrants, legal and illegal, pose to the nation's economy, culture, social stability, and system of government—to any reader of Samuel Huntington's book or Hoover Institution historian Victor Davis Hanson's *Mexifornia,* or any reader of Pat Buchanan or watcher of Lou Dobbs on CNN or listener to Rush Limbaugh or the scores of other radio talkers who've made illegal immigration their prime issue—the warnings of the immigration restrictionists of the nineteenth and early twentieth centuries have to be eerily familiar. The nation is being "flooded"—another old metaphor—by people from backward places that make them culturally or politically unfit for assimilation. They are people (mostly men) who come here only to make money to send back to the old country, have dismally low levels of education, bring leprosy and other dangerous diseases, drive up crime rates, and never have much interest in becoming Americans. The "Palatine boors" who would Germanize Pennsylvania have become Mexicans polluting the language with Spanglish. In recent years, the use of the word *illegal* as a noun has itself carried overtones of—even become a synonym for—*Mexican.*[24]

Like John Tanton, most of our contemporary immigration restrictionists vehemently deny that they are either nativists or racists. And since both are fuzzy words, the defense is often hard to refute. In the age of Obama, the overt, nearly ubiquitous racialism of the Victorian era, like eugenic science, is largely passé and certainly no longer respectable. Eugenic sterilization is gone. The race-based national origins immigration quotas of the 1924 Johnson-Reed immigration act have been formally repealed. But modern arguments against immigration echo, often to an astonishing degree, the theories and warnings of their nativist forebears. In Tanton's journal *The Social Contract,* the blatantly predatory image of Rome that ran through nativist tracts in the nineteenth century has been replaced by more subtly worded (and imaged) but equally inflammatory renditions of the Vatican as the two-faced exploiter of immigration to further its own imperious (and imperial) strategy.

Although few of the arguments are new, there's not much awareness of their long history. The gloomy warnings about the threat of Mexican *reconquista* to what Huntington calls the "Anglo-Protestant culture that has been central to American identity for three centuries" go back even farther than the Progressive era: in Boston in the 1840s, Catholic priests were alleged to be using young girls for their sexual pleasure and Rome was conspiring with the Hapsburgs to take over the American West. Henry Cabot Lodge, Theodore Roosevelt, and countless others warned about the foreign threat to Anglo-American culture at the turn of the last century. And as early as 1928, sixty years before Huntington put pen to paper, Harry Laughlin reported to Congress that "during the last few years [the Mexican] has come here in such great numbers as almost to reverse the essential consequences of the Mexican War. The recent Mexican immigrants are making a reconquest of the Southwest more certainly . . . than America made the conquest of 1845, 1848 and 1853."[25]

None of this is to say that the great numbers of undocumented immigrants—much less the total of all immigrants living in the United States, at 14 percent roughly equal, as a percentage of the total population, to the immigrant population in the peak years of a century ago—aren't a legitimate national policy concern, whether economically, culturally, politically, or psychologically. How many immigrants, particularly low-skilled immigrants, can the nation assimilate in what period of time? How much is a society still dominated by non-Hispanic white voters willing to tax itself to support generous services for people regarded not merely as "others" but in many cases "others" who have no legal right to be here? No developed society can tolerate totally uncontrolled borders next to an underdeveloped nation—now a nation also battered by drug-gang corruption and violence—and the unchecked immigration of unskilled people that it produces. Conversely, in the coming decades, when retiring American baby boomers are going to leave huge gaps in the labor force, and when the proportion of Americans of working age will decline precipitously even as the rank of retirees shoots up, who will do the work or support the health and pension benefits of those retirees? As a growing body of research is making clear, the answers to these questions will almost certainly depend on multinational strategies, not merely on fences, walls, and sweeps of fields and factories.

• • •

The politics of immigration restriction and American nativism from the colonial era—and particularly since the mid–nineteenth century—to the immigration battles of the twenty-first is one of the most complex and confounding stories in U.S. history. As historians like the great Oscar Handlin have pointed out, in many ways the narrative of immigration *is* American history. But the immigration battles of the past also constitute a great cautionary tale. Within eight years of the passage of the 1924 Johnson-Reed national origins quota immigration law, immigrants of the prior four decades and their children, long spurned by Republicans and often disengaged from national politics, were so closely attached to the urban (Democratic) machines of New York, Boston, Baltimore, Chicago, Cleveland, Philadelphia, and countless other cities that they became central to the New Deal coalition that swept into office in 1932 and that would control national politics for most of the following three decades.

The 2008 election of Barack Obama, in which so-called minorities made the crucial difference, underlines the long-range consequences of anti-immigrant politics. George W. Bush and his political "boy" genius Karl Rove, for all their other political miscalculations, understood that, which is why they pushed so hard for immigration reform. ("Some in the party seem pleased," said former Bush speechwriter Michael Gerson with prophetic accuracy, after the defeat of the comprehensive immigration reform bill in 2007. "They should be terrified.")[26] Our history seems to tell us that nativism and a fierce backlash to immigration, however harsh, are frequently rearguard tactics of groups that feel besieged. In a healthy democracy—by definition—they rarely have a future. Obama's election in 2008, which would not have been possible without the overwhelming voter support of African Americans and Latinos, should have made that perfectly obvious.

As I hope this book makes clear, American nativism and our historic ambivalence about immigration—at times vigorously seeking newcomers from abroad, at other times shutting them out and/or deporting them—is deeply entangled both in economic cycles and in the uncertainties of our vision of ourselves as a nation. A self-proclaimed "city upon a hill," a shining model to the world, requires a certain kind of people. But what kind? Do they have to be pure Anglo-Saxons, whatever that is, which is what many reformers at the turn of the twentieth century believed? Or could it include Tom Tancredo's grandfather and all those "inferior" southern Italians, the Greeks, the Slavs, the Jews, even finally, the Indians, Filipinos, the Chinese, and the dirty Japs of 1942? Did American democracy begin at Runnymede in 1215? Was the frontier the great shaper of the American character, as Frederick Jackson Turner believed? Or was it formed by the Enlightenment Englishmen who invented the country in 1787? Can America take the poor, the "tempest-tost," the "wretched refuse" "yearning to breathe free" and make them a vital part of that city? If we began in perfection, how could change ever be anything but for the worse?

As far back as the 1840s, even a sympathetic foreign observer like Alexis de Tocqueville expressed concerns that American cities contained "a multitude of Europeans [chiefly Irish] who have been driven to the shores of the New World by their misfortunes or their misconduct; and they bring to the United States all our greatest vices, without any of those interests which counteract their baneful influence. As inhabitants of a country where they have no civil rights, they are ready to turn all the passions which agitate the community to their own advantage." He worried that the size of cities was "a real danger which threatens the future security of the democratic republics of the New World" and that might not be contained without a federal "armed force."[27]

Conversely, it's equally hard to ignore the unvarnished racial, religious, and xenophobic bigotry that was so often laced through American nativism and sometimes still is. Among the other ironies of that history is that immigration restriction in the twentieth century—along with World War II—was probably a major contributor to the assimilation, and what some historians call "the whitening," of the millions of southern and eastern European immigrants who had once been widely regarded as a serious danger to the vigorous Nordic "germ-plasm" that had made the country great. Low levels of immigration probably also made it easier to enact the great New Deal and Great Society social programs of the 1930s, 1940s, 1950s, and 1960s, just as the existence of those programs today—welfare, health, state and federal support for higher education—probably reinforces pressure to restrict immigration and drive out illegal aliens now. Obama's decision in the summer of 2009, when he was trying to enact a major federal health-care program, to put off until 2010 the immigration reform he'd promised during his campaign, may well have been partly based on similar considerations. Putting undocumented immigrants on the road to legalization even as a broad federal health program was being negotiated would have been an explosive political mix.

Among the most frequently cited differences between the European immigrants of a century ago and today's mostly Latino and Asian immigrants is the relative ease of long-distance travel and the proximity of the Mexican border, and thus the continuing effect of the Spanish language and alien cultures. But similar arguments were made a century ago—about lingering native languages and cultures and about people just coming to earn money here and then returning to the old country with no interest in, or loyalty to, America. Indeed, a great many did go back, Italians and Poles in particular. In the modern case, according to most research, efforts to tighten immigration enforcement at the Mexican border in the past two decades—the quadrupling of the Border Patrol, the fences, the electronic sensors and other technology, the surveillance aircraft—paradoxically have increased the resident population of illegal aliens. By making the crossing more expensive and dangerous, the stepped-up enforcement has discouraged seasonal north-south migration. Instead, more and more workers simply stay in the United States, send for their families, and become permanent de facto residents, even when they began with—or in some cases still have—no intention of becoming Americans.

The Herrnstein-Murray argument that modern immigration is easier than at the turn of the twentieth century, when there were "no guarantees, no safety nets" and "the immigrant had to make it on his own" and thus made for "a crackerjack self-selection system" for attracting "brave, hard working, imaginative, self-starting—and probably smart" men and women, is as fatuous now as it was in 1994 when they published it.[28] Nativists of a century ago also argued that the introduction of the steamship and the groundwork of the early pioneers had made things too easy for recent arrivals. Those early pioneers had been the true settlers, while all who came after were mere immigrants. But ask any of the tens of thousands of Latinos who've risked the Arizona desert or the mountains beyond or extortion by the smugglers who brought them here, or those who crossed the Pacific from China in sealed shipping containers, or the Haitians who risked drowning in leaky boats off the Florida coast—ask them how easy it was and what guarantees or safety nets they enjoyed.

• • •

This book is not about the history of immigration per se, but rather about America's twenty-first-century immigration debates in the context of the politics, ideas, organizations, and movements that have sought to restrict immigration since the mid–nineteenth century and in some instances long before. It's about the lessons we should have learned from the past, written in the hope that as immigration policy is again debated, as it must be, those lessons will finally be part of the conversation. Because ideas, groups, and in some cases individuals often defy chronological classification—many of the ideas and ambiguities this book is concerned with are woven through the generations—this story itself sometimes transcends chronology. Questions about who belongs here, dilemmas about race and citizenship—like questions about who we are as Americans—resonated through American history even before Hector St. Jean de Crèvecoeur's classic attempt in 1782 at defining "this new man [who] is either an European, or the descendant of an European," yet who was also a creature of a process where "individuals of all nations are melted into a new race of men."[29]

Yet the controversies over immigrants and immigration policy can nonetheless roughly (if somewhat arbitrarily) be divided into historical periods. With one exception, the book's chapters correspond to that chronology.

Chapter 1 (A City upon a Hill): From the early settlements through the adoption of the Constitution and the first naturalization laws when only whites of "good moral character" could be naturalized, through the Alien and Sedition Acts of 1798, and the xenophobia and anti-Catholicism of Know-Nothingism to the Civil War.

Chapter 2 ("This Visible Act of Ingurgitation"): From the Civil War through the turmoil of industrialization and urbanization, and the accompanying waves of "new immigrants" from southern and eastern Europe, to World War I; Henry Cabot Lodge and the Immigration Restriction League; the Chinese exclusion laws; Madison Grant's *Passing of the Great Race.*

Chapter 3 ("Science" Makes Its Case): The interplay between intelligence testing and eugenics, on the one hand, and preexisting beliefs and prejudices about race and ethnicity on the other; their effects on immigration policy.

Chapter 4 (Preserving the Race): The Red Scare of 1919 and the roundups of radicals in the Palmer Raids that followed the war; the individuals, ideas, and events that shaped the Johnson-Reed national origins quota act in 1924 and other immigration policy in the 1920s.

Chapter 5 (The Great Awhitening): From 1924 through the Depression and the peak years of the Ku Klux Klan, the anti-Semitism of Father Charles Coughlin and Gerald L.K. Smith, the growing movement to exclude and deport Mexicans and other Hispanics, to the passage of the Hart-Celler Act in 1965 repealing the national origins scheme; the effects of immigration restriction on the success of the New Deal in enacting its programs and in the Americanization of the once-unacceptable southern and eastern European immigrants through hard times and World War II.

Chapter 6 ("They Keep Coming"): The backlash against the growing numbers of illegal immigrants; anti-immigrant laws in Texas and

California; the Immigration Reform and Control Act of 1986; the failure of Congress to enact comprehensive immigration reform in 2007; the wave of state and local laws beginning in 2007 to drive illegal aliens out, and the wave of federal raids on worksites and other places where illegal aliens were concentrated.

Chapter 7 (A Border without Lines): Controlling immigration; our current immigration controversies and the changed geographic, economic, and political landscape that confounds the debate; the nation's latter-day anti-immigration organizations and the media figures who retail their material; the possibility—perhaps the necessity—of creating a North American community.

Epilogue: The lessons, ironies, and paradoxes of a complex immigration history unfortunately too often forgotten in our contemporary immigration debates.

Necessarily, this story touches on a great range of issues. Transgenerational ideas, institutional links, and controversies run through it. It's tied up with national expansion and nationalism itself, with intelligence testing and eugenics, with foreign policy and economic cycles, with the coming of the North American Free Trade Agreement, with globalism and offshoring, with the growing diaspora of third-world immigrants moving from California and the Southwest into the South and Midwest, and with the contradictions inherent in advocating equal treatment for immigrants on the one hand and ethnic-group rights and affirmative action on the other.

In order to limit my scope, I've focused on the events, ideas, and politics that seem particularly relevant to and instructive for our contemporary controversies and dilemmas: questions about the assimilability of different groups, about language and culture, about the capacity (or needs) of the economy for foreign workers and the countervailing fear of disease, terrorists (née Mafiosi and anarchists), and crime. Some of this history has been told elegantly in other books and in other research on which I partially rely and that I gratefully acknowledge elsewhere. But to my knowledge, no one source has explicitly traced the more than two centuries of ironically telling contradictions and historical currents to our present immigration debates and to the greatly altered political and economic landscape in which we will conduct these debates in the future. These are the issues I hope to explore and the story I hope to tell.

CHAPTER I

A City upon a Hill

From the beginning, Americans' perceptions about who they were and their hopes for whom they wanted to be necessarily embodied a deep strain of ambivalence. If this New World "shall be as a Citty upon a Hill," a beacon to the world, as the Puritan John Winthrop devoutly hoped it would become, where the "eies of all people are upon us," how do we judge others of varying degrees of difference who want to come among us? How do we decide who does and does not fit the decreed model, religiously or ethnically or racially, and with what justification? If the Puritans had come for the freedom to practice their religion, could others of different faiths—or those who, like Roger Williams, the religious separatist who professed "soul liberty" not subject to the established authorities—come to practice theirs in the Puritan community as well?

Winthrop's sermon, delivered on the *Arabella* during, or perhaps before, the long Atlantic crossing in 1630, professed that "when God gives a special commission He looks to have it strictly observed in every article," a hefty self-imposed burden. But it was also Winthrop, as governor of Massachusetts Bay Colony, who decided seven years later that Anne Hutchinson was "not fit for our society," not because she was a theologically liberal heretic—far from it—but because, like Williams, she was an anticlerical dissenter who, in Winthrop's judgment at her trial, had "spoken divers things, as we have been informed, very prejudicial to the honour of the churches and ministers thereof."[1]

Hutchinson's crime, if that's what it was, came closer to civic sedition than to religious heresy. Hutchinson, a midwife, had been running weekly meetings of women who, in trusting their own theological reasoning, chafed against the doctrines and laws of what had become an established state church in a society where only church members could vote, where church attendance was compulsory, and where inner religious belief had to bend to the Bible and the ministers officially ordained to interpret it. "As I understand it," she is said to have replied to one of the charges leveled against her, "laws, commands, rules, and edicts are for those who have not the light which makes plain the pathway." So what was her offense? She had the light, it just wasn't theirs. But that statement made it easy for her judges to conclude that she was a "thing not tolerable nor comely in the sight of God, nor fitting for your sex."[2]

The ambivalence about who belonged was almost inevitable. Americans were creating something out of a wilderness, a vast territory of great natural riches and beauty hidden from European civilization from the beginning of time, and now providentially revealed. Some thought that what the country was or would be was a given, but in fact Americans were making it up as they went along. "The land was ours," as Frost wrote, "before we were the land's."[3] To the west was all that open territory, ready (if you ignored the Indians) for the taking, a gift from God. It wasn't surprising, then, that a lot of Americans believed they were divinely blessed above all others. As early as 1837, in a Phi Beta Kappa address at Yale, the influential Yankee clergyman Horace Bushnell observed that America's God-ordained destiny was no "less sublime than to be opened, at a certain stage of history, to become the theater wherein better principles might have their action and free development. Out of all the inhabitants of the world, too, a select stock, the Saxon, and out of this the British family, the noblest of the stock, was chosen to people our country; that our eagle, like that of the prophet, might have the cedars of Lebanon, and the topmost branches of the cedars, to plant by his great waters."[4]

It soon became clear to people like Bushnell that Providence alone wouldn't take care of that. The chosen people of the New World would have to do a little choosing of their own. While "the free mingling and crossing of races would doubtless be a great benefit to the stock," Bushnell continued, "the constant importation, as now, to this country, of the lowest orders of people from abroad, to dilute the quality of our natural manhood, is a sad and beggarly prostitution of the noblest gift ever conferred on a people. Who shall respect a people, who do not respect their own blood? And how shall a national spirit, or any determinate and proportionate character, arise out of so many low-bred associations and coarse-grained temperaments, imported from every clime?"

Maybe, in fact, the American settlers had been led to a new Garden of Eden, even the original Garden, as the Mormon prophet Joseph Smith Jr. regarded Jackson County, Missouri, the place where, in the 1830s, Mormons "planned to build a kingdom of God that would eventually redeem the United States and, finally, the world."[5] But if this was a providentially bestowed Garden, a place of perfection, soon to be narrowed to Anglo-Saxon perfection, as Bushnell already had it, and as generations of subsequent American thought would have it, then it would inevitably also be beset by snakes, demons, and, of course, witches. Principal among the despoilers, depending on the time and place, was an ever-changing list of outsiders. Benjamin Franklin's worries (in 1751) about the effect that "Palatine boors" might have in "Germanizing" Pennsylvania echoed controversies dating back to the first decades of the eighteenth century, when Mennonites, having fled Swiss persecution, first to Alsace, then to London, began, along with a growing number of Germans, to emigrate to the New World. Pennsylvania governor William Keith (in 1723) had at first welcomed German workers from New York who chafed over that colony's defective land titles and what they regarded as abusive treatment. But the resulting spike in immigration to Keith's colony quickly generated fear—what one writer called "a panic"—that "Pennsylvania might cease to be a British province. . . . [The] great number of foreigners from Germany, strangers to our language and constitution [Governor Keith told his council], daily dispersed themselves immediately after landing, without procuring certificates from whence they came or what they are [a practice that] might be of very dangerous consequence, since by the same method, any number of foreigners, from any nation whatever, enemies as well as friends, might throw themselves upon us."[6]

The colonial assembly passed a bill prohibiting all foreign immigration, but Keith vetoed it as excessively harsh. In the meantime, "to counteract the German element, every inducement on the part of England was employed to encourage the transportation of English servants to the colonies," which, among other things, meant shipping convicts as indentured servants: seven years' service for ordinary crimes, fourteen years for those sentenced to death. That in turn led to new measures in the colony prohibiting the importation of "Old persons, Infants, Maimed, Lunatics or Vagabonds or Vagrant persons."[7] But by midcentury close to half the colony was of German extraction, and so much German was spoken and read, so much business conducted in German, and so many books published in German—in 1732, Franklin himself printed Philadelphia's first German-language newspaper (which soon failed)—that despite all the attempted restrictions, German probably came as close to being an accepted language as Spanish is in contemporary California or Texas. In 1831, barely a century after Keith vetoed the anti-German immigration bill, the Commonwealth authorized bilingual education in German and English in Pennsylvania's public schools. "I suppose in a few years [Franklin had wryly observed in 1753] it will also be necessary in the Assembly to tell one-half of our legislators what the other half says. In short, unless the stream of importation can be turned from this to the other colonies . . . they will soon so outnumber us, that all the advantages we have, will, in my opinion, be not able to preserve our language, and even our Government will become precarious."[8]

The ambivalence about foreign immigrants—often the vacillation from welcome to calls for exclusion in the same generation or even the same decade—bordered on the commonplace. America needed to attract people to work—if not the Palatine German then the East London cutpurse and prostitute. Jefferson's words in the Declaration of Independence indicted King George for trying to "prevent the population of these States; for that purpose obstructing the Laws for Naturalization of Foreigners; refusing to pass others to encourage their migrations hither, and raising the conditions of new Appropriations of Lands." But six years later, in 1782, Jefferson warned of the dangers of immigrants who knew nothing of democracy. This country, he wrote, "is a composition of the freest principles of the English constitution, with others derived from natural right and natural reason. To these nothing can be more opposed than the maxims of absolute monarchies [whose emigrants] will bring with them the principles of the governments they leave, imbibed in their early youth; or, if able to throw them off, it will be in exchange for an unbounded licentiousness, passing, as is usual, from one extreme to another. It would be a miracle were they to stop precisely at the point of temperate liberty."[9] Democracy itself might not be capable of assimilating these alien elements.

What made such doubts most notable was their articulation, even in this case by the author of the Declaration of Independence, on behalf of a nation among whose founding ideals was the belief that all men were born equal and presumably had equal potential. It was the radicalism of the American Revolution and the great ideals in whose name it was fought that resounded around the world, made us that city upon a hill, and gave the New World its special meaning. In revolution we became Americans by choice, no longer Englishmen. From that moment on, becoming an American was far removed from the classic determinants of nationality and citizenship—nativity, ethnicity, religion. It was and would continue to be an affirmative act, something previously unknown in the world and in many places still unknown.

• • •

In loud echoes of the doctrinal battles of the Old World, the most suspect of the immigrant elements were Catholics. The first Americans, in New England as in New York and Virginia, were children of the Reformation and the brutal battles that accompanied it. What nearly all shared, despite their differences, was "the fear and hatred of Rome."[10] In his draft of the first postindependence New York State Constitution (1777), John Jay, one of three authors of *The Federalist* and later the first chief justice of the United States, included the requirement that, in order to be naturalized, immigrants "shall take an oath of allegiance to this State, and abjure and renounce all allegiance and subjection to all and every foreign king, prince, potentate, and State in all matters, ecclesiastical as well as civil."[11]

Jay, the grandson of French Huguenots persecuted by Catholics, was a firm believer that Catholics couldn't maintain their allegiance to the Church, and hence the pope, and still be loyal American citizens. As a member of the New York provincial congress, Jay wanted to "build a wall of brass around the country for the exclusion of Catholics" and proposed harsh restrictions in the New York charter but was deterred by his fellow delegate, Gouverneur Morris, among others. The singular American exception was Maryland under Lord Baltimore and the Calvert family, which was founded as a haven for English Catholics. But Maryland quickly became embroiled in religious strife and Puritan persecution of Catholics and Anglicans, which didn't end until the restoration of the fifth Lord Baltimore as colonial governor in 1658. He swore that he was a Protestant.

America's providential destiny, of course, also encompassed the question of slavery and race, which would haunt the nation from its beginnings. Indians, "not taxed" (and fit for removal or worse), and black slaves were not citizens at all. Blacks were officially recognized in one of the Constitution's great compromises—and in the first example in a long history of census tampering and race confusion—as three-fifths of a person. In 1790, Congress passed one of the world's most liberal naturalization laws, requiring only two years of residence in the country—extended to five in 1795—and one year's residence in a particular state, provided that the applicant was a white person of "good moral character." The law allowed any court, state or federal, to grant citizenship, a policy that "led to a motley array of more than five thousand high and low courts exercising such jurisdiction by the turn of the twentieth century."[12] The law's liberality probably wasn't surprising since eight members of the Constitutional Convention were born abroad, as were eight signers of the Declaration of Independence—and who knows how many thousands of other Americans of their time?[13]

Nonetheless, it took only three years for the nation to have second thoughts, not for ethnic or religious reasons but because President John Adams and his Federalist allies in Congress were determined to check the growth of the immigrant vote, most of which went to the Jeffersonian Republicans. Their instrument was the Naturalization Act of 1798, part of the Alien and Sedition Acts, which lengthened the period required for citizenship to fourteen years and authorized the president to deport foreigners considered dangerous. In 1802, after winning the presidency in 1800, the Jeffersonians revised the Naturalization Act to restore the five-year requirement. Again, as in 1790 and 1795, naturalization was limited to "free white persons" of "good moral character," limits that wouldn't change, for blacks, until the adoption of the Fourteenth Amendment after the Civil War and, for Asians, until the middle of the twentieth century.[14]

As a practical matter, the question of naturalization wasn't all that important in the antebellum years because citizenship was still primarily a state matter in which the federal government concerned itself very little, if at all. The issue was left, with virtually no guidance, to those hundreds of state and local judges. Nor did the question of citizenship include immigration. Until well after the Civil War, in the words of the official historian of the U.S. Immigration and Naturalization Service, "the United States achieved a policy of free and open immigration largely by failing to legislate on the subject."[15]

But the questions, confusion, and controversy about race that began even before the 1787 convention—at first just about the black-white/north-south dichotomy, then about a growing multiplicity of ethnicities—have long since crept into countless national policy areas, including, for the past 150 years, questions about immigration. Who qualified as white—not just in the one-drop-of-blood sense—but in determining whether Arabians or Armenians or Syrians or Punjabis or Filipinos or Hawaiians were white and thus eligible for naturalization? Was the Mexican white or, as part (or maybe largely) Indian, something else? (Under the Treaty of Guadalupe-Hidalgo, Mexicans in the territory taken from Mexico after the war in 1848 could choose to become Americans, so essentially they became white.) Was a person who was half white and one-fourth Chinese and one-fourth Japanese white? From the last decade of the nineteenth century to the 1940s, federal courts confronted more than fifty such questions.[16] In the early years of the twentieth century, Congress drew a map with a line around northern Europe to help determine which people from which "nations" should be eligible for naturalization and immigration and which should not. In the case of Mexicans, Latino advocates who "fought to be included on one side or the other of the American racial divide" have alternately played it both ways, first pushing for whiteness to avoid the stigma of being seen as black, then for nonwhiteness when affirmative action seemed to open the way for significant economic or political advantages.[17]

Through much of the nineteenth century and the first half of the twentieth, Americans, if they thought at all about people from other countries, tended indiscriminately to conflate race, ethnicity, nationality, and class. The definitions changed over time as new generations of immigrants and their descendants from southern and eastern Europe—Jews, Italians, Slavs, Greeks—became Americanized and thus inferentially whitened. But for most of three centuries there was also the fuzzy line between American (meaning white Anglo-Saxon Protestant) and other (meaning mostly Catholic and, when it suited the occasion, Jewish). And as the Irish, impoverished by the potato famine, began to arrive in great numbers in the late 1840s and 1850s, and a great many others—Germans and French for the most part—came after massive crop failures on the continent and the failed revolutions of 1848; as the Chinese came to California during and after the Gold Rush; and as some eighty thousand Mexicans in the newly annexed territories of the Southwest became American citizens after the Mexican War and the Treaty of Guadalupe-Hidalgo, the line became brighter and the backlash more virulent.

Roughly 143,000 immigrants arrived in the United States in the 1820s. In the 1830s, that number jumped to nearly 600,000; in the 1840s, to 1.7 million; and in the 1850s, the decade before the Civil War, to 2.3 million, including an exploding proportion from Ireland. In the two decades between 1820 and 1840, about 700,000 Irish immigrants arrived in the United States; in the next two decades, more than 1.7 million came. By 1850, counting the second and third generations, New York was more than one-third Irish. In Boston, from 1845 to 1855, the Irish-born population increased from one in fifty to one in five. There were similar increases in other eastern cities.[18]

It would have been surprising if those millions, many of them radically different from the way older Americans imagined themselves, had been greeted with complete equanimity. The newly arrived Irish, many of them with limited skills and education, were crammed into filthy, overcrowded housing, sometimes ten to a room, sometimes in backyard sheds that once housed tools or animals, as thousands of Latinos would be 150 years later. As William Shannon, himself the son of Irish immigrants, put it in his masterful history of the American Irish, they "challenged the code of the community at almost every point." In competing for jobs, they threatened "the old occupational structure of master, journeyman and apprentice." They did not seem to practice the Yankee virtues of thrift, self-denial, and sobriety. Although the Irish were a crucial source of labor for the nation's expanding industries, the proper people, who then called themselves "native Americans," saw "that the Irish . . . posed problems in housing, police, and schools; they meant higher tax rates and a heavier burden in the support of poorhouses and private charitable institutions. . . . They seemed drunken, dissolute, permanently sunk in poverty."[19] At the very least, said a writer in the establishmentarian *North American Review* in 1835, we had better consider "the ignorant and improvident refugee in the light of a pupil whom we have five years given us to form into an intelligent and virtuous citizen. If we fail in any considerable degree to attend to his wants, to supply his defects, to enlighten his darkness, we must of course expect that our chalice will be returned in time to our own lips, charged with the ingredients of insubordination, recklessness and venality."[20]

Assimilation rarely worked as smoothly as succeeding generations imagined it. As Shannon and others have pointed out, "appearances were partly deceiving."[21] It was rare for first-generation Irish workers to have rags-to-riches stories. To rise economically in the customary American fashion (which, in fact, was not all that customary), said Shannon, "demanded more in terms of relentless perseverance, financial acumen, familiarity with new ways, and plain good luck than the first Irish generations were able to summon from themselves or their environment. . . . But within the bounds of what was humanly possible, the Irish laborers and housemaids of the first generation were not so thriftless as the native stereotype of them suggested."[22] But the stereotype, which began to spread even before the great midcentury wave of Irish immigration, stuck. It would be applied to other generations of immigrants from that day to this, often based on the same realities of immigrant life. To be that special creature, the American, there always had to be the Other.

• • •

The anti-immigrant, anti-Irish, anti-Catholic reaction began well before the peak years of Irish immigration, much of it—though hardly all—concentrated in the northeastern states and directed against the Irish and German Catholics who had concentrated there, men and women who, in their drinking and debauchery, seemed to have no respect for the Puritan mores around them (whiskey for the Irish, as the cartoonists portrayed it, beer for the Germans). In August 1834, a nativist mob, many with Indian-style painted faces, broke into the Ursuline convent and school in Charlestown, near the site of the battle of Bunker Hill across the Charles River from Boston, and torched it. The spark was the rumor that a young nun, a former Protestant, was being held there against her will. But much of the fuel was provided by increasingly virulent sermons by prominent Protestant ministers, among them the celebrated Reverend Lyman Beecher (father of Harriet Beecher Stowe and Henry Ward Beecher), who warned of the dangers of creeping "Popery" and foreign immigration. A few years earlier, Beecher had accepted the presidency of Lane Theological Seminary in Cincinnati to carry on his battle against what he and many others were certain was a popish plot, perhaps with the support of the Hapsburg emperors and other European despots, to swamp the American West with a flood of Catholic immigrants and destroy American democracy. Beecher had come east on a speaking tour to raise money and sound the alarm.

What made the Ursuline convent a particularly inviting target was that it had been educating both Catholic girls and the daughters of upper-crust liberal Boston Protestants, most of them Unitarians, which added class animosity to religious hatred. As a dozen nuns and sixty pupils fled out a back door, and as the growing crowd of spectators cheered, the mob burned the place nearly to the ground. In the days following, they returned to torch whatever was left of the Ursuline property, while other rioters roamed through Boston. The violence was widely condemned by proper Bostonians, even by ministers like Beecher, who a few days earlier had fanned the flames. "The soul sickens," said the *Boston Evening Transcript,* "the heart grows faint—the whole man is unmanned, at the very thought of the abomination. The perpetrators of the outrage must be ferreted out, and summarily punished as they merit." But the arson trial of the "perpetrators"—those who were brought to trial—was so slanted against the prosecution and so laced with further rumors about the Catholic iniquities at the convent that the jury quickly acquitted them.[23]

Two years later, in 1836, perhaps prompted by the Charlestown savagery and the story about the captive nun that helped provoke it, came the publication of *The Awful Disclosures of Maria Monk, as Exhibited in a Narrative of Her Sufferings During a Residence of Five Years as a Novice and Two Years as a Black Nun, in the Hotel Dieu Nunnery in Montreal,* a purportedly true story similar to hundreds of other priest-nun scandal tales dating back to the Middle Ages. (Monk's story had been preceded shortly before by the publication of Rebecca Theresa Reed's much less sensational *Six Months in a Convent,* which was about her brief sojourn with the Charlestown Ursulines.)[24] In *The Awful Disclosures,* the innocent Maria, a Protestant convert to Catholicism, was told by her mother superior that her duty "was to obey the priests in all things; and this I soon learnt, to my utter astonishment and horror, was to live in the practice of criminal intercourse with them."[25] The priests weren't allowed to marry and sacrificed their worldly pleasure for the faith, she was told. Thus it was the nuns' duty, in this clerical harem (she said it was housed in a great gothic edifice with secret doors and hidden passageways, including one from the priests' seminary nearby), to sacrifice for them. After being impregnated by a priest, she said, she escaped from the Hotel Dieu with her baby and fell into the welcoming arms of some New York Protestants.

The 1830s and 1840s saw the publication of a long list of anti-Catholic tracts and books, among them Beecher's own *Plea for the West* and a collection of letters to the *New York Observer* by the painter Samuel F.B. Morse, who was then working on his telegraph, about the alleged Catholic plot to conquer America. Morse called it *A Foreign Conspiracy against the Liberties of the United States.*[26] But far and away the biggest sensation was *The Awful Disclosures.* The book, heavily promoted by the nativist journal the *American Protestant Vindicator,* went through scores of printings in the United States and abroad—it sold some three hundred thousand copies within months of its publication, feeding the anti-Catholic passions that had been simmering for years and prompting an equally inflammatory sequel. A modern edition is still available. Shannon called it the *Uncle Tom's Cabin* of the Know-Nothing movement.

Charlestown was only the beginning. In succeeding years, there would be more anti-Catholic, anti-Irish riots in the textile-mill city of Lawrence, Massachusetts, in Baltimore, and in New York, among other places. But the most deadly and dramatic came in Philadelphia, the City of Brotherly Love, in May 1844, even before the heyday of the Know-Nothings and before large numbers of Irish potato famine immigrants began to arrive. Battles over prohibition, partisan animosity, literature like Maria Monk's *Awful Disclosures,* and fear of the growing "foreign influence" of the Catholic hierarchy in Philadelphia public schools triggered a wave of anti-Catholic demonstrations that quickly turned violent. The immediate spark in Philadelphia was the partial success of Bishop Francis Patrick Kenrick's insistence that Catholic public schoolchildren not be forced to read the King James version of the Bible but be allowed to read the Catholic Douai Bible instead. He eventually got the Philadelphia school authorities to rule that children whose "parents were conscientiously opposed" to the King James version might be excused from class, which immediately produced the fear that Protestant kids might also be deprived of the Bible. It brought a manifesto from ninety-four Protestant clergymen calling "the attention of the community to the dangers which . . . threaten these United States from the assaults of Romanism."[27]

The clergymen got help from an unlikely source: Lewis Levin, a nativist Philadelphia lawyer and politician who was the son of a Jewish South Carolina family. Said to be a brilliant orator, Levin, a leader of both the city's temperance movement and its American Republican Party, would soon be elected to Congress. As the editor of the nativist *Philadelphia Sun,* Levin appears to have been the key figure in organizing the nativist protest march into the Third Ward of the working-class (largely Irish) suburb of Kensington. As the demonstrators gathered, Levin mounted a box and called on the crowd to battle "the deleterious effects of Popish interference in the elective franchise," which predictably brought a barrage of rotten vegetables and rocks from neighboring residents, most of them Irish weavers, who drove the marchers off. In the ensuing riot, Levin appears to have done his best to calm the crowd and spare one of the churches under attack. Barely a day later, however, another nativist demonstration triggered three more days of rioting in which Protestant mobs burned homes and two churches and in which scores of people were badly beaten and several killed.[28]

Two months later, on July 4, there was yet another nativist demonstration, staged by a crowd estimated at between five thousand and thirty thousand people, inflamed by a report that the priest of St. Philip de Neri Church in the Philadelphia factory suburb of Southwark, fearing an attack, had stored guns and ammunition in his church. (The arms delivery had in fact been legally sanctioned by Governor David Rittenhouse Porter for use by militia in defending the church.) Word about the mob, "those near the church composed of the worst class of mankind, the very dregs of the canaille of a large city," brought the militia to restore order, though not until after a prolonged shootout outside the church with the demonstrators, who had managed to find their own cannon, and not until thousands of Catholics had fled. All told, according to one credible study, some 45 were killed in the May and July riots and 145 wounded. Most were nativists shot by the militia. Property damage was substantial.[29]

The 1844 riots were not the first episodes of civil unrest in Philadelphia—there had already been attacks on blacks and abolitionists, and there would be more, both in Philadelphia and elsewhere on the East Coast. At the same time, as Shannon points out, each week during the spring and summer in the antebellum years, "vessels arrived in Atlantic Coast seaports carrying more Irish to America. While the battle raged intermittently in the streets between the Irish and natives, the reinforcements poured forth from steerage. The Irish were slowly winning the battle for the city against the Protestant lower class by sheer force of numbers."[30] But those numbers didn't check the nativist politics of the American Party, the American Republican Party, the fraternal Order of the Star Spangled Banner, the Order of United Americans, the American Patriot Party, and the various other orders, clubs, groups, and publications that were part of the Know-Nothing movement of the 1850s. Predictably, the arrival of the new immigrants only reinforced the warnings of clerics like Beecher, who saw the West as the new Eden: "If the potentates of Europe have no design upon our liberties, what means the paying of the passage and emptying out upon our shores of such floods of pauper emigrants—the contents of the poor house and the sweepings of the streets—multiplying tumults and violence, filling our prisons, and crowding our poor houses, and quadrupling our taxation, and sending annually accumulating thousands to the polls to lay their inexperienced hand upon the helm of our power?"[31]

But Shannon was probably right that what had been happening on the streets in the 1830s and 1840s was increasingly channeled into political-cultural movements and into the groups that were spawned by them, the Know-Nothings paramount amount them. Know-Nothings—the label came from the organized refusal of early adherents to answer questions about the group—were pledged to resist "the insidious policy of the Church of Rome, and all other foreign influence against our republican institutions [and] to place in all offices of honor, trust, or profit, in the gift of the people, or by appointment, none but native-born Protestant citizens"[32]

The Know-Nothings were a strange animal, a conglomerate of largely Protestant blue-collar workers in the Order of the Star Spangled Banner and similar fraternal Masonic-like organizations. Beginning as the Native American Party in New York—in most places it ultimately called itself the American Party—it drew in part on the remains of the Whigs (who were fracturing over slavery), in part on the status anxieties of an urbanizing age, in part on reaction to high levels of Catholic immigration, and in part on reaction to (or avoidance of) the bitter sectional battles over slavery in the admission of new states in the western territories. In retrospect, the American Party also served as a halfway house for voters confused by the crazy quilt of parties growing out of the slavery dispute and the fight over the new territories, or abandoning the old parties on the way to the new Republican Party in 1860. In the 150 years since, it's also become clearer that religious bigotry was hardly the only contributing impulse to the formation and success of the movement.[33] Among working men and women, many of whom were themselves badly exploited, there was a genuine fear that foreign immigration would jeopardize their jobs and welfare, and would be used to further undermine their rights and wages. But whatever the prime impulse, the core of the American Party program was nativist, rooted in a fear of "the imminent peril of Freedom, both from internal and external foes," perhaps even fear for the Union itself. The call, as in the platform of the Massachusetts party, was for:

1. An essential modification of the naturalization laws, so that the immigrant shall not be permitted to exercise the elective franchise until he shall have acquired a knowledge of our language, our laws, and institutions, by a residence in this country of at least 21 years.
2. Stringent penalties against the fraudulent transfer of naturalization papers, and such a description of the peculiarities of the person applying for naturalization as shall render such transfer impossible.

3. Opposition to all attempts to establish foreign military or political organizations to perpetuate old national prejudices; but encouragement of such a policy as shall tend to assimilate the foreign population, in sentiment and feeling, with the mass of American citizens.
4. Efficient laws to prevent the deportation of criminals and paupers, by foreign authorities, to our shores; but a hospitable reception to the persecuted and oppressed of every clime.
5. The withholding of grave diplomatic and political trusts from persons of foreign birth.
6. The right to worship God according to the dictates of one's conscience to be preserved inviolate. Resistance to any politico-ecclesiastical hierarchy, which, through its agents, be they pope, bishops or priests, who attempt to invade this right, or acquire political power. Hence, we rebuke all attempts to appropriate the public funds to the establishment of sectarian schools, all attempts to exclude the Bible as a text-book therefrom, and all attempts to wrest from the laity and give to the priesthood the control of church property. We also rebuke in indignant terms such sentiments as those put forth by the representatives of the Papal Power. That "Protestantism has no rights in the presence of Catholicism," "that Religious liberty is only to be endured until the opposite can be established with safety to the Catholic world," and that "the Catholics of America are bound to abide by the interpretation put upon the constitution of the United States, by the Pope of Rome."
7. That the Bible as the source and fountain of all true and rational liberty should be made the basis of all popular education, and should be open to, and in the hands of every man, woman and child. And the man or men who may attempt directly or indirectly to shut it out of our schools, or to keep it from the hands and hearts of our people or any portion of them, should be deemed guilty of a crime against society, and of treason against liberty itself.[34]

There were other versions of the creed, though the underlying anxieties and motifs were fundamentally the same: "The strange, cruel monster of Rome," as one tract put it, "can never amalgamate with the fair and beautiful form of America. Liberty and Despotism are two eternal opposites."[35] Some party documents called for "the repeal of all Naturalization Laws," the election of "none but native Americans to office," "war to the hilt on political Romanism," and "more stringent and effective Emigration [*sic*] Laws," among other planks.[36] In Pennsylvania, in what (again) seemed more like a Masonic initiation than enlistment in a political party, prospective members were required to swear "before Almighty God, and these witnesses, that you will not divulge or make known to any person whatever the nature of the questions I may ask you here, the names of the persons you may see here or that you know that such an organization is going on as such, whether you become a member or not!" They were also to promise on oath "to elect only native-born citizens to office, to the exclusion of all foreigners and Roman Catholics."[37]

The focus on excluding immigrants from elected office and denying them voting rights, either for twenty-one years or maybe forever, was partly based on pure nativism—call it a principled belief in the incompatibility between the freedom of republican government and the despotic power of the Church—but also in part on the fact that the Democratic Party was more hospitable to immigrants and Catholics, organized them, and got the lion's share of immigrant votes. Shortly after the election of 1844, in which Democrat James K. Polk narrowly beat Henry Clay, the Whig, Horace Greeley's Whiggish *New York Tribune* complained:

> Our Country's greatest living Statesman has just been defeated . . . and the benignant system of Nation Policy with which he is identified has been frustrated by what is termed the Foreign Vote. That is, the Man and the Measures preferred by a large majority of Americans born have been crushed by the vote of Two Hundred Thousand Immigrants from Europe whom we have admitted to an equality of Political Rights with us. While we Americans born are nearly all in some degree educated and informed on questions of National policy, these are in good part unable to read or write, and many of them unable to speak our language. While we very generally consider and discuss the great Political questions of the day, these concern themselves very little, inform themselves less, with regard to the Tariff, the Annexation of Texas, or whatever may be the ruling topics of the time, but band together as Irishmen, Germans, or whatever they may be, to secure personal or clannish ends.[38]

None of this should sound strange in the context of the nation's current immigration debates, with their demands for stricter immigration laws, a "Real ID," policies to discourage voting by immigrants and ethnic minorities who might not be citizens (or maybe are), and insistence on Christian—meaning Protestant—Bible reading in public schools. There are only two major differences. One is that many states in the antebellum years *did* allow noncitizens to vote—as did the federal government in the Kansas and Nebraska territories under the 1854 act organizing the territories, providing that the voter intended to become a citizen and took an oath to support the Constitution. The other difference is that the Know-Nothing parties of the 1850s were often prolabor in their economic positions—many of the rank and file were clerks, mechanics, teachers, and preachers, nearly all Protestant, of course. They condemned "all attempts to appropriate the public funds to the establishment of sectarian schools," which meant Catholic schools, since the public schools were, for all intents and purposes, Protestant schools.

In Massachusetts, the party also strongly opposed slavery, favored the regulation of industry and laws to protect workers, and promoted women's rights. But when they won control of the governor's office, both houses of the legislature, and most other high state offices, the Know-Nothings, few of whom had any political experience, proved themselves hopelessly incompetent and often corrupt. Thus, despite the passage of some appeals to Congress on tightening naturalization laws, so little was accomplished that the session became a joke. The legislature's so-called Nunnery Committee, in its attempt to investigate convents, not only visited schools, convents, and colleges, but lavishly entertained itself at dinners in the company of women who were associated with nunneries only in the Elizabethan sense. (The diocesan *Boston Pilot* took delight in pointing out that one committee member had visited nuns "of the type who got him intoxicated and stole $71 from him.") Most of the Know-Nothing legislators did not survive the next election.[39]

Notwithstanding the mess in Massachusetts, what may be most telling about the Know-Nothings in their various political incarnations is the degree of electoral success they quickly achieved and how quickly they vanished as a political movement. In the short ten years of their existence—roughly the decade of the 1850s—they elected not only governors in Delaware and Massachusetts, but also captured all the top state offices as well as a majority in their legislatures. In the mid-1850s, 43 of the 234 members of the U.S. House were Know-Nothings. Know-Nothings also held mayoral and other city offices in Boston, Salem, Chicago, and Philadelphia. Most surprising were the elections in 1855 of American Party members J. Neely Johnson as governor of California—a majority of the legislature was also captured by nativists—and Stephen P. Webb as mayor of vigilante-plagued San Francisco. Those successes led to the growing expectation that the American Party, which would nominate Millard Fillmore as its candidate the next year, would win the presidency in 1856. But, like the nation a few years later, the party's convention broke apart over the slavery issue, with the northern wing joining the new Republican Party in supporting John C. Fremont. In November, Fillmore won just 23 percent of the popular vote and carried only one state, Maryland, with eight electoral votes. In that same election, only fourteen Know-Nothings were elected to Congress.

Just a year earlier, Abraham Lincoln had written a letter to his longtime friend Joshua F. Speed, declaring that he was not a Know-Nothing:

> How could I be? How can anyone who abhors the oppression of negroes be in favor of degrading classes of white people? Our progress in degeneracy appears to me to be pretty rapid. As a nation we begin by declaring that "all men are created equal." We now practically read it "all men are created equal, except negroes." When the Know-Nothings get control, it will read "all men are created equal, except negroes, and foreigners and catholics." When it comes to this I should prefer emigrating to some country where they make no pretence of loving liberty—to Russia, for instance, where despotism can be taken pure, and without the base alloy of hypocracy.[40]

Lincoln's implicit recognition of the incompatibility between nativism and the country's founding ideals would have been an appropriate epitaph for Know-Nothingism. Yet after the Civil War ended in the triumph of the industrial north, and the rate of immigration resumed its upward trend, Know-Nothing's ghost refused to rest. On the contrary, as immigration increased in the decades after the war—and as the country tried to deal with hundreds of thousands of former slaves, as the railroads and the Homestead Act opened great expanses of the West, as the cities and all they brought with them grew, and as demands from bishops for public support of parochial schools inflamed the controversies over religion in schools—questions about who belonged and who did not, about the designs of Rome, about race and nationality, and about what was and was not American became increasingly intense and unsettling. These were the same questions Crèvecoeur had tried to answer a century before. Now they were more perplexing and divisive than ever.

• • •

The great nineteenth-century exception to the patterns of nativism in Boston and Philadelphia was the West Coast, California particularly, where most foreign immigrants were non-European and where, from the start, race and ethnicity could be more easily defined to delineate who qualified—or might eventually qualify—as American and who didn't. The first California constitution, drafted at a convention that included Californios—Mexicans whose residence preceded annexation—and adopted in 1849, gave the right to vote to "every white male citizen of the United States, and every white male citizen of Mexico, who shall have elected to become a citizen of the United States."[41] Tellingly, in light of later controversies about official languages, it was published in both English and, as the "Constitucion del Estado de California," in Spanish. Its forty-seven signers included one Carrillo, one Dominguez, one Rodriguez, one Covarrubias, one De La Guerra, one Pico, one Vallejo, one Sansevaine, and one Pedrorena.

Because slavery and the fate of free blacks—not Mexicans, much less the Chinese, who were not yet a major presence—was the overriding issue of the time, especially in the territories, it was the question of slavery and the in-migration of blacks, free or slave, that dominated the California constitutional debate. One delegate "had heard of gentlemen having sent to the States for their negroes, to bring them here, on condition that they should serve for a specified length of time. He was informed that many had been liberated with this understanding. After serving a few years, they were to be set loose on the community. He protested against this. If the people of this Territory are to be free against the curse of slavery, let them also be free from the herds of slaves who are to be set at liberty within its borders."[42]

But the link with other races would soon become obvious. In the West, the nation's long-established white-black dichotomy almost immediately set the pattern for the treatment of any class of people defined as something other than white, among them the "mongrel" Latinos and the Chinese who, in 1849, were just beginning to arrive.

• • •

Like the rest of the nation, California in the early Gold Rush era needed immigrant labor but wasn't quite sure whether to welcome Chinese workers, even for hard, dangerous low-status jobs—first in mining, then in the construction of the Central Pacific Railroad through the Sierra, later in construction of the Sacramento River levees—or to shut them out to protect white workers. Beginning in 1849, the Gold Rush brought thousands of people from every part of the world—Frenchmen and Brits across the Atlantic; Chilean miners up the West Coast; Americans traveling overland from the East or by ship down one coast, by land across the isthmus of Panama, and by ship up the other; Australians and Chinese across the Pacific. While many were welcomed, for the Chinese the welcome quickly wore off.

Unlike the Irish in the East or even Latinos in the Southwest, the Chinese (and as they began to appear in the West, all Asians) were a truly alien breed. "Prior to the Gold Rush," as historian H.W. Brands put it, "few Americans had ever encountered a Chinese outside the pages of Marco Polo; as a people, the Chinese seemed almost as exotic as Martians would have been to a later generation of Americans."[43] They were not Christians of any sort. Their language, dress, grooming, diet, gambling, use of opium, and, paradoxically, their willingness to work incredibly long hours as contract laborers under terrible conditions put them in a class far beyond any that most Americans had ever encountered. Even black slaves were Christians and spoke English. But as more Chinese women arrived in the generation following the Gold Rush, what probably made the Chinese most "exotic" was the common practice of polygamy and the easy acceptance of prostitution, both of which were deeply offensive to most Americans—and certainly not part of any version of a city upon a hill.[44]

Shortly after admission to the Union in 1850, California enacted the Foreign Miners' License Tax Law, which imposed a twenty-dollar monthly fee—an exorbitant sum at the time—on any foreigner engaged in mining in California. The law, despite its name and its impact on angry Mexican miners, many of whom had only a few years before regarded this territory as theirs, was primarily aimed at Chinese miners. (Ironically, because it proved a major source of revenue for state and local government, and because the Chinese miners, being almost all single men, required little in the way of schools or other public services, the law briefly protected them from the exclusionary pressure of the mid-1850s.)[45] But the law proved hard to enforce and was repealed less than a year later.

That hardly ended the animosity toward "coolie laborers"—so labeled because of a misreading of the terms that bound those who were contract workers—and the "tide of Asian immigration" that Governor John Bigler warned about in his 1852 message to the legislature. The lawmakers, he said, should ask Congress for a measure prohibiting the Chinese from mining. In the interim, he also wanted another tax on foreign miners—a new version was duly enacted—and, since the Chinese would never honor an oath, he also called for the disqualification of Chinese people as jurors and witnesses in California courts. Although he didn't specifically propose it, he also made clear his interest in some sort of law that would more or less exclude Chinese immigration altogether. States had a right, he reasoned, to bar the entry of dangerous classes.[46]

Two years later, the state Supreme Court would grant part of his wish, racially classifying Chinese with Indians, blacks, and mulattoes, thus preventing them from testifying at trials involving white people in the state's courts. In this particular case, George Hall, a white man, had been convicted of murdering a Chinese gold miner, in large part on the testimony of Chinese witnesses. The court overturned the conviction, adding the dictum that, in the words of Chief Justice Hugh C. Murray, "even in a doubtful case, we would be impelled to this decision on grounds of public policy. The same rule which would admit [the Chinese] to testify would admit them to all the equal rights of citizenship, and we might soon see them at the polls, in the jury box, upon the bench, and in our legislative halls."[47]

Along the way, Murray also came up with the novel thesis that because Columbus thought that San Salvador, where he first landed, was an island in the China Sea, the Chinese were really Indians.[48] In effect, Murray's decision was a license for whites to harass and abuse Chinese immigrants, both in the goldfields and elsewhere, with near impunity. Two years after the *Hall* case, Mariposa County ordered all Chinese to leave the county. Those failing to comply were to be "subjected to thirty-nine lashes and removed by force of arms."[49] As a growing number of Chinese miners succeeded in claims abandoned by whites, there were increasing demands that the Chinese be run out, sometimes formalized in petitions and local votes in the gold country, many of them coming against a background of increasing anti-Chinese violence in the camps.

The demands didn't go unchallenged. In San Francisco and in the Central Valley, newspaper commentaries lauded the industrious, moral, and orderly Chinese—not surprisingly since many enterprises depended on them and since they were wanted for domestic labor and the hot, backbreaking work of clearing and reclaiming agricultural land. In some counties, revenue from the 1850 tax on foreign miners was the largest source of income, larger than the property tax. In the words of the *San Joaquin Republican,* a Stockton newspaper, "Have not this race of men . . . discovered new placers, and been . . . the hewers of wood and drawers of water for our citizens? In the cities are they not our attendants in our houses, and in our public rooms? Do they not wash our shirts? The Chinese, in this city alone, must expend, and thus throw into circulation, money to the amount of $500 a day, at the very smallest calculation. This money goes into the hands of our merchants."[50]

And there were protests from the Chinese themselves. After one of Governor Bigler's speeches came a pointed reminder from a leader of San Francisco's Chinese community that "when your nation was a wilderness, and the nation from whom you sprung barbarous, we exercised most of the arts and virtues of civilized life." Some showed signs that, at least when it came to absorbing American racial attitudes, the Chinese were acculturating quickly. A few months after the *Hall* decision, another representative of the Chinese community complained that "your honorable people have established a new practice. They have come to the conclusion that we Chinese are the same as Indians and Negroes, and your courts will not allow us to bear witness. And yet these Indians know nothing about the relations of society; they know no mutual respect; they wear neither clothes nor shoes; they live in wild places and [in] caves."[51]

Later in the decade, the California legislature debated a "Negro Exclusion Bill . . . an Act to restrict and prevent the immigrations to and residence in this State of Negroes and Mulattoes" (marked in the accompanying report as the "nigger bill"), which was similar to laws in a number of other states, most of them in the South and Midwest. Those laws, often in response to workers' petitions, were officially promoted to protect whites from cheap labor, and (paradoxically) because, as in the California proposal, "the negro is by nature indolent and in a state of freedom [and thus] becomes a ready prey to vice." This law would thus protect the state from Negro laziness and the social burdens associated with it, even as it shielded whites from competition in the labor market. But because the legislators couldn't figure out how to distinguish between "legal" black residents who had arrived before passage of the bill (it was proposed that they register and wear tags) and "illegal" immigrants who arrived after its adoption, the bill was dropped.[52]

But that, too, was a temporary reversal. In Salem, Oregon, in 1851, a black saloon keeper and boarding house owner named Jacob Vanderpool was arrested as an illegal resident and jailed for moving into the territory in violation of a law passed by the territorial legislature in 1849 that prohibited the immigration of free blacks after it was passed. He was tried five days later, convicted, and ordered deported.[53] In 1857, the year of *Dred Scott,* Oregonians adopted a constitution that rejected slavery and that was in many ways respectful of civil rights (of whites), that was liberal in its voting qualifications, but that reiterated and broadened the prohibition on the entry of free blacks. "No free negro or mulatto, not residing in this State at the time of the adoption of this Constitution," it said, "shall come, reside or be within the state, or hold any real estate, or make any contracts, or maintain any suit herein. . . . The Legislative assembly shall provide by penal laws for the removal . . . of all such negroes and mulattos." Voters approved that provision by a margin of 8,640 to 1,081. The constitution also called for the "punishment of persons who shall bring them into the State, or employ or harbor them" and provided that "no Negro, Chinaman or mulatto shall have the right of suffrage."[54] Oregon, like many others, wanted to be a white state.

All Negro exclusion laws eventually fell with the ratification of the Fourteenth Amendment in 1868 and the Fifteenth Amendment in 1870. They nevertheless served as models for the rapidly growing movement to exclude Chinese (and later all Asians) from immigration, naturalization, and, in many parts of the nation, from the right to own property and enjoy other civil and commercial rights. In 1859, the California Supreme Court, under a different group of justices—Hugh Murray died in 1857—struck down as unconstitutional California's "act to prevent the further immigration of Chinese or Mongolians to this State," passed by the legislature the year before, which imposed severe penalties on anyone found guilty of helping Chinese to enter California.[55] That provision, too, presaged congressional legislation in the twenty-first century.

The drift was clear: what states like California couldn't do under the federal Constitution, Congress could. It took just over thirty years from the Gold Rush to passage of the federal Chinese Exclusion Act in 1882. The growing pressure in the West and the laws passed by territorial and state legislatures in the intervening decades had often lumped blacks with Chinese (and eventually all other non-Caucasians) on the list of races to be excluded from immigration, naturalization, and the franchise. In 1869, during debate on the Fifteenth Amendment conferring voting rights on all citizens regardless of "race, color or previous condition of servitude," the California Democratic State Central Committee issued an "address to the Voters," asking "Shall Negroes and Chinamen Vote in California?" a question that left no doubt about what the answer should be.[56] What was happening, said historian Najia Aarim-Heriot, was the "Negroization of the Chinese."[57]

• • •

For all the great differences through two centuries of antebellum history among the Northeast, the South, and the Midwest, and the short pre–Civil War decade of white settlement on the Pacific Coast, the fused narratives of those histories generated an almost fully evolved nativist legacy. It's that legacy that set the terms of the nation's self-definition and its immigration and racial policies for the 150 years since. Americans had in effect been preparing for 200 years their response to the immigrant generations of the industrial age and beyond long before they had any clear idea that they were coming. The nation was a gift from God to his chosen people, but a gift that imposed great obligations. "Providence has raised up, and sustained, and qualified the Anglo-Saxon race," as one anonymous mid–nineteenth century writer put it in the *American Whig Review,* a journal that was obsessed with the subject. That Providence required its members "to perform a great work in reclaiming the world; has guided and protected them from temptation, or brought them from it purified, and ennobled by every scene of trial; and has given to them the destinies of the world."[58]

What was never clear—and couldn't be clear—was whether we were engaged in the pursuit of perfection or merely engaged in its nurture and preservation. Our great institutions were themselves ambivalent. The same founding document that, within four years of its drafting, promised freedom of worship and the separation of church and state, reduced blacks to part-persons or, maybe more realistically, to nonpersons, and Indians to less than that. It guaranteed citizens' rights and protections that no prior society had ever promised, if it thought of them at all, but never fully defined who in the future would be entitled to become a citizen. Nor were we sure whether Americanism rested on acculturation, reform, education, and what the Germans called *Bildung,* or whether it would rely primarily on the screening and exclusion of undesirables by race and genes and what, in the first decades of the twentieth century, was to be selective breeding. Notwithstanding those constitutional rights and protections, would the nation's ideals permit state-imposed sterilization of inferiors—in essence doing the Lord's work on the fallopian tubes? It was around these fundamental chasms that so many of our political battles would be fought.

CHAPTER 2

"This Visible Act of Ingurgitation"

The Civil War, like most American wars since, was a powerful assimilator. The two-million-man Union Army, in addition to its black units (most of them commanded by white officers), included at least five hundred thousand foreign-born troops—Irish, British, Canadian, Hungarian, Russian, French, Indian. Among them were Louis Blenker's regiment of Germans, the Italian Garibaldi Guards, and the Irish Brigade, New York's "Fighting Sixty-ninth," which, flying a green banner with the harp of Ireland, established a reputation for its gallantry, most famously at the First Battle of Bull Run. After taking heavy casualties from Confederate fire at Fredericksburg, much of it from Irish troops fighting for the South, it was reorganized under General Thomas Meagher to fight again.[1] Many of those units of immigrants, like Meagher's and Blenker's, were commanded by military veterans of the European uprisings of 1848. Some thirty-eight Union regiments called themselves Irish.

The urban Irish responded quickly to Lincoln's call for volunteers after the attack on Fort Sumter in 1861. But given their intense hatred of blacks, with whom they often competed for low-end jobs, they had never been abolitionists. Most were Democrats, as they remained for more than a century. After the war, William Shannon said in his history of the American Irish, "native-Irish antagonism never again flared in the open violence that had been almost habitual in the generation of 1830–1860. On the fields of Antietam and Fredericksburg and Gettysburg, old hatreds had been submerged and a larger unity forged."[2]

With the coming of the war and the corresponding decline in foreign immigration, Know-Nothingism vanished as an organized movement as rapidly as it had begun a decade before.

But immigrant assimilation was hardly smooth, much less complete. By 1863, the Irish who had rallied to the colors in great numbers at the start of the war had begun to turn against it. After the casualties Irish volunteers suffered, they bitterly resented the Conscription Law of 1863, in part because, like other Americans of the time, they detested any sort of draft, and in part because it allowed the affluent to buy their way out of service. As low-wage workers, the Irish couldn't afford the three-hundred-dollar bounty the law imposed to recruit a replacement, intensifying long-standing class hatreds. The resentment was aggravated by the belief that New York's Irish wards had been assigned larger draft quotas than others (which turned out to be true but probably wasn't intentionally discriminatory), and by Lincoln's Emancipation Proclamation, issued in January 1863, which appeared to turn the war to preserve the Union into a war to free the slaves. Worse, in April 1863, Negro scabs had been hired to break a strike of Irish stevedores on the New York waterfront. The resulting five days of draft riots in July, directed largely at blacks but also at Chinese peddlers, turned parts of the city into a combat zone. There was widespread damage, with an estimated 120 people killed and 2,000 wounded. The riots, it was widely (and incorrectly) believed, were generated by an anti-Union plot organized and fanned by Confederate sympathizers. They were, in fact, far more indigenous.

There was also the growing belief in the North that, because of their role as financiers and suppliers to the Union forces, the biggest war profiteers were Jews—dry-goods merchants, clothing manufacturers, bankers—who had considerable success in getting government contracts, in part because the Union was so broke that many of their established competitors, fearing nonpayment, shunned the business. The belief was so strong that General Ulysses S. Grant issued a directive from his headquarters in Tennessee (which Lincoln overruled a few weeks later) that "the Jews, as a class violating every regulation of trade established by the Treasury Department and also department orders, are hereby expelled from [the territory within Grant's command] within twenty-four hours from the receipt of this order."[3] In fact, it was more than probable that Jewish entrepreneurs, as much as profiteering, were major creditors to the financially struggling Union and essential in keeping the war effort funded. After the war, one of the greatest of them, banker Joseph Seligman, himself an immigrant from Bavaria who had been paid in high-risk government bonds and who would be instrumental in settling the Union's debt, had Grant and General Pierre Gustave Beauregard, the Confederate commander who directed the attack on Fort Sumter, to dinner.[4] (In 1862, the same year that Grant tried to expel Jews from the territory under his control, California, foreshadowing efforts in other states to block employment of illegal aliens in a later era, enacted its "Anti-Coolie Act" to discourage Chinese immigration by imposing a tax on any employer who hired them.)

For all "the larger unity" forged between natives and immigrants and among immigrants during the war—indeed, by virtue of their war service, Irish (and other) immigrants would thereafter regard themselves as complete Americans—the racial and nativist patterns of the prewar generations cast long shadows. As would happen again and again with later arrivals, to the extent that native-Irish unity existed in the last decades of the 1800s, it was nourished in large part by the arrival of new groups of immigrants who seemed even less acceptable than the Irish. There were no notorious church burnings or torchings of convent schools, as there had been in Philadelphia and Charlestown in the 1840s. But the phrase "Irish need not apply" did not vanish from the help-wanted signs in Boston, Harvard did not throw open its doors to arriviste Harps, the battles over religion in the schools continued, and, as the Irish gained political strength in the eastern cities, the Protestant establishment tried to create new governmental institutions to divert and dilute their power. In the 1884 presidential election, Democrat Grover Cleveland narrowly beat James G. Blaine in part because of Catholic reaction to a Republican politician's reference to Cleveland as the candidate of the party of "rum, Romanism, and rebellion."

But it would take another century before a man could, in Al Smith's famous words after his loss to Herbert Hoover in the presidential election of 1928, "say his beads in the White House." The Know-Nothings were gone, but suspicion of Catholics and Catholic plots, especially the shadow they supposedly cast on the "secular" schools, was alive and well. "The Roman Catholic peasantry, who have flowed over into America," said a writer in the establishment *North American Review* in 1879, "are poor, ignorant creatures, who care nothing for the Constitution, whose interests, so far as they have any, are in Ireland and in their creed, and who vote as their priests direct them. . . . The Constitution guarantees liberty of speech and of the press. The Pope says this is the liberty of perdition, and should not be tolerated." If Catholics ever became predominant, the resulting crisis would not be solved with "balloting-papers" but with bullets.[5] "We are not a lot of bigots or of fools," went the poem of the American Protective Association, like the Know-Nothings a semisecret fraternity with Masonic rituals. "But ye Roman Catholic hordes,/We will buckle on our swords,/If you dare meddle with our public schools."[6]

Those nativist attitudes would soon be directed, often in even stronger terms, to the long string of other groups who followed the Irish to America's ports and borders. Old racial stereotypes would be rationalized by the new social "sciences" gaining prominence toward the end of the century and institutionalized into new forms that became the dominant influence in immigration policy for generations. In freeing the slaves, the victory of the Union not only brought potential new competitors into the labor market. It also set the nation more firmly than ever on its steady long-term course to urbanization and industrialization that would bring millions of new immigrants, and ultimately turn the nation away from its agricultural and small-town roots and put it on the iron road to a national economy. The Union victory also hastened the perhaps inevitable extension of America's classic black-white racial dichotomy to the lines that would be drawn between Anglo-Americans and the Italians, Poles, Russians, Greeks, Chinese, Japanese, Syrians, and the scores of other groups who came, or wanted to come, to America's city upon a hill. The attempt to extend the black-white model to other "races" was often a long stretch that brought no end of confusion.

The war itself committed the federal government to the active encouragement of immigration to replace the men serving in the military. In December 1863, Lincoln called on Congress to establish

> a system for the encouragement of immigration. Although this source of national wealth and strength is again flowing with greater freedom than for several years before the insurrection occurred, there is still a great deficiency of laborers in every field of industry, especially in agriculture and in our mines, as well of iron and coal as of the precious metals. While the demand for labor is thus increased here, tens of thousands of persons destitute of remunerative occupation are thronging our foreign consulates and offering to emigrate to the United States if essential but very cheap assistance can be afforded them.[7]

The resulting bill, passed in 1864, provided for the immigration of contract workers who would be committed to repaying their travel expenses out of their first year's wages. In squinting toward indentured servitude, the act quickly ran into unexpected problems and was amended several times. It also produced a backlash when authorities in at least one Swiss canton were reported to be offering to release convicted felons if they emigrated to America. It was repealed in 1868.[8] Federal laws dating back to 1819 had regulated shipping coming into American ports, imposing minimum safety and sanitary conditions and requiring shipmasters to deliver manifests listing all aliens landing in the United States. Among the early opponents of one of those laws requiring better conditions on ships was Lewis Levin, the nativist Philadelphia rabble rouser, elected to Congress in 1844 on a nativist platform, who called it "a bill to afford additional facilities to the paupers and criminals of Europe to emigrate to the United States."[9] Nonetheless, the 1864 act represented the first real federal entry into immigration policy.

Almost (but not quite) by coincidence, the war also brought the Homestead Act, fulfilling the promise of "Free Soil," which before the war had been regarded as a politically powerful weapon to keep not just slaves but blacks generally from the territories, but which had been blocked by the South. The act opened millions of acres of federal land to settlement by native Americans and immigrants both—"land for the landless"—160 acres free to anyone who would build a home, sink a well, and, after five years of the homesteader's own labor, turn those acres to productive use.

• • •

What the historian Henry Nash Smith called the virgin land of the West had long been regarded as the safety valve protecting America from the urban class and labor conflicts plaguing Europe.[10] But during and after the war, the safety valve got a lot of help from public policy. Even during the 1840s and 1850s, some states and territories had actively sought both domestic and foreign immigrants and investors. After the war, the manpower drain of the conflict, the rapid industrialization in the East and Midwest, the new railroads increasing access to the West, and the Homestead Act all opened so much territory and required so much labor that state and territorial legislatures—among them those of Arizona, Kansas, Minnesota, Missouri, Nebraska, Iowa, and Colorado—named commissioners of immigration and/or created boards or bureaus of immigration. Their charge was to advertise abroad or, as in the Kansas law of 1864, "to appoint one or more agents to visit Europe for the purpose of encouraging and directing immigration to this State, to make contracts with railroad and packet companies for the purpose of securing a low rate of fare . . . and perform such other functions as may be necessary."[11] In the same year, Missouri passed legislation "to repair as rapidly as possible the losses of population sustained through the desolation of war" through "the introduction of a people recommended by their loyalty, their industry, and their intelligence. And in order to secure this end every inducement should be offered that class of immigrants, come from whatever portion of the civilized world they may."[12] Never had the nation's governmental policies been so energetic in trying to draw immigrants.

The states also had help from aggressive advertising by railroads—often wildly exaggerated—of cheap acreage (once federal land) and from transatlantic steamship companies, whose fares, reflecting technological improvements and the shorter, easier crossings they allowed, continued to go down. Thus, even as the nation was urbanizing in the East and in California, it was growing in the rural interior. Between 1863, the year the Homestead Act went into effect, and 1900, some six hundred thousand claims were filed for a total of eighty million acres. Those acres and the towns to which they gave life spawned the next great generation of American reformers—Progressive, nativist, and often both in the same person and groups.

Running through and beyond the need for settlers—beyond the advertising of railroads and land companies and, as industrialization progressed, beyond the need for strong backs to work farms, mines, and factories and to build railroads, bridges, sewers, water systems, and streetcar lines—there was the fundamental (and equally radical) idea, going back to the Revolution, that America was a place to get ahead, to make money, and in the process to remake oneself. Open borders were an integral element sustaining that hope. Especially in the half century after the Civil War, nativism in America, despite its centrality in defining national identity, had to struggle as never before against the headwinds of economic interest, local boosterism, and individualistic ambitions.

Nonetheless, the official postwar programs to draw immigrants, "come from whatever portion of the civilized world they may," had a remarkably short life. Within a few years, in the words of historian John Higham, "friendliness turned into fright."[13] Immigration—ever an estimate at best—had dropped from the prewar peak of 428,000 in 1854, a spike primarily driven by the effects of the crop failures on the European continent, the Irish potato famine, and the failed revolutions of 1848, to a low of 92,000 in the first years of the war. The numbers then climbed back to 459,000 in 1873 and to nearly 800,000 in 1882. The swings were far from constant, fluctuating wildly according to (though usually lagging behind) economic cycles, the numbers declining sharply after the depression of 1873, then rising again in the early 1880s. After the doubts had begun to set in about the unalloyed blessings of immigration, Alabama's law of 1907 was far choosier than those of the states that opened their doors in the years during and just after the Civil War. It directed "that immigrants shall be sought from desirable white citizens of the United States first, and then citizens of English-speaking and Germanic countries, France and the Scandinavian countries, and Belgium, as prospective citizens of this State, and conformable with the laws of the United States."[14]

Higham believed that undifferentiated xenophobia rather than dislike of particular "races" and classes of new immigrants underlay the opposition to immigration in the years after 1880. But judging from popular literature and political rhetoric, the national, racial, religious, and class backgrounds of the new arrivals—and sometimes several of them combined—were as important in the nation's declining enthusiasm for open borders as a general dislike of foreigners, concern about the numbers of immigrants, or even the growing pressure from labor organizations fearing competition from low-wage newcomers. Roughly one million Germans arrived between 1881 and 1885, among them a sizable number of Jews. But beginning in the mid-1880s, the sources of that immigration shifted dramatically from northern and western Europe to southern and eastern Europe, bringing millions—Sicilians and other southern Italians, Russians, Poles, Czechs, Hungarians, Romanians, Greeks, Turks, Armenians—who spoke no English. If they weren't more foreign to Anglo-Protestant culture and society than the pre- and postwar Germans, the predominantly middle-class Jews who came with them, and the scruffy Irish of the previous generation, they were nonetheless widely regarded as hopelessly alien by proper Americans like Representative (later Senator) Henry Cabot Lodge of Massachusetts and the Harvard men who were shortly to form the Immigration Restriction League.[15]

Of the roughly 9 million immigrants who arrived in the years 1898–1910, 1.9 million, the largest single category, were listed by the U.S. Immigration Commission (the Dillingham Commission of 1907–10) as "Italian, South," and 1.1 million as "Hebrew." By the commission's calculations, in 1896, 57 percent came from southern and eastern Europe and only 40 percent from the traditional sources. In the first decade of the twentieth century, the ratio grew to a nearly incredible 72:22. This new class of immigrants was also predominantly—and visibly—poor. These were the people whose arrivals at New York's Castle Garden and, after it opened in 1892, at Ellis Island have been so movingly recorded in the classic American immigration photographs and in books and articles like those of Jacob Riis (himself a Danish immigrant) on the wretched conditions in New York's tenements.

Not surprisingly, the founding of the Immigration Restriction League in 1894 coincided almost perfectly with the time when the old Yankees began to lose their grip on northeastern cities, places they'd regarded as theirs by birthright for 250 years. In 1885, Hugh O'Brien had become the first Irish-born mayor of Boston, signaling the beginning of the end of Yankee demographic, cultural, and political domination in the city of the bean and the cod. And then, for the two generations beginning in 1900, Irish mayors were more the rule than the exception: Patrick Collins, elected in 1901; John "Honey Fitz" Fitzgerald, John F. Kennedy's maternal grandfather, elected in 1905 and again in 1909; and, in 1914, James Michael Curley, who had run for his first public office, alderman, from prison and later served part of his last mayoral term in prison again. During his fifty-year career as council member, congressman, and mayor, Curley—the model for Frank Skeffington in Edwin O'Connor's great novel *The Last Hurrah*—turned ethnic politics into an art form. In New York, William Marcy Tweed, though not Irish himself, harnessed the immigrant Irish into the great Democratic political machine that Tammany Hall became. In Chicago, until 1930, when Anton Cermak fused them into one machine, there were three Democratic organizations, Irish, Polish, and Italian. For most of the half century after Cermak was killed in the assassination attempt on Franklin D. Roosevelt in 1933, the mayor's office would be filled by a procession of Kellys, Kennellys, Byrnes, and, for some twenty years, the archetypal Richard J. Daley.

The American "race" was always assumed to be Anglo-Saxon, the world's great civilizer, with America as its greatest and noblest home. And Anglo-Saxon, it went without saying, meant Protestant. In 1848—maybe also the peak year for antebellum anti-Catholicism—two of the nation's most respectable highbrow journals, the *American Whig Review* and the *North American Review,* had published celebratory articles identically titled "The Anglo-Saxon Race." In 1879 came the Reverend William Henry Poole's goofy hypothesis that the British nation, meaning the Anglo-Saxons, consisted of the lost tribes of Israel.[16] But it wasn't until after the publication of Charles Darwin's *On the Origin of Species* in 1859, his *Descent of Man* in 1871, the accompanying (and growing) influence of Social Darwinism, and the arrival of the new immigrants in the 1880s that Anglo-Saxonism became central to American nativist thinking and politics. In his best-seller of 1885,

Our Country: Its Present Crisis and Its Possible Future, the Reverend Josiah Strong, secretary of the American (Congregational) Home Missionary Society, a leader in the Social Gospel movement, a passionate imperialist, and one of the great advocates of social reform of the 1880s, brightly predicted the ultimate triumph of the Anglo-Saxon race in its great American home. Citing Darwin, he saw that triumph as verification of natural selection in producing superior individuals:

> There can be no reasonable doubt that North America is to be the great home of the Anglo-Saxon, the principal seat of his power, the center of his life and influence. Not only does it constitute seven-elevenths of his possessions, but his empire is unsevered, while the remaining four-elevenths are fragmentary and scattered over the earth. But we are to have not only the larger portion of the Anglo-Saxon race for generations to come, we may reasonably expect to develop the highest type of Anglo-Saxon civilization. If human progress follows a law of development, if "Time's noblest offspring is the last," our civilization should be the noblest; for we are "The heirs of all the ages in the foremost files of time," and not only do we occupy the latitude of power, but our land is the last to be occupied in that latitude. If the consummation of human progress is not to be looked for here, if there is yet to flower a higher civilization, where is the soil that is to produce it?[17]

Strong also warned darkly of the dangers of Romanism, Mormonism, socialism, intemperance, and class warfare in cities crammed with crime-prone immigrants, the last especially. "The typical immigrant," he wrote, "is a European peasant, whose horizon has been narrow, whose moral and religious training has been meager or false, and whose ideas of life are low. Not a few belong to the pauper and criminal classes. . . . [The immigrant] is isolated in a strange land, perhaps doubly so by reason of a strange speech. He is transplanted from a forest to an open prairie, where before he is rooted, he is smitten with the blasts of temptation. . . . Our population of foreign extraction is sadly conspicuous in our criminal records."[18] If that couldn't be brought under control, the whole happy scenario was in jeopardy.

The economist and statistician Francis Amasa Walker, the first president of MIT, former superintendent of the Census Bureau, and sometime president of the American Statistical Association, had an even gloomier combination of economic, evolutionary, and environmental theses on the evils of the new immigration. That immigration, he wrote in 1896, of "vast masses of peasantry degraded below our utmost conceptions, is a matter which no intelligent patriot can look upon without the gravest apprehension and alarm. They are beaten men from beaten races. They have none of the ideas and aptitudes such as belong to those who were descended from the tribes that met under the oak trees of old Germany to make laws and choose chiefs." He wrote elsewhere, "When was it that native Americans first refused to do the lowest kinds of manual labor? I answer, When the foreigner came. Did the foreigner come because the native American refused longer to perform any kind of manual labor? No, the American refused because the foreigner came."[19]

All "intelligent men admit," he concluded, that "the cutting down of our forests, the destruction of the tree-covering of our soil, has already gone too far; and both individual States and the nation have united in efforts to undo some of the mischief which has been wrought to our agriculture and to our climate from carrying too far the work of denudation." Whether that was a metaphor for the negative environmental effects of excessive foreign immigration or was meant literally, which would have made him an environmentalist ahead of his time, wasn't clear. But beginning in the early 1890s, as Walker worked with a century of census data, he became increasingly certain that, as the foreigners came, the birthrate of good native American stock declined because Americans didn't want to bring children into the world to compete with that cheap immigrant labor. Foreign immigration, he contended, rather than augmenting native births, was replacing them.[20] In the view of many later academics, writers, and politicians, that was race suicide.

Fear of immigration took all manner of forms, expressed in countless ways: as complaints about the burdens immigrants placed on charitable institutions and the numbers of immigrants in prisons and asylums; as the problems of immigrant children in schools; with photographs of urban slums; with muckraking exposés of political corruption and the city bosses who thrived on immigrant votes; with liberal complaints about immigrants as the exploited labor pool of the economically privileged; and, beginning in the first decades of the twentieth century, with intelligence test scores. All of these fears would be the subtext—a mixture of social reform and nativism—of the immigration restriction movement and policies to this day.

The traumatic events of the era—the wave of labor conflicts accompanying the intense union busting that began in the 1880s; the Chicago Haymarket Riot in 1886, which was set off when someone threw a bomb at police trying to break up a demonstration; the 1891 lynching in New Orleans of eleven Italians alleged to be Mafiosi; the attempted assassination by Alexander Berkman, a Jewish Russian-born anarchist (and Emma Goldman's lover), of industrialist Henry Clay Frick in 1892; the assassination of President William McKinley in 1901 by Leon Czolgosz, a homegrown anarchist with a very foreign name; the dynamiting in 1910 of the then rabidly antilabor *Los Angeles Times* by a couple of Irish union activists, in which twenty-one were killed and many more injured (the *Times*, rather prematurely, called it "the crime of the century")—all fell into a context that linked industrial and urban unrest with anarchists and/or immigrants. (The fact that Czolgosz was a native American didn't deter Congress from immediately enacting the Anarchist Exclusion Act to block those judged to be radicals from admission.)

No one ever determined who'd thrown the Haymarket bomb that killed one police officer and injured seven others. Countless civilians were killed in the melee that followed, some almost certainly by police bullets. But since German anarchist newspapers had urged their readers to make bombs, and since the suspects were Germans and thus obviously part of the bomber's conspiracy, no further evidence was needed.[21] Eight men, all anarchists, all but one foreign-born, were arrested, tried, and convicted of murder. Four were executed. One committed suicide the evening before his scheduled hanging. In 1893, the Progressive governor of Illinois, John Peter Altgeld, issuing a seventeen-thousand-word statement outlining his belief that the men never had a fair trial—he said the judge was biased, the jurors unqualified—pardoned the other three.[22]

The Haymarket affair reenergized American nativism as no event had since the Civil War. "Anarchy's Red Hand" was the headline in the *New York Times*. "Rioting and Bloodshed on the Streets of Chicago. Police Mowed Down with Dynamite," it continued. The article cited the "bravery of the police" but did not point out that most of those killed or injured had probably been shot by those same police.[23] Other publications were less polite about this "invasion of venomous reptiles," as one paper put it, or "the long-haired, wild-eyed, bad-smelling, atheistic, reckless foreign wretches who never did an honest hour's work in their lives." "Our National existence, and, as well, our National and social institutions are at stake."[24] These immigrants were importing the European class conflicts and radicalism that America was supposed to be immune to and against which it had been created.

• • •

Many immigrants, wrote Henry Cabot Lodge in 1891, were "mere birds of passage. They form an element in the population which regards home as a foreign country, instead of that in which they live and earn money.

They have no interest or stake in the country, and they never become American citizens. . . . In a word, the continued introduction . . . of four hundred thousand persons annually, half of whom have no occupation and most of whom represent the rudest form of labor has a very great effect in reducing the rates of wages and disturbing the labor market."[25] Among the worst, according to the government officials and academics on whom he relied, were the Slovaks, the Bohemians ("violent ultra-socialists," "illiterate and ignorant in the extreme"), and the Italians, especially the swarthy southern Italians who were "generally rustic and of the lowest type of the Italian as to character and intelligence." A lot of European welfare groups, Lodge and others charged, were paying to ship misfits—"criminals, vicious characters, paupers"—to the United States to get them off the charity rolls abroad.[26]

Lodge, a graduate of Harvard three times over and sometime professor there, was an Anglophile down to his shoe tops. In Congress he carried the agenda of the Immigration Restriction League, created by a small group of Boston patricians like himself, whose prime policy objective was the imposition of a literacy test for would-be-immigrants, which its elite membership expected would screen out the worst of the misfits. Lodge left no doubt who he meant. Such a test would hit most heavily, he said in a floor speech in 1909, "Italians, Russians, Poles, Hungarians, Greeks and Asiatics. . . . In other words [races] with which the English-speaking people have never hitherto assimilated, and who are most alien to the great body of the people of the United States."[27] Perhaps even more telling was his response, echoing many others, to the lynching of the eleven Italians in New Orleans in 1891. Lodge, as a proper Bostonian, would be presumed to be both well mannered and properly institutional. But he could not restrain himself from justifying the crime.

> There is no doubt [he wrote] that every intelligent man deplores the lawless act of the New Orleans mob. But to stop there would be the reverse of intelligent. To visit on the heads of the mob all our reprobation, and to find in its act alone matters of anxiety and regret, would not only be unjust, but would show a very slight apprehension of the gravity and meaning of this event. Such acts as the killing of these eleven Italians do not spring from nothing without reason or provocation. The mob would have been impossible if there had not been a large body of public opinion behind it, and if it had not been recognized that it was not mere riot, but rather that revenge which Lord Bacon says is a kind of wild justice.[28]

After that it takes Lodge some twisting and turning to get to the main point: The New Orleans prisoners were not lynched because they were

Italians. Americans liked Italians. Nor did the guilt lie with the New Orleans mob, which had concluded that the Italians, imprisoned for the murder of the New Orleans police chief but acquitted by a (possibly suborned) jury, were criminals, but with the lax American immigration policy that had let them into the country:

> Whatever the proximate causes of the shocking event at New Orleans may have been, the underlying cause, and the one with which alone the people of the United States can deal, is to be found in the utter carelessness with which we treat immigration to this country.
>
> The killing of the prisoners at New Orleans was due chiefly to the fact that they were supposed to be members of the Mafia, but it would be a great mistake to suppose that the Mafia stands alone. Societies or political organizations which regard assassination as legitimate have been the product of repressive government on the continent of Europe. They are the offspring of conditions and of ideas wholly alien to the people of the United States.[29]

Having issued his disagreement with the conventional explanations for the lynching, few of them sympathetic to the victims, Lodge goes on to list a whole series of dangerous immigrant groups—Polish secret societies, the Molly Maguires in Pennsylvania, the anarchists of Chicago—and then expands the categories to their national origins and to the miserable personal qualities that characterized those national groups. Worse, "they have not, as a rule, a cent of money after paying their fare." The same applied to low-class immigrants from the "Far East"—Lodge specifically cited Syrians and Armenians, since the Chinese had been excluded for nearly a decade. But the "Slovacks" were just as bad and, quoting the American consul in Budapest, "not a desirable acquisition for us to make, since they appear to have too many items in common with the Chinese. Like these, they are extremely frugal, the love of whisky of the former balanced by the opium habit of the latter. Their ambition lacks both in quality and quantity. They will work similarly cheap as the Chinese and will interfere with a civilized laborer's earning a 'white' laborer's wages."[30] Lodge did not explain the reason for the quotation marks around the word *white* or whether they were his own or those of the American official in Budapest.

Those fears didn't quite square with Lodge's view that many of the newcomers, arriving without a cent to their name, were "mere birds of passage," either shuttling back and forth between the United States and their native country, taking their earnings with them, or going back permanently after earning enough money to set themselves up in the old country. This in turn didn't quite square with the claim that, in many European countries, the authorities or "benevolent societies" were encouraging felons to emigrate, sometimes helping them to get new clothes or even the fare to go to America. (In light of the British practice of sentencing felons to transportation to the colonies in the eighteenth and the first decades of the nineteenth centuries, most of them presumably solid Anglo-Saxons, the practice would have hardly been new, assuming it was at all common.) And then there was the miserable condition of the Russian Jews, which, said Lodge, was even worse than that of the paupers from Hungary, Italy, and Poland: "Yet it has been stated in the newspapers that plans are on foot to remove these unfortunate people from Russia to the number of four millions and land them in the United States." Since "one half the pauper population of Massachusetts and New York is of foreign birth . . . we can see how deeply alarming the present condition of affairs is."[31]

Lodge's conclusion, like that of countless other politicians, journalists, labor leaders, charitable groups, government officials, and academics, some of them leading Progressive social reformers, was predictable: unrestricted immigration, especially immigration from eastern and southern Europe, was no longer tolerable. As early as 1888, the Progressive economists who had formed the American Economic Association put up a $150 prize for the best paper on the evil effects of unrestricted immigration.[32] There were no doubts about the unfitness of these new immigrants to become Americans, or about their criminality, their immorality, the diseases they brought, their depressing impact on wages and living standards, and the burdens they imposed on charitable organizations. The newcomers were also, in the words of the U.S. immigration commissioner in 1903, "generally undesirable because unintelligent, of low vitality, of poor physique, able to perform only the cheapest kind of manual labor."

> I believe [he said] that at least 200,000 (and probably more) aliens came here who, although they may be able to earn a living, yet are not wanted, will be of no benefit to the country, and will, on the contrary, be a detriment, because their presence will tend to lower our standards; and if these 200,000 persons could have been induced to stay at home, nobody, not even those clamoring for more labor, would have missed them. Their coming has been of benefit chiefly, if not only, to the transportation companies which brought them here.
>
> [Those companies] are inducing through agencies that spread like a vast network over all Europe, having representatives of all classes in every town, village, and hamlet, who are local centers for the distribution of enticing literature showing with all the art of the advertiser and illustrator the glories

> of the Eldorado on the west of the Atlantic—to which the great majority may gain entrance without hindrance, and from which even the poor, diseased, and helpless cannot always be excluded.[33]

Higham was right on one point. The doubts of leading Americans like Lodge, bolstered by statistics on poverty, urban misery, and the high failure rates of immigrant children in schools, raised questions about the nature of the American society and economy and about the nation's capacity to assimilate that had rarely been raised before. In 2008, Mark Krikorian, executive director of the prorestriction Center for Immigration Studies and grandson of the kind of Armenian immigrants that Lodge regarded as unfit in 1891, published a book called *The New Case against Immigration—Both Legal and Illegal.* His thesis is that immigration should be stopped not because today's immigrants are different from those of a century ago but because the country is different and no longer has the social and economic institutions fostering assimilation. The problem, he says in the first line of the book, isn't the immigrants—"it's us."[34]

But that, too, is an old argument. Although they didn't explicitly make the distinction, as early as the last decades of the nineteenth century and the first years of the twentieth, restrictionists implicitly invoked both sets of arguments: Was the problem the number and character of the immigrants, or was it the nation's limited capacity (or maybe willingness) to accommodate them? Krikorian, in contending that the nation no longer had the capacity to absorb immigrants, cites the 1890 finding of the superintendent of the census that the frontier was closed and historian Frederick Jackson Turner's famous essay, "The Significance of the Frontier in American History," attributing American democracy to the influence of the frontier. The Turner essay was pegged to that census finding and first delivered as a paper at a conference of the American Historical Society in 1893.[35] What, Turner wondered, would replace it to sustain democracy in the future? In fact, even the alarm about democracy in peril was sounded a decade earlier by the single-taxer Henry George, who, echoing the growing anxiety of western farmers, warned that the country was running out of the open land "that has given scope and freedom to our American life and relieved social pressure in the most progressive of European nations." An explosion could be coming.[36]

The geographical abstraction that led to the census conclusion that the frontier was "closed," essentially the end of a continuous line demarcating settled from unsettled land, also accompanied earlier arguments for reducing or shutting down immigration. To quote Lodge's 1891 articles again: "Conditions have changed utterly from the days when the supply of vacant land was indefinite, the demand for labor almost unbounded, and the supply of people very limited. . . . Our labor market, if we may judge from the statistics of the unemployed, is overstocked in many places, and that means a tendency toward a decline in wages. This tendency is perilous both socially and politically." The "dreadful condition of things" in cities like New York, Lodge said, "is intensified every day by the steady inflow of immigration, which is constantly pulling down the wages of the working people of New York and affecting in a similar way the entire labor market of the United States."[37] Maybe the power of the Anglo-Saxon race, carrying the white man's burden and marching to instruct and civilize the inferior peoples of Africa and Asia, was not sufficient even to absorb and Americanize the Europeans now arriving in their growing numbers at the nation's Atlantic ports.

The novelist Henry James may have been most eloquent in his doubts. Though a proper Bostonian, James had lived abroad for much of his life. In 1904–5, he returned for a tour of America and recorded his misgivings and ambivalence, melding equal portions of sympathy, disorientation, revulsion, and horror in his description of "the terrible little Ellis Island":

> Before this door, which opens to them there only with a hundred forms and ceremonies, grindings and grumblings of the key, they stand appealing and waiting, marshalled, herded, divided, subdivided, sorted, sifted, searched, fumigated, for longer or shorter periods—the effect of all which prodigious process, an intendedly "scientific" feeding of the mill, is again to give the earnest observer a thousand more things to think of than he can pretend to retail.
>
> It is (a poignant and unforgettable) drama that goes on, without a pause, day by day and year by year, this visible act of ingurgitation on the part of our body politic and social, and constituting really an appeal to amazement beyond that of any sword-swallowing or fire-swallowing of the circus.
>
> The simplest account of the action of Ellis Island on the spirit of any sensitive citizen who may have happened to "look in" is that he comes back from his visit not at all the same person that he went. He has eaten of the tree of knowledge, and the taste will be for ever in his mouth. He had thought he knew before, thought he had the sense of the degree in which it is his American fate to share the sanctity of his American consciousness, the intimacy of his American patriotism, with the inconceivable alien; but the truth had never come home to him with any such force. In the lurid light projected upon it by those courts of dismay it shakes him—or I like at least to imagine it shakes him—to the depths of his being; I like to think of him, I positively *have* to think of him, as going about ever afterwards with a new look, for those who can see it, in his face, the outward sign of the new chill in his

> heart. So is stamped, for detection, the questionably privileged person who has had an apparition, seen a ghost in his supposedly safe old house. Let not the unwary, therefore, visit Ellis Island.[38]

For the native, James wrote, the result is a sense of "unsettled possession . . . the implication of which is that, to recover confidence and regain lost ground, we, not they, must make the surrender and accept the orientation. We must go, in other words, *more* than half way to meet them. . . . There was no escape from the ubiquitous alien into the future, or even into the present; there was an escape but into the past." Yet in the process of observing these new aliens, James also sensed the alien in himself. "Who and what is an alien, when it comes to that, in a country peopled from the first under the jealous eye of history?"[39] A century later, Krikorian tried to say the same thing, but James said it better.

Not surprisingly, nineteenth-century calls for restrictions on immigration were rarely supported by the men who ran the nation's great industrial enterprises and who grew great on that low-wage immigrant labor. (Lodge, in his references to the depressing effect of immigration on wages, did not trouble himself with the union-busting practices, often reinforced by gun-toting Pinkerton agents and other cops, of the corporate robber barons who employed those workers.) Nor was it surprising that immigration restriction got no support from Tammany Hall and the other urban political machines that depended in large part on immigrant votes and that, in an age before public welfare, in turn provided social services, jobs, and—in what these days would be called identity politics—embraced and celebrated the newly arrived ethnics, most of them Irish. In April 1892, a year after Lodge's articles appeared, the *North American Review* ran a piece called "Our National Dumping Ground: A Study of Immigration" by U.S. Immigration Commissioner John B. Weber—it had a concurring codicil by Charles Stewart Smith, the president of the New York Chamber of Commerce, which, though not explicitly naming Lodge, countered every one of his points. Industry needed the immigrants.

The purported evils of immigration, Weber said, "are purely imaginary in some features, greatly exaggerated in others, and susceptible of nearly complete remedy by the amendment of existing laws." As a member of a commission on immigration visiting Europe, he found no evidence that paupers and criminals were being dumped on the United States; most of those crowding American cities weren't immigrants but Americans from rural areas, and there was still plenty of land and untouched natural resources. "We are in no danger of being Germanized,

Frenchified, Italianized or Europeanized."[40] Four years later, in 1896, another U.S. immigration official seconded the assurance with a backhanded endorsement: Italians, as a nationality, he wrote, "certainly do not belong per se to an undesirable class of immigrants. There are vast regions in the South and West and on the Pacific coast for the colonization of which they are unquestionably and pre-eminently adapted, and as manual laborers for many varieties of work which Anglo-Saxons are very loath to undertake they are beyond a doubt excellently fitted."[41] If that was damning with faint praise, it also was not the last time the argument was made.

Another, stronger demur, published in 1900 by Kate Holladay Claghorn, one of the earliest women to get a PhD from Yale and a vocal feminist, could have been written last week:

> Our people, even while, as a whole, they are cherishing a conscious dislike to foreigners, and a theoretical objection to their incoming, are constantly, as individual employers, calling them here, either by name and expressly, or through the great general clamor for labor of all kinds that is always going up. Here is a half-worked country in need of a larger labor force; across the sea is a labor force in need of employment. It will be as impossible to keep these apart, under modern conditions of intercommunication, as to shut out a rising tide with a board fence; the water will force its way in, either over, or under, or through the cracks.[42]

But the objections didn't mute the mounting chorus demanding tight immigration restrictions rooted in familiar fears. In part, those fears arose from the unpredictable but gradually increasing numbers of immigrants. In part, they grew out of a series of severe depressions—the panic of 1873, which lasted some four years (and drove immigration from a high of 460,000 in 1873 to a low of 178,000 in 1879), and the four-year depression that began in 1893—and the plight of the millions of workers affected by them and the generally miserable conditions and pay even in good times. The petitions of the patrician Immigration Restriction League, founded in 1894, citing "the unhealthy competition in the labor market [from] the introduction of foreign workers living under degraded conditions incompatible with the standard of living of American workingmen" and asking for tighter immigration laws, were endorsed by scores of labor groups—the Brockton Clothing Cutters and Trimmers Union, the Hoisting Engineers Association of Chicago, the Core Makers International Union, the Journeymen Tailors Union of Bloomington, Illinois, and countless others, most of them affiliates of the American Federation of Labor.[43]

After the turn of the century, Samuel Gompers, founding and longtime president of the American Federation of Labor—himself a Jewish immigrant born in London who grew up in a New York tenement—joined the Harvardians Lodge and the three founders of the Immigration Restriction League, Prescott Farnsworth Hall, Robert DeCourcy Ward, and Charles Warren, in demanding toughened immigration laws.[44] In fact, even as the labor petitions were circulating, immigration—as ever, responding to hard times—dropped from 579,000 in 1892 to 229,000 in 1898.

But as Lodge and his friends made consistently clear, it was the ethnic, religious, and class background of the immigrants that underlay their resistance. Lodge's "illiteracy test" for potential immigrants, as he said in 1909 in his Senate argument for the bill, "will bear most heavily" on the new immigrants. Many weren't even Christians or Europeans. As would be the case a century or more later, suddenly there were new faces with new complexions and the sounds of new languages on streets, in factories, and in schools where they'd never been seen or heard before.[45] They were not fit for our society

Among those newly visible were Jews. The first wave, which had arrived in the decades before the Civil War, came mostly from Germany. Some, highly educated, many not, most of them from cities, began as small tradesmen and itinerant peddlers and quickly made their way as retailers, garment manufacturers, and bankers. By the first decades of the twentieth century, there was hardly a city in America that didn't have a department store begun and often still run by Jewish ex-peddlers: Goldwater's, Weinstock's, Altman's, Gimbels, Kaufmanns, Lazarus's, Gottschalk's, Spiegel's, and dozens of others. But the business success of Jews in the Gilded Age, rather than assuaging anti-Semitism, and contrary to the generic depiction of the new immigrant as economically unfit, seemed to inflame the image of the Jew as a conniving, social-climbing interloper.

Probably the most famous target was the banker Joseph Seligman, who a decade earlier had entertained Generals Grant and Beauregard and had apparently been offered the job as Grant's secretary of the treasury, a job in an administration he was probably wise to reject. In 1877, in what became a cause célèbre, Seligman, who, with his family and an entourage of servants had made periodic summer visits to the Grand Union Hotel in Saratoga Springs, New York, then among the most lavish of the society watering spots, was turned away on arrival and informed that, as an "Israelite," he was no longer welcome. Nothing personal, he was informed, but "business at the hotel was not good last season," in the words of the hotel's manager, professedly because there had been a lot of Jews staying there, and "Christians did not like their company and thus shunned the hotel." Accordingly, Judge Henry Hilton, who controlled the trust that owned the hotel, had ordered that no Jews be admitted. The hotel was run for the proper guests who did not want to associate with Jews like the Seligmans, who, in Hilton's words, all published in the *New York Times* and other papers, "brought down public opinion upon themselves by a vulgar ostentation, a puffed-up vanity, a lack of those considerate civilities so much appreciated by good American society, and a general obtrusiveness that is frequently disgusting and always repulsive to the well-bred."[46] Not fit for our society. Simon Rosedale, in Edith Wharton's novel *The House of Mirth,* was precisely the kind of ill-mannered Jewish social climber that Hilton and probably much of the New York upper crust imagined (or maybe wanted) all Jews to be. Yet in her subtle way, Wharton renders Rosedale as less viperous and more direct and kinder than most of the members of the social set whose acceptance he sought.

The Seligman story was both a sensation and something of a mystery. Did Seligman, who was in a nasty business battle with the trustees of the Grand Union and who was trying to fight the Tweed political machine with which they were associated, deliberately provoke the incident? If he did, it brought unexpected consequences for New York's middle-class Jews. A lot of prominent New Yorkers, including Henry Ward Beecher, came to Seligman's defense. But the uproar, in spawning restrictive policies at other resorts and hotels, particularly in the Adirondacks, and later in clubs and real-estate deeds—and the overt anti-Semitism that came with them—set back the cause of Jewish assimilation far more than advanced it. In the view of social historian Stephen Birmingham, while Jews "had been snubbed by hotels and clubs before . . . now it was out in the open and a fact of life: certain areas of America were closed to Jews."[47] A few years later, when Seligman's grandnephew Theodore was rejected for membership in New York's Union League Club, he was told it was nothing personal regarding either him or Jesse Seligman, Theodore's father, who had been a member. "It was purely racial."[48]

By the 1890s, most of the Jews of the new immigration were Ostjuden—eastern European peasants, tradesmen, and working people from the shtetl—and thus far more visible in the streets, schools, and tenements, who, in thereby reinforcing anti-Semitic bias, tended to be resented and disparaged almost as much by the established Jewish middle class as by American Gentiles. As in Germany, the older generation of

German Jews, many of them nearly indistinguishable from their Gentile neighbors, regarded the newcomers as an embarrassment, though they did often provide assistance to the new immigrants through charitable organizations. One of those assimilated Jews, the immensely rich banker and Democratic Party heavyweight August Belmont, née Schoenberg in Germany, could have been the model for Wharton's Simon Rosedale. But the anti-Semitism, which had been festering since the Civil War and began to flare in the years after, and which would institutionalize itself for over a century in corporate board rooms, law firms, social clubs, and university admissions offices, spared no Jew.

• • •

The alien-ness of the new immigrants was unmistakable in the tenements, on the streets, in the sweatshops and construction gangs, and among the (mainly Irish) ward heelers of the political machines of the big cities. Government in the Gilded Age had grown more corrupt at all levels. There had to be something wrong with Darwin's theory, Henry Adams would observe in *The Education of Henry Adams* in 1918, if the presidency had gone from George Washington to Ulysses S. Grant.[49] The cities were visibly dirtier, the burdens on charities heavier, the politics more corrupt, corporate behavior more rapacious and arrogant. In turn, the magazines and the burgeoning circulation (and circulation wars) of the penny press, which thrived on "weepers" and scandals, became more frenetic in documenting them. The Immigration Restriction League got a lot of pickup in newspapers, with headlines like "The Perils of Immigration . . . Startling Figures on Illiteracy." From the end of the Civil War until 1886, when *Harper's,* which had been his home since the Civil War, tried to defang him and he quit, cartoonist Thomas Nast, among the most influential American figures of the second half of the century, himself a German immigrant, had been flaying the city bosses and the Catholic Church with equal ferocity. He drew the now-classic 1875 cartoon ("The American River Ganges") depicting Catholic bishops as crocodiles snapping at the ankles of innocent schoolchildren.[50]

Nast wasn't remotely unique in that respect. Few cartoonists of his time hesitated to portray the Church as a demonic seducer, or immigrants as pirates and rats slipping off ships at America's ports, or as Irish drunks, or as Jewish peddlers with drums strapped on their backs labeled "Sabbath Desecration," or toting carpetbags of "poverty," "disease," and "anarchy," or as a predatory bat looming over American workers.

There was the figure of a prelate casting a shadow over a classroom of schoolchildren. And when some Chinese workers were found crossing the Mexican and Canadian borders in the years after passage of the Chinese Exclusion Act, thus becoming the nation's first illegal immigrants, cartoonists brought their readers "the wily Chinese sneaking over the Northern frontier." In the San Francisco–based *Wasp* in 1889, foreshadowing twenty-first-century theories about terrorists disguising themselves as illegal Mexicans, the illegal border crosser became a grinning Chinese man in a bullfighter's outfit entering the United States over the caption "Now They Come as Spaniards." Or, as in a later headline in the *Buffalo Evening News*, "Wily Tricks Played by John Chinaman and His Smugglers."[51] Cartoonists loved drawing ships with lowered gangplanks discharging hordes of unsavory-looking figures while Uncle Sam or customs officials slept on the docks.

By now, the link between the filth, dislocations, and corruption of industrialization and urbanization, on the one hand, and the great waves of reformist thought and action that followed, on the other, is a long-familiar story. Chicago's Hull House, founded by Jane Addams and two others in 1889, inspired the creation of settlement houses to expand the educational, cultural, and social horizons of thousands of poor women in scores of cities. Edward Bellamy's enormously popular and influential novel, *Looking Backward,* a "fairy tale of social felicity" published in 1888, looked longingly toward a future (in 2000) of social equality in which the private trusts have been replaced by a form of democratic capitalism and where conflict, most crime, wars, and want have been engineered away, and all people are educated to their maximum potential.

Looking Backward was followed by a wave of other utopian literature. It also led to the creation of Bellamy clubs and a Nationalist Party and appears to have considerably influenced the populism of the 1890s, which in turn flowed into and gave way to the Progressivism and the accompanying muckraking of the last decades of the century and the first years of the twentieth. This was the era of *McClure's* magazine and *Colliers* and *Cosmopolitan;* of Frank Norris's *The Octopus* (1901), whose villain, S. Behrman, the slippery dealer-manipulator who represents the railroad, may or may not have been intended to be Jewish; of Lincoln Steffens's pieces on urban corruption that became *The Shame of the Cities* (1904); Ida Tarbell's series for *McClure's* exposing the Standard Oil Company (1902–4); Upton Sinclair's *The Jungle* (1906); and a long list of others. Appropriately for fanciers of anti-immigrant paranoia,

Sinclair's novel was the story of the progression of Jurgis Rudkus, a Slavic immigrant, from his employment under abusive foremen in the Chicago stockyards, and the accompanying disease and brutality of his life in a heartless society, to the shining light of socialism.

Progressivism and social and political reform generally could be both a check on nativism and immigration restriction and a cheerful companion at their side. William Allen White, the editor of the *Emporia (Kansas) Gazette,* perhaps the most genuine voice of Progressivism, seemed to be on both sides: the Anglo-Saxon legacy could cut both ways. "We hold to the racial institutions that made us conquerors of the Mongol and the Semite," he said in 1910.

> What is this universal movement in our American cities for home rule but the old race call for the rule of the folk? . . . And now that the Greeks and the Slavs and the Armenians and the Huns and Poles are pushing the Latin races up from the slums and deeper into our civilization, we need not tremble for our institutions. For these strangers are all of the old blood. They will merge into the old blood again. The American is no sport, no chance child, no woods colt in the races of men. He is the flower of the purest blood on earth, the youngest blood on earth. And the unseen hand of fate that is weaving the garment will weave ignorance and greed out of its warp, and make it strong and fine and clean.[52]

Many were with Theodore Roosevelt in their belief that, through instruction in English and in the basics of democratic government, even these new immigrants could be properly Americanized. The tilt of the Bull Moosers in the 1912 election was clearly toward the protection and nurture of immigrants. But as historian Richard Hofstadter said so well, "One senses again and again in the best progressive literature on immigration, that the old nativist Mugwump prejudice is being held in check by a strenuous effort of mind and will."[53] Acceptance of immigrants did not, in short, come easily, especially since many immigrants themselves were more comfortable with the ethic of clan and personal loyalty of the city political bosses and, more generally, with the culture of the village, the clubhouse, and the saloon, than with abstract WASP principles of good government and personal self-discipline.

Nor did the new immigrants make eager candidates for the ministrations of social workers and settlement houses. Unwittingly, the Progressive reformers—in creating civil-service systems, writing the initiative, referendum, and recall into western state constitutions, and moving power away from political parties toward their ideal of nonpolitical politics—also reinforced ethnic identity politics. In Boston, as elsewhere, the old Yankee establishment, trying to check the political clout of the upstart Irish, created new governmental institutions, transferring authority from city hall to state commissions, still controlled by the old crowd, to make it harder for the new political gang to run things. In Boston, this involved a restructuring of the Finance Commission, latterly appointed by the governor, to make it independent of the city council.[54] But paradoxically, because the parties that had been mediating institutions were weakened, "conflict between Yankee and Irish," in the words of social historian James J. Connolly, "now defined the city's public as never before."[55] In the end, of course, the Yankee efforts were mostly for naught, as the Irish captured most of the establishment redoubts and learned to turn even the presumably nonpolitical civil-service systems into instruments of personal and ethnic privilege and loyalty.[56] A generation later, ethnic identity politics evolved in New York, Chicago, and many other cities into a system of "balanced tickets" drawn to appeal to a spectrum of ethnic identities.

Still, the mismatch between the ethic of immigrant loyalties to family and clan, on one side, and WASP principles of the rule of law and impersonal nonpartisanship, on the other, was always more a reflection of old biases than a source of new ones. After a half century of anti-Chinese prejudice, California Progressives were perfectly comfortable with the classic good-government reform agenda—civil service, the initiative, referendum and recall, public ownership of utilities—even as they took for granted the inferiority of Asians and lobbied hard for their exclusion. In 1905, San Francisco mayor Eugene Schmitz, going one race further, declared that he'd rather lower the bars on "the heathen Chinese" than suffer "the many great evils that would at once beset our industrial welfare if the brown toilers of the Mikado's realm were permitted to swarm through our gates unhindered."[57] In 1913, two years after Governor Hiram Johnson secured voter approval of his Progressive reforms, the California legislature weighed in with yet more anti-Asian bills. Defying pleas from President Woodrow Wilson, who feared a diplomatic confrontation with Japan, the state passed the Alien Land Act that prohibited Japanese aliens, as people not eligible for naturalization, from owning land or other real property.[58]

In Wisconsin in 1907, where he was an intellectual force for Progressive reform, John R. Commons was probably the leading labor economist of his day. Commons, whose left-wing views had earlier cost him a university teaching job, was nonetheless an unequivocal subscriber to Francis Walker's race-suicide theory and to the belief that native Americans refused either to work with, or compete with, low-wage immigrant workers. Commons supported further restrictions on immigration and proposed sharply increased fines on steamship companies that brought "unfit" immigrants—defined by an ever-increasing official list as diseased, idiots, lunatics, and carriers of defective genes—to America. With expanded accountability, wrote Commons, echoing other immigration restriction advocates, "every agent of the steamship companies in the remotest hamlets of Europe would be an immigration inspector."[59] But beyond those particulars, Commons entertained a more fundamental doubt: now that the nation was beset by non-Anglo-Saxon races and great numbers of peasants whose presence in American society was never contemplated by the founders, was the original faith in democracy and the belief that all men are created equal still justified? Because the nation had a common language, which made many other things possible, education in particular, Commons was inclined toward the affirmative (except about blacks), but he was certain that it would take a lot of doing.[60]

Sociologist Edward Ross, Commons's colleague at the University of Wisconsin and a key member of Governor Robert M. La Follette's brain trust of Progressive intellectuals, was less optimistic. Race suicide, the phrase he coined, seemed to him entirely likely. "The superiority of a race," Ross, then still a professor at the University of Nebraska, said in 1901, "cannot be preserved without *pride of blood* [italics his] and an uncompromising attitude toward the lower races."[61] (This was three years after the war with Spain, roughly at the same moment when William Howard Taft, then the governor of the newly conquered Philippines, was famously telling President McKinley that it would probably take at least fifty years of supervision before "our little brown brothers" were ready for self-rule.) Good government was an Anglo-Saxon legacy. In places like the Philippines, which we had captured from Spain in 1898, it imposed on us a God-given mission to govern "these children" because, in the words of the Progressive Senator Albert J. Beveridge of Indiana, "He has made us the master organizers of the world."[62] In North America, Ross said in a lecture, "the Spaniard absorbed the Indians (through inter-breeding), the English exterminated them by fair means or foul. . . . Whatever may be thought of the latter policy, the net result is that North America from the Bering Sea to the Rio Grande is dedicated to the highest type of civilization; while for centuries the rest of our hemisphere will drag the ball and chain of hybridism." The American farmhand, mechanic, and operative "might wither away before the heavy influx of a prolific race from the Orient, just as in classic times, the Latin husbandman vanished before the endless stream of slaves poured into Italy by her triumphant generals." He ended the lecture with a forced optimism for which he had laid no foundation.[63]

A dozen years later, Ross returned to the Roman allusion, but the optimism was now all gloom. "Europe retains most of her brains," he wrote in 1914, "but sends multitudes of the common and the sub-common. . . . The fewer brains they have to contribute, the lower the place immigrants take among us, and the lower the place they take, the faster they multiply." Meantime, the low moral tone of the immigrant in the workplace—his example was the female raisin packers of Fresno, California—was driving respectable American workers away to inferior jobs. "Thus the very decency of the native is a handicap to success and to fecundity." Nor was it just old-stock Americans who were "becoming sterile" in the face of the new immigrants—"the older immigrant stocks," he wrote, "are becoming sterile" as well. In a book that's as gloomy in outlook as it is angry in tone, immigration was driving down every aspect of American life. A nation willing to let immigrants replace its own kind was doomed. "A people that has no more respect for its ancestors and no more pride of race . . . deserves the extinction that surely awaits it."[64]

The gloom was somewhat unusual for a Progressive sociologist and reformer; it didn't seem to leave a lot for reformers to do. But the ideas were hardly unusual. By the time Ross's *Old World in the New* appeared in 1914, it was just one voice in a great chorus—books, articles, lectures, conferences, petitions, government commission reports—about race suicide and the destructive effects of the flood of new immigrants on America. These effects included long lists of particulars:

- That the prisons, almshouses, and lunatic asylums were "stuffed to repletion by new arrivals from Europe." That a high number of immigrant children were falling behind in school. And, most of all, that American citizenship needed protection "from degradation through the tumultuous access of the vast throngs of ignorant and brutalized peasantry from the countries of eastern and southern Europe."[65]
- That parents were so busy trying to earn a living that their children were neglected. Was it therefore surprising that "the children of immigrants [were] the most criminal class in the community?"[66]
- That "backward and benighted provinces from Naples to Sicily" were sending a "flood of 'gross little aliens' who gave Henry

James, on revisiting Boston, the melancholy vision of 'a huge applied sponge—a sponge saturated with the foreign mixture and passed over almost everything I remembered and might still have recovered.'"[67]

- That the Slavs exhibited "excessive alcoholism," brutality, and "reckless fecundity." That eastern European Hebrews were pushy, "willing to break any ordinance they find in their way," and known for "their slipperiness and their reputation for lying." That "pleasure-loving Jewish business men spare Jewesses but pursue Gentile girls [which] excites bitter comment."[68]
- That some states still allowed aliens to vote. That immigrants were examples of the "ignorance of the mass of voters—ignorance of things in general, and especially of the moral and political truths underlying our government."[69]
- That it was likely that the Tammany Hall political machine would never have grown as powerful or lasted as long had it not been for foreign voters. That political organizations with "hyphenated names" were proliferating. That Poles, Slovaks, Jews, and Italians tended to vote not as Democrats or Republicans but as members of ethnic groups. That "the heterogeneity of [the Greek, Italian, and Hebrew] races [tended] to promote bossism, localism, and despotism, and to make impossible free cooperation for the public welfare." That identity politics has in cities become the very essence of the political process.[70]

Some of these themes were pure fear; some were laced with messianic exceptionalism that went back to the first landing of the Puritans in 1620; some were an undifferentiated mix of both. Many were infused with supercilious—and long familiar—attempts to justify class privilege, some with unmitigated Social Darwinism. Some seemed to arise from an upper-class version of the anxieties of place and status that beset the small-town midwestern Progressive. "It is our duty to the world," wrote Prescott Farnsworth Hall in 1906, the Boston lawyer who was one of the founders of the Immigration Restriction League, "not only to preserve in this country the conditions necessary to successful democracy, but to develop here the finest race of men and the highest civilization."[71] In its messianic exceptionalism, that "duty" was an almost perfect echo of the declaration of faith sixty years earlier that Providence had fitted Anglo-Saxons "to perform a great work in reclaiming the world."[72] Because biology had shown that heredity was far more determinative than environment or education, Hall said, that could only be accomplished, as in animal husbandry or in producing seedless fruits and new grains, by careful selection of the breeding stock: "Natural selection cannot be trusted by itself to bring about the best results. 'Survival of the fittest' means that those survive who are fittest for survival, but not necessarily fittest for any other purpose. This is seen when we compare a statesman or college president who has two children and educates them so they take useful and important places in society with some poor drunkard in the slums who has a dozen children and gives them no advantages at all."[73]

Some advanced persons, said Hall, talked of regulating marriage "with a view to the elimination of the unfit . . . yet most people fail to realize that in the United States, through our power to regulate immigration, we have a unique opportunity to exercise artificial selection on an enormous scale." We began, he said, with "immigrants of the best stock in Europe selected naturally by the perils of the voyage and the hardships of life in a new country." (This, too, we would hear again.) By carefully selecting our future immigrants, we could begin to fulfill our duty to the world and produce that "finest race of men and the highest civilization."[74]

• • •

By the beginning of World War I, the campaign to select the right stock was well under way, not only at the immigration ports, but in efforts to encourage the proper American women to produce more children. Theodore Roosevelt, despite his belief in the Americanization of immigrants, talked a lot about race suicide. He may have been the nation's greatest cheerleader in encouraging the Anglo-Saxon woman to overcome the selfishness, the life of ease, which he regarded as among its principal causes. She should be "a good wife, a good mother, able and willing to perform the first and greatest duty of womanhood, able and willing to bear, and to bring up as they should be brought up, healthy children, sound in body, mind, and character, and numerous enough so that the race shall increase and not decrease."[75] All those WASP women were certified breeding stock. The Eugenics Record Office (about which more in the next chapter) was established in 1910, and the first National Conferences on Race Betterment were held in Battle Creek, Michigan, in 1914 and 1915. The states, in the meantime, were imposing varied restrictions on aliens in licensing attorneys and accountants; Michigan even began to deny barber's licenses to aliens, and other states imposed heavy fees on hunting licenses for aliens, or banned them altogether.[76] Banking in New York became largely an ethnically segregated, mostly WASP business, as were law firms and gentlemen's clubs. Admission to Ivy League universities and other selective colleges was subject to a conflated mix of racial-ethnic-religious-class quotas and would continue to be until well after World War II.

But the policy emphasis leading up to World War I was still on immigration. Responding to pressure from western politicians and nativist organizations, Congress had passed the Chinese Exclusion Act as a ten-year bill in 1882, extended it another ten years in 1892, and made it permanent in 1902. California had tried to regulate Chinese and "Mongolian" immigration in a series of laws beginning in 1855, including one pertaining specifically to the arrival of "lewd or lascivious women," but all had been struck down as unconstitutional by the courts. The power to regulate immigration, the U.S. Supreme Court ruled in 1875, belonged to Congress alone.[77] President Chester Arthur vetoed one bill in 1881 that would have excluded all Chinese. Congress then amended it to ban Chinese laborers but to allow the entry of professors, students, merchants, and their servants and passed it again. This time, President Arthur, who had been besieged by attacks and hung in effigy after his veto, signed it. Yet, in the words of the late historian Iris Chang, "far from appeasing the fanatics, the new restrictions inflamed them." In the years following the bill's passage, mobs in Washington, Oregon, Wyoming, and elsewhere burned Chinese homes and shops, and stoned and murdered hundreds of Chinese in an effort, often successful, to drive those already here out of the country.[78]

Even the exceptions in the Chinese-exclusion laws—particularly the right of return for U.S.-born Chinese Americans or legal U.S. residents, most of whom had been in the country before the exclusion laws were passed—were accompanied by humiliation and often outright rejection. After it opened in 1910, Angel Island in San Francisco Bay, which was called the "West Coast Ellis Island" but wasn't remotely like it, became a notorious detention camp where during the succeeding thirty years an estimated 175,000 transpacific arrivals, most of them Chinese, were held for weeks, and sometimes for more than a year. Many did in fact carry fraudulent documents falsely certifying them as U.S. natives or as children of American citizens born abroad—a fraud made easier after all San Francisco birth records were destroyed in the earthquake and fire of 1906. But many others who were legal U.S. residents, and sometimes citizens, were caught in the bureaucratic web created to screen out those illegal "paper sons" and were subject to extended interrogations, strip searches, and housed in tight cells with inadequate food and little medical care. And since they often had to prove that they were U.S. natives, the lost records were as much a handicap to them as they were a boon to the "paper sons."

The arguments for shutting out the Chinese, going back almost to the beginning of the Gold Rush, and later for shutting out all Asians, were based primarily on the constitutional provision limiting naturalization to whites (and, after the Civil War, to blacks). But they also rested on the presumed ethnic mismatch between American society and "Mongolians" and the resulting corrosive consequences, also taken from the black-white legacy of slavery, of "mongrelization." In much of the racial theorizing, it wasn't just that the Chinese were unfit to become Americans but that any racial mixing would have negative consequences on both: it was them *and* us. In 1907, again responding to pressure from the western states and territories, but trying to avoid a diplomatic blowup—the same concerns that would motivate Woodrow Wilson to oppose California's Alien Land Act in 1913—Roosevelt negotiated what became known as the Gentlemen's Agreement with Japan, under which Japan restricted (but did not end) emigration by refusing to issue passports to Japanese laborers and the United States agreed not to officially exclude Japanese.

The lion's share of Washington's attention, however, understandably remained on immigration from Europe. Between 1881 and 1890, 3.7 million immigrants arrived. In the following decade, when the population (in 1910) was roughly 92 million, of whom roughly 13.5 million were foreign-born, the number of arrivals increased to nearly 9 million. That influx prompted one of the most massive studies ever undertaken by the federal government, the forty-one-volume report of the U.S. Immigration Commission. The panel, which worked from 1907 to 1910, and (of course) included Henry Cabot Lodge, was composed of nine men, three each named by the president pro tem of the Senate, the Speaker of the House, and the president. Chaired by Senator William P. Dillingham, a moderately progressive Vermont Republican, its mission was to gather and analyze the information on which all future immigration policy was to be based.[79]

The report covered every conceivable aspect of the issue: conditions affecting emigration from Europe; the jobs held by immigrants in American factories, mines, and agriculture (it found, among many other things, that 57 percent of workers in manufacturing and mining were foreign-born); historical immigration statistics by year and "race" or national origin; data on the problems of immigrant children, again by "race," in American schools; data on the "fecundity" of immigrant women; information on conditions in the steerage quarters of immigrant ships; data "on the importation and harboring of women for immoral purposes" (mostly presumed to serve Chinese workers); the number and national origins of immigrant inmates in jails, charitable hospitals, and asylums; an abstract of the government's official "dictionary of races and peoples" that was used to classify new arrivals; plus a vast range of other statistics that, to this day, still provide the most comprehensive picture of U.S. immigration before the twentieth century and the most complete picture of the immigration concerns that agitated the nation. The Dillingham Commission report also remains a useful inventory of the social priorities, attitudes, limitations, and biases of its time. Some of the concerns originated in the legitimate complaints of overburdened charities and urban reformers; some were pure nativism; some were both.

The commission concluded that 63 percent of schoolchildren with a southern Italian background were "retarded"—meaning two or more years behind the norm for their age groups in school—exceeded only by the children of Polish Jews, at nearly 67 percent. The best performers were the offspring of Dutch and Swedish immigrants, who did better than their native-born white peers.[80] The report also included a long list of recommendations, with various degrees of commission enthusiasm, of reform measures that had been "suggested" to the panel. Among many other items: reducing the immigration of unskilled workers and excluding those who "by reason of their personal qualities or habits" would least readily be assimilated or would make the least desirable citizens; subjecting aliens who "attempt to persuade immigrants not to become citizens" to deportation; vigorously enforcing the laws against "the importation of women for immoral purposes"; adopting measures, in cooperation with the states, "to secure better distribution of alien immigrants throughout the country" (i.e., to reduce the concentration of ethnic voters in the cities); the strict regulation of "immigrant banks" (which transferred funds from alien workers to their families or to their accounts in their home countries); imposing the literacy test that the Immigration Restriction League had been calling for since its founding in 1894; and limiting "the number of each race arriving each year to a certain percentage of the average of that race arriving during a given prior period of years."[81] Its essential message was the danger from, and need to curb, the new immigration.

The commission report never fully served its purpose. By the time it was released in 1911, three years before the start of the Great War in Europe, events in Washington had already partially overtaken it. As early as 1881, the year before passage of the Chinese Exclusion Act, Congress had started to exclude some European immigrants—contract laborers at first, meaning those whose transportation was prepaid by their employers, and those with what was to become a growing list of purportedly negative characteristics: "lunatics," paupers, and people likely to become public charges and continuing (in 1891) with "persons suffering from a loathsome or dangerous disease," those convicted of a crime of "moral turpitude," and polygamists.[82] In 1903, Congress expanded the list to include "idiots, insane persons, epileptics and persons who have been insane within five years previous; persons who have had two or more attacks of insanity at any time previously; paupers, persons likely to become a public charge, professional beggars." The list, beginning with the McKinley assassination in 1901, also included anarchists or anyone who "advocated or believed in the overthrow of the United States government by force or violence or of all government or of all forms of law or the assassination of public officials." It covered prostitutes and, what was by then a hardy perennial, "persons who procure or attempt to bring in prostitutes or women for the purpose of prostitution." Masters of ships were held responsible for meeting those conditions; aliens not qualifying were to be deported forthwith at the expense of the steamship company that brought them across. At the same time, the law also provided that "skilled labor may be imported if labor of like kind unemployed can not be found in this country."[83]

What may be most remarkable about the 1903 law, as about virtually all other congressional acts before World War I, excepting only those concerning Asians, was the unwillingness of Congress to write into law any of the racial, religious, or national distinctions that had colored attacks on immigrants during the prior half century. Pursuant to the demands of Henry Cabot Lodge and the Immigration Restriction League, Congress had passed a number of bills establishing literacy tests requiring all adult aliens seeking to immigrate to be able to read in some language, but all were vetoed. A bill was finally enacted early in 1917, twenty years after Grover Cleveland had issued his first veto, by a Congress that succeeded in overriding Woodrow Wilson's veto—actually his second on a literacy bill. The bill bowed to the strong opposition of American Jews by exempting Russian Jews fleeing pogroms. Aliens escaping political persecution got no such exemption.[84]

But as the bill was passing, so many of the illiterate immigrants that Lodge, Hall, Ross, and others complained about, even those benighted southern Italians, were learning to read and write that, once the war ended and immigration rose again, the literacy test wasn't much of a screen. It was nonetheless evidence that in an age that knew little political correctness in its public discourse, Congress, with its eye on the immigrant vote, fearing yet another a presidential veto and probably still in deference to the nation's founding ideals, seemed averse to institutionalizing the overtly racist program that the public discussion pointed to and that would become national policy with the Immigration Acts of 1921 and 1924. It was the new human "sciences"—intelligence testing, eugenics—that, as much as anything else, helped break the ice.

• • •

The last word before America's entry into World War I—more accurately, perhaps, the first loud off-stage call forewarning of postwar nativist and eugenic virulence—came from Madison Grant, that most eminent of pedigreed old-family patricians, lawyer, world traveler, ardent conservationist, friend of two presidents, a founder of the New York Zoological Society and the Bronx Zoo, cofounder of the Save the Redwoods League and scores of other naturalist groups, trustee of the American Museum of Natural History, a collaborator (with Theodore Roosevelt) in the creation of the nation's system of national parks, and member of virtually every major gentlemen's club on two continents. Grant, also a longtime member of the Immigration Restriction League and a budding eugenicist, was even gloomier than his fellow nativist Edward Ross, who, despite his racism, had seen the American as "destined to play a brilliant and leading role on the stage of history."[85] And he was far gloomier than his friend Roosevelt, who at various times in his career favored excluding anarchists and the unfit but who famously declared that "if the immigrant who comes here does in good faith [with the help of education] become an American and assimilates himself to us he shall be treated on an exact equality with every one else, for it is an outrage to discriminate against any such man because of creed or birth-place or origin."[86]

Grant had no such hopes. He was angrily certain that the horde of immigrants he saw all around him in New York, Jews especially, was evidence, as he would put it in his magnum opus of 1916, of "the passing of the great race." In a later time, the conservationist interests to which his nativism was closely (if perversely) linked might have led him to call the great race, primarily Nordics, an endangered species. Grant, almost certainly unaware of the irony, had in fact written an article in the 1890s called "The Vanishing Moose."[87]

Grant's *Passing of the Great Race* embraced nineteenth-century European (primarily French) racial theorizing, refined in 1899 by a young MIT economist named William Z. Ripley, who in his book *The Races of Europe* divided whites into three distinct groups—the Nordic (or Teutonic, but always the superior race), the Alpine (from central and eastern Europe), and the Mediterranean. Grant's book was packaged as an ethnographic history of the rise and fall of Europe's racial preeminence, but its impetus seemed to originate in the author's revulsion at what the new immigrants had done to his America. Like others of his era, Grant, subscribing to Francis Walker's dark racial Darwinism, actually a Social Darwinist drama of the survival of the unfittest, also saw the ominous prospect of race suicide before him. He fervently believed that, unless drastic measures were taken, the American stock was finished. In a book loaded with facile anthropological theorizing, he concluded that the nation was in thrall to the "widespread and fatuous" belief in the power of environment or education, "which arises from the dogma of the brotherhood of man," to alter heredity:

> It has taken us fifty years to learn that speaking English, wearing good clothes and going to school and to church does not make a negro into a white man. Nor was a Syrian or Egyptian freedman transformed into a Roman by wearing a toga. . . . We shall have a similar experience with the Polish Jew, whose dwarf stature, peculiar mentality and ruthless concentration on self-interest are being engrafted on the stock of the nation.
>
> What the Melting Pot actually does in practice can be seen in Mexico where the absorption of the blood of the original Spanish conquerors by the native Indian population has produced the racial mixture we call Mexican and which is now engaged in demonstrating its incapacity for self-government. The world has seen many such mixtures of races and the character of a mongrel race is just beginning to be understood at its true value.[88]

Any cross of races is a member of the lower race. Thus a cross between a white man and a Negro produces a Negro. "The cross between any of the three European races and a Jew is a Jew," Grant wrote. The European war where, by his classifications, Nordics opposed Nordics, was a "civil war" fought largely by tall blond types who were slaughtering each other while the "brunets" who stood on the curb and avoided combat survived and became part of "the social discards" who had been immigrating to America.[89] He would likewise regard "the Bolshevist movement in Russia" as "a war of races. The Alpine peasantry, under Semitic leadership, are engaged in destroying the Nordic bourgeoisie, and with it the only racial elements of value in that great sodden welter of quasi-European peoples called 'The Russias.'"[90]

Grant, who seemed to prefer rule by an aristocracy of quality, complained bitterly about the leveling effects on government produced by a democracy accessible to people inferior in class, learning, or race, who didn't speak the proper English and were bereft of classical learning. "*Vox populi* . . . thus becomes an unending wail for rights, never a chant of duty," he said.[91] The fatuous belief in the power of American "institutions or environment to reverse and obliterate immemorial hereditary tendencies" had led America to welcome these new immigrants, the sweepings of European jails and asylums, "the weak, the broken, the mentally crippled of all races drawn from the bottom stratum of the Mediterranean basin and the Balkans, together with hordes of the wretched submerged populations of the Polish ghettoes" and to give them "a share in our land and prosperity." Grant continued:

> The American taxed himself to sanitate and educate these poor helots and as soon they could speak English, encouraged them to enter the political life, first of municipalities and then of the nation.
>
> The result is showing plainly in the rapid decline of the birth rate of native Americans because of the poorer classes of Colonial stock will not bring children into the world to compete in the labor market with the Slovak, the Italian, the Syrian and the Jew. The native American is too proud to mix socially with them and is gradually withdrawing from the scene, abandoning to them the land which he conquered and developed.[92]

The native American is vanishing from much of the country, Grant said, "being literally being driven off the streets of New York City by the swarms of Polish Jews. . . . He will not marry with inferior races and he cannot compete in the sweatshop and in the street trench with the newcomers. . . . From the point of view of race, it were better described as 'the survival of the unfit.'"[93] The "altruistic ideals," he concluded, and the "maudlin sentimentalism" that made America "an asylum for the oppressed" (a phrase he put in quotes), were leading the nation to the "racial abyss." If the melting pot were allowed to boil without control and the nation deliberately blinded itself to all "distinctions of race, creed or color" (again a phrase he put in quotes), the native American of colonial descent "will become as extinct as Athenians of the age of Pericles and the Viking of the age of Rollo."[94] There was a remedy: state-managed eugenic sterilization of those who were weak or unfit—the "social failures." That would solve the problem within a century and "enable us to get rid of the undesirables who crowd our jails, hospitals and insane asylums." It was a "practical, merciful and inevitable solution" that could be applied to an ever-widening circle of "discards," beginning with criminals and continuing through a range of "weaklings and defectives," extending "ultimately perhaps, to worthless race types."[95] Grant, pursuing his theory and its consequences, came to the logical conclusion that the ultimate problem was the American ideal of equality itself.

The Passing of the Great Race didn't get much attention when it was first published, but some ten new editions in the 1920s and 1930s drove U.S. sales up to an estimated sixteen thousand by the time of Grant's death in 1937, and many more overseas, a lot for a volume of prolix anthropological theorizing. The book, which was published in Munich in 1925 as *Der Untergang der grossen Rasse,* and has been reprinted several times in this country since World War II, influenced a great deal of subsequent writing and helped shape and feed racism and race-based laws both in the United States and in Europe for more than a generation. Adolf Hitler was said to have sent Grant a letter telling him that "the book is my Bible."[96] That may or may not be correct, but there's no doubt that *Mein Kampf* echoed some key Grant passages. "It is almost inconceivable," Hitler wrote for example, "to think that a Nigger or a Chinaman will become a German because he has learned the German language and is willing to speak German for the future, and even to cast his vote for a German political party."[97] Madison Grant was a man ahead of his time.

CHAPTER 3

"Science" Makes Its Case

In its extensive surveys of immigrants in the United States in the years 1907–10, the Dillingham Commission's determination of the high percentage of "retarded" immigrant children in American schools, like its numbers about immigrant paupers, inmates of public asylums, and other data, coincided with a great deal of popular belief about the inferiority of the new immigrant stocks.[1] Its surveys didn't control for the fact that native Americans were far more likely to be able to afford better private hospitals and institutions, and that immigrant children from southern and eastern Europe were growing up in homes where Yiddish or Italian was the primary language: those kinds of issues would be left to later generations. At the time of the Dillingham Commission investigations many American schools, particularly in the Midwest, were still offering programs in German or Polish—not schools, of course, that Jews attended—even as the parents were still reading one or more of the hundreds of foreign-language papers—Yiddish, German, Italian, Polish, Slovak—that served immigrants in the nation's major cities.

If there had been any doubts about either the survey data or the beliefs they reinforced, the new biological and social "sciences" beginning to proliferate in the decade before the lights went out all over Europe would serve to assuage them, if not end them. The early years of the new century saw the rediscovery of Gregor Mendel's genetics, with its inference that crossing breeds (in Mendel's case, smooth peas with wrinkled peas) produced an inferior new generation and with it the rise of the erroneous belief "that all human traits would behave like the color, size or wrinkling of Mendel's peas."[2] Concurrently, intelligence testing was imported from France and eugenics, which in the United States evolved into "race betterment," from England. Francis Galton, Darwin's cousin, who invented the word *eugenics,* believed, like William Graham Sumner and other American Social Darwinists, that sheltering weak individuals in social-welfare institutions would permit undesirable reproduction by the unfit. But Galton never proposed forced mass sterilization and never would have much to do with the American eugenicists who carried his banner; later, some of his followers in England would savagely attack American eugenics. Galton's cause was what would be called "positive" eugenics—biologically promising family planning, perhaps state mandated, based on genetic data conducive to good offspring. Although Theodore Roosevelt later squinted toward negative eugenics, presumably segregation or sterilization of the unfit, his injunction to good-stock American women to stop being selfish and have babies was essentially Galton's message.[3]

In America, however, and later in Germany, there was a more ambitious, grandiose goal: the revival of the great nation and culture that was being defiled by alien degenerates. The creation of the Eugenics Section of the American Breeders Association, many of whose members were prepared to be convinced by the eminent Harvard zoologist (and Galton admirer) Charles B. Davenport that breeding a superior human stock was no different from breeding better bulls or horses; the establishment of the Eugenics Record Office under Davenport and Harry H. Laughlin at the Carnegie-funded Station for Experimental Evolution at Cold Spring Harbor, New York, in 1910; the founding in 1914 in Battle Creek, Michigan, of the Race Betterment Foundation by John H. Kellogg, a physician and brother of the father of corn flakes; and later the establishment of the California-based Human Betterment Foundation all testified to the rapidly growing acceptance of eugenics not only as sound science but as the way to restore a better society by perfecting a better race. For the eugenicists, the objective was primarily restorative, even purgative—cleansing the society of its flawed genetic strain. But it was also a perfect fit for—even a *reductio ad absurdum* of—the older American hope of human and social perfectibility.

In the first decades of the twentieth century, eugenics drew many of the nation's most distinguished people. The speakers at the Race Betterment Foundation's second international conference in San Francisco in August 1915 included David Starr Jordan, the first president of

Stanford University; Irving Fisher, Sumner's former student and great admirer who became a distinguished economist at Yale; and the plant breeder Luther Burbank, who spoke about the importance of good nourishment but concluded that the benefits were transient. "Only by constant selection of the best can any race ever be improved," Burbank said.[4] At the same conference, Paul Popenoe, the editor of the *American Journal of Heredity,* talking about the natural selection of man, said there were only two ways to "improve the germinal character of the race." One was to "kill off the weaklings born in each generation." The other was to substitute a "selective birthrate for Nature's death rate. That means eugenics."[5] Madison Grant's friend and colleague Henry Fairfield Osborn, president of the American Museum of Natural History, which hosted the Second International Congress of Eugenics in 1921, was named president of the conference; Alexander Graham Bell was named its honorary president. "As science has enlightened government in the prevention of disease," Osborn said in his opening address, "it must also enlighten government in the prevention of the spread and multiplication of worthless members of society."[6]

Among the most devoted of the eugenicists was the psychologist and psychometrician Henry H. Goddard, director of the Vineland (New Jersey) Training School for Feeble Minded Boys and Girls, who in 1908 had translated the Binet-Simon IQ scale into English (it would soon become the Stanford-Binet test). In his study of the pseudonymous "Kallikak" family, tracing the offspring of a normal man and a woman with supposedly defective genes—a study characterized by later critics as "little more than guesswork"—he had already made his case for the heritability of feeblemindedness and, resonating with it, the dangers of interracial breeding.[7] (*Die Familie Kallikak* was published in Germany in 1914 and reprinted there shortly after the Nazis came to power in 1933.) In 1912 Goddard, regarded as a kind man—he came from a devout Quaker family in Maine—who saw his professional work as a calling to advance his Quaker ideals, was invited to Ellis Island to develop a way of screening out "imbeciles" and the other mentally unfit aliens barred by immigration laws. But Goddard, who seems to have doctored his photos of the Kallikaks to make them look more like depraved "morons"—a word derived from Greek roots that he coined for the purpose (he concluded they were not "imbeciles or idiots")—contended it was easy to spot the unfit; just a glance, he said, would do it.

In the course of his work at Ellis Island, Goddard and two colleagues from the Vineland School examined a sample of "average" immigrants that had already been purged of "defectives" by inspectors. In that group, which included a representative spectrum of immigrants of the time, 40 percent were classified as feebleminded; 60 percent of Jews were classified as morons. "Two Immigrants Out of Five Feebleminded," said the headline in *The Survey*, a generally sober journal.[8] Morons, Goddard hopefully observed, "if taken early and trained carefully and so kept from becoming vicious and criminal, could be successfully employed if the employer understood them, and realizing that they are children, excused their faults and mistakes, [and] was watchful of, and patient with them." Yet even here, Goddard said, his screen—a combination of tests—"is too lenient. The standard would seem to be too low for prospective American citizens."[9]

From the start, Goddard must have been a little uncomfortable with his methods. His only major summary table, based on one part of his analysis, classified 82 percent of Russian immigrants (presumably non-Jewish) as morons, followed by Hungarians (80 percent morons), Italians (79 percent), and Jews (76 percent). Nonetheless, he confidently reported:

> We believe that this study has demonstrated that it is entirely feasible to test with considerable degree of accuracy the mentality of the immigrant. When we say feasible we do not mean easy. Dr. Williams, chief medical officer at Ellis Island in 1914, has ably set forth the difficulties. Nevertheless he shows that, beginning at about the time of our experiment, the number of aliens deported because of feeble-mindedness (not insane or epileptic) increased approximately 350 per cent in 1913 and 570 per cent in 1914 over what it had been in each of the five preceding years.[10]

In the spring of 1917, shortly after America entered the war (and before his article on mental tests and immigration appeared), Goddard, collaborating with Harvard's Robert Yerkes, president of the American Psychological Association, and Stanford psychologist Lewis Terman, committed eugenicists all, began a more ambitious project. Working at the Vineland School, they developed what became the army Alpha and Beta intelligence tests. The Alpha test was to be given to all World War I recruits who were literate in English. The Beta test, a picture test, was designed for recruits, many of them immigrants, who couldn't speak or read English. It included drawing lines through mazes, counting cubes in a pile, fitting two pieces together to make a specific geometric figure, and sketching missing elements on a picture—a missing finger on a hand, a missing leg on a table, a cat missing its shadow. A third test consisting of "construction puzzles," with instructions given by gestures and measured on a "performance scale," was developed for those who couldn't complete either the Alpha or Beta test. All three tests involved a lot of psychometric guesswork; both the Alpha and Beta required a fair degree of cultural literacy that boys off the farm or recently off the boat probably had never been exposed to. (How many would know that Crisco was a food product and not a "patent medicine or a toothpaste"?) After Yerkes persuaded the army to let him proceed, he and his team administered the tests to some two million soldiers.

The test results were first published in 1921 in Yerkes's 890-page National Academy of Sciences monograph, *Psychological Examining in the United States Army*.[11] Then, with Yerkes's blessing, the results were further analyzed in 1923 in *A Study of American Intelligence*, by the young Princeton psychologist Carl C. Brigham, one of the participating testers and later to become a principal author of the Scholastic Aptitude Test, now the SAT that millions of American college applicants take every year.[12] As might have been expected (by the testers perhaps most of all), most of the results came out with near-perfect predictability. Commissioned officers showed more intelligence than officer candidates, who showed more intelligence than the sergeants, who scored higher than the corporals. Most famously, perhaps, the tests showed that the mental age of the average American adult was just over thirteen, a finding that seemed to surprise even the testers, since Terman had previously estimated it at sixteen. The reports devoted many pages to alternately embracing and trying to explicate that finding away, arguing essentially that "mental age" was merely a testing abstraction invented by Alfred Binet, who first devised the test for French schoolchildren, and didn't really mean that the average American adult had the mentality of a child.[13] At the same time, as Terman said, many testers were certain that "all feebleminded are at least potential criminals. . . . Moral judgment . . . is a function of intelligence."[14]

Army recruits born in England scored higher than all other groups (including native-born white draftees). Far down on the intelligence scale (in descending order), and thus high in the moron category, were draftees born in Belgium, Ireland, Austria, Turkey, Greece, Russia, Italy, and Poland, who in the overall rankings were just above black draftees. ("Thus," wrote an acerbic critic, "is the white race saved from complete disgrace!") The testers also concluded that the decline in American intelligence was due to two factors: the "change in races migrating to this country" and "the sending of lower and lower representatives of each race."[15] That deterioration of intellectual ability, Brigham calculated from the army test data, "would give us over 2,000,000 immigrants below the average negro."[16]

The testers were initially surprised that the longer that foreign-born recruits had been in this country, the higher their intelligence scores were. After twenty years' residence here, the average foreign-born draftee had closed the gap with native-born draftees. One hypothesis was that the stupid immigrants went home while the intelligent ones stayed. More likely, Brigham concluded later in his book, it was because the more recent immigrants, being predominantly southern European rather than Nordic, were of inferior intelligence compared to those who'd arrived earlier. (It apparently didn't occur to them that after twenty years residence in the United States, immigrants had become more literate in English and American culture.) The testers acknowledged that much was speculation. "At best," they said, "we can but leave for future decision the question as to whether the differences represent a real difference in intelligence or an artifact of the method of examination."[17] They also worked hard to explain why northern blacks had higher scores than those from the South. They acknowledged that education and economic conditions had something to do with it, but adamantly refused to admit that there wasn't also a difference in innate intelligence. Maybe the result came from "the greater admixture of white blood."[18]

But such matters seemed not to raise any doubt in Brigham's mind that "interpreting the army data by means of the race hypothesis support Mr. Madison Grant's thesis of the superiority of the Nordic type." And of course the testing ambiguities didn't deter Brigham from echoing Grant (and probably Hitler, who was writing almost the same thing in *Mein Kampf* at just about the same time): "The Fourth of July orator can convincingly raise the popular belief in the intellectual level of Poland by shouting the name of Kosciusko from a high platform," Brigham said, "but he can not alter the distribution of the intelligence of the Polish immigrant." Moreover, since roughly half of recent Russian immigrants were Jews, he said, "our data would tend to disprove the popular belief that the Jew is highly intelligent."[19] Nor was Brigham deterred from making extended analyses of intraracial differences—was the Alpine type superior to the Mediterranean?—or extensive elaborations on the inferiority of the American Negro and the pernicious effects of whites marrying partners from inferior races.

But the real burden of Brigham's book was how to arrest the decline of American intelligence, and that "of course must be dictated by science and not by political expediency. Immigration should not only be restrictive but highly selective. And the revision of the immigration and naturalization laws will only afford a slight relief from our present difficulty. The really important steps are those looking to the prevention of the continued propagation of defective strains in the present population."[20]

It was almost certainly this issue, reinforced again by a potent dose of intellectual elitism, racism, and class snobbery, rather than anything having to do with military efficiency, that was the major reason for the testing to begin with. "The author presents not opinions but facts," said Yerkes in his foreword to Brigham's book. "It behooves us to consider their reliability and their meaning, for no one of us as a citizen can afford to ignore the menace of race deterioration or the evident relation of immigration to national progress and welfare."[21] In 1923, almost at the same time the book was published, Yerkes wrote a piece for the *Atlantic Monthly* reiterating the case for its nonprofessional readers: the tests showed that the intelligence of the new immigrants was inferior. Nor was there any doubt about the link of inferior intelligence to crime and delinquency. That had been "clearly established."[22] Intellectuals have well tended the roots of American anti-intellectualism for generations.

From their publication on, the racist inferences drawn from the army studies, and from Brigham's book in particular, got no more than a lukewarm reception from critics and often much less than that. Some responses came from liberal journalists like Walter Lippmann, who, in debates with Terman and in a series of *New Republic* articles, listed a whole array of flaws, some technical, some definitional (what is "intelligence" anyway?), some logical, among them the simple fact that "the average adult intelligence cannot be less than the average adult intelligence, and to anyone who knows what the words 'mental age' mean, the conclusion that the average American has a mental age of 14 is precisely as silly as if [the author] had written that the average mile was three quarters of a mile long."[23] More critiques came from members of the scientific community. Kimball Young, a Stanford psychologist and a student of Terman's, savaged Brigham for embracing Grant's antiquated race theory dividing Europeans into distinct Nordic (northern) Alpine and Mediterranean groups and for drawing unwarranted inferences from what might well have been skewed military samples. The testing left out groups, presumably including many of the better-educated, who had been exempted for work in war-related industries, which Young argued (correctly) impugned all responsible testing. "We shall never pass to this second, advanced stage of work," he wrote, "if we rest our case as psychologists on the shifting sands of an antiquated, outworn and mythological race hypothesis."[24]

The oddest and probably the most devastating attack, however, came from what, to Brigham, was an entirely unexpected quarter. Yerkes had asked his Harvard colleague, psychologist Edwin G. Boring, who'd actually read portions of Brigham's manuscript, to write a review, which Boring agreed to do. In a letter to Brigham, Boring had offered congratulations on having "presented a difficult subject in a wonderfully clear and careful manner," and he promised a favorable review.[25] (No ethical qualms about lack of academic objectivity or collegial incest there.) The review, which was also to appear in the *New Republic,* with which Boring said he had an arrangement, might leave "less for Lippmann . . . to jump on."

Before he finished the review, however, Boring changed his mind, probably because he felt a need to justify some of his earlier writing. His piece, "Facts and Fancies of Immigration," which ran in the spring of 1923, put much of the blame on the data in the Yerkes team's original army studies, which "were not collected with an ultimate scientific analysis in mind." The data might be scientifically sound, but could the authors really draw the broader inferences about whole populations in their conclusions? There was a "mountain of statistical material" in the army reports, which brought forth only "a timid mouse."[26] Brigham's book was also sharply criticized in *Science, Scientific Monthly,* the *American Journal of Psychology,* and the *Educational Review,* in part for misinterpretations of data and in part for its conclusion that the declining intelligence of recent immigrants was based on the native inferiority of the new "races" rather than on the difference in the class of immigrants who had been arriving.[27] By 1924, contra Goddard's findings at Ellis Island before the war, even Terman, while sticking to all his other racial theories about the worst immigrants being the biggest breeders, included Jews with northern and western Europeans as "the most prolific of gifted children." The worst, as always, were the "Mediterranean races, the Mexicans and the Negroes."[28]

A more fundamental challenge came from the eminent Columbia University anthropologist Franz Boas, a German-Jewish immigrant who would spend the coming years debunking not only beliefs in racial differences or the artificial divisions between superior Nordics and benighted Mediterraneans but teaching the world that the idea of race was itself a social, not a scientific, construct. Humans of all nations, Boas contended in sharp and often explicit contradistinction to the Madison Grants, were equally capable of growth and development. All men were created equal. (In the 1930s, as they were awarding American eugenicist Harry

Laughlin an honorary degree from Heidelberg, and reprinting the German version of Grant's *Passing of the Great Race,* the Nazis would pay Boas the ultimate compliment of burning his book on culture and race and revoking the doctorate he'd earned in physics and geography from the University of Kiel in 1881.)

• • •

The doubts of some respected scientists and the other critics, however, were hardly proof against eugenics and a racial "science" that reinforced a century of nativist belief, lately amplified by the dislocation, traumas, and hypernationalism unleashed by the war and the immediate postwar years. Americans had turned against everything German during the war, which led not only to the overnight cancellation of bilingual (German) education in hundreds of midwestern schools but to the harassment and sometimes forced sale of German American–owned meatpacking plants and other businesses, the conversion of sauerkraut into "liberty cabbage," and the banishment of Bach, Beethoven, and Brahms from concert halls. The war prompted states like Nebraska to pass "Babel Acts" banning the use of any language but English in public. "Let those who cannot speak or understand the English language," famously declared Governor William L. Harding of Iowa, who called for a ban on German speech anywhere, even in churches and on the phone, "conduct their religious worship in their home."[29] Not surprisingly, the war against those who were then often called "the Huns" also caused some discomfort for the theorists of Nordic superiority who had contended that America's great germ-plasm and its superior culture had come largely from the Teutonic forests.

The nationalism, xenophobia, and messianic furor unleashed by the war, rather than ending with the armistice, were quickly reinforced by the postwar industrial strikes and demonstrations—some for better wages and conditions, some for the nationalization of factories and mines—that swept the nation. Those strikes and the associated workplace tensions helped pry business leaders from their resistance to tougher restrictions on the immigration of cheap labor and seemed to intensify the nostalgia, especially in the outback, for simpler times. On January 16, 1919, two days before Woodrow Wilson was to give his opening address at the Paris Peace Conference—and two months after the armistice was signed ending the war to end all wars—Utah became the thirty-sixth and deciding state to ratify the Eighteenth Amendment, allowing Prohibition to become the law of the land. It was a signal victory not only for the Anti-Saloon League and old Puritan America against the urban boozers, not all of them Irish Catholics, and against modernism generally. It also created a huge market for the bootleggers, many of them immigrants, and their sons, who were most reviled by the temperance thumpers and the Elmer Gantrys who got Prohibition passed and for many of whom the law promised to be the first step toward restoration of the dream of American purity.

Later in that spring and summer of 1919, more labor unrest and a string of noisy protests by American communists and anarchists, many of them also immigrants, and the resulting street riots in Cleveland and other cities, seemed to validate the fears of Bolshevism spreading west from the Russian Revolution of 1917. More menacingly, there was the bombing of the Washington, D.C., home of Attorney General A. Mitchell Palmer and the discovery of some three dozen mail bombs addressed to leading businesspeople and public officials—Supreme Court justices, cabinet officers, the commissioner of immigration, as well as J.P. Morgan and John D. Rockefeller, a list whose eminent membership indicated the naiveté of the would-be bomber. All the bombs were found before they did any damage, but they certainly got plenty of attention.

Combined, the events of 1919 sparked the great wave of crackdowns that became known as the Palmer Raids on alleged communists and other suspected radicals, many of them aliens. (In the course of those arrests, Palmer's agents found three guns and no explosives whatever; a few hundred radicals were deported, but most were eventually released for lack of evidence. The best known were Alexander Berkman and the Russian-born Emma Goldman, who, though a U.S. citizen, had been convicted of conspiring to obstruct the World War I draft. At the direction of J. Edgar Hoover, then Palmer's assistant, both were shipped back to Russia in 1919.)[30] The violence, real and only feared, also reinforced dark rumors from Palmer's office of yet more Red plots—among other things, Palmer said, the Bolsheviks were preparing to take away Americans' savings, including the Liberty Bonds that the government sold during the war. Combined, the strikes, bombings, demonstrations, and the rumors that spread from them created the panic that became the Red Scare, which, in Frederick Lewis Allen's wonderful social history, persuaded "millions of otherwise reasonable citizens" that "a Red revolution might begin in the United States the next month or next week [making them] less concerned with making the world safe for democracy than with making America safe for themselves."[31]

The resulting pressure to conform and the accompanying fear of being attacked as a communist spread everywhere—into schools and college classrooms, to the theater, even to suspicions raised about the Americanism and loyalty of the League of Women Voters, the newly formed Foreign Policy Association, and the National Council of Churches. But the Red Scare's most memorable symbol remains the Sacco-Vanzetti case, in which two Italian immigrant anarchists, Nicola Sacco, a shoemaker, and Bartolomeo Vanzetti, a fishmonger, were executed for the murder of a payroll clerk and a guard in connection with what began as a little-noticed payroll robbery in 1920 in Braintree, Massachusetts. After extensive coverage in left-wing newspapers in Europe, the case became an international sensation. The men were convicted and went to the electric chair in August 1927, following a trial before a hanging judge named Webster Thayer, who did little to conceal his biases about "Bolsheviki" outside the courtroom, and after a string of appeals whose fairness and impartiality continues to be questioned to this day. Among those named to a panel to review the defendants' pardon application by the governor of Massachusetts were the presidents of Harvard and MIT, who, despite the questionable evidence and Thayer's obvious bias, found the men guilty. For the McCarthy generation of the 1950s, the events of the Red Scare would have been familiar stuff.

Given that climate and the accompanying flurry of anti-Semitic, anti-black, anti-Catholic, and generically nativist messages coming from the Allied Patriotic Societies, the American Legion, the American Defense Society, the Ku Klux Klan, and countless other sources, the nation wasn't too fussy about what Franz Boas or Walter Lippmann thought about race, or what was and wasn't good science. The xenophobic climate also helped weld the particular biases against Italians, Poles, Greeks, and all the rest into an undifferentiated suspicion of all foreigners. In 1920, even before Brigham's book appeared, Lothrop Stoddard, another Boston Yankee with a family dating back to colonial times, had published his *Rising Tide of Color against White World-Supremacy*, a book that grew out of his Harvard doctoral thesis on the black slave uprising and ensuing slaughter of whites in Haiti, which he regarded as the first omen of what was to come. There was no more "absurd fallacy," Stoddard wrote, "than the shibboleth of the melting pot. As a matter of fact, the melting-pot may mix but does not melt. Each race-type, formed ages ago, and 'set' by millenniums of isolation and inbreeding, is a stubbornly persistent entity. Each type possesses a special set of characters: not merely the physical characters visible to the naked eye, but moral, intellectual, and spiritual characters as well. All these characters are transmitted substantially unchanged from generation to generation."[32]

Stoddard followed that up in 1922 with a similar volume, *The Revolt against Civilization: The Menace of the Under Man,* based in part on Yerkes and Goddard's army studies. The book's chapter called "The Iron Law of Inequality" begins with the declaration that the idea of natural equality "was one of the most pernicious delusions that has ever afflicted mankind."[33] Madison Grant, who advised Stoddard on his first book and whose ideas echo through both, wrote a lengthy introduction for it. Expressing horror at the postwar creation of "Alpine states" like Czechoslovakia and Yugoslavia in central Europe, no longer subject to the control of the superior Nordics, Grant's introduction was even more grimly racist than his own *Passing of the Great Race* four years before. Yet Stoddard's book, despite negative reviews, may have been more influential than Grant's with American readers. It went through a number of printings and got enough currency in the general culture that Stoddard (with a slight change of name) was immortalized in the words of *The Great Gatsby*'s rich, vacuous Tom Buchanan: "'Civilization's going to pieces,' broke out Tom violently. 'I've gotten to be a terrible pessimist about things. Have you read "The Rise of the Colored Empires" by this man Goddard? . . . It's a fine book and everybody ought to read it. The idea is if we don't look out the white race will be—will be utterly submerged. It's all scientific stuff; it's been proved.'"[34]

Many psychologists and social theorists of the 1920s, little troubled by the doubts about the army tests or by Madison Grant's racial stereotypes, associated themselves with eugenics organizations or projects: the Race Betterment Foundation, the American Eugenics Society and its twenty-eight associated state committees, Grant's overtly racist Galton Society, and several others. In the 1920s, fairs around the country offered "Fitter Families Contests," many sponsored by the American Eugenics Society and defined (at one Kansas fair) as "a legitimate outgrowth of scientific agriculture. [The contest] is the application of the principles of scientific plant and animal husbandry to the next higher order of creation, the human family, and contemplates the development of a science of practical human husbandry."[35]

There were exhibits on hygiene and posters on "the right to be well born," books on eugenics and marriage, and charts showing the genealogy "of a feebleminded woman sterilized in California." Journals were full of pieces with titles like "Mental Differences in Certain Immigrant Groups," "Intelligence as Related to Nationality," "Intelligence Tests of

Foreign Children," and "Race Differences in New York City," many of them echoed in the popular media. Eugenics was the science of the Polish joke, the moron joke, and the ethnic vaudeville routine. Selective immigration, said one sympathetic writer with unintended irony, was the new mercantilism.[36] In 1922, the *New York Times* unblushingly ran a lengthy book review by Madison Grant extolling the virtues of race purity and the historical superiority of the Nordic race and warning "native Americans whose traditions are threatened with submergence by the incoming hordes of immigrants." It was headlined "Failures of the Melting Pot."[37]

More dubiously still, hundreds of colleges, including Harvard, Columbia, Brown, and Cornell, offered biology courses on eugenics; eugenics was written into high school biology texts as a legitimate science. The young John Scopes was using one in his classroom in Dayton, Tennessee, when he agreed to be the defendant in the American Civil Liberties Union test case challenging that state's laws against teaching evolution. The book, *A Civic Biology Presented in Problems,* which characterized "the Caucasians, represented by the civilized white inhabitants of Europe and America" as "the highest type of all" the races, had an extended section on heredity based in part on Charles Davenport's discussion of the Jukes in his book on eugenics, and in part on Henry Goddard's Kallikak family and other families of "degenerates," complete with diagrams:

> The cost to society of such families is very severe. Just as certain animals or plants become parasitic on other plants or animals, these families have become parasitic on society. They not only do harm to others by corrupting, stealing, or spreading disease, but they are actually protected and cared for by the state out of public money. Largely for them the poorhouse and the asylum exist. They take from society, but they give nothing in return. They are true parasites.
>
> If such people were lower animals, we would probably kill them off to prevent them from spreading. Humanity will not allow this, but we do have the remedy of separating the sexes in asylums or other places and in various ways preventing intermarriage and the possibilities of perpetuating such a low and degenerate race.[38]

To this day, in the view of some scholars, it was the eugenic and Social Darwinist elements, not Darwinism per se, that most enraged William Jennings Bryan, the Nebraska populist, three-time presidential candidate, and former secretary of state who had been the biggest promoter of the nation's antievolution laws. Bryan, who could never resist a platform, volunteered to be the lead prosecutor at the Dayton "monkey trial," and as such became the "walking malignancy" of H.L. Mencken's famous obituary, "a vulgar and common man, a cad undiluted . . . ignorant, bigoted, self-seeking, blatant and dishonest." As Matthew Brady, the Bible-thumping true believer in the Mencken-influenced play *Inherit the Wind,* Bryan was a burned-out case more to be pitied than to be detested or lampooned.[39]

But in the full context of the case and Bryan's motives, the story is neither simple nor devoid of long-term consequences. The Harvard paleontologist Stephen Jay Gould, a vigorous defender of evolution against creationism, argued that at least part of Bryan's quarrel was not with evolution per se but grew from Bryan's misreading of evolution as the might-makes-right philosophy that Bryan believed drove Germany's aggression in World War I. Gould quotes the text of Bryan's "Last Evolution Speech," the long closing argument drafted for the Dayton trial but never delivered: "By paralyzing the hope of reform [evolution] discourages those who labor for the improvement of man's condition," Bryan planned to say. "Its only program for man is scientific breeding, a system in which a few supposedly superior intellects, self appointed, would direct the mating and the movements of the mass of mankind—an impossible system."[40] It was eugenics that Bryan was quarreling with.

• • •

Far and away the most important and influential "scientific" eugenic enterprise of the postwar era, however, was the Eugenics Record Office (ERO), which was attached to Charles Davenport's Carnegie Institution Station for Experimental Evolution at Cold Spring Harbor on Long Island. It would be run from its founding in 1910 until 1939 by the hyperactive eugenicist Harry Laughlin, who like many of his fellow reformers seemed well pedigreed for the role. Son of a preacher father in Kirksville, Missouri, and a mother who was both a temperance activist and a suffragist, Laughlin began his career as a high-school teacher and principal and a normal school agriculture teacher in his hometown. It was at the normal school that his interest in animal breeding led him to his true calling. He would later write a thesis on cytology for his doctor of science degree from Princeton, but other than his devotion to eugenics he had no special qualifications in 1910 when Davenport hired him.[41]

At its start, the ERO was generously funded by Mary Averell Harriman, the widow of railroad tycoon Edward H. Harriman (who had controlled both the Union Pacific and the Southern Pacific railroads), who, after her husband's death, became a prominent philanthropist associated with environmental causes.[42] The ERO, which would soon be underwritten even more lavishly with Carnegie Institution funds, became the center and wellspring of a great network of eugenicist activists and projects. The projects, some Orwellian, some just silly, included collecting reams of physical data on thousands of Americans and using that data to chart hereditary traits through families; categorizing and ranking "races"; compiling "the Geographical and Ancestral Records of Members of the United States Senate"; and studying "the Approaching Extinction of Mayflower Descendants," "the Direct Cost of the Socially Inadequate to New York State," and "Juvenile Delinquency as Related to Immigration." There was also a "Corn Breeding Experiment to Demonstrate Human Heredity"; the compilation of "an index of inventiveness," with the French and Swedes at the top and Italians, Poles, Belgians, Latin Americans, and Africans at the bottom; work toward defining "the socially inadequate" in the United States; studies of the feebleminded in Connecticut and of "Race Descent and Crime in the United States."[43]

In the course of those projects, the ERO trained hundreds of young interns, most of them from the Ivy League, to gather data and become good eugenic scientists. Along the way, Laughlin, Davenport, and others published countless papers, letters, and articles on immigration, sterilization, and eugenics. Most important, they gathered data to promote the forced sterilization of "defectives" and generated the "science" supporting immigration laws that excluded inferior individuals from inferior races. From its creation in 1910, the ERO's basic assumptions were clear. Unless conditions changed, Davenport wrote, "The population of the United States will, on account of the great influx of blood from South-eastern Europe, become rapidly darker in pigmentation, smaller in stature, more mercurial, more attached to music and art [all those Italians?], more given to crimes of larceny, kidnapping, assault, murder, rape and sex-immorality and less given to burglary, drunkenness, and vagrancy than were the original English settlers. . . . It seems probable that, under present conditions, the ratio of insanity in the population will rapidly increase."[44]

The ERO listed among its initial board of "scientific directors" Alexander Graham Bell, who would have second thoughts and withdraw, and Yale's Irving Fisher, who was deeply committed to the cause. The "expert" advisors to the ERO's "Committee to Study and to Report on the Best Practical Means of Cutting Off the Defective Germ-Plasm in the American Population" in 1914 included Robert DeCourcy Ward, who had been a founder of the Immigration Restriction League; Henry Goddard, on psychology; Fisher, on "public affairs"; and Johns Hopkins University geneticist Raymond Pearl, whose expertise was listed as "thrematology," which the dictionary defines as the branch of biology dealing with the breeding of domestic animals and plants but which the committee defined as "the efficacy of sterilization of hereditary degenerates to raise the average of the race." The committee's "suggested remedies" ranged from "eugenical education" and "general environmental betterment" to "life segregation," polygamy, sterilization, and euthanasia, some of which were rejected as unacceptable to a modern society. Nonetheless, the committee concluded that "a successful society must at all hazards protect its breeding stock, and since, under modern conditions, a vigorous program of segregation supported by sterilization seems to present the only practicable means for accomplishing such end, a progressive social order must in sheer self-preservation accept it."[45]

The dour Davenport leveraged his high-prestige positions and influence at major educational and zoological institutions—Harvard, the American Museum of Natural History, and the new Eugenics Section of the American Breeders Association, among others—to get support for his Faustian ambition to create a superior race. He had close connections with the noted paleontologist and eugenicist Henry Fairfield Osborn, a fellow trustee of the museum; with his longtime friend Madison Grant, who was also a trustee of the museum; and with a range of other eugenicists, race theorists, and eugenics associations both in the United States and in Europe. Through Laughlin, who in 1921 would be named by Chairman Albert Johnson as the "expert eugenics agent" of the House Committee on Immigration and Naturalization, the ERO would also become the semiofficial immigration research arm of Congress. In 1923, Johnson would be elected president of the Eugenics Research Association.[46] Laughlin and Johnson would get along famously.

The ERO's ranking of the strengths and defects of the races picked up where the Dillingham Commission and the army testers had left off (although the ERO sometimes relied on the army data in its own reports). In elaborating on the related eugenic theories regarding the inheritability of degeneracy, the ERO also produced a prodigious amount of other material—reports, articles, the periodical *Eugenical News,* testimony before governmental committees, and papers at academic conferences—some of which was directed to the eugenics field, some to the general public, and some, particularly in the late 1920s and 1930s, to state policy makers who were developing and campaigning for compulsory eugenic sterilization. Laughlin was the author of the model Virginia law that allowed for the sterilization of any institutionalized person maintained at public expense who was feebleminded, insane, epileptic (which, it later appeared, would have included Laughlin himself), inebriate, "criminalistic," blind, and/or who exhibited other traits regarded as "socially inadequate." It was this law that would be upheld in 1927 by the U.S. Supreme Court in the 8–1 *Buck v. Bell* decision in which Justice Oliver Wendell Holmes famously declared that "three generations of imbeciles are enough."[47]

Laughlin's own contribution to the *Buck v. Bell* case, in addition to the Virginia statute, was a deposition for the state in a lower court, written without Laughlin having seen any member of the "three generations" they were supposedly members of—"the shiftless, ignorant, and worthless class of anti-social whites of the South." (And though it is Justice Holmes's quote that is justly enshrined in the annals of juridical infamy, those voting to affirm the law and who signed Holmes's opinion included two other giants of the court, Louis D. Brandeis and Harlan Fiske Stone.) Eugenic sterilization had been enacted into law in several states in the first decade of the century; in some, the courts struck the laws down—it was their legal defects that Laughlin's model Virginia statute sought to remedy.

Nonetheless, the widespread acceptance of compulsory sterilization after the war was a clear indication, and maybe the most frightening, of the extent to which eugenics had become accepted in the United States—though it was never embraced to anywhere near the same extent in Francis Galton's England, where the theory was born. Between the 1920s and the early 1970s, when the practice of forced sterilization finally ended, there would be some sixty thousand eugenic sterilizations in thirty-three states, among them an uncounted number of epileptics who were regarded as feebleminded. An estimated twenty thousand of the total were eugenically sterilized in California alone.[48]

It may thus have been hardly surprising that even liberal reformers—Margaret Sanger, founder of Planned Parenthood, not least among them—would join earlier feminists like Victoria Woodhull in the belief that if a better society were to be created, better people had to be bred and inferior ones kept from reproducing. Like some of her contemporaries in the movement, Sanger regarded birth control and eugenics as inseparable and she unequivocally supported much of the eugenics agenda:

> The emergency problem of segregation and sterilization must be faced immediately [she wrote in 1922]. Every feeble-minded girl or woman of the hereditary type, especially of the moron class, should be segregated during the reproductive period. Otherwise, she is almost certain to bear imbecile children, who in turn are just as certain to breed other defectives. The male defectives are no less dangerous. Segregation carried out for one or two generations would give us only partial control of the problem. Moreover, when we realize that each feeble-minded person is a potential source of an endless progeny of defect, we prefer the policy of immediate sterilization, of making sure that parenthood is absolutely prohibited to the feeble-minded.[49]

In a speech in 1931, later published as an article in her *Birth Control Review,* she again called for a program "to apply a stern and rigid policy of sterilization and segregation to that grade of population whose progeny is already tainted or whose inheritance is such that objectionable traits may be transmitted to offspring" and "to give certain dysgenic groups in our population their choice of segregation or sterilization." The segregated would be given farms or homesteads "where they would be taught to work under competent instructors for . . . their entire lives." Sanger also embraced the eugenic taxonomy with her call to "keep the doors of immigration closed to the entrance of certain aliens whose condition is known to be detrimental to the stamina of the race, such as feebleminded, idiots, morons, insane, syphilitic, epileptic, criminal, [and] professional prostitutes."[50] In the late 1920s, Sanger, whose *Birth Control Review* was always open to eugenicists, even proposed some sort of alliance between her birth-control groups and eugenics organizations, which she regarded as part of the same movement.[51]

Although Sanger's defenders point out that in her struggle to liberate women she was never a racist, the opponents of abortion and birth control to this day suggest that through the Sanger link—and through her close associate, the New York University sociologist Henry Pratt Fairchild, author of the savagely nativist and racist *Melting Pot Mistake* (1926) and *The Alien in Our Midst* (1930)—Planned Parenthood carries a dreadful legacy. Her book, *The Pivot of Civilization,* can still be read as her inadvertent contribution to the case against abortion on the Web sites of some right-to-life organizations.[52]

In the 1930s, Laughlin would use the *Eugenical News* to advance eugenics in both domestic policy and immigration and, after Hitler came to power in 1933, to cheer on the ruthless sterilization law that the Nazis adopted. Laughlin and other American eugenicists claimed that the American laws and legal sanctions "provided the experience which

Germany used in writing their new sterilization statute." (By the time the Nazis came to power, there had been some thirty thousand eugenic sterilizations in the United States, giving Laughlin's claim some credibility.) It was difficult to see, Laughlin wrote in 1933, how the German law "could, as some have suggested be deflected from its purely eugenical purpose and be made an 'instrument of tyranny' for the sterilization of non-Nordic races." Until the law was to go into effect in January 1934, Germany would, in accordance with American sterilization laws, "work out a census of its socially inadequate human stocks." Thus, while "one may condemn the Nazi policy generally . . . it remained for Germany in 1933 to lead the great nations of the world in the recognition of the biological foundations of national character." Laughlin's article also included the full text of the Nazi law, which had been signed by Hitler himself.[53]

In 1936, the Nazis would return the compliment, recognizing Laughlin with "the very high honor," as he put it, of an honorary degree from Heidelberg. He enthusiastically accepted, especially since it came from a nation "which for many centuries nurtured the human seed-stock which later founded my own country and thus gave basic character to our present lives and institutions." His only regret was that he couldn't attend the ceremony "to receive this highly honored diploma in person."[54] By then, some of his partners in the cause had become jealous of the Nazis for outdoing America in their sterilization program. Laughlin lived until 1943. Did the memory of that mutual back-scratching ever make him cringe?

In the 1920s, however, most of the ERO's attention was directed to the restriction of immigration. Laughlin first appeared before the House Committee on Immigration and Naturalization in 1920, when, in his testimony on the "biological aspects of immigration," he told the committee that "the character of a nation is determined primarily by its racial qualities: that is, by the hereditary physical, mental, and moral or temperamental traits of its people."[55] It was that testimony that got him named the committee's "expert eugenics agent," a post that he used for an extended trip to Europe and for legitimizing his contacts overseas. The "expert" designation brought him before the committee several more times as the panel was working on what eventually became the national origins quota immigration bill of 1924, and then again as the committee and various government agencies were struggling with the tangled problem of working out the exact quota numbers. Laughlin's gauge of degeneracy "which characterizes the several nativity groups of the United States," he told the committee in 1922, "is not a direct measure of relative racial values, but a measure of the degree to which each racial and nativity group must be culled or sifted by the Federal Government in preventing immigration, and later, if this fails, in deporting degenerate individuals and families of whatsoever nationality. Still later, if all these attempts at prevention fail, and the degenerate individuals and families become established in a given State, the particular State must grapple with the problem of preventing the reproduction of these degenerate individuals and families."[56]

The priorities for human betterment in America thus were (1) keeping the unfit out of the country; (2) deporting them; and, if all else failed, (3) keeping them from reproducing. In pursuit of those goals, Laughlin presented Congress with statistics on feeblemindedness, "dependency," insanity, and crime rates by "race" or national origin, all based on his calculated "quotas"—bar graphs showing the percentage of immigrants in jails, prisons, lunatic asylums, and other institutions compared to their proportion of the general population. With 100 being "normal," northern Europeans—the Swiss (at 27 percent of their quota), the Germans, the Dutch, the Scandinavians, the British, even the Irish—fell far under their "quotas" for "social inadequates" in the crime category, while immigrants from Portugal, Italy, Turkey, "All Asia," Greece, the West Indies, "All Balkan States," China, Bulgaria, Mexico, Spain, and Serbia, along with the "American Negro," were the worst. The score was 185 for Portugal, 207 for the "American Negro," 549 for Mexico, 660 for Spain, and 1,400 for Serbia.[57]

Laughlin should have been more than a little uncomfortable with his table for "feeblemindedness," which showed that Ireland, Switzerland, and "All Asia" registered far under their "quotas," as he would probably have expected. But then came the "American Negro" at 15 percent, far better than native whites (at 107 percent), native whites with foreign-born parents, and, of course, Serbia, which was the worst of the worst. Since he himself pointed out in passing that only 5 percent of the feebleminded get institutional care, the rest being cared for by their families (and thus not counted), he should have been even charier about presenting the numbers at all.[58] He tried to explain away part of his problem with a convoluted eugenic rationale, wrapped in a thin layer of Grantian bigotry:

> We in this country have been so imbued with the idea of democracy, or the equality of all men, that we have left out of consideration the matter of blood or natural inborn hereditary mental and moral differences. No man who breeds pedigreed plants and animals can afford to neglect this thing, as

> you know. But in adding to our human breeding stock by immigration that is what we do: We keep out fairly well the individually feeble-minded immigrant, but, because we have ignored inborn quality, when the next generation arrives, children of immigrants make a very poor showing by being relatively very numerous in this particular type of degeneracy. According to our findings while the foreign born themselves only fulfilled their institutional quota for feeble-mindedness by 31.56 per cent, the native white, one parent foreign born and one native born, fulfilled their quota by 190.27 per cent—nearly twice the normal quota, or six times the quota of the present immigration generation.[59]

This argument, however, didn't account for the low proportion of blacks among the "feebleminded," much less address the larger inferential problem resulting from the huge percentage of people who weren't institutionalized and thus couldn't be counted through institutional censuses. Laughlin's fellow eugenicist Paul Popenoe, the editor of the *Journal of Heredity* and soon to become secretary of the Human Betterment Foundation, pointed out these problems but was not deterred in his general enthusiasm for Laughlin's "pack . . . of interesting information."[60]

Laughlin had an even more glaring problem with his contention that a large proportion of the inmates of mental institutions came from southern and eastern Europe even as his own number showed much larger percentages for the Irish (who had been low in the crime category) and Germans. His analysis also had anomalies regarding the army intelligence tests, which (as he would have expected) showed men born in England, Scotland, and men called up in the "white draft" heading the list of those with "superior intelligence," and Russia, Greece, Italy, Belgium, and Poland just above "Southern American Negroes" at the bottom. But since commissioned (white) officers, noncommissioned officers, and Negro officers scored highest in the army tests, all the tests seemed to prove was that the army had attracted volunteers who scored marginally better than draftees.[61] Laughlin also used the army data to project the "natural intelligence" of the entire U.S. population in the year 1920 from "very superior" through seven grades to "very inferior." Predictably, he established that while 24 percent of the whole white population were "inferior" or "very inferior" in intelligence, nearly 46 percent of the foreign-born fell into those categories—altogether more than six million of the fourteen million who were foreign-born. Since "native intelligence does not depend upon opportunity or education [and] is inborn [and] consequently transmitted from generation to generation," Laughlin told the committee, if there had been a mental test for native intelligence, all those immigrants of inferior intelligence could have been refused admission.[62]

Laughlin's chart listing "all types of social inadequacy" had similar problems. American blacks were ranked just below "native whites" in adequacy and above people from Canada, Germany, the Netherlands, Great Britain, and Ireland, who, along with immigrants from Mexico, Spain, and Serbia, were shown to be the very worst. Nor did Laughlin seem troubled that his census of mental institutions omitted many states with low numbers of immigrants and thus had few immigrant inmates, which of course would further skew his numbers and increase the statistical probability of error, something he appears to have deliberately overlooked.

Laughlin also ignored the fact that immigrant males tended to be far younger than the national average for men and thus were of the ages more prone to crime. He jiggered the base year for feeblemindedness and insanity to increase his "quota" for immigrants from northwestern Europe but not for immigrants from southern and eastern Europe. "Facts were . . . selected in such a manner and the methods of interpretation so chosen," wrote Joseph M. Gillman of the University of Pittsburgh in 1924, "as to yield the desired support for their preconceived conclusions."[63] In some cases, as in Laughlin's data for "dependency," which showed precisely the reverse, he simply ignored the numbers and concluded that "in the matter of thrift, if not in personal industry, the immigrants of former generations were superior to those of the present time."[64] Laughlin, Gillman said, "has ventured out from behind the screens of the generalities of our forefathers and has attempted to conceal his preconceptions in the elusiveness of technical statistical inaccuracies."[65]

None of those anomalies or the statistical inferences Laughlin drew from his samples, however, seemed to deter either him or his friend Chairman Johnson from their conclusions. The rankings, Laughlin told the House committee, "represent real differences in inborn values of the family stocks from which the particular inmates have sprung. These degeneracies and hereditary handicaps are inherent in the blood."[66] In subsequent testimony in March 1924, as the committee was working on what would become the definitive national origins law, Laughlin contended that the arrival of hordes of inferior immigrants was similar to, and in some ways worse than, an invasion by conquest, foreshadowing arguments that would be made eighty years later:

> When one people move from their home territory into the territory of another country, the ultimate result depends not so much upon whether the movement is a sudden military invasion, as contrasted with a more insidious invasion by immigration, as upon variation of the incoming individuals in the factors of race, sex, numbers, age, distribution, mate selection, differential fecundity, and ultimate family stock qualities of body, mind, and morals. The immediate difference between military conquest and immigration is tremendous, but in the perspective of history, by which we judge the lives of nations and races, the difference is not nearly so great. In the long run, military conquest by a superior people would be highly preferable to a conquest by immigration by peoples with inferior stock endowments.
>
> Immigration is an insidious invasion just as clearly as, and works more certainly in national conquest than, the invading army which may or may not come and go without supplanting national population. If the immigration is of a closely related racial type, and possesses inborn talents higher than those of the native stocks, then the national type is preserved and the character improved. But if, on the other hand, the racial type is not assimilable, and the inborn traits of character are less ideal than those of the foundation stocks, then immigration works toward ultimate disaster.[67]

Our latter-day Cassandras of *reconquista* couldn't put it any better.

The appearance of feeblemindedness, epilepsy, and other forms of "degeneracy" among immigrants who had passed the screens at Ellis Island, or among their children, demonstrated the need, in Laughlin's view, for the stationing of agents overseas who would more thoroughly investigate the backgrounds and the family and genetic histories of those seeking to immigrate. "If the country is to be protected against inferior immigrants and is to select and welcome superior strains," he told the committee in March 1924, the nation's future laws "should provide by statute for the determination of individual and hereditary qualities by requiring modern pedigree examination in the home territories of the would-be immigrant. Our standard should ultimately eliminate not only the positively feeble-minded, but also all those who are below the American average in natural intelligence." His charts showed, he said, that "our recent immigration, as a whole, has not served to raise the intelligence level of the total white portion of the United States."[68]

To better the situation and to "admit only sound metals," he suggested not only eliminating "all dross" but sifting would-be immigrants for "desirable . . . national traits, such as truthfulness, inventiveness, initiative, dependability, altruism, honesty, religious feeling, artistic sense, and many other talents and moral qualities, the bases of which are inborn in the individual and which vary greatly in family strains." There were, in addition "the physical qualities of stature, strength, comeliness, [and] longevity." All of these traits could be located and measured by clinical examination "supplemented strongly by field investigations."[69] At almost the same moment, Lewis Terman, the pillar of intelligence testing, then at Stanford, made his jaw-dropping prediction "that if the present differential birth rate continues, 1,000 Harvard graduates will at the end of 200 years have but 50 descendants, while in the same period 1,000 South Italians will have multiplied to 100,000."[70]

• • •

Eugenics had been mostly junk science from the start. As early as 1913, long before Boas and others challenged the eugenicists and their race theories, the stuff coming out of the Eugenics Record Office had been torn apart by the English followers of Francis Galton, the man who Charles Davenport had tried so desperately to befriend and in whose footsteps he pretended to follow. Galton himself seemed to believe that "our friend Davenport [was] not a clear strong thinker."[71] The ERO's papers show, wrote David Heron, a fellow at the Galton Eugenics Laboratory at London's University College, in the Galton Lab's series *Questions of the Day and of the Fray,* that the group's research

> has been collected with a decided bias in favour of a particular theory of heredity; that it is presented with extraordinary carelessness; that it is, on internal evidence, repeatedly contradictory; that it is not treated in any adequate statistical manner, and that the conclusions reached are not justified by the data . . . those of us who have the highest hopes for the new science of Eugenics in the future are not a little alarmed by many of the recent contributions to the subject which threaten to place Eugenics with the older "social science" and much of modern sociology entirely outside the pale of true science.[72]

Heron regarded his own article as a defense of eugenics against the bad science the ERO practiced in its name. But he also made clear, in a long piece written for the *New York Times* based on his article in the British journal, lampooning the vagueness of the ERO's conception of "feeblemindedness" and the arbitrariness of the traits supposedly associated with it, "that the time is far from ripe for [eugenic sterilization] except in those grave cases of sexual violence where the Swiss have, apparently with some success, adopted this treatment. In America, however, the case is different; the initial steps have already been taken and it is an extension of the laws permitting sterilization that is demanded [by people like Davenport]."[73] Three years after Heron's articles appeared, a St. Louis psychologist named J.E.W. Wallin gave Henry Goddard's version of the Binet-Simon test to a group of successful people, among them several farmers, a businessman, and a housewife, and found that the test rated them all as feebleminded.[74]

Charles Davenport contended that Heron had taken some of the quoted statements out of context, that the ERO was far ahead in its application of practical eugenics, and that "the United States is the only place where, on a large scale, eugenics is being worked out from observations of living people in relation to their community . . . and we are the only country which is attempting with any measure of success to put the findings of the eugenics expert into practical everyday use."[75] The exchange set off a debate in the field, much of it technical, about misapplied Mendelian genetics and eugenics but apparently had little impact on policy or on the credibility of most American eugenicists.

The same appeared to be true of the growing doubts—in some cases, the unequivocal public renunciations—of the American psychologists and psychometricians who had been major forces in the early days of the eugenics movement. Long before the Nazi experiments began, and before the world had a chance to learn where the doctrines of eugenics would lead, both Carl Brigham and Henry Goddard would recant.

> Frankly, [Goddard wrote in 1928] when I see what has been made out of the moron by a system of education, which as a rule is only half right, I have no difficulty in concluding that when we get an education that is entirely right there will be no morons who cannot manage themselves and their affairs and compete in the struggle for existence. If we could hope to add to this a social order that would literally give every man a chance, I should be perfectly sure of the result.
>
> It may still be objected that moron parents are likely to have imbecile or idiot children. But there is not much evidence that this is the case. The danger is probably negligible. . . . As for myself, I think I have gone over to the enemy.[76]

Sadly for Goddard, the reprinting of *Die Familie Kallikak* by the Germans in 1933 and the Nazis' emulation of his work, and the subsequent embrace of Goddard's book by the Columbia University psychologist and racialist Henry Garrett in 1961, left it hard for Goddard's reputation ever to escape his earlier work. He wanted to go over to the enemy but his earlier allies never fully allowed it. Later he would become a strong supporter of the New Deal, and he worked to help

Jews escape from Germany and joined Einstein's group opposing the use of the atomic bomb.[77]

In 1930, Brigham, the Princeton psychologist who had done so much to publicize the racist inferences of the army tests, and who had since become the father of the Scholastic Aptitude Test, issued a more sweeping recantation than Goddard's.[78] He renounced his earlier analysis of the army tests completely, acknowledging that they were culturally biased and that since the Alpha and Beta tests measured different things their results couldn't be combined. Since, as Brigham confessed, "this method was used by the writer in his earlier analysis of the Army tests as applied to samples of foreign born in the draft, that study with its entire hypothetical superstructure of racial differences collapses completely." Moreover, because the samples of recruits who were tested weren't in any way statistically representative, they couldn't be used for national comparisons. But perhaps the most important acknowledgment was Brigham's declaration that "tests in the vernacular must be used only with individuals having equal opportunity to acquire the vernacular of the test." That condition is "frequently violated here in studies of children born in this country whose parents speak another tongue." Nor may comparative studies be made with existing tests. And then, the clincher: "One of the most pretentious of these comparative racial studies—the writer's own—was without foundation."[79]

By 1937, long after Harry Laughlin and others had read Brigham's version of the army test data into the record of Johnson's House Committee on Immigration and Naturalization, and from there into the pseudoscientific rationale for the 1924 immigration law and the quotas attached to it, Lewis Terman of Stanford, another of the stars of American psychometrics who'd helped design the army tests, would change his position as well. Terman had long warned about sloppy administration and misreadings of intelligence test results. But a major revision, prepared after ten years' work, of his *Measuring Intelligence*—the basic guide to the Stanford-Binet IQ test and the standard in the field—was, in Stephen Jay Gould's assessment, "so different from the original volume of 1916 that common authorship seems at first improbable."[80]

Terman's new edition was virtually silent on the heredity of intelligence; in it, as Gould said, "all potential reasons for differences between groups are framed in environmental terms." Terman also noticed—and was honorable enough to point out—that the IQ of rural children dropped after they began school, while the IQ for urban children of working-class parents rose. The explanation, he said, would "require extensive research," but he left little doubt that he suspected that the explanation had more to do with the quality of schooling than with innate intelligence.[81] The recantations, mea culpas, caveats, and corrections, needless to say, would as often be forgotten by the testers and the policy makers who followed the Brighams and Goddards as they were observed. Eugenic sterilizations continued until well after World War II; the national origins quotas would remain in immigration law until the 1960s—and in spirit well after that.

The recantations certainly didn't discourage the hard-line eugenicists. In 1937, Laughlin became the first president of the racist Pioneer Fund, which he cofounded with the New England textile-machine heir Wickliffe Draper and which continues to fund research on race differences. In the same year, speakers at the Eugenics Research Association conference, again at New York's Museum of Natural History, urged the isolation and sterilization of "feeble-minded females." And because the birthrate of the socially desirable was "dropping like a plummet," one of the association's officers also urged a tax "on the childless for the benefit of large families," presumably only those with superior genes.[82] Nor had the recantations deterred Laughlin, whose blatant racism and shoddy science had been the targets of mounting criticism for some twenty years, from preparing a "study" for the New York State Chamber of Commerce in 1934 that no special immigration consideration should be given Jews or other European refugees, or to any groups who were not "all members of the white or Caucasian race."[83] And in May 1939, when, in historian John Higham's estimate, eugenics (thanks, probably, to the Nazis) "had shrunk to the status of a dedicated but ineffectual cult," and when the Nazis' persecution of Jews was absolutely clear, the New York State Chamber of Commerce published Laughlin's lengthy "report," *Conquest by Immigration* (also *Immigration and Conquest*).[84]

The report, echoing Laughlin's speeches, papers, and congressional testimony of the 1920s, argued that because Jews were counted in immigration quotas as Poles or Germans, not as Jews, far too many were allowed to enter the country.[85] It was first publicized by the chamber of commerce on June 8, 1939, five days after the ship *St. Louis* left Havana with 907 Jewish refugee passengers, who, having been promised temporary asylum in Cuba and permanent U.S. asylum when their turn in the quota came up later, were denied the right to land, ultimately sending many of them to death in the gas chambers.[86]

The timing may have been only coincidence. It was no coincidence, however, that Laughlin proudly sent copies of the report to a group of

Nazi eugenicists, among them Interior Minister Wilhelm Frick.[87] Laughlin listed as a "loophole" in American law a decision by the attorney general that the conviction by a Nazi court of a German Jew attempting to smuggle some of his money out of Germany did not constitute "moral turpitude" that would bar immigration. The report was full of lengthy recitations about protecting the American "seed stock" to make certain that "every future immigrant will constitute a very definite asset by race, inborn soundness and capacity to the reproductive stock of the American people. The nation can then settle down to the business of building up its own racial type and cultural character."[88]

Laughlin's report was vehemently denounced by a group of leading scholars, Franz Boas among them, for its racism, its unscientific use of the term "race," and its professional shoddiness. Far from supporting his conclusions, the critics said, a lot of Laughlin's data in fact showed that native Americans, not foreigners, constituted a disproportionate share of the inmates of mental and other institutions.[89] The denunciation had no immediate effect on policy, but it was probably the penultimate straw for Laughlin. His racism had by then become so blatant, his "science" so blatantly false, that patient tolerance of his ability to embarrass himself, the ERO, and their funders at the Carnegie Institution had run out. At the end of 1939, Carnegie finally pulled the plug, the ERO was shut down, and Laughlin was forced to retire. He moved back to Kirksville, Missouri, from where, as president of the Pioneer Fund, he supervised its race research program until 1941. He lived until 1943, by which time he should have become just a little queasy about his work and his romance with the Nazis, but there was no sign that he ever did.

Many years later, Nobel laureate James D. Watson, the codiscoverer of the structure of DNA, recalled that when he first came to Cold Spring Harbor where the Eugenics Record Office had been housed, "nobody would even mention the 'E word.'" But by then the damage had been done. Eugenics had badly discredited the real science of human genetics. Far worse, "not only had Laughlin's sterilization law provided Hitler with the model for his ghastly program," Watson wrote, "but his impact on immigration legislation meant that the United States would in effect abandon German Jewry to its fate at the hands of the Nazis."[90] What made this assessment doubly ironic is that Watson, having become director of the Cold Spring laboratory and making it one of the world's premier genetics research institutions, was himself forced to retire after he expressed doubts about the intelligence of Africans.[91]

• • •

It may always be a matter of debate how much the eugenic spin on nativism and the dark warnings of racial extinction cranked out by the Madison Grants, the Lothrop Stoddards, the Charles Davenports, and other Nordic supremacists helped drive the national origins laws about which Harry Laughlin and other eugenicists testified in the 1920s. "Science" certainly had no bearing on the Chinese Exclusion Act, which preceded American eugenics by nearly thirty years. Nor could it have had much bearing on the first quota law, enacted in 1921 (about which more in the next chapter). Arguably, American racism and nativism—indeed, our long history in pursuit of perfection and the search of reforms to achieve it—may have shaped the American version of eugenics as much as eugenics reinforced the political and social tendencies that preceded it. The same probably goes for Hitler and the Nazis, regardless of how convenient they found the American model. They didn't need the cover of American eugenics to initiate the racist brutalities that led to the Holocaust.

But eugenics surely helped make the case: In 1922, Robert Yerkes wrote the manager of the Princeton University Press urging him to hurry the publication of Carl Brigham's book "because of its importance in connection with practical immigration problems that are to be considered by Congress during the next few weeks." In January 1924, four months before the big national origins law was passed, Brigham was quoted warning of "the wholesale importation of low-grade people and the exportation of talent," which meant "that the level of intelligence in this country is declining." One form of population control, he said, though not the only one, was restriction of immigration.[92]

As eugenics became entangled in a bundle of other ideas, policies, and their politics, the dubious science also cast two additional shadows that may last indefinitely: the one, through Margaret Sanger and her undeniable eugenicist views, on family planning, birth control, and abortion, a bloody shirt that opponents of family planning, birth control, and abortion continue to wave with glee; the other on the teaching of evolution in American public schools. Stephen Jay Gould, in *Rocks of Ages,* his book trying to reconcile evolutionary science with religion, contended that while women's suffrage, the graduated federal income tax, and various other Progressive reforms would have been achieved even without William Jennings Bryan's strenuous efforts, "the legislative attempt to curb [the teaching of] evolution was his baby, and he pursued it with all his legendary demoniac fury. No one else in the ill-organized fundamentalist movement had the inclination, and surely no one else had the legal skill or political clout." Gould and a growing number of other modern historians saw (and see) that campaign as entirely consistent with Bryan's Progressivism, not a retreat from it. Yes, he badly misread Darwin, but "when he said that Darwinism had been widely portrayed as a defense of war, domination and domestic exploitation, he was right."[93]

Gould's moral is a plague on the excesses of both houses: on the partisans of creationism for attempting to impose their dogma on the "magisterium of science," but, as the eugenics story should illustrate, on the scientists as well. If the scientists—or in this case, often nativists wearing the mantle of science—had maintained some restraint in their interpretations and exercised (in Gould's words) "proper humility in resisting invalid extensions of their findings into the inappropriate domains of other magisteria," our conversations about what are probably our three most contentious subjects—race, religion, and abortion—might be a little more like real conversations. "The average American male reader in 1900," as Gould wrote, "probably accepted racism, with his group on top, as a dictate of nature, and probably supported imperial expansion of American power. The claim that evolution justified the morality of both conclusions seemed to him both evident and reasonable. And if a prominent biologist accepted such a statement, then the argument became even more persuasive."[94]

There is, finally, one other legacy and its accompanying shadow: intelligence testing in particular and standardized educational testing in general. It took the Educational Testing Service, which administers the SAT, more than a half century to acknowledge that the test, which Carl Brigham had shaped out of the World War I army intelligence tests, was neither a test of innate intelligence nor an "aptitude" test. Long before that acknowledgment, a whole test-preparation industry—the Princeton Review, Kaplan, and others—effectively exploded the claim that the SAT, which was once promoted as a way to increase fairness in the college admission process, was uncoachable. Thus the upper-class WASPs from exclusive prep schools who had been routinely favored by selective colleges before World War II (and often much later) and who, in theory, then had to compete on the testers' level playing field, have in the past generation been forced to purchase their competitive edge from the test-prep companies and/or from even more costly private tutors and counselors.[95] Ethnic advantage had been minimized: if they have the money, ambition, and cultural wherewithal, immigrants and their descendants—Jews, Poles, Italians, and all the other inferior "races," even blacks—can now buy their children the same advantages as all others. As ever, the deck remains stacked: what had been pushed as an instrument of fairness (for Jews particularly) now is exhibit A in the case for the intellectual inferiority of blacks. But if the SAT and its cousins ultimately cease being centerpieces of the admissions process and the totems of inborn ability, even that last legacy of the testers' "science" may finally be forgotten.

CHAPTER 4

Preserving the Race

The nativist ideology and the mountains of "scientific" data generated on the immigration issue and on the consequences of the new waves of arrivals in the half century after 1880 made the outlines of the immigration laws enacted in the 1920s almost predictable. If Americans could just get into the habit of using the "term 'the American race,'" Harry Laughlin told Congress early in 1924, "their foreign and their immigration problems would be greatly simplified. We could have a standard to go by, and we could recruit to this standard from different European nationals in accordance with the qualities and proportions needed."[1]

Through most of the first century after independence, naturalization decisions had been casually left to the inconsistent and sometimes contradictory decisions of state and local judges. But by 1900, naturalization had begun to be subject to gradual federalization and the imposition of uniformity. As of 1906, prospective citizens were required to know English. The old Bureau of Immigration was expanded into the Bureau of Immigration and Naturalization. But two related sets of difficulties made the response to the growing pressure to restrict immigration complex and the progress toward what would become the big 1924 national origins quota immigration law hesitant and uncertain. One was Americans' historic faith in equality and the powers of what soon would be called the melting pot to assimilate newcomers—to take the poor, the tired, the huddled masses from wherever they came and make them into productive, decent citizens. The other was the related political concern about not offending American voters from disfavored groups and not complicating international diplomacy by subjecting some foreign nationals to unequal treatment and implying that certain immigrants were inferior "races."

Concern about racial discrimination didn't deter Congress in 1882 when it passed the Chinese Exclusion Act, or when the law was extended in succeeding decades, not only because the Chinese were obviously of a different "race," but at least in part because the endemic chaos within China diverted its shaky rulers to more urgent matters. The revolts against the corrupt and widely hated Qing dynasty and the plotting and intrigues inside the government allowed outside powers to do pretty much as they wanted. But similar race-based discrimination against other groups worried American presidents from Teddy Roosevelt to Calvin Coolidge. Coolidge would have much preferred to have Japanese immigration restricted through an extension of the 1907 Gentlemen's Agreement than through the outright restriction of an act of Congress.

In effect, the post–Civil War Congresses tacked up to immigration and the many questions associated with it, beginning with Chinese exclusion and the exclusion of "lunatics" and people likely to become public charges in 1882, through the Alien Contract Labor law of 1885 that prohibited any company or individual from bringing in workers under contract, excepting only domestic workers—the proper people in New York, Boston, and Philadelphia wanted their Irish maids—and those with the skills required to establish a new industry in the United States. During the twenty-five years after passage of the Chinese Exclusion Act, the list of undesirable characteristics gradually grew until, in the updated immigration act of 1907, it included

> idiots, imbeciles, feebleminded persons, epileptics, insane persons, and persons who have been insane within five years previous; persons who have had two or more attacks of insanity at any time previously; paupers; persons likely to become a public charge; professional beggars; persons afflicted with tuberculosis or with a loathsome or dangerous contagious disease; persons not comprehended within any of the foregoing excluded classes who are found to be and are certified by the examining surgeon as being mentally or physically defective, such mental or physical defect being of a nature which may affect the ability of such alien to earn a living; persons who have been convicted of or admit having committed a felony or other crime or misdemeanor involving moral turpitude; polygamists, or persons who admit their belief in the practice of polygamy, anarchists, or persons who believe

> in or advocate the overthrow by force or violence of the Government of the United States, or of all government, or of all forms of law, or the assassination of public officials; [and] persons coming for immoral purposes.[2]

Screening was done at the ports of entry, but because shipping lines were responsible for returning those who were rejected, and later subject to fines, they were under some constraint to make certain, within the limits of the crude definitions of the law and the diagnostic techniques then available, that all their passengers were qualified. Later, much of this screening would be done abroad before visas were issued.

The 1907 law, which President Roosevelt signed, was in some respects true to the nation's tradition of political liberty. It specifically provided that "nothing in this Act shall exclude, if otherwise admissible, persons convicted of an offense purely political, not involving moral turpitude."[3] It again exempted domestic servants as well as actors, artists, professors, and clergymen from the contract-worker exclusion. But, reflecting the widespread belief that European nations were dumping undesirables on the United States—or, as Laughlin later reported from his visit to Italy, that they were making emigration of surplus labor attractive, treating it as an "export" that would return remittances to "replenish the treasuries of the Italian people, just as surely as if Italy were a great exporter of manufactured goods"[4]—anyone whose passage was paid for by a foreign government or a corporation was not to be admitted (assuming, that is, that such a contract came to the government's attention). In the same period, Congress also tried repeatedly to pass the literacy test that the Immigration Restriction League had been pushing for since the early 1890s—a test always strongly opposed by business groups in pursuit of cheap unskilled workers—only to be blocked each time by a presidential veto. It wasn't until 1917, two months before America's entry into the war, that Congress overrode President Wilson to enact a mild requirement that applicants be able to read forty words in some language.

The 1917 bill also included what may have been the most bizarre immigration provision in U.S. history. It was based on a gerrymandered global map that created a so-called Asiatic Barred Zone, also called the Asia-Pacific Triangle, from which no person could immigrate or be naturalized. It ran from Turkey to Southeast Asia (including what's now Indonesia) and included all of the Middle East, most of China (though that was redundant), the Philippines, and all of South Asia, but (again for diplomatic reasons) not Japan. The Fourteenth and Fifteenth Amendments and the implementing bills of the post–Civil War era granted citizenship and the franchise to anyone born or naturalized in the United States, and that now included blacks and "aliens of African nativity or persons of African descent."[5] But they did not guarantee the right to naturalization to Asians or anyone else, regardless of ethnicity, who came from the excluded zone, or indeed, to anyone who wasn't white or black. Since federal law already denied naturalization to Asians, and because immigrants from China and (by way of the Gentlemen's Agreement) many from Japan as well were already excluded, the 1917 act created more legal confusion than it resolved. Who was white and thus entitled to naturalization and, by extension, to immigration, and who was something else?

Lawsuits seeking to answer the racial question had begun in 1878, three decades before creation of the barred zone—suits in which the courts ruled repeatedly that the Chinese weren't white, that the Japanese weren't white, that Hawaiians weren't white, that Filipinos weren't white, and that Burmese weren't white. There were also decisions that Armenians were white. But the confusion among the judiciary and the immigration and naturalization bureaucrats picked up after the barred zone was created, not only about categorization, but about the reasons for it. In 1919 two courts ruled that Asian Indians were white (one other court, in 1919, ruled they probably weren't). After 1923, the courts ruled that Asian Indians, sometimes "Hindoos," weren't white and (in 1925) that Punjabis weren't white. Four pre-1917 decisions had ruled that Syrians were white, and three that they weren't. Then came rulings that Koreans weren't white; that Afghanis weren't white, followed in 1945 by a decision that they were; and that "Arabians" weren't white, again followed by a Board of Immigration Appeals ruling (in 1941) that, because European civilization had originated in the Middle East, that they were white.[6]

By the late 1930s, Mexicans were considered white for most official purposes. Court decisions going back to the turn of the century also held that persons who were half white, one-fourth Chinese, and one-fourth Japanese weren't white. Following what appeared the one-drop-of-blood standard, there were similar decisions for all mixed-race individuals, including one, as late as 1938, that ruled that a person who was three-fourths American Indian and one-fourth African was not African and thus not entitled to naturalization.[7] In 1922, an appellate court in Alabama, overturning a conviction for miscegenation between a black man and a white woman, at the time a very serious offense, ruled that there had been no proof that the woman, a Sicilian, was white.[8] One often-repeated story, from the *Detroit News* in 1891, was about a black whitewasher who was asked by a reporter if he worked with any white men. "No," he replied, in the reporter's version of Negro dialect, "dere's no white men. Dere's some Polacks, but they ain't white men."[9]

There were more than fifty such court cases between 1878 and 1938, and countless more in the federal immigration and naturalization agencies, in which judges and administrators relied on a crazy quilt of rationales—congressional intent, "common knowledge," what the judge regarded as scientific evidence, whether the applicant came from within the Asiatic Barred Zone, pure prejudice, and, of course, legal precedent often based on some combination of the others. The cases never settled anything definitively, since the racial and national origins categories on which the statutory and judicial distinctions were based rested on biological and anthropological quicksand.

The problem was further compounded by the interethnic marriages, regarded by most eugenicists of the 1920s as the certain road to racial inferiority, whose rapid increase became the source of still more categorical fuzziness and confusion. Nonetheless, wrote University of Utah law professor John Tehranian in the *Yale Law Journal,* while the "litigation over whiteness often grew absurd, with judges delving into the depths of antiquity, reconstructing history, and spouting rigid ideologies in order to justify their rulings, the reification of whiteness had a profound impact on shaping the immigrant experience in the United States."[10] Tehranian also argued that, in their decisions, the courts made assimilability within Anglo-white culture—what he called "performing white"—into a determinative criterion:

> Successful litigants demonstrated evidence of whiteness in their character, religious practices and beliefs, class orientation, language, ability to intermarry, and a host of other traits that had nothing to do with intrinsic racial grouping. Thus, a dramaturgy of whiteness emerged, responsive to the interests of society as defined by the class in power—an "evolutionary functionalism" whereby courts played an instrumental role in limiting naturalization to those new immigrant groups whom judges saw as most fit to carry on the tradition of the "White Republic." The courts thereby sent a clear message to immigrants: The rights enjoyed by white males could only be obtained through assimilatory behavior.[11]

In the process, the law and the judges struggling to interpret it, and rarely recognizing that race was from the start a social construct, further confused the historic black-white dichotomy. The question wasn't just who was white or black—were those Dagoes, Wops, Guineas, Polacks,

Micks, Spicks, Hunkys, Kikes, and Canucks really white, and what made them white? What of "Mexicans" or the catchall "Asiatics" or "Hispanics," the latter an artificial category created by the Nixon administration in the 1970s and unknown in any of the nations from which so-called Hispanics come? The question of whiteness continues to rattle around American domestic policy debates to this day—in the census and other official statistics, in affirmative action, in criminal law. "Is 'white' one race," Kenneth Prewitt, the former director of the U.S. census, would ask, "or a residual category for everyone not noticeably something else?"[12]

• • •

The first great turning point came on May 19, 1921, when President Wilson's successor, the insouciant Warren G. Harding, in one of the earliest (and one of the few) major acts of his brief presidency, signed the first immigration quota law, which for the first time in U.S. history restricted the numbers of aliens who could enter the country in any given year. It did so by limiting immigrants of any nationality to 3 percent of the foreign-born from that nation who were living in the United States in 1910. The act, as historian Mae Ngai would note, was part of a larger global postwar "consolidation of the international nation-state system, based on [rigid ideas of] sovereignty, hardened borders, state citizenship, and passport controls."[13] But it also reflected a growing recognition in the United States that the literacy test and other restrictions were porous screens.

The House of Representatives had initially, and hurriedly, passed the bill in the midst of the great spike of postwar immigration that newly available ships, which had in 1919 still been required for the returning troops, made possible. Those ships brought, among others, large numbers of war refugees and Jews fleeing a savage wave of Polish pogroms. At times the backup and crowding at Ellis Island were so great that passengers were not allowed off ships, bringing the crowds waiting at dockside for the arrival of their relatives to the verge of riot. Some ships were diverted to other ports. "The exodus of these Jewish people from Poland," Frederick A. Wallis, New York's federal immigration commissioner told the *New York Times* in 1920, "amounts to a stampede. They are coming too fast for their own good." U.S. Jews, he said, were trying to organize a movement, which he hoped would "discourage this unbusinesslike method of turning loose thousands of the Jewish people all at once upon the tide of immigration."[14]

Then, in February 1921, during the last full month of the Wilson presidency, the discovery in lower Manhattan of typhus-infected immigrants, most apparently from Poland and Galicia, panicked New York health authorities. Urgent pleas for help were dispatched to the ailing president; cables were sent to ship captains at sea to delouse their steerage passengers before landing—presumably the upper crust in the first- and second-class cabins wouldn't be infected; and at least four ships with a total of five thousand passengers were diverted to Boston because the immigration inspectors at Ellis Island were too busy to examine all the new arrivals. To check them, the railroads were asked to set up their own inspection facilities "to prevent infected persons from slipping into New York."[15]

The national climate in 1920–21 was ripe for tougher restrictions in any case. The Red Scare was on the wane, but the fever of wartime nationalism remained high, now inflamed by Prohibition's success in the ratification of the Eighteenth Amendment and reinforced by a brief depression and high postwar unemployment—running to an estimated five million Americans in 1921—which in turn brought a nationwide wave of social and economic disturbances and the xenophobia, isolationism, and anti-Semitism that came with them. Why couldn't the nation return to normalcy? Pressed by groups ranging from the American Federation of Labor and the American Legion to the Ku Klux Klan—the so-called second Klan, then at the height of its power—and influenced by the apocalyptic race-suicide theorizing of the Madison Grants and Lothrop Stoddards, the virulently anti-immigrant articles of novelist Kenneth Roberts then running in the mass circulation *Saturday Evening Post,* and the dubious racist-eugenicist statistics in "the biological aspects of immigration" that Laughlin dumped on the immigration committee, the House was more than ready to act. The spike in immigration and the turmoil in New York—all those Jews coming off those ships—which occurred just as the Senate was working on its version of the 1921 immigration bill, made the pressure for passage of committee chairman Albert Johnson's "emergency" measure (which was how the House bill had first been conceived) all the more intense.

Johnson was the right man for the job. Like Laughlin, he was a native of a small midwestern town. Trained as a printer in Kansas, he later had a career as a newspaper editor in St. Louis, Washington, D.C., New Haven, Tacoma, and Seattle, after which he became the editor and publisher of the *Gray's Harbor Washingtonian* of Hoquiam, Washington, where he'd been since 1907. He was a rabid enemy of both monopolies and organized labor, each of which he denounced as menaces to small-town values to build his political career. He joined vigilante groups that attacked socialists, Wobblies, and other union members and that called for mob action against a labor leader who'd been charged with a felony. He was also an enthusiastic supporter of women's suffrage (as was Laughlin's mother); harbored a strong hatred of non-European "races," particularly the Japanese whom he "studied" through his years in western Washington; and vehemently opposed immigration of all but old-stock Europeans, starting a second xenophobic newspaper called *The Home Defender* to further the cause. He was first elected to the House as a (William Howard) Taft Republican in 1912 from a district in western Washington, a post he would hold until he was defeated, like many other conservatives, in the New Deal sweep in 1932.

In December 1920, in his effort to secure passage of his proposal for a two-year suspension of all immigration, Johnson submitted a report to the House that 55,000 people had landed at Ellis Island the previous September. By October, he said, the "rising immigrant tide" had increased to 74,000, of whom "more than 75 percent were of the Semitic race." The document included as an appendix a nation-by-nation (sometimes city-by-city) State Department summary of reports from U.S. consular officials abroad, which, in describing the wretched postwar conditions in Europe, declared that virtually all potential immigrants of whatever "race" were unfit to become Americans. From Florence: Italy is "so honeycombed with socialistic ideas" that the only way to weed them out is to stop immigration altogether. From Rotterdam: Most of those passing through (to embark) are "Russian Poles or Polish Jews of the usual ghetto type. . . . They are filthy un-American and often dangerous in their habits." From Poland: Those seeking to emigrate are "physically deficient . . . mentally deficient . . . economically undesirable . . . socially undesirable." There was, in addition, the threat of Bolshevism and typhus. But the central message in virtually every case was that the overwhelming number of would-be emigrants were low-class Jews who always congregated in the cities and who, as a class, "have proved to be inassimilable."[16] The subtext of the whole report was Jews.[17]

The resulting immigration bill was driven in part by the rush to finish before Congress adjourned on March 4, 1921, and in part by fear that, in Johnson's estimate, ten million Europeans, many of them carrying fraudulent passports and visas, and many of them Jews, were poised to come as more ships became available. It was therefore a hasty patchwork of compromises between the House, which had in the meantime written a bill suspending all immigration for fourteen months, and the leisurely Senate, which was more responsive to farmers and industry still seeking cheap labor than to the national mood.[18] Nonetheless, as the clock ran down, the Senate began to feel the pressure as well, particularly from the South and West, and approved a token quota limiting annual immigration from each country to 5 percent of the foreign-born from that country in the United States as recorded in the 1910 census. That would have changed the "race" composition of immigration somewhat but would have decreased total immigration by only about 40 percent from the million people who had arrived in the last prewar year.

In February 1921, the Senate Committee on Immigration, reminded of the New York typhus scare by a member from Mississippi and warned by an Alabamian that "agents of Lenin and Trotsky are now either here or trying to get in to preach this devilish work [of Bolshevism] in the United States," then worked out the 3 percent national origins quota formula with the House.[19] In a gesture of good neighborliness and, more importantly, in response to the demand of cotton and beet growers and other farmers for cheap field workers, of the expanding railroads for labor to lay track, and of mountain west mining companies for strong backs, the immigration bill exempted all of the Western Hemisphere, never regarded as a major source of immigrants anyway, from the quotas. Wilson, near the very end of his term, pocket-vetoed this compromise, but soon after Harding was inaugurated in March, he called a special session of Congress, which forthwith repassed the act and sent it to the new president.

Although the 1921 act was always regarded as a temporary measure, in setting numerical limits and quotas on how many people could immigrate from each nation, it put a permanent end to the nation's history of virtually open borders and set a radically new pattern for the immigration ideology that lasts to this day. The act set a limit of roughly 350,000 a year, with the greatest quotas allotted to the countries of northern and western Europe. But as a "temporary" measure that would sunset in 1922 and that, in using the 1910 census, still allowed too much immigration from southern and eastern Europe to satisfy the nativists, the act required further congressional attention almost at once. Worse, because the law allowed only one-fifth of any nation's annual quota to immigrate in any single month, it created a great rush of ships for Ellis Island that would arrive in the first days of the month, creating even more crowding and chaos, while ships arriving at the end of the month had to anchor in the harbor waiting for the clock to start running again.[20]

Against a background of buck-passing between the government and the various steamship lines, some immigrants were refused admission; ships were ordered to stand outside the three-mile limit before the end of the month, while other ships were turned away.

One set of *New York Times* headlines (on December 20, 1921) told much of the story: "Notified too Late, Cunard Line Says, *Aquitania* at Sea When Company Was Informed That Quota Had Been Exhausted. Ellis Island Congested—1,190 Aliens Awaiting Deportation and 2,190 More in the Harbor Will Have Cheerless Christmas." In the *Aquitania* case, involving some three hundred Hungarians, the Labor Department, which was then in charge of the immigration system, claimed that shipping lines had been informed. The shipping companies, which competed furiously for the reduced business but would face large fines and be stuck with the cost of feeding and/or returning over-the-quota passengers, said the problem was in Washington. With the Labor Department overseeing the immigration service and the State Department issuing visas, and with what appeared to be an increasingly overworked and undertrained staff at Ellis Island, the confusion was hardly surprising.[21] At times, the monthly immigrant quotas for certain nations ran out, and, as they did, Americans returning from abroad on the same ships had to wait it out with the new arrivals.

Despite the chaos partly created by the 1921 law, indeed in part because of it, Congress did nothing but extend the law for another two years while it figured things out, negotiating among competing domestic lobbies—the manufacturers, the farmers, the immigrant groups, labor, the American Legion and other patriotic societies—and shuttling between the conflicting objectives of its new policy direction and the historical American ideals of equality and fairness. Total suspension wasn't possible, though some in Congress favored it—indeed there had been a string of suspension bills even before the 1921 act. But with widespread popular support for reducing immigration, the question was never what to do, but only how to do it without seeming too blatantly racist and/or ruffling too many diplomatic feathers abroad. The 1921 law left Japanese immigration policy to the restrictions negotiated in the Gentlemen's Agreement of 1907, but by 1924, when a new bill was ready, even the concern about offending Tokyo, believed by some influential Americans to have flagrantly violated the agreement, was giving way to a policy not subject to the weaselly dealings of diplomats and foreign bureaucrats.[22]

The initiative for the 1924 revision came from Johnson's committee, whose prime objective was always tighter restriction, and particularly restriction of "races" that might further mongrelize and weaken the hardy American stock. By 1922, Johnson had the benefit not only of Harry Laughlin's warnings about the entry of "degenerates" in his racist "Analysis of America's Modern Melting Pot" and his other "scientific" data but of close associations with many others in the nativist establishment—among them Grant, Stoddard, and two Immigration Restriction League founders, Robert DeCourcy Ward and Prescott Farnsworth Hall, the author of one of the earliest books warning of the dangers the new immigration posed to the survival of the American race. In 1923, Johnson's friends in Cold Spring Harbor would choose him to succeed Grant as president of the Eugenics Research Association.

In 1921, Charles Davenport's friend Henry Fairfield Osborn, president of the American Museum of Natural History and a highly regarded paleontologist, devoted his address as president of the Second International Congress of Eugenics to the subject of immigration, which he summarized in a later letter to the *New York Times:*

> We are engaged in a serious struggle to maintain our historic republican institutions through barring the entrance of those who are unfit to share the duties and responsibilities of our well-founded Government. The true spirit of American democracy that all men are born with equal rights and duties has been confused with the political sophistry that all men are born with equal character and ability to govern themselves and others, and with the educational sophistry that education and environment will offset the handicap of heredity.[23]

The most enterprising, vigorous, and creative Italians, Frenchmen, Spaniards, and Poles—Dante, Leonardo, Lafayette, Rodin, Kossuth, Cervantes, even Napoleon—were all of Nordic blood, Osborn maintained, and it was that Nordic heritage that America had to preserve in its immigration policy. Even some of the liberal members of Congress (many of them, like Fiorello LaGuardia of New York) who opposed the national origins bills were willing to admit that the "Asiatic races" should be excluded. Either way, however, they were overmatched by the Nordic supremacists.

The key figure in developing the quota formula that would emerge in the Johnson-Reed immigration act of 1924, and that would become the long-term successor to the 1921 law, was a New York lawyer named John B. Trevor. Like Grant and Osborn, his fellow trustees of the American Museum of Natural History, and many other leading immigration restrictionists, Trevor belonged to an old East Coast family. He would shortly become a member of the Eugenics Research Association, and was one of the most thoroughgoing nativists of the lot. As a captain in military intelligence during World War I—he was based in New York City—Trevor suspected early on that the blatantly anti-Semitic *Protocols of the Elders of Zion* was the czarist fabrication it proved to be. But he nonetheless freely circulated rumors that the Warburgs, the Schiffs, Kuhn and Loeb, and other Jewish bankers were influencing the Wilson administration and the Federal Reserve to favor Germany and, later, that a secret "Jewish International," headed by Justice Louis D. Brandeis, which backed the "Bolsheviki" in the United States (most of them, of course, Jews), had also "embraced Zionism."[24] Trevor's experience in intelligence during the war also persuaded him that the greatest concentrations of radicals lived in New York's Jewish neighborhoods.

That each nation's immigration quota would be further reduced in the 1924 legislation, probably from 3 to 2 percent, never seemed in serious doubt. From the start, the object of immigration policy had been to replace what Laughlin in his House testimony characterized as "the dross" with the "metals . . . as would alloy well with the earlier American elements already in the crucible."[25] The question was 2 percent of what? If the percentage was based on the number of foreign-born in America in the immediately preceding (1920) census, the quotas would tilt too far toward the inferior races from southern and eastern Europe to achieve their real purpose. There had been a similar problem with using 1910 as a base year. Thus the House committee chose the 1890 census, when Italians, Greeks, Poles, Hungarians, Russians, and Jews, though always part of the eastern European contingent, were still a relatively small part of total immigrant numbers.

But as Congress appeared to be heading for resolution early in 1923, the bill, which Johnson hoped to pass before the March 23 adjournment date, hit an unexpected snag when the sluggish postwar economy turned sharply up, wages increased, and groups like the National Association of Manufacturers and the U.S. Chamber of Commerce complained that even the 1921 law was depriving their members of urgently needed workers, unskilled workers particularly. In April, Elbert H. Gary, chairman of the board of U.S. Steel, told his shareholders that the law was "one of the worst things this country has ever done for its economic future." (Presumably he didn't advance his case when he announced at the same meeting that the corporation was worth a billion more than its initial capitalization of $1.4 billion in 1901.) The next day, President Harding, who had signed the 1921 law, was reported to be convinced that there was indeed a labor shortage, but he either agreed with his secretary of labor, James J. Davis (a Welsh immigrant), that "it is a short sighted policy to seek cheap labor through immigration," or the widely beloved Harding was just being his famously indifferent and unengaged self. Whatever the cause, he did nothing.[26]

Industry, in any case, didn't want a further reduction in the quotas but a loosening, to which at least some members of the Senate were inclined to be responsive. The result was yet another stalemate until Congress reconvened in 1924. American industry and agriculture had comfortably survived the prior year under the 1921 restrictions—survived in part because of technological improvements that reduced the need for labor and in part by employing workers who, in the words of Secretary of Labor Davis, were "bootlegged" into the country by sneaking them over the land borders at a rate he estimated to be between one hundred and one thousand a day. The shortage of workers, Davis told Harding, had prompted "a perceptible movement of common labor of a low grade from a contiguous country" into American mills and factories in Pittsburgh, Youngstown, Detroit, and elsewhere, none of whom could do a fraction of the work that "an upstanding American workman" could do. He didn't specify which contiguous country.[27]

But by the spring of 1924 it was also evident that the 1890 base proposed for the 1924 law was so blatantly discriminatory against southern and eastern Europeans, who in 1890 still represented a relatively small minority of the foreign-born, and that by implication the law was so disrespectful of their descendants in the United States, many of them voting citizens, that some adjustment was required. There was, as historian John Higham wrote, "a certain crassness about shifting to an old census in order to achieve a desired discrimination."[28] It was here that Trevor came to Chairman Johnson's rescue. Trevor, working with Senator David A. Reed of Pennsylvania, who with Johnson would coauthor the final 1924 bill, used census data to produce statistics, subsequently appended to the House report, not for the number of the foreign-born in any given census year, but for the number of *descendants* of the different immigrant groups. Following an analysis of U.S. population data by Clinton Stoddard Burr, who in 1922 had published his *America's Race Heritage* and was another great admirer of Madison Grant's Nordic supremacist theories, Trevor fashioned a sort of ethnic genealogy going back to the first census in 1790, which brought him (not surprisingly) to the conclusion that the overwhelming majority of Americans in 1920 were descended from northern Europeans. In the process, Trevor created a chart dividing the U.S population in the 1920 census into five groups according to their national origins:

- Descendants of "colonial stock," as enumerated in the first census, and descendants of arrivals between 1790 and 1820, all of whom were from Britain or Northern Ireland, Germany, the then Irish Free State, the Netherlands, France, or Sweden.
- Foreign-born "white stock," native-born of foreign parentage, and native-born of mixed parentage, of whom—excepting only Italians, Czechs, Poles, and Russians—the largest numbers also were descendants of northwestern Europeans (and Canadians, who would again be covered under the exemption for the Western Hemisphere, as they had been in the 1921 law).
- Native-born of native parentage, contributed by arrivals between 1820 and 1900, who were again overwhelmingly northern European and Canadian.
- "Colored Races," who were not divided by national origins at all but categorized as black, mulatto, Indians, Chinese, Japanese, and "all others" and who, with only a few exceptions, were excluded from immigration.[29]

What was most original about Trevor's plan, however, was that the quotas would be allocated not according to the number of foreign-born from any nation in the 1890 or any other census but based on the proportion of present-day Americans who traced their origins to the various nations from which their forebears came. The new system was to go into effect in July 1927, when calculations for national origins breakdowns were expected to be ready.

Trevor acknowledged that his original numbers were only estimates, but they were not far off. Either way, the total annual immigration quota for all countries would not exceed 150,000, less than 15 percent of the total in the years just preceding the war. Until the 1927 date, immigration would be limited to the 2 percent of the foreign-born from each country in the 1890 census that Johnson's committee had written into the original draft of the bill. The final bill also took some major steps to avert future chaos and congestion of the kind that hit Ellis Island in 1921 and that left a lot of immigrants in a no-man's sea of confusion and heartbreak. Henceforth the quota limits would be enforced in the issuing of visas at U.S. consulates abroad, not by counting heads at Ellis Island. The beauty of the Trevor scheme was that the quotas for each nation would hardly be any different when calculated on the basis of national origins in the U.S. population in 1920 than they were when calculated according to the number of foreign-born in 1890. As Trevor proudly pictured it in a couple of pie charts, calculating quotas apportioned by the 1890 census limited immigrants of "South and East European Stock" to 15.5 percent of the total. Under the national origins formula, the proportion increased slightly, to 16.3 percent. And, as Johnson argued in response to complaints from ethnic groups, using the 1920 numbers of foreign-born as a base for the quotas would have actually discriminated against the British and the other northern Europeans whose descendants still far outnumbered those of the newer immigrants. And since the Trevor scheme used the emblematic 1920 census, the formula stuck.

The final Johnson-Reed Act reaffirmed all the earlier restrictions against admission of "persons liable to become public charges" (subsequently shortened by the immigration service to "LPC"), imbeciles, epileptics, anarchists, polygamists, carriers of "loathsome" diseases, and all the rest. The new 1924 act set a token minimum of one hundred for each country, exempted spouses and minor children of American citizens from the quotas, and, despite complaints from the Southwest—complaints that would become louder in the years that followed—again left immigration from Mexico and other countries in the Western Hemisphere theoretically unrestricted. No matter how the act was viewed, it went a long way toward achieving Laughlin's objective that there be "race quotas."[30]

For the first time in the history of immigration policy, the new law also deleted the statute of limitations on deportations, previously two years, for illegal entry or virtually any other reason. Congress, ignoring diplomacy, also acceded to heavy lobbying from the Japanese Exclusion League of California and other westerners and wrote Japanese exclusion into the act along with all the other Asians from nations that had previously fallen into the Asiatic Barred Zone. To do otherwise, argued league president V.S. McClatchy, publisher of the generally progressive *Sacramento Bee* and friend of former governor, now senator, Hiram Johnson, "would insure, under existing conditions and within a few generations, the inundation of the white population in this country by the yellow race." Moreover, he said in a long plea endorsed by the state legislature and most of the California congressional delegation, "The advantages possessed by the Japanese in economic competition are such that the whites are speedily driven out of communities and industries and must in time succumb to such competition in all sections where the Japanese are permitted to gain a foothold. . . . The Japanese, with a few individual exceptions, and even when born in this country, are for various reasons inassimilable and a dangerous element, either as residents or citizens."[31]

Since ethnic Chinese had long been excluded, it was argued, and since all other Asians were also shut out, how could this be racial discrimination? It was clear that when he got the bill, Calvin Coolidge, who had become president on Harding's death in August 1923, would have much preferred to have Japanese immigration restricted through an extension of the old Gentlemen's Agreement than through the outright restriction of an act of Congress. He devoted most of his signing statement to those misgivings, but since the bill passed with only a few dissenting votes in each house, he signed it. The law brought an eloquent protest from Masanao Hanihara, the Japanese ambassador in Washington, reminding Americans of their own professions of equality and fairness: "It has been repeatedly asserted in defense of these discriminatory measures in the United States that persons of the Japanese race are not assimilable to American life and ideals. [But] the process of assimilation can thrive only in a genial atmosphere of just and equitable treatment. Its natural growth is bound to be hampered under such a pressure of invidious discriminations as that to which Japanese residents in some States of the American Union have been subjected, at law and in practice for nearly twenty years."[32]

Secretary of State Charles Evans Hughes responded disingenuously if courteously that Japanese exclusion indicated no hard feelings toward Japan and that the act should not "derogate in any degree the mutual good-will and cordial friendship that has always characterized the relations of the two countries."[33] Others, including Senator David Reed, the act's coauthor, would remind the Japanese that they themselves excluded, and discriminated against, Koreans and many other "races."

It would take until 1929, in the early days of the administration of Herbert Hoover, for government demographers to calculate the specific national origins quotas. But when Hoover proclaimed them, most were remarkably similar to Trevor's estimates, despite subsequent questions about Trevor's demographics. The quota for Italy would be 5,802, not 5,716; for Poland it would be 6,524, not 4,535; for Russia 2,784, not 4,002; for Great Britain and Northern Ireland 65,721, not 85,135; for Germany 15,957, not 20,028. The only significant proportional difference was in the numbers for Ireland, which the official calculation set at 17,853, not Trevor's 8,330.[34]

Given the volume of intermarriage through the prior three hundred years, the changing European borders, and the other difficulties of establishing national origins—the melting pot, contra the assertions of the nativists, had in fact been working—both the 1929 numbers and Trevor's estimates were always arbitrary. The 1924 law provided for the allocation of quotas according to changed national boundaries, but doing all that reallocating through three centuries of history was still a squishy process. Were Alsatians French or German? Shouldn't immigrants from the free city of Danzig, as it was for the twenty years after the post–World War I redrawing of Europe's boundaries, but rarely before or since (it's now Gdansk, Poland), have been counted as Germans or Poles, which most of their ancestors had in fact been? When did Serbs become Yugoslavs and cease being Austrians? And who did all those millions of new immigrants, two-thirds of whom were men, marry? How could the census really decide how to categorize the offspring of an immigrant Pole and a native WASP? Nonetheless, the 1924 act and the resulting quotas achieved their objectives, legally limiting overall annual immigration to 150,000 (because of the Depression, in the 1930s it was a lot less) and, as Trevor had calculated in his pie charts, ensuring that the total would be overwhelmingly made up of applicants from what he called the "colonial stock" (i.e., Nordic) nations.

The objectives were no secret. In a long *New York Times* piece published even before Coolidge signed the law, Reed, then just a Senate freshman, made clear that while the melting pot had worked, its best days were gone. The new immigrants didn't know our language, didn't understand our institutions, and couldn't be expected to assimilate as their predecessors had. Reed invoked the specter of the Roman Empire, where the "inpouring of captives and alien slaves" undermined the willingness of once vigorous Roman citizens to do manual labor, producing a "toga class," none of whom would lower himself to do hard work. "From that day the power of Rome waned and she sank into an impotency which made her the prey of every barbarian invader."[35]

To prevent such a fate, wrote Reed, who as a graduate of an exclusive Pittsburgh prep school and Princeton University was surely a member of the "toga class" himself, America must not be deterred by the cries of those who claimed that the "labor supply" must ever be brought in afresh. America, he wrote, was "also beginning to smart under the irritation of her 'foreign colonies'—those groups of aliens either in city slums or in rural districts who speak a foreign language and live a foreign life and who want neither to learn our common speech nor to share our common life. From all this has grown the conviction that it is best for America that our incoming immigrants should be of the same races as those of us who are already here." Reed's piece was headlined "America of the Melting Pot Comes to End . . . Chief Aim, He States, Is to Preserve Racial Type as it Exists Here Today."[36] A year after the law was enacted, Trevor, in a letter to the *Times,* declared it "nonsense to assert that [the law] was aimed specifically at the Italians or the Jews," notwithstanding the fact that "partisans of both races shout from the housetops that restriction of immigration is tantamount to prejudice." The law was conceived, Trevor wrote, for "the protection of our institutions and the development of American solidarity."[37]

Although Trevor's "analysis" celebrated the 1924 act as the closing "of an epoch in the history of the United States," he immediately went out of his way to show that it was entirely consistent with the ideas of the founders, quoting the concerns of Jefferson, Franklin, and Washington about unrestricted immigration from countries whose inhabitants didn't speak English or were monarchies whose emigrants would not likely be suited to democracy. In any case, Trevor said, American naturalization law, excepting only the former slaves, had always been limited "to those races of mankind who by tradition, ideals and habits of life, would tend to support and perpetuate the principles of Republican Government in this nation." As to the vehement protest submitted by Tokyo's ambassador about Japanese exclusion, Trevor had two responses. First: that the Japanese, by withholding information on the issuing of visas, hadn't lived up to the Gentlemen's Agreement, which in any case was really a treaty and thus violated the Constitution. Second: (a simple reiteration of earlier contentions)"that where the white and yellow races live side by side, in direct economic competition, the white succumbs. It is not necessary that we should discuss the reasons for this condition, but it is a fact."[38] For a Nordic supremacist, it was a strange concession.

• • •

The Immigration Act of 1924 represented, as Trevor said, the end of an epoch, but it was hardly the end of the issue. Laughlin, Trevor, and countless other individuals and organizations worked intensely in the decades following the law's enactment defending the immigration restrictions against appeals to ease the quotas to allow European refugees, Jews particularly, to enter the country, even as Nazi atrocities made it likely that to do otherwise was to send millions to their deaths. At the same time, pressure mounted from the American Legion and a spectrum of other patriotic and nativist organizations to further restrict immigration and tighten enforcement of existing restrictions, especially against the Chinese coming across the land borders and Mexicans, the "mongrelized" mix of Spaniard, Indian, and African who, by eugenic doctrine, were likewise an inferior race.

Even before the 1924 act was passed, federal immigration officials were reporting sharp increases in smuggling across both the Canadian and Mexican borders, consisting in part of bootleg liquor, much of it whiskey coming across the Canadian border, in part of Chinese and European immigrants who either did not qualify under the 1921 quota law or who wanted to avoid the various tests of intelligence, disease, morality, and the other screens imposed by prior laws. The smuggling also included a growing number of Mexicans who couldn't, or wouldn't, go through the health examinations and other formalities required for a nonquota visa or who couldn't afford the eight-dollar head tax and ten-dollar visa fee required of all immigrants. It was a lot easier simply to walk around the immigration inspection stations and across an amorphous and nearly open border dividing a region that a century earlier had been all Mexican or colonial Spain and that was still inhabited by thousands of people who'd lived there for generations. One writer at the time described the border inspection system (at El Paso, San Ysidro, and elsewhere) as a set of locked doors with no connecting walls in between. But before World War I, Mexican immigration had been of little interest to anybody.

In 1923, Secretary of Labor Davis reported that, in response to the boom of the Harding era and the growing demand for workers, there had been a significant increase both in immigration of legal nonquota immigrants from Mexico and Canada and in the creation of "far-reaching organizations that take the alien from his home in Europe, secure a passport for him (a fraudulent one if necessary), purchase his steamship passage, place him on the ship, arrange for his entry into Cuba, Canada, or Mexico, and later conduct him by various underground routes into the United States—all for a fixed price. If we would successfully prevent wholesale smuggling and the unlawful entry of inadmissible aliens, our wholly inadequate border guard or patrol must be increased." In the fiscal year 1922–23, 3,600 people were deported (of whom more than 1,000 were Mexicans), nearly all of them for having become public charges or committing felonies and only rarely for illegal entry. With better funding, Davis said, many more could have been removed.[39] It was the immigration quota laws of the 1920s and the enforcement machinery that followed that, in combination with

Prohibition, gave birth to the bootlegger-cum-coyote, the illegal alien, and the beginning of mass deportations.

In 1924, two days after passage of the national origins act, Congress, responding to the cross-border influx of undocumented immigrants, the liquor runners, and appeals like Davis's, approved the first appropriation for the formal creation of the U.S. Border Patrol. Since 1904, immigration officers had mounted hit-or-miss border-enforcement efforts to stop Chinese workers from slipping across the southern border, but, in the official words of the Border Patrol's contemporary Web site, "their efforts were irregular and undertaken only when resources permitted."[40] Occasionally the army, as part of its training exercises, mounted patrols or garrisoned border towns to protect them from Mexican raiders. But the only significant military action came in response to the abortive 1916 attack launched by the Mexican revolutionary and bandit Pancho Villa on the town of Columbus, New Mexico, and its army garrison. In the months following, on orders from President Wilson, General John Pershing and his ten-thousand-man "expeditionary" force pursued Pancho Villa deep into the Mexican interior. But despite nearly a year of sporadic fighting, some by a black cavalry regiment, Pershing never caught Villa. (Ironically, after Pershing's withdrawal, the provisions of the Chinese exclusion law were waived to allow him to bring back some five hundred ethnic Mexican Chinese who had helped in his campaign; most of them settled in San Antonio, where they became known as the Pershing Chinese.)[41]

In its first years, the Border Patrol was a motley crew with a high rate of turnover, some recruited from sheriff's deputies, the Texas Rangers, and railroad guards but often just made up of converted cowboys. They provided their own horses (the government furnished the oats to feed them). Nor was the enforcement emphasis on the southern border, or on immigrants, but on the smuggling of booze from Canada. Nonetheless, immigration from Mexico, prompted in part by the long years of revolutionary upheavals there and in part by the booming American economy of the 1920s, began to climb. In theory, Mexicans were not subject to immigration quotas, but the head tax and the complications of meeting all the health and other requirements of U.S. immigration law prompted growing levels of illegal immigration.

What was certain was that the Latino population in California and the Southwest was going up, and the backlash, both from nativists who'd always wanted Mexican immigration restricted and from small Southwest farmers complaining about the competitive advantages big growers derived from cheap Mexican labor, was going up along with it. As early as 1928, four years after passage of the national origins act, and before it went into effect, Harry Laughlin was back before Albert Johnson's House committee warning about "a racial problem that has become acute in the Southwest." The region, he said, giving history his own mythic twist, grew out of "a western migration of fine American pioneers, who took possession of the country and started its settlement under law and order." But now, as the demand for cheap labor increased,

> there have been established a great many Mexican immigrants who seem to be driving out the Americans. How will this situation ultimately work out? The common Mexican, of course, is, as we know him, of mixed racial descent—principally Indian and Spanish, with occasionally a little mixture of black blood. The Mexican comes in freely because there is no quota against him. And during the last few years he has come here in such great numbers as almost to reverse the essential consequences of the Mexican War. The recent Mexican immigrants are making a reconquest of the Southwest more certainly . . . than America made the conquest of 1845, 1848 and 1853.[42]

Laughlin urged three improvements to the immigration law: the imposition of higher standards for the intelligence of potential immigrants; investigation of each applicant's "family stock" to make certain of suitable offspring (an old Laughlin favorite); and "limitation of immigrants to the white races." Algiers, he told the committee was included in the French quota, but "in Algiers there are many black bloods, as well as many Moors and Arabs." The same applied to Mexicans or West Indians, "who can come in regardless of race or numbers." The "Mexican, so far as he is white, could come in," Laughlin allowed. But in a memo to the committee attached to the record, he also urged restoration of the naturalization law of 1790 limiting naturalization to white persons, meaning "one all of whose ancestors are of Caucasian stocks." Since only people eligible for naturalization could immigrate, he said, that would pretty much solve the immigration problem.[43]

Albert Johnson, who had by now joined Carl Brigham, the Reverend Harry Emerson Fosdick, Henry Goddard, David Starr Jordan, Harry Laughlin, Gifford Pinchot, Lothrop Stoddard, Lewis Terman, Robert Yerkes, and two dozen other notable Americans as a member of the American Eugenics Society, seemed inclined to agree. "The task of our committee," he said after Laughlin's testimony, "is to prepare proposed statutes which will develop the American people along the racial and institutional lines laid down by the founders of the country, so far as the control of immigration can do it."[44]

There had in fact been a serious push in the House to apply immigration quotas to Mexico. In 1926 and 1928, Johnson's committee held hearings on a bill by Representative John Box, a Texas Republican, which would have ended the Western Hemisphere exemption. But the State Department, fearing Mexican retaliation against, among other targets, the growing number of U.S.-owned businesses south of the border, deterred Congress, substituting, among other things, stricter border inspections and tighter enforcement by consular officials of the long-standing restrictions on contract labor and on the entry of those likely to become public charges. That not only slowed legal immigration but also became a crude—and in the wholesale deportations of tens of thousands of Mexicans during the Depression an extralegal—way of reinforcing the cyclical economy-driven flows of workers in and out of the country and, incidentally, a paradigm for restricting European immigration during the Depression as well.[45] In 1929, Congress also made unlawful entry a crime—a misdemeanor for the first offense, a felony for subsequent offenses. That gave the immigration service an additional club in forcing aliens who had not been convicted of an ordinary crime to leave voluntarily and drove the number removed from the country from fewer than 2,800 in 1920 to nearly 39,000 a decade later, most of them officially categorized as EWIs, "entered without inspection."

The provision against unlawful entry supports the contention of historian Mae Ngai that the immigration system established in the 1920s not only created the "undocumented immigrant" but also helped define him as a criminal, reflecting the broader postwar "historical moment" that "loosened the links between birth and nation, human being and citizen." The view of the illegal alien as a criminal "situated the principle of national sovereignty in the foreground [and] made state territoriality—not labor needs, not family unification, not freedom from persecution, not assimilation—the engine of immigration policy." But the difficulties of distinguishing between illegal aliens and the legal residents, many of them citizens, that they lived among, and who were often their spouses or children, also fed the growing fear that the illegal aliens, as Ngai writes, "were an invisible enemy in America's midst."[46]

The law's provision that Europeans who had lived for five years in Canada or elsewhere in the Western Hemisphere could enter as nonquota immigrants allowed thousands—Greeks, Italians, Poles, Czechs, and, among them, many Jews—into the country as legal residents, but it didn't stop the increase of illegal aliens or reduce fears of an "invisible" internal enemy, especially if he was brown-skinned and clearly visible.

At the same time, Ngai contends, as the growing Depression-fueled pressure of the late 1920s and the 1930s for restricting the Mexican presence in the Southwest sharpened the focus on the southern border, it "rearticulated the U.S.-Mexican border as a cultural and racial boundary [and thus] as a creator of illegal immigration." The tightening of border checks also brought increasingly humiliating inspection rituals requiring immigrant laborers—but not those arriving first class by train—to be stripped for bathing and delousing, to file in the nude past an official for medical inspection, and to have their clothes and luggage fumigated. Commuters who lived in Mexico and worked in the United States were required to report weekly for the bathing, "a hated requirement" that Ngai says "gave rise to a local black market in bathing certificates."

More important, the Depression and the growing enforcement machinery of immigration inspectors and Border Patrol agents created in the wake of the 1924 law brought intense searches both at the border and in the interior for deportable aliens, Mexicans, and others. And given the long list of immigration restrictions enacted during the prior forty years and the absence of formal due process rights, the legal threshold justifying deportation became both murkier and easier to cross. How, for example, did you know who had been an immigrant "liable to become a public charge"? Was an employed widow liable to become a public charge because she didn't have a husband to support her? Was a mother in a stable long-term relationship with, but not married to, the father of her children thereby guilty of entering the country for immoral purposes? Did the inspectors have to inform the suspect that he had a right to a lawyer?

The bureaucratic rules seemed to change almost by the day. According to the findings of the high-level eleven-member National Commission on Law Observance and Enforcement, appointed in 1929 by President Hoover and chaired by former attorney general George P. Wickersham, the searches and subsequent detention and deportation process were equally arbitrary, constituting a clumsy administrative review and hearing process in which the detaining officer frequently acted as interpreter, prosecutor, and presiding officer. The closed-door hearings that were usually critical in deciding whether or not to deport, and that the commission characterized as "inquisitorial examinations," were sometimes stenographically transcribed, sometimes not, according to the whims of the inspector.[47] The Palmer Raids of 1919–20 in pursuit of radicals had been replaced by raids on meetings and by warrantless "checkups" by immigration inspectors of boardinghouses, restaurants, and pool rooms, where "any persons who seem to the inspectors to be aliens are stopped and interrogated" and, if thought to be suspicious, "taken to the immigration station for further questioning."[48] The interrogators, especially of women, asked irrelevant questions about "illicit relations" and other sex habits, rarely informed suspects that they had a right to an attorney, asked leading questions, referred to witnesses they didn't have, and relied on various other forms of prosecutorial deceit. The Wickersham Commission found that in cities with organized immigrant groups (mostly European) 20 percent of detainees were represented by lawyers; on the Mexican border, only 1 or 2 percent were. In some hearings, detainees were actively discouraged from asking for a lawyer.[49] Many legal residents, mostly but not all Mexicans, were arrested and deported for illegal entry after crossing from the United States into Mexico, sometimes for only a few hours, and failing to return through an official inspection station. (The commission cited the case of a longtime Texas laborer, a legal resident, with an American wife and eight children, who wandered into the Rio Grande to fish and was apprehended wading back. Notwithstanding his pleas about having to support his family, he was expelled for life.) Thousands of families, including many American citizens, were divided, sometimes because one member was falsely judged to be deportable.

Although it was silent on the national quotas, probably because they didn't formally apply to Mexicans, the commission made clear that deportation was necessary to enforce laws "to protect the United States from being inundated by defective, diseased, incorrigible and delinquent persons" and to deter the smuggling that brings them here. But the arbitrariness and abuses motivated by the inspectors' urge to "deport as many aliens as possible," in the commission's words, "can only be described . . . as a star-chamber proceeding. . . . It is no defense for the use of despotic methods, at least in our country, to say that they accomplish results."[50] And because the courts had ruled that deportations were based on the nation's sovereign powers and were not criminal proceedings, there was no right to judicial review, excepting only habeas corpus petitions that were rarely granted. Suspects thus were subject to the "despotic powers of the administrative agency," according to the commission. "The execution of the laws involves the most important rights of personal liberty; the processes of deportation reach more than 100,000 persons a year, many of whom are aliens lawfully in this country or United States citizens. In the administration of these laws one agency of the United States Government acts as investigator, prosecutor and judge, with despotic powers. Under the present system not only is the enforcement of law handicapped but grave abuses and hardships have resulted."[51]

Nor, as the Wickersham panel concluded in the large part of its 1931 report dealing with crime, was there any demonstrable link between crime and the foreign-born. "In proportion to their respective numbers," said one of the commission's researchers, "the foreign born commit considerably fewer crimes than the native born."[52] The commission also went to considerable lengths to tear apart Harry Laughlin's House testimony, citing the "numerous fallacies" in his statistics (and noting that far more complete data were available from the census at the time he compiled his data, which made Laughlin's own estimates of the number of "degenerates" in U.S. asylums unnecessary). The commission also pointed out that the Jukes, the Kallikaks, and the other classic families of "degenerates" invoked by Laughlin and other eugenicists as arguments for immigration restriction were all of old American stock.[53]

When the commission's report was released, the *New York Times* headlined its page-one story "Dark Age Cruelty Charged in System for Deportations."[54] But given that the commission's principal reason for existence had always been bootleggers, gangs, and the enforcement of Prohibition, even the report's strong language about star chambers and despotic proceedings didn't generate much in the way of sympathy or action. This was the bottom of the Depression, less than two years after Black Monday, four years after the Italian anarchists Sacco and Vanzetti were executed, an era when most Americans weren't inclined to be particularly tender about abuses of the deportation process or the injustices and anomalies of a half century of immigration laws.

The strongest response came from John Trevor, who had helped formulate the 1924 law and was now chair of the American Coalition of Patriotic Societies. Trevor, who'd seen a draft before the Wickersham report was officially released (and would soon commission Laughlin's racist Chamber of Commerce document urging no leniency in the immigration quotas), complained vehemently to commission chairman Wickersham that Reuben Oppenheimer, who wrote most of immigration and deportation part of the report, was working for the American Civil Liberties Union, which, Trevor insinuated, was a communist front. (Coming from Trevor, the charge was almost certainly also intended as a reminder that the author was a Jew.) Trevor asked Wickersham to strike the report's recommendation that the government create a board of alien appeals with broad discretion to review cases. Such a panel would "curtail the ability of the United States to rid itself of illegal entries, criminals and the generally undesirable aliens."[55] The recommendation stayed, but it would be a long time before any real flexibility was introduced into the system.

Even reformers, historian Ngai writes, didn't call for leniency in cases of unlawful entry because "the idea of transgressing the nation's sovereign space stood out as an absolute offense. Thus while European immigrants with criminal records could be construed as 'deserving,' Mexicans who were apprehended without proper documents had little chance of escaping either the stigma of criminalization or the fate of deportation."[56] Rather than reform, the 1930s saw increasing pressure to shut down the southern border and drive Mexicans out, often without too much concern about their legal status or even their citizenship. "It is evident that, unless an end is put to the influx of Mexicans, this country will have merely substituted a low-grade Westerner for a European immigrant, with a new race problem thrown in," said the journal of the Order of the Native Sons of the Golden West. "The effect of this Mexican influx on the already over-burdened taxpayer should be considered. Los Angeles County . . . is the dumping ground for poverty-stricken Mexicans."[57] In the double vision of American nativists, Mexicans were strong as oxen and fit to do hard labor even as periodic outbreaks of typhus, typhoid fever, and tuberculosis in the 1920s and 1930s intensified arguments, especially after 1924, when the Johnson-Reed Act was passed without a Mexican quota, that Mexicans were carriers of dangerous diseases and should be much more carefully screened.

In attempts to rebut employer arguments that Mexican workers were a net asset, officials like Edythe Tate-Thompson, director of California's Bureau of Tuberculosis, contended that Mexicans were biologically less able to fight off TB, putting great burdens on public hospitals. Her arguments resonated with other restrictionists who claimed that Los Angeles had become a place to dispose of Mexico's poor. Beginning in the mid-1920s, Tate-Thompson wrote articles and sent letters to Albert Johnson, urging him not only to restrict Mexican immigration but also to push for the removal of Filipinos, whom she regarded as an equally dangerous threat to health and to the budgets for public medical resources.[58] Elsewhere, officials—many in towns close to bankruptcy themselves—complained they could no longer afford to educate Mexican children, could not pay the cost of relief, such as it was, and just had to get them out.

A few years after Tate-Thompson launched her campaign, another prominent Californian, the multimillionaire Charles M. Goethe (pronounced gay-tee) of Sacramento, joined the anti-Mexican campaign. Like Grant, a committed conservationist—he is credited with launching the park guides for Yosemite National Park—and, like Laughlin, an admirer of the Nazis, Goethe was a member of the Sierra Club, the head of the Pasadena-based Human Betterment Foundation, and the cofounder of the Eugenics Society of Northern California. Barraging newspapers and Washington officialdom with letters and articles on the dangers of Mexican immigration, Goethe got down to the racial basics. "Peons," he said in a 1935 handout to the press, "multiply like rabbits. It is this high birthrate that makes Mexican peon immigration such a menace." And in a letter to the *New York Times* the same year, he declared that "marihuana, perhaps now the most dangerous of our narcotics, is a direct by-product of unrestricted immigration. . . . Bills for our quota against Mexico have been blocked mysteriously in every Congress since the 1924 Quota Act. . . . We are supporting millions on the dole. Why should we not enact against Mexico the same quota we have against Great Britain, Germany Scandinavia, Italy?"[59] (The image of Mexicans multiplying "like rabbits" was hardly new. A few years earlier, Kenneth Roberts described them as breeding "with the reckless prodigality of rabbits.")[60]

The Mexican, Goethe wrote elsewhere, is "eugenically as low-powered as the Negro. . . . He not only does not understand health rules: being a superstitious savage, he resists them."[61] In 1934, Goethe had spent six months in Europe, returning with glowing reports about French deportations that "weed out the eugenically low-powered," leaving France with "practically no unemployment problem." He was also effusive about how the German eugenics program was giving Germany "an advantage over us as to future leadership." His thirty years of research, he said, "makes profound the conviction that we should (1st) pass a Quota Act against Latin America, (2nd) register all aliens [and] (3rd) deport, like France, aliens to make jobs for the old American stock."[62] In an article in *Current History* in 1934, he also warned that Filipino immigration was a "peril."[63]

Goethe wanted to use the marijuana-Mexican link both ways. Mexicans were evil because they were bringing marijuana in; meanwhile, the refer-madness prohibitionists were trying to show that marijuana was evil because Mexicans used it. By the time he wrote his letter, most states—many, but not all, in the Southwest—had already outlawed marijuana. The bans resulted not from any finding that it was medically more dangerous than any other drug but because of the growing belief that marijuana, sometimes described as "Mexican opium," was the drug of choice of Mexicans, blacks, and other lower types.[64] The Colorado law, for example, seemed to arise primarily from hysterical newspaper stories about bloody killings by "crazed" Mexican "dope fiends" and about imported Mexican farmworkers who, finding bootleg alcohol too expensive, were smoking pot in the sugar beet fields. The marijuana scare was fanned by thousands of news stories, lurid magazine pieces, and films, but particularly by William Randolph Hearst's then-powerful newspaper chain. The prime target wasn't marijuana but Mexicans.

Citizen Hearst appears to have had personal reasons for his campaign: not only did he hate blacks and Mexicans, especially after Pancho Villa seized a huge stand of Hearst's Mexican timber during the Mexican Revolution, but because reefer madness was a great circulation booster.[65] In part because of that campaign, which more or less coincided with the end of Prohibition and put a lot of T-men out of business, Harry Anslinger, who, as the first head of the federal Bureau of Narcotics, was the nation's drug czar, shed his earlier indifference to marijuana and became a vigorous retailer of the reefer-madness hysteria sweeping the country. Spicing his error-riddled congressional testimony with Hearst's atrocity stories of ax murderers under the influence of pot, and with a colorful collection of other tales about wild sex and crime, Anslinger worked hard for passage of the federal Marijuana Tax Act in 1937, which in effect added marijuana to the nation's list of contraband substances. But mostly pot was bad because it was associated with nonwhites. Black jazz musicians, Mexicans, and Filipinos went crazy smoking marijuana; Africans and Arabs chewed it. "The primary reason to outlaw marijuana," Anslinger was quoted as saying, "is its effect on the degenerate races."[66] The propagandists' version of the Mexican word itself, *marihuana,* not the more universal *cannabis* or *hemp,* became the name of choice because it made for an easy connection.

Goethe needn't have worried about the lack of a Mexican immigration quota. As he was writing his letters and articles, hundreds of thousands of aliens, many of them Europeans from eastern cities but also many thousands of Mexicans, were being or had already been detained and deported under a Hoover administration program euphemistically called repatriation. The estimates of the number of Mexicans deported in the 1930s ranged up to four hundred thousand and sometimes much higher, but the numbers are fuzzy because of the statistical uncertainty about who was actually deported, who left under pressure, either from the immigration authorities or simply because their jobs had vanished in the Depression, and who never intended to stay. Some of the deported were undocumented, some were legal residents, not a few of them citizens, many of them U.S.-born children.

The repatriation program was run by Hoover's labor secretary, William N. Doak, a longtime union member who, as a former railway switchman and later vice president of the Brotherhood of Railway Trainmen, was under particular pressure to make his administration look like it was addressing the nation's horrendous rates of unemployment and the other dislocations of the Depression—officially unemployment stood at 16 percent in 1931 and would rise to nearly 24 percent in 1935. In places like Gary, Indiana, most of the thousands of Mexican workers who had been recruited by the steel mills during World War I—as others had been brought to Detroit by the auto industry—were destitute as the mills shut down. They lived in hovels, many of them ill, in "agony and suffering," in the words of a story in the *Gary Post-Tribune* in the winter of 1932, "that is beyond comprehension of any who have not experienced it."[67] The kindest thing "that could be done for these people," said Horace Norton, the head of U.S. Steel's Gary Works, which had employed them, "would be to send them back to Mexico. They do not assimilate and are unhappy here." He disclaimed any responsibility for bringing them to Gary. Most, he said, "just drifted in." Given their desperate circumstances in that Depression winter, many were content to be shipped back home. Others, who had been in the country for many years, were harassed and coerced to leave.[68]

Most of the Europeans who were expelled were charged, not always fairly, with a specific element of the older immigration laws—with a crime committed after (or before) immigration, or with being a person likely to become a public charge. But in the government's pursuit of Latinos, Doak's Labor Department sent hundreds of agents, sometimes tipped off by workers in overstressed local welfare agencies, to raid homes and to close off city squares and other public places where Latinos congregated and round them up. Strikes and other labor demonstrations led by aliens were monitored. Those without proper documentation were arrested, locked into trains and school buses, sometimes called "Mexican gun boats," and shipped south or, if they were Europeans, to the Atlantic ports. Others, frightened by the sweeps and unable to find jobs with employers who—given the millions of unemployed American workers and under pressure from unions—stopped hiring Latinos altogether, left on their own. Still others, most of them small barrio business owners, were caught in the wake of both.

Although Frances Perkins, who became Franklin D. Roosevelt's labor secretary after his inauguration in March 1933, softened Hoover's deportation program and often found ways to legalize European (but not Mexican) illegal immigrants, many western and southwestern states continued with their own programs. To this day, there are still thousands of American-born citizens like Ignacio Piña, then six years old, who watched as the immigration inspectors raided his home in Montana, where his father and older sister worked harvesting sugar beets.

"They came in with guns and told us to get out," Piña, a retired railroad worker, told reporter Wendy Koch of *USA Today*.[69] "They didn't let us take anything," not even the trunk with the documents proving that he and his five siblings were U.S.-born citizens. "The family was thrown into jail for ten days before being sent by train to Mexico," Koch wrote. "Piña says he spent 16 years of 'pure hell' there before acquiring papers verifying his Utah birth and returning to the USA." No one knows how many thousands like him fought, after their deportation, not just the immigration system but also their parents to be able to return. The removal of the Piña family took place in 1931, the same year as publication of the Wickersham deportation report, which, in hindsight, was only prologue. Americans would eventually get a vivid picture of what the nation, California especially, had done to the Okies; but it rarely heard much about what it had done to Mexicans.[70]

And yet, while the racism that didn't much trouble with the legality of many who were deported, provided only that they were "Mexicans," is obvious—as is the difference between the legal help provided some European aliens and the star chamber process to which many Latinos were subject—it's too easy to forget the panic and the larger economic desperation against which these things took place. The same is true about the racism on which a great deal of the nation's basic immigration policies and practices rested. In 1931–33, when the U.S. unemployment rate was climbing to 25 percent—in 1936, despite the New Deal, it was still around 15 percent—it didn't take admirers of the Nazis like Harry Laughlin or Charles Goethe to understand that during the Depression no nation embraced immigrants, and many expelled them if they could only find grounds for expulsion and places to ship them.

America had been trying to withdraw from the world since World War I. In large part because of the efforts of people like Henry Cabot Lodge, America didn't join the League of Nations even though (or perhaps because) it was Woodrow Wilson's baby. In 1930, Congress enacted the Smoot-Hawley Tariff Act, which in inspiration and spirit was not all that different from the immigration restrictions that Hoover and Doak were trying to enforce at the same time, although probably still more ill-advised in its disastrous effects on both the nation's and the world's economy.[71] What gave the American immigration and deportation policies their special irony is that they represented such a sharp break both with prior laws and practices and with the nation's welcoming traditions and beliefs, always among its greatest glories. That there would be a break was almost inevitable. A country that a century before had been crying for people to work couldn't forever absorb unlimited additional others, especially in terrible economic times when both the economy and its basic relief system were under stress. The irony lay not in that the restrictions came, but in how and on what basis they were imposed. It's with those things especially that we continue to struggle.

CHAPTER 5

The Great Awhitening

The melting pot had always involved a more complicated chemistry than the metaphor suggested, and the forty years following the adoption of the 1924 immigration act—the decades of the Depression, the New Deal, and two wars—demonstrated how complicated assimilation was. Historian Mathew Frye Jacobson contends that "the saga of European immigration [as] proof of the openness of American society . . . and the robust health of American democracy" is "a pretty story [that] suddenly fades" when one recognizes "how crucial Europeans' racial status as 'free white persons' was to their gaining entrance in the first place; how profoundly dependent their racial inclusion was upon the racial *ex*clusion of others; how racially accented the native resistance was even to their inclusion for something over a half century; and how completely intertwined were the prospect of becoming American and becoming Caucasian. Racism now appears not anomalous to the working of American democracy, but fundamental to it."[1]

Jacobson's assessment may give the story an even darker hue than it deserves. But it's surely true that one of the unadvertised expectations on admission into the United States was for the greenhorns to adopt the attitudes about, and habits of, ethnicity, race, and class of those who preceded them. As fellow victims of WASP discrimination, many of the children and grandchildren of the shtetl Jews, like many German Jews, made common cause with southern blacks in the civil rights movement of the 1960s, and some died in the cause. But their cousins in New York patronized the *shvartzes* who cleaned their apartments as much as the Gentiles upstairs looked down on the coloreds who did the same work for them. New immigrants were no more hesitant about using ethnic and racial stereotypes than those who'd arrived a generation earlier—and they often invoked these stereotypes proudly, sometimes affectionately, because it showed they were now also 100 percent American.

Vaudeville entertainers—Irish, Italian, Jewish, among them, perhaps most memorably, Al Jolson, born Asa Yoelson in Srednik, Lithuania, to Cantor Moishe Yoelson—put on blackface and did black dialect even as real blacks were still trying to get on the same stages. And sometimes, like Chico Marx, they did each other's dialects. Immigrants brought some of their prejudices with them; others were acquired in the process of assimilation. (Chico learned his Italian dialect on the streets of New York to avoid trouble with the Italian kids when he crossed into their territory.) In Fresno a century later, the Hmong gangs who fought with Latino gangs spoke English with the same Hispanic inflections as the gang members they fought.

Yet even before the 1924 immigration law was passed, and with a vengeance in the decades after, immigrants and their children, a few of them Irish like George M. Cohan, many of them Jewish—George and Ira Gershwin, Irving Berlin, Richard Rodgers, Jerome Kern, the men who made Tin Pan Alley—joined Scott Joplin, Jelly Roll Morton, Billie Holiday, Duke Ellington, Louis Armstrong, and scores of other African Americans and a parade of other Jewish and Irish vaudevillians and comics to *become* the entertainment industry. (The greatest exception on Tin Pan Alley who proved the rule was Cole Porter, the Yalie from Peru, Indiana.) On the "coast," Sam Goldwyn, Louis B. Mayer, David O. Selznick, and the four Warner Brothers (born Eichelbaum) in Hollywood, along with a large cast of immigrant directors and actors—Frank Capra, Erich von Stroheim (son of a Jewish hat manufacturer in Vienna), Otto Preminger, Ernst Lubitsch, Billy Wilder, close friend of Peter Lorre (née Loewenstein)—became the pushcart peddlers of the American dream.

Ethnic names were changed, not just at Ellis Island but by movie industry managers and agents who were sure that Rita Hayworth would go over better than Margarita Carmen Cansino and that Tony Curtis would be an improvement over Bernard Schwartz. Jack Benny, son of a Polish immigrant haberdasher, was born Benny Kubelski. Eddie Cantor began as Israel Iskowitz; Fred Allen, the son of Irish Catholic immigrants, as John Florence Sullivan; Karl Malden as Mladen Sekulovich, son of a Yugoslav immigrant steelworker. Goldwyn was born Shmuel

Gelbfisz in Poland. Mayer, who began his movie career as the New England distributor of D.W. Griffiths's racist classic *Birth of a Nation,* started life as Eliezer Meir in Minsk. (One actor, John Hodiak, who first appeared in plays at the age of eleven at the Ukrainian Catholic Church in Hamtramck, Michigan, refused to change his name because, he said, it sounded like what he looked like.) The play *Abie's Irish Rose* opened in New York in 1922 and before it closed in 1927 had become one of the longest-running hits on Broadway up to that time. In 1928 it became a movie; in 1946, after a two-year run as a radio comedy, it again became a movie.

The children of the immigrants who dug the sewers and laid the tracks for the streetcar lines in Albany, Boston, and Chicago took over the civil-service machinery that turn-of-the-century reformers had designed in part to check the upstarts' political power. In some cases, as noted in chapter 2, the civil service itself became an enduring ethnic enclave in which family ties, personal friendships, and just plain cronyism became more reliable tickets to entry and promotion than high scores on civil-service examinations and the other meritocratic formalities that the reformers had established. Jimmy Walker, Fiorello LaGuardia and the O'Dwyers, Paul and William, in New York, Tommy D'Alessandro in Baltimore (father of future House speaker Nancy Pelosi, the first woman to hold that post), James Michael Curley and the Kennedys in Boston, and Anton Cermak and the Daleys in Chicago spanned the bridges between identity politics and assimilation to make their way in government (and sometimes to jail) or, like George Meany, grandson of Irish immigrants, worked their way up to lead the great national labor unions that, along with the public schools and, later, the military, became the greatest instruments of Americanization.

From California came sons of immigrant Italians named A.P. (for Amadeo Peter) Giannini and Joe (born Paolo Giuseppe) DiMaggio, brother of Dom and Vince. Lee Iacocca, later to become an auto industry hero, was the son of an Italian immigrant steel worker. The father of Leon Panetta, who became Bill Clinton's chief of staff and later director of the CIA (which a generation earlier had been the paradigmatic WASP institution), was, like DiMaggio's, an immigrant Italian fisherman. The children of Irish cops and Italian grocers went to Fordham, Holy Cross, Boston College, St. John's, Loyola, or St. Michael's if they could afford it or if the parish priest kicked in. The offspring of sweatshop seamstresses, tailors, and kosher butchers went to City College and Brooklyn College, and later, if they met the admission quota requirements and managed to get financial aid, to Harvard and Columbia and became lawyers and doctors, physicists and literary critics, who, like Alfred Kazin, were among the great celebrators of national letters. Sometimes their children would take their children, now named Elliot, Irving, Shelley, and Norman, from the Upper West Side or from Great Neck back to Rivington Street on the Lower East Side for sentimental shopping trips and to calibrate their own achievements.

And in due course, the children and grandchildren of slaves and the "new" immigrants—James T. Farrell, Clifford Odets, Bernard Malamud, Norman Mailer, Arthur Miller, Saul Bellow, Philip Roth, Isaac Bashevis Singer, Richard Wright, James Baldwin, Langston Hughes, Ralph Ellison, Toni Morrison, later to be joined by the children of Latinos and East Indian and Chinese immigrants—entered the pantheon of great American writers, infusing a heavy charge of new energy into the nation's literature. In the process, the theme of migration and immigration, the impact of culture on culture and race on race—and the process of assimilation per se—established itself more firmly than ever as an essential narrative in American literature. What the children of the new immigrants brought to American literature, and what the great black jazz artists coming out of the South were infusing into the national idiom, the émigré immigrants of the 1930s and 1940s, those who were able to get in, often brought with them, helping American music and visual arts become increasingly creative and confident on their own, instead of looking anxiously to Europe for leadership. Together they brought into being what Emerson had only dreamed about a century before.

Some were temporary refugees who returned to Europe after the war ("birds of passage"), some became permanent residents: Arturo Toscanini, Gian Carlo Menotti, Bruno Walter (born Schlesinger), Rudolf Serkin, Jascha Heifetz, Arnold Schoenberg, Kurt Weill, André Previn, Mark Rothko, Jacques Lipschitz, Marc Chagall, Darius Milhaud, plus countless other performers, composers, writers, academics, sculptors, painters, art dealers, and scholars, many Jewish, many not. But permanent or not, they energized and enriched American culture as it had never been before and, in the grim postwar years, in turn reenriched all of Western culture. And, of course, there were the scientists: for better or worse, the United States would not have produced an atomic bomb when it did without immigrants named Bethe, Einstein, Fermi, Rabi, and Szilard, three of them Jewish, one half Jewish, one married to a Jew. One arrived as a young child, the others were distinguished enough to be admitted as adults despite the national origins quotas and the increasingly difficult bureaucratic immigration hurdles of the 1930s.

• • •

Assimilation was rarely easy. Everywhere in America, nativism, racism, and anti-Semitism, in part fanned by economic and social turmoil and later by the very success and prominence of the new generation of immigrants and their children, remained the favorite flavors of bigotry. Between 1920 and 1927, when a libel suit forced him to apologize, Henry Ford's *Dearborn Independent* relentlessly spewed anti-Semitic venom about an imagined Jewish conspiracy to take over the world.[2] Ford, who as a visionary industrial pioneer had a stature and a cultural impact in 1920s America that were greater than Bill Gates's eighty years later, had not only persuaded himself that Jews had engineered World War I—he would believe the same a generation later about World War II. Immigrants in general were destroying the country. "Melting Pot Dross," said one *Dearborn Independent* headline, "Takes Fifth of Tax Dollar." But it was the menace of the Jews that most obsessed him. Through ninety-one consecutive articles that were collected by Ford and published in four volumes as *The International Jew: The World's Foremost Problem,* Ford became the nation's leading retailer of classic anti-Semitic dogma. The pieces were laced with references to the *Protocols of the Elders of Zion,* the fabrication of the czarist secret police about an alleged meeting of Jews planning domination of the world.

Jews, according to Ford, were the principal profiteers of World War I: "In New York City alone," said the *Independent* in 1920, "fully 73 per cent of the 'war millionaires' are Jews," with financier Bernard M. Baruch as the chief power broker. "Baruch could probably do a better job than Trotsky did. . . . Before Mr. Bernard M. Baruch got through, he was the head and center of a system of control such as the United States Government itself never possessed and never will possess until it changes its character as a free government."[3] The (Jewish) banker as Bolshevik and vice versa. In the article "Jewish Element in Bootlegging Evil," Ford's paper noted that "'Rabbinical wine' is a euphemism for whisky, gin, Scotch, champagne, vermouth, absinthe, or any other kind of hard liquor." Jews, according to the *Independent,* corrupted baseball; Benedict Arnold had Jewish associates; Jews dominated the press; "Jew wires" controlled "Tammany's Gentile Puppets"; there was "an all-Jewish mark on 'Red Russia'"; and Jewish financial manipulators, who "have simply grabbed American-produced wealth and made American consumers pay and pay and pay, have been able to operate almost openly because of the sheer blindness of the American people."[4]

As to democracy, in 1920, "Jewish nature is autocratic. Democracy is all right for the rest of the world, but the Jew wherever he is found forms an aristocracy of one sort or another. Democracy is merely a tool of a word which Jewish agitators use to raise themselves to the ordinary level in places where they are oppressed below it; but having reached the common level they immediately make efforts for special privileges, as being entitled to them."[5] And in 1922: "The subversive Jewish influence supports the oligarchy of unserviceable wealth at one end of the social scale, while it stimulates the baser elements of industrial unrest at the other end. And the race thus rent asunder to its own undoing, does not see this—capital does not see, and labor does not see—that the leaders of chaos are alien in blood and soul."[6]

Although Ford, after sneering at or just ignoring extended public criticism from a wide spectrum of leading Americans, was forced to settle the libel suit, issue his apology, and shut down the paper, *The International Jew* and its anti-Semitism lived on. The collection appears to have considerably influenced Hitler, who, according to reports widely circulating in Germany in the early 1920s—more than a decade before he seized power—was getting both ideas and substantial financial help from Ford for his fascist and anti-Semitic campaign. A large picture of Ford hung in Hitler's private office; copies of the German translation of *The International Jew* were prominently scattered in the adjacent office in his "splendidly furnished" Munich headquarters.[7] In 1938, the year before Hitler attacked Poland, he would return the favor by awarding Ford the Grand Cross of the German Eagle, a medal adorned with swastikas that the Nazis created to honor worthy foreigners. At the same time, *The International Jew* and the *Protocols* were also becoming the urtexts for generations of lesser bigots.

If Ford tried to impose his dogma on the country from the top down, the Ku Klux Klan, "the second Klan," founded in Atlanta in 1915 and only an indirect descendant of the night-riding Klan of the Reconstruction era, grew from the bottom up. Espousing a broader Anglo-Protestant nativism—antiblack, anti-Catholic, anti-Semitic, anti-immigrant, and militantly prohibitionist—it reached its peak in the mid-1920s. In 1925, the year when some forty thousand Klan members marched down Pennsylvania Avenue, it had between two and five million members and countless other sympathizers, many of them drawn by its temperance position, making it a major force not only in the politics of Oregon, Indiana, Texas, Oklahoma, and other southern and midwestern states but in presidential politics. A series of sexual and financial scandals and ugly internal fights reduced its influence in the 1930s, but the cross burning and lynching continued.[8]

Beyond organized groups like the Klan, the 1930s were a fertile field for individual economic and social crackpots and rabble-rousers, left and right (and sometimes both at different times), who worked xenophobia, racism, nativism, and anti-Semitism with renewed vigor. Many have been forgotten. One of the unforgotten is Gerald L.K. Smith, the peripatetic Arkansas preacher who shuttled between the left-wing populism of Huey Long, a man he idolized, to William Dudley Pelley's fascist Silver Shirts and the virulent anti-Semitism that, following Long's assassination (by a Jewish dentist), would mark the rest of his career. In 1936, as part of the quixotic National Union Party to elect an obscure North Dakota congressman named William Lemke president, Smith, who was regarded by H.L. Mencken as the "best breast-beater" of them all—better than William Jennings Bryan or Billy Sunday—promised to rid the country of "Franklin D. Jewsevelt."

To battle communism, the labor unions, and Jews, and to keep blacks in their place, Smith launched the Christian Nationalist Crusade, the America First Party, the Christian Nationalist Party, and a monthly publication called *The Cross and the Flag*. After running unsuccessfully for the Senate and for president, he ended his career by creating what was, in essence, a Christian theme park in Eureka Springs, Arkansas. It included a seven-story "Christ of the Ozarks" statue, a Bible museum, and the performance of a hugely successful passion play, "the only presentation of its kind in the world," in Smith's words, "which has not diluted its content to flatter the Christ hating Jews."[9] In the 1950s, Smith also published the first of a string of postwar editions of Henry Ford's book, which to this day remains a featured item on the Web sites of neo-Nazi and other anti-Semitic groups, among them several maintained by Arab extremists who find comfort in Ford's association of Zionism with the Jewish scheme for world domination.

Another of the great rabble-rousers of the 1930s and a precursor of today's radio frothers, was the Irish Catholic priest Charles Coughlin of Royal Oak, Michigan, a Canadian immigrant who, in his newspaper *Social Justice*, serialized the *Protocols* and, in his weekly preaching on national radio, accused Jews of financing the Russian Revolution.

Fifty-six of the fifty-nine members of the Communist Party's Central Committee, he said, were Jews. The Depression was the work of an international conspiracy of Jewish bankers.[10] "Every cannon forged [in World War I]," wrote Coughlin, "every shell exploded was trademarked with the sign of decadent capitalism. It was a war fought to make the world safe for Wall Street and for the international bankers."[11] Among these bankers, again, was "Bernard Manasses Baruch whose full name has seldom been mentioned but which name from this day forth shall not be forgotten in America. This was the name which his parents gave him, the name Manasses. This is the name of your prince of high finance. Him with the Rothschilds in Europe, the Lazzeres in France, the Warburgs, the Kuhn-Loebs, the Morgans and the rest of that wrecking crew of internationalists whose god is gold and whose emblem is the red shield of exploitation—these men I shall oppose until my dying days." The list of names by itself left no doubt who he was talking about.[12]

Along with Gerald L.K. Smith, Coughlin was one of the strange bedfellows who composed the short-lived National Union Party, which grew out of Coughlin's National Union for Social Justice and which ran Lemke for president. (Among their compatriots was the wacky left-winger Frances E. Townsend, the California doctor who promulgated the Townsend pension plan. The plan, which would have imposed a 2 percent national sales tax to pay every American $200 a month, a lot of money in the thirties,[13] is widely believed to have spurred Franklin D. Roosevelt's creation of the Social Security system. But because Townsend regarded Roosevelt's program as insufficient, he joined the campaign to defeat him.)

Coughlin, who in the early 1930s had an enormous following—in 1934, the year his collection of talks sold more than a million copies, he made the cover of *Time* magazine—had begun as a strong supporter of Roosevelt in 1932; it was, he famously said, "Roosevelt or ruin." But by 1936, the praise for FDR and Coughlin's own left-wing populism in his weekly talks on the CBS network had turned first to castigation of Roosevelt for his failure to carry out the radical anticapitalist program that Coughlin had called for, and then to embittered attacks and dark conspiracy theories. In the process, Coughlin's talks veered away from sermonizing and became ever more blatantly political, isolationist, and anti-Semitic.

In a talk in December 1938, later published as a pamphlet, Coughlin deplored the Nazi persecution of Jews even as he expressed understanding that Nazism "was conceived as a defense mechanism against communism." Communism, he contended, complete with long lists of

Russian names, was the work of Jews. Despite the persecution of Catholics in Russia, Coughlin complained, the press gave their attention to the persecution of German Jews because Jews controlled the press.[14] "Must the entire world go to war," he asked early in 1939, "for 600,000 Jews in Germany who are neither American, nor French, nor English citizens, but citizens of Germany?"[15] With the approach of the war, as he lost the major radio networks, church authorities, who, despite growing criticism from a large number of prominent Americans, had long left him to his political sermonizing, finally shut him down.

The noisy rants of the Smiths and the Coughlins both reflected and incited the xenophobia and the broader racism and anti-Semitism of the era and almost certainly contributed to the failure to liberalize national immigration policy during the Depression and war years. These were the years of Charles A. Lindbergh's flirtations with the Nazis: In 1938, two years after Laughlin got his honorary degree, and just a few months before Henry Ford got his Grand Cross of the German Eagle, Field Marshal Hermann Göring, whose Luftwaffe had shocked the world in 1937 with its vicious bombing of the Spanish city of Guernica, would award Lindbergh the Nazi Service Cross of the German Eagle. (Just two weeks earlier, Hitler, with the concurrence of British prime minister Neville Chamberlain that forever gave appeasement its ugly name, had marched into the Sudetenland.) It was the heyday of the German American Bund and of the isolationists, some of them well-meaning idealists, of the America First Committee. Notwithstanding the ebbing respectability of eugenics, it was in 1937 that Laughlin and Wicliffe Draper, the New England textile millionaire, established the Pioneer Fund to pursue an agenda of race science that continues to this day. In 1939, as the war in Europe was beginning, Lindbergh urged America to stay out. This, he said, wasn't our fight. "We can have peace and security," he wrote in the *Reader's Digest,* "only so long as we band together to preserve that most priceless possession, our inheritance of European blood, only so long as we guard ourselves against attack by foreign armies and dilution by foreign races. . . . Our civilization depends on a Western wall of race and arms which can hold back . . . the infiltration of inferior blood."[16]

Beneath all that noise, and perhaps as influential, was the quiet and subtler anti-Semitism—and, needless to say, the racism—in the executive suites of corporations, in the law firms, in the social clubs, in the selective private universities and prep schools, and in the sale and rental of apartments and private homes. Much of the Ivy League continued to maintain Jewish quotas into the 1960s; the great Wall Street law firms excluded Jews, blacks, and often other minorities as well, almost always as partners and often as associates; clubs continued to be segregated—and some still are. Until the Supreme Court struck them down in the late 1940s, restrictive antiblack, anti-Jewish covenants that real estate boards had actively promoted in the 1920s riddled the housing market. When Althea Gibson, having already taken both the French Open and the British Open, won the U.S. Open tennis championship at the West Side Tennis Club in Forest Hills, New York, in 1957, neither she nor any other black or woman, nor any Jew, could become a member. When she returned the following year to defend her title, someone had made a sign telling her to "Go back to the cotten plantation, nigger." Somebody, she supposedly told a companion, can't spell "cotton."[17]

In 1947, when *Gentleman's Agreement,* the Oscar-winning film based on Laura Z. Hobson's best-selling novel about subtle upper-crust anti-Semitism, was released, *New York Times* critic Bosley Crowther, though praising it, deplored the naiveté of the hero who discovers bias in all the expected places and among a lot of proper people that, as a journalist, he should long have been aware of. The *Times*'s literary reviewer called the book, which included references to Gerald L.K. Smith and some other contemporary bigots, a "Grade-A tract masquerading as a novel," but one that was still "required reading for every thoughtful citizen in this parlous century."[18] As if to reinforce the point of both the novel and the film, when Darryl F. Zanuck, a Nebraska boy who wasn't remotely Jewish, was preparing to make the film, many of Hollywood's Jewish powers, already intimidated by the shadow of McCarthyism, tried to dissuade him, fearing it would stir up unnecessary trouble. Zanuck disregarded the warnings and produced what turned out to be Fox's biggest hit of the year. Two weeks after the film opened, the Hollywood writers and directors who, after refusing to testify before J. Parnell Thomas's House Committee on Un-American Activities about their alleged communist affiliations and friends and came to be known as the Hollywood Ten, were cited for contempt, indicted, convicted—and were eventually blacklisted in Hollywood by some of the same studio executives.[19]

• • •

Given the nation's racial consciousness, being—or becoming—white had long been one of the essentials of Americanism. And as the litany of court cases in the three generations after the 1880s demonstrated, the definition of whiteness was often mutable and rarely certain. In the

American scorebook, the Greeks, Italians, Slavs, and Turks of the new immigration weren't black, but they weren't white either. They occupied, in historian David R. Roediger's phrase, a state of "racial inbetweeness."[20] The Depression tended to further complicate that uncertainty, often adding yet more fuel to the fires of anti-Semitism and generating complaints like that of Representative Martin Dies of Texas, chairman of the House Committee on Un-American Activities and another of the great nativists, who blamed the whole Depression on immigrants.[21] The stresses of hard times on families, particularly on recent immigrants, were almost certainly also partly responsible for urban legends like the common belief that children of southern Italian immigrants had particularly high rates of truancy and delinquency. Yet paradoxically, the sharp reduction in immigration that followed enactment of the 1924 quota law and, in many instances (though hardly in all), the shared economic hardships the Depression brought, also generated an emergent class solidarity that allowed the industrial labor movement to grow. It helped drive immigration-related ethnic consciousness (though rarely race) into the background. The Hoovervilles and soup kitchens of the 1930s were also melting pots.

Where a decade or two earlier Samuel Gompers and his craft unions had been muscular opponents of the new immigration, both on economic and ethnic grounds, the new industrial unions composed of unskilled and semiskilled workers in the steel mills, the mines, the glass works, and the auto plants now necessarily embraced the Hunkies, Polacks, and Italians who made up large parts of their memberships—and often, if reluctantly, these unions recognized blacks as well, even as they continued to be fiercely opposed to competition from additional immigrants. Among the surnames of the successful organizers for the United Steel Workers in western Pennsylvania in the late 1930s (to choose just one example) were Busarello, Chartok, Danko, Dwardetto, Grecula, Medrick, Nunes, Petrak, Tafelski, Timko, and Tormayo, not to mention the Burkes, Feeneys, and McGarrys. These were not the Sons of the American Revolution or members of the General Society of Mayflower Descendants. Nor were Julius Hochman, David Dubinsky, Luigi Antonini, and Rose Pesotta, the executive board members of the International Ladies Garment Workers Union, or James C. Petrillo, the organizer and muscular boss of the musicians' union, or the officers of many of the nation's other unions as they grew under the protection of the National Labor Relations Act (the Wagner Act) in the friendly climate of the New Deal.

In drawing new immigrants and their children to the mostly Democratic political machines of the big cities, political organizations had long been the Harvards and Yales of immigrant Americanization and political education. Now the unions became the Princetons and Browns. The Sidney in Roosevelt's once often-quoted (and possibly apocryphal) phrase "clear it with Sidney" referred to Sidney Hillman, the onetime rabbinical student from Latvia who had turned the Amalgamated Clothing Workers of America into a major political force. Hillman, frustrated by the American Federation of Labor's (AFL's) antiquated emphasis on skilled crafts workers, had joined with the fiercely combative John L. Lewis of the United Mine Workers—Lewis was the son of Welsh immigrants—to form the Congress of Industrial Organizations (CIO). Hillman, who soon became the CIO's vice president, was a major organizer for FDR, who in turned appointed him to a string of federal boards and commissions.

Hillman's relationship with Roosevelt didn't assuage the nation's residual anti-Semites. On the contrary, like the appointment of upper-class Jews like Henry Morgenthau Jr. as FDR's secretary of the treasury or of Felix Frankfurter to the Supreme Court, or FDR's association (again) with the financier Bernard Baruch, it only reinforced the paranoia about an incipient Jewish takeover. Beginning in 1933, Roosevelt's liberal Secretary of Labor Frances Perkins and her immigration commissioner, Daniel MacCormack, although facing opposition from southern conservatives for any formal changes, had exploited administrative devices in existing law to legalize the status of what eventually totaled some two hundred thousand illegal European immigrants already in the country—no one then called it amnesty. Nonetheless, the America First miasma of xenophobia and anti-Semitism, combined with Depression-era (and later wartime) priorities and pressures, made Roosevelt, who had long been indifferent to the plight of Jews in Nazi Germany, especially skittish about anything that might increase immigration or that seemed to extend special privileges to the European Jews who were desperately trying to escape from Hitler.[22]

In one paradigmatic incident in October 1943, after the outlines of the Holocaust had become horribly clear, a prominent group of Orthodox rabbis marched to the White House hoping to see the president and present their pleas for help. Earlier they'd met with House speaker Sam Rayburn and Senate majority leader Alben Barkley. But the president, acting on the advice of two high-profile Jewish leaders—Sam Rosenman, a senior member of the American Jewish Committee, and Rabbi

Stephen Wise, president of the American Jewish Congress, who both feared that the meeting would inflame anti-Semitism—refused to see them.[23] Even before the war, the State Department (then still a WASP-dominated institution), reflecting that anti-Semitism and suspicion of refugees, had been making the application procedures for visas more difficult, reducing immigration well below the legal quotas for Germany and eastern Europe. After the European war began, in a classic catch-22, no doubt intended, the American consul in Marseille, then in Vichy France, would not issue a visa until the applicant had an exit visa; the French, collaborating with the Nazis, wouldn't issue the exit visa until the applicant had an immigration visa.

It wasn't until after the war, when some eight million European war refugees were crowded into camps in Austria, Germany, and Italy, that President Harry S. Truman ordered the admission of some thirty-eight thousand displaced Europeans and that Congress, under pressure to take some leadership, passed the Displaced Persons Act of 1948, which allowed the admission of some two hundred thousand Europeans over a two-year period, but only by in effect charging them against future quotas. Worse, the law also drew such tight limits that Truman only signed it, he said, "with great reluctance." The legislation, Truman charged, "discriminates in callous fashion against persons of the Jewish faith. This brutal fact cannot be obscured by the maze of technicalities in the bill or by the protestations of some of its sponsors." The bill's "niggardly restrictions," he said, reflected "a singular lack of confidence by the Congress in the capacity and willingness of the people of the United States to extend a welcoming hand to the prospective immigrants."[24]

It's highly likely that the Depression and then the war would have sharply reduced immigration even without the 1924 quota act, as had similar economic crises before. Because of the Depression and the administration's bureaucratic tightening of the immigration process, even national quotas for northern Europe often went unfilled. At the same time, notwithstanding pleas from a few Jewish organizations and humanitarian groups for some easing of the quotas to admit more refugees, the sharp reduction in immigration almost certainly made it easier for the New Deal to institute its liberal economic measures—Social Security, the WPA, school lunch and other nutrition programs, the Wagner Act—and appease its labor constituencies without fear of a backlash about, as Ford's *Dearborn Independent* complained a decade earlier, melting pot "dross" taking a big chunk of the tax dollar. In 1910, 14.7 percent of the U.S. population was foreign-born. In 1940 the proportion was down to 8.8 percent. In 1960 it would be 5.1 percent, a little over a third of what it had been a half century before and just 72 percent of what it had been in absolute numbers.[25]

The incorporation of immigrants and their descendants into the voter rolls, far from ending identity politics, sanctified, institutionalized and formalized it. In the Northeast particularly, where party organizations controlled nominations, the balanced ticket was an election staple, especially for the urban Democrats: an Irishman, an Italian, a Jew, occasionally a Slav, like Mayor Anton Cermak of Chicago, with more consonants than vowels in his name, but more often than not a Scully or an O'Dwyer—and occasionally a Wagner or a D'Alessandro—at the top. Because of those urban machines, the unions, and the cultural (wet, Catholic) impact of Al Smith's failed but important 1928 presidential campaign, millions of those older immigrants and their American-born children were now voters, the overwhelming proportion of them Democrats. For the previous half century, the political clubs and precinct committees had taught thousands of immigrant ward heelers how to get voters to the polls, how to run meetings, manipulate opinion, skewer opponents, distribute favors, allocate public jobs and contracts, and appeal to the respective sensibilities and pride of their communities. In 1932, it paid off big.

But the biggest whitener of the decades after the Immigration Act of 1924 was World War II, when millions of the in-betweens were called up and when the nation's war propaganda systems—official from the military and the Office of War Information and unofficial from Hollywood, the radio networks, newspapers, and countless other sources—celebrated the white commonness of the effort against the Germans, the Japanese, and, somewhat sub voce, the Italians, who were more often lampooned for their incompetence and cowardice than for their sadistic villainy. (Q: What do you call an Italian submarine commander? A: A chicken of the sea.) Conversely, Winston Churchill was often quoted about our émigré allies, now in exile in London, to the effect that wherever one found three Poles, there was one prime minister and two leaders of the opposition. In the war movies, every bomber and every submarine was manned by a balanced ticket: Jones, Bartolucci, O'Brien, Levine, Kowalski, Burns, Hennessey, Alvarez, Schmidt, with an occasional black mess boy thrown in. For many who were not yet citizens, military service could speed the path to naturalization. If we were white-skinned (more or less), we all belonged.

Wartime assimilation was hardly perfect. Americans didn't hear much about the Nisei battalion in the bloody fighting at Cassino and

Anzio, or the all-black squadron of Tuskegee Airmen, or the many other segregated African American units that fought honorably all over the world. Even after the war, it took pressure from black leaders and some courage for Truman, already facing a split in his party over civil rights, to order the integration of the military and stare down the resistance and the complaints both from within the officer corps and from outside, later echoed in the battle over gay service members, that integration would destroy morale and fighting effectiveness—and it took another fifteen years to accomplish it.[26]

Nor were most Americans troubled when 110,000 Japanese Americans living on the West Coast, 60 percent of them U.S. citizens, were summarily stripped of their rights, freedom, and property and shipped off to Manzanar, Gila River, Poston, Minidoka, Topaz, Granada, and the other "war relocation camps," some of them as far east as Arkansas, where many were interned for the duration of the war. (Interestingly enough, in Hawaii, which, having already been attacked, was a much more plausible target for future attacks, and where more than one-third of the population was of Japanese descent, only 1,800 were interned because Japanese laborers were needed on the sugar and pineapple plantations.) In California and many other places, there were cheers—from farmers who wanted to be rid of the competition, from politicians, among them California attorney general Earl Warren, then preparing to run for governor,[27] from the newspapers, which had long campaigned to be rid of the Japanese, and from many ordinary citizens. "Ouster of All Japs in California Near!" said a headline in the *San Francisco Examiner*, whose exclamation point left little doubt about the celebratory sentiment behind it. When the first evacuees returned from the camps at the end of the war, many were harassed, sometimes shot at, and told to get lost.

In contrast with World War I, when all things German were suspect, World War II rarely demonized any but the Japanese and occasionally the "Nazis." In the days after the "sneak attack" on Pearl Harbor, a few Germans and Italians, who appeared on an FBI list of suspected enemy aliens, were detained but in most cases were soon released, despite the fact that German subs had been spotted off the East Coast and that in the spring of 1942 two had actually landed small groups of clumsy saboteurs (soon caught), one on the beaches of Long Island, the other in Florida. But by then, as many writers have pointed out, the new immigrants and their children had been whitened—meaning Americanized—enough to possess the political clout that immunized them against the sort of discrimination leveled at the Japanese.

As Americans, the new citizens, even the would-be citizens, felt comfortable, and probably proud, in lampooning and sometimes beating up blacks in Harlem and Detroit or, in their sailor's uniforms, roaming the streets of Los Angeles in search of Mexicans and Filipinos they could attack, Latinos who, in turn, would be described as "youth gangs" by the mayor, the police, and the papers. Who threw the first punch in the 1943 "Zoot Suit riots" or wielded the first chain and bottle was never clear. But there was little question that it was the sailors, later joined by soldiers, who in succeeding days went looking for Hispanics.[28] The presence, as the Harvard political scientist Jennifer L. Hochschild writes, of the semiofficially certified lesser races—Asian, black, and Latino—made becoming a white American that much easier. You were white because you were a citizen, spoke English, served in the war alongside (or under) other Americans, including Mayflower descendants (or your kids did), and you weren't a spade or a Jap, races that in Hochschild's words, "could not traverse the same path."[29] Albeit, now that the Chinese were our allies and far and away the greatest victims of Japanese atrocities, they too would soon be (slowly) brought out of the shadows. The war, like the Depression, helped glorify the idea of America as a nation of immigrants, turned Ellis Island into a symbol of historic triumph and belonging, and made the whole idea of immigration less toxic. Arguably, it set the stage for the liberalization of immigration policy that came in the 1960s.

• • •

Trying to construct a counterfactual history is always a slippery undertaking, but historian David Roediger has a strong case when he tries to imagine what would have occurred in America in the Depression had there been no immigration restrictions. What would have happened to the labor movement, or "racial formation," he asks, if the Depression had begun before immigration restrictions were in place? "What if a dozen years of depression had begun in 1920, not 1929? How powerful might the Ku Klux Klan and fascist organizing generally have become? How widespread might the animus against existing immigrant communities have grown? How lastingly divisive to the cause of labor unity might the American Federation of Labor's embrace of anti-immigrant racism have been under such conditions?"[30]

On a less hypothetical but equally telling point, Roediger is surely right that the great migration of southern blacks to Chicago, Detroit,

Cleveland, Pittsburgh, and other northern industrial centers in the 1920s might have been a lot slower had the supply of immigrant labor not been reduced. Something similar was true for the Latino and Filipino immigrants who were recruited into the fields and canneries of the South, Southwest, and West in the half decade before the 1929 crash, many of them the same people who would be forcibly repatriated when the Depression hit. But neither the black migration north nor the Latinos who had come to El Norte resolved any of the lingering racial questions. On the contrary, blacks, Mexicans, sometimes Jews, and, for many more years, Asians were the necessary Other in the great awhitening of the people who would for generations themselves still be called "ethnics," even, in social philosopher Michael Novak's phrase, "unmeltable ethnics." Writing in 1971, Novak, like millions of others, was awed by the fearful price his grandparents—in his case Slovaks from the onetime Austro-Hungarian empire—had to pay to become Americans. "What price," he asked, "is exacted by America when it sucks into its maw other cultures of the world and processes them? What do people have to lose before they qualify as true Americans?"[31]

But for all the costs in humiliation and, often, in the blood of the hundreds of thousands who died for what was not yet their country, most didn't pay the price that the Others almost necessarily paid and in many cases still pay for the legitimization of the new whites. Nor, as suggested earlier in this chapter, did their parents' or grandparents', and sometimes their own, experiences with discrimination keep a lot of the newly whitened from demeaning the officially certified Others of their time. In some instances, they even adapted the tactics of Jewish and African American antidiscrimination organizations to their own causes—learned from the the Anti-Defamation League and NAACP to organize protests against those who associated Italians with the Mafia and Poles with the endless dumb Polack, dirty T-shirt, and light bulb jokes that some Americans still tell. The sensitivities, real or feigned, and the political correctness set off by ethnic slurs, real or perceived, now often seem overdone. There was a kind of freedom and often a warm recognition in those jokes, recognition of other groups as equals in their Americanness, as well as proud recognition of one's own. If you could call your Italian buddy "wop" and he called you "yid," it certified true American acceptance.

"As it happened," Roediger wrote, "the Depression . . . proved how well (from the restrictionists' viewpoint) the changes made in the 1920s actually worked."[32] But it wasn't just the tightened immigration restrictions or the deportations that drove down the number of foreign-born. To an incalculable extent, it was also the Depression and the war that coincided with those changes. The absolute low points of twentieth-century immigration came in 1933 (23,000), four years after the quotas were formally implemented, and in 1943 (23, 700), the depth of World War II, when it would have been hard, regardless of the nation's indifference to the plight of European Jews, to bring many refugees to this country. Nor do we have any reliable data on illegal immigration—a category that didn't exist in the 1930s—or other officially uncounted immigrants. To the extent that the immigration changes enacted in the 1920s worked, they worked in an era when most of the left, like the New Deal itself, was struggling to help unemployed workers feed, house, and clothe their families and to check the racism and latent fascism that had taken over much of Europe.

• • •

For nearly thirty years after the passage of the Johnson-Reed national origins quota law of 1924, Congress fiddled with the details of immigration provisions, passed the Alien Registration Act (the Smith Act), added new classes of aliens who could be deported, but did little to alter the broader naturalization and immigration regime that had been evolving since the turn of the century. There were three exceptions. One came in 1929 when the Registry Act amended existing immigration law to, for a twenty-dollar fee, permit legal residence to anyone who had arrived before 1921 but who had no documentary proof of having gone through U.S. ports of entry and passing the medical and mental requirements in effect when the immigrant arrived. Under the amendment an estimated two hundred thousand "illegal" European immigrants were legalized, contributing, in historian Mae Ngai's words, "to a broader reformation of racial identity, a process that reconstructed 'the lower races of Europe' into white ethnic Americans."[33] In contemporary terms, it was "amnesty."

Another, enacted in part to counter Japanese wartime propaganda reminding the nation's Chinese allies that they were still the targets of U.S. racism, was the repeal in 1943 of the Chinese Exclusion Act and the establishment of a token Chinese immigration quota.[34] The third—hardly a change in policy or ideology—came in 1942, when what farm groups and other employers described as, and probably was, a desperate wartime shortage of workers persuaded Congress to enact the emergency labor legislation that became the umbrella for the Bracero

Program. Until it was finally shut down in 1964, far later than first intended, American agriculture and industry recruited as many as four million desperate and exploitable guest workers under the program, some for the railroads, many more for the cotton farms and other fieldwork in the South and Southwest. Some came for a few months, some for longer periods; many came and went back home in a seasonal cycle that later became almost the norm.

Because of its push-pull nature, bringing people when they were most needed, then forcing them out when they were not, the Bracero Program also brought in its wake an increasing number of undocumented people. Some were braceros who just slipped away when their jobs were done. Some crossed into the country without documents, establishing the trails from the villages of Michoacan, Zacatecas, Guanajuato, and Jalisco (or from their counterparts in Guatemala and El Salvador) to El Norte—paths on which people from the same villages came to the same U.S. towns, and often to the same job sites—that continue to be followed to this day. The process imprinted the image of the Mexican as a useful but disposable outsider more indelibly than ever. In 1954, reaction to the flood of agricultural workers that the Immigration and Naturalization Service (INS) had admitted in 1951 in retaliation for Mexico's suspension of the Bracero Program prompted Operation Wetback, in which a combination of INS and Border Patrol agents rounded up hundreds of thousands of Latinos and shipped them south, a number augmented by the additional thousands who fled in fear of deportation. Pull-push.

The growing number of low-wage farmworkers, legal and illegal, many of them first drawn by the Bracero Program in the years after the war, became a growing source of concern through much of the nation. It particularly worried struggling U.S. farmworker unions and even established Mexican American civic and advocacy groups. In 1948, leaders of the League of United Latin American Citizens (LULAC) sent telegrams to President Truman complaining that illegal workers were "a direct danger to our own citizens."[35] The (Latino) American GI Forum, along with a number of farmworker unions, asked for tighter border controls. In 1953, with support of the Texas Federation of Labor, the unions produced a booklet called *What Price Wetbacks?* prompted, in the later words of one of its authors, by illegal immigrants who

> would come on over here and pick cotton and take jobs away from our own people that were either legal immigrants already well documented and everything, or our citizens. As a result of that, our own people had to migrate away from South Texas and go up north to pick cotton, follow agricultural

> crops of different kinds. And the wetback, or the illegal alien, took their place in the cotton fields around the valley and so forth. They were paid anywhere from 15 to 20 cents an hour, and our people couldn't live for that kind of money.[36]

More generally, the Latino groups, which had begun to battle in the courts and the public arena for better schooling and other rights for Latin Americans, were also uncomfortable with the influx of generally poor and ill-educated workers who not only would lower wage levels but also, they feared—as did the established German Jews of the Northeast on the arrival of the eastern Jews in the 1880s—would bring still more racist animosity down on them. That many members of those established groups were descendants of Mexicans who had been in Texas or California long before the Anglos came made the anxiety all the more intense. But it wasn't until 1954 that the concern about this "wetback invasion," in the words of an article in the *Stanford Law Review,* reached a critical mass powerful enough to overcome the clout of the growers "who look on this fugitive army as an economic blessing and a vested right" and who, long after the end of World War II (and even after the end of the Korean War), were still complaining about their dire need for workers.[37] The 1954 roundup and deportations were hardly the first of the push-pull cycles in the treatment of Mexican workers, but they were an unmistakable indication of the cyclical pattern of the nation's nonpolicy and of the see-saw political and social ambivalence that governed it. As Philip Martin, an agricultural economist at the University of California at Davis, would say many years later, we wanted workers but we got people.

The first serious piece of post-1924 immigration legislation, the McCarran-Walter Act of 1952, wrote some of the discretionary flexibility into the deportation system that the Wickersham Commission had recommended more than twenty years earlier. The new legislation eliminated the old Asiatic Barred Zone, ended the racial restrictions on naturalization that were as old as the Republic, and created a token annual quota, albeit still based on race, not nativity, of 105 for Chinese and Japanese immigrants. Those changes were probably predictable given that the ban on the naturalization of ethnic Chinese, who came from an allied nation, had ended during World War II. And since, with the coming of the Cold War and the Korean War in 1950, Japan was now an ally in the Far East, overt discrimination became much less defensible. But in the immigration quotas, an ethnic Chinese citizen of France was still Chinese.[38]

The pugnacious Senator Pat McCarran of Nevada, the legislation's principal author, was an anti–New Deal Democrat who, like Father Coughlin, had developed an increasingly anti-Semitic tilt in the late 1940s. McCarran, who had been a leader in blocking the admission of thousands of Holocaust survivors and other European refugees, had two major priorities: The first, bordering on obsession, was the menace of communists and fellow travelers—he was the author of the Internal Security Act of 1950 that all but outlawed the Communist Party and that even some congressional Republicans regarded as the gravest danger to personal liberty in America since the Alien and Sedition Acts.[39] McCarran's second priority was the demands of ranchers in his home state of Nevada for enough good Basque sheepherders that, given the 131-person Spanish quota, they couldn't get. Twice before the 1952 act, McCarran, a son of Irish immigrants, had managed to pass bills enlarging the quota for the Basques. The new law enlarged that quota further. In the process, it also established the principle of giving preferences to certain occupations.

Despite the pleas, however, of congressional liberals like Representative Emmanuel Celler, the New York Democrat who had railed against national origins formulas ever since his fierce but futile fight against the Johnson-Reed Act in 1924—in 1943, he'd called U.S. refugee policy "cold and cruel"—the national origins quota system remained, and would for another thirteen years.[40] In the latter-day language of an official State Department summary, the bill's authors, McCarran and his coauthor, Representative Francis Walter of Pennsylvania, like McCarran a conservative Democrat, feared (or claimed they feared) that "the United States could face communist infiltration through immigration and that unassimilated aliens could threaten the foundations of American life. To these individuals, limited and selective immigration was the best way to ensure the preservation of national security and national interests."[41] And Communists were more likely to come from southern and eastern Europe, and of course, from China, than from England, Scandinavia, or West Germany, now also an ally.

The 1952 law, coupled with McCarran's Internal Security Act of 1950, also provided for the deportation of aliens, including naturalized aliens, who were Communists or suspected subversives, or who had "become a member of any organization, membership in which at the time of naturalization would have raised the presumption that such person was not attached to the principles of the Constitution of the United States and not well disposed to the good order and happiness of the United States." It banned anyone presumed to hold such views from entering the country.[42] Among those regarded as excludable or actually barred from entry, even as visitors or visiting scholars, in the years following were the Nobel laureates Pablo Neruda, Gabriel García Márquez, and Carlos Fuentes as well as Doris Lessing, Farley Mowat, and scores of other internationally recognized scholars, writers, artists, and scientists. President Truman, arguing that the national origins quotas, which he called the work of Republicans, had always been unjust, and calling the McCarran-Walter bill not only racist and discriminatory but a barrier to the nation's efforts to alleviate the European refugee problem, vetoed it. The claims of the sponsors that it would fight communism, he also declared, was only a flimsy excuse for "prejudice against people with foreign names from foreign backgrounds."[43] But Congress, with the help of Democrats, overrode him.

• • •

Fittingly, it would be Emmanuel Celler, part Jew and part Catholic, who had campaigned for civil rights and nonracist immigration laws since he arrived in Congress in 1923, who would be the prime mover of the law that put the formal national origins regime to an end. Celler and his coauthor, Senator Philip Hart, a Michigan Democrat, received strong support from President Lyndon Johnson, who announced the outlines of the new bill in January 1965 and had probably worked with the authors before he did. But this was chiefly Celler's cause. The bill would abolish national origins quotas over a five-year period and assign them to a general pool, imposing an Eastern Hemisphere limit of 170,000 and a Western Hemisphere limit of 120,000. The bill would also establish a set of priorities based on skills and family unification, subject only to Labor Department certification that U.S. workers wouldn't be displaced by the new immigrants.[44]

President John F. Kennedy had proposed a similar set of changes a couple of years earlier, which never got out of committee in either house. But in 1965, after the Kennedy assassination in 1963 and Johnson's landslide victory over Barry Goldwater in 1964, the new president was in a much stronger position. The Hart-Celler Act of 1965 came in the same wave of optimism and liberalism that drove the Great Society programs in the same years—the Civil Rights Act of 1964, the Voting Rights Act, the Elementary and Secondary Education Act, both passed in 1965, and Johnson's ambitious poverty program. (Celler, as chairman of the House Judiciary Committee, was a major player in the passage of most of Johnson's civil rights legislation.) In the context of that great surge of progressivism, it would have been surprising if Congress hadn't acted on immigration. After the whitening that took place during the Depression, the war, and the brief euphoria of the early Johnson years, immigration problems had nearly vanished as a national issue.

When it passed, the Hart-Celler Act, though moderately raising the total number of legal immigrants—and clearly a break with the past—wasn't expected to have much effect on immigration. Nonetheless, the law also seemed to reflect the fact that the prior immigration restrictions had done their work, sharply reducing the number of foreigners in the United States and reducing the tensions that had historically been associated with them: in 1960, the nation had 9.7 million foreign-born residents, roughly 5 percent of the total U.S. population, the lowest in absolute numbers since 1890, when the foreign-born comprised nearly 15 percent of the total U.S. population, and far and away the lowest number as a percentage of the total population since the census began counting the foreign-born in 1850. The nation had in the meantime assimilated many millions of immigrants, nearly all of whom were now generally regarded as Americans and, under what sociologists Richard Alba and Victor Nee described as "racial/ethnic boundaries [that] can blur, stretch and move," had become officially white. "Indeed," as they concluded, "were it not for the fluidity of boundaries, there might be no racial/ethnic numerical majority in the United States today."[45] Despite all the efforts of the old nativists and eugenicists, the descendants of the old WASPs had long ago become a minority. But millions of people descended from once-disparaged immigrants were now as American as the descendants of those who came with John Winthrop on the *Arabella*.

Most of the children and grandchildren of those not-so-new immigrants—though they might make an occasional vacation visit abroad, or a pilgrimage to Israel, or even find a cousin or a church register in Ireland, a shtetl in Poland, or a family village in Italy—knew little about the old country, its language, or culture. By the end of the 1960s, Yiddish, once the lingua franca of the Lower East Side, was vanishing in America. The children of immigrants had all gone to American schools; many had fought in World War II and often attended college on the GI Bill afterward. Many still identified themselves as hyphenated Americans—Italian Americans, Polish Americans. Others contributed to the support of the state of Israel, as many still do. Some American Jews even went to fight or to become hard-line settlers on Israeli kibbutzes. Some children of immigrants sent money to Sinn-Féin or the Irish Republican Army; many more marched in the St. Patrick's Day parades. But for most, nearly every contact with foreigners, even among blacks like the writer James Baldwin during his years in Paris, reminded them that they were Americans. Ethnic identity, Nathan Glazer and Daniel Patrick Moynihan would maintain in their classic book *Beyond the Melting Pot* (1963), was as much "a matter of choice as of heritage; of new creation in a new country, as well as of the maintenance of old values and forms." Assimilation comprised "a disinclination of the third and fourth generation . . . to blend into a standard, uniform type."[46]

But that disinclination, too, was a mark of Americanness. Even earlier—a decade before Hart-Celler—the theologian-sociologist Will Herberg had observed that the children of the immigrants, if not the immigrants themselves, had begun to identify themselves not so much by ethnicity as by religion, defined, as in the title of Herberg's now-classic book, as *Protestant, Catholic, Jew.* Nor, in his analysis, was the nation so much a single melting pot as three melting pots. But each denomination also tended to be a sort of secular religion: to be American, at least in the 1950s when he was writing, required what Herberg called "faith in faith." Herberg also contended that because being Jewish implied a distinct cultural heritage as well as religion, third-generation Jews could return to and identify with their "Jewishness" in ways that Italians couldn't return to their "Italianness" or Poles to their "Polishness."[47]

Glazer and Moynihan began their book by declaring that at least in New York City, which was their focus, the melting pot "did not happen." But they go on to implicitly acknowledge that it did, only not quite as Israel Zangwill's romantic formulation in his 1908 play, *The Melting Pot,* and its accompanying mythology had it. The Cold War, of course, also helped. It turned the inhabitants of Russia's satellites into captive freedom-loving peoples, thus miraculously westernizing Poland, Czechoslovakia, Hungary, and all the other places from which many of the presumptively inferior arrivals of a half century before—the Hunkies and Polaks and Bohunks—had come. With some exceptions, European immigrants had evolved into their new American identity (or perhaps identities), and for a brief moment in the nation's history, the prior century, or even the one and a half prior centuries, of nativism and xenophobia ceased to be a major force in the nation's policies. But it was destined to be a brief hiatus.

CHAPTER 6

"They Keep Coming"

Hart-Celler didn't come close to working as expected. Even as it was being passed, the world had begun to change in altogether unexpected ways. Economics and events abroad—religious persecution in England, the Irish and German potato famines, the failed revolutions of 1848, the Russian pogroms, Stalin, Hitler, the two European wars, the strong post–World War II recovery of western Europe and Japan, the creation of the state of Israel, and, as ever, boom and bust—had always influenced immigration. But in combination with spiking third-world birthrates, the rapidly growing economic gaps between the booming developed world and the underdeveloped world brought great waves of new faces—yellow, black, brown—to places that had never seen them before. People who once wanted to come to America by the millions, western Europeans especially, weren't nearly as interested in emigrating, while tens of millions of others—Poles, Chinese, Vietnamese, Indonesians, Indians, Iranians, Pakistanis, Algerians, Moroccans, Turks, Ethiopians, Kenyans, Sudanese—were trying to move north or toward the west.

For the United States, the new wave was overwhelmingly Latino, Caribbean, and Asian. In 1970, five years after the passage of Hart-Celler, the foreign-born population, at 9.6 million, was still lower than it had been at any time since 1900 and, at 4.7 percent of the total population, lower as a percentage than at any time in recorded American history. By 1980, a short decade later, the number of foreign-born had increased by nearly 47 percent, to almost 14.1 million, many of them undocumented. In 1990, it stood at 19.8 million, double what it had been twenty years before, of whom nearly 5 million were born in Asia, among them more than 900,000 Filipinos; 8.4 million came from Latin America or the Caribbean, half of them Mexicans. The numbers also included some 700,000 Cuban refugees, more than a half million Vietnamese and 170,000 Laotians who came after the Vietnam War and who were not part of any long-term immigration strategy or policy except, in the case of the Southeast Asians, acknowledgment of wartime responsibility, and, in the case of the Cubans, a combination of humanitarian generosity and Cold War politics. Nor did anyone in 1965 expect that within four years Lyndon Johnson would be gone, that the nation would become fearfully and often violently divided over both Vietnam and domestic policy, and that the Great Society, like the optimism that produced it, would be a thing of the past.

In a process that segued smoothly and almost unnoticed from the World War II–era Bracero Program to a system of increasingly organized illegal immigration, the growing gap between the booming postwar U.S. economy and the lagging, preindustrial Central American agricultural economy sucked ever more Mexicans, Salvadorans, Guatemalans, and Hondurans into California and the Southwest. Those new immigrants and their children began to show up in growing numbers in schools, public clinics, and hospital emergency rooms; their rickety cars were usually uninsured. As a result, they were increasingly regarded as nuisances, and often a burden, on taxpayers, schools, and the established residents with whom they (sometimes literally) collided. In the 1960 census, the native language of most foreign-born Californians was English, people who had come from either the United Kingdom or Canada. But that quickly changed, and it was noticed. What right did these newcomers have to be here?

The generation after passage of Hart-Celler would thus see the start of new state and federal attempts to gain control of immigration—and eventually local attempts as well—few of them with much success, and some bringing totally unexpected and increasingly costly and painful consequences. The first clear sign came, probably not surprisingly, in Texas, where in May 1975, just a decade after Hart-Celler, the legislature revised the education code to deny state funding to local districts for any pupil not "legally admitted" to the United States and to authorize any district to deny enrollment to such children. In the landmark case of *Plyler v. Doe,* the U.S. Supreme Court in 1982, though recognizing that the Texas legislature may have been reacting to the fact that "the increases in population resulting from the immigration of Mexican nationals into the United States had created problems for the public schools of the State, and that these problems were exacerbated by the special educational needs of immigrant Mexican children," struck down the Texas law by a hair-thin 5–4 margin. Under the Fourteenth Amendment, the Court ruled, all residents of the United States were entitled to equal protection of the laws, meaning that the undocumented children in Tyler, Texas, on whose behalf the case was brought, could not be excluded from schools open to all other children.[1]

In 1978, three years after Texas passed its law, 65 percent of California voters passed Proposition 13, rolling back and severely limiting local property taxes, a large share of which had gone to schools whose enrollment was increasingly Latino. Because of prior state court rulings that, in an effort to equalize school funding between rich and poor districts, resulted in the decoupling of local taxes from school support, voters in affluent communities no longer had much incentive to oppose property tax cuts: because their schools were now subject to "revenue limits," any tax increases in affluent communities would be offset by loss of a corresponding amount of state aid. So while funding was gradually leveled, it was leveled down, not up. It also meant that any boost in taxes would increasingly go to the growing population of immigrant children, not to the children of white taxpayers who made up the vast majority of the voters' rolls. While many places in California (as in Arizona) had long been laced with romantic Spanish street and real estate development names, hardly anyone had ever heard a word of Spanish, except maybe from the maid who came in once a week to clean. But now it was being heard on those same streets, and brown faces were appearing in hospital emergency rooms, in the discount stores, and at the DMV.

Clearly immigration wasn't the prime issue driving Proposition 13: most immediately the tax revolt was fueled by spiking property taxes driven by inflated property values. But that inflation, itself partly the result of in-migration, foreign and domestic, was accompanied by increasing awareness of the negative side effects of California's ebullient postwar growth: crowding, traffic congestion, smog, racial tension, and general disillusionment with the California dream. But immigration was surely part of it. Where "immigrants" had formerly been Iowans, Kansans, and Okies (once also unwanted), they were now Mexicans and other Latinos. Three months after Proposition 13 passed, the curmudgeonly Howard Jarvis, who was its principal author, would write a newspaper opinion piece in which he complained about "illegal aliens who just come here to get on the taxpayers' gravy train."[2]

The clearest sign, however, of where the country wanted to go and of the deep national ambivalence about how to get there, was passage of the Immigration Reform and Control Act of 1986 (IRCA). Authored by Representative Romano Mazzoli, a Kentucky Democrat, and Senator Alan K. Simpson, a Wyoming Republican, IRCA was a complex and intensely negotiated compromise among business and agriculture (which wanted more workers), immigration rights groups (which sought amnesty to legalize those already here), and restrictionists (who were demanding tighter controls and opposing anything that seemed to reward the illegal behavior of those who were here without documents). Although IRCA initially extended amnesty only to illegal residents who could document that they had been working in the United States for at least five years, pressure from agriculture opened amnesty to anyone who could show he or she had done ninety days of farm work in the year before May 1, 1986. In addition, IRCA opened the country to three hundred thousand additional Mexican agricultural guest workers. In return, the law provided for tighter border enforcement and criminal penalties for employers who knowingly hired undocumented workers. Its authors promised that there would never be another amnesty.[3]

But because so many different kinds of documents—rent receipts, utility bills, and drivers' licenses, which had been widely available to anyone who passed the tests—were judged acceptable by employers as proof of legal residence, employer sanctions were rarely enforced, even when businesses flagrantly violated labor laws. To compound the problems, because identifying documents could be and were easily forged, and because of the clout of employers dependent on low-wage immigrant workers in agriculture, in hotel and restaurant kitchens, in meatpacking plants, and increasingly in landscaping and construction, employer sanctions soon lost almost all meaning.[4] Nor was there any serious increase in either state or federal enforcement of labor laws that might have reduced the exploitation of workers (and thus reduced the incentive to hire undocumented workers). While the IRCA rules seem to have lowered wages, they didn't reduce the employment of illegal aliens. Employers, said sociologists Douglas S. Massey of Princeton and his coauthors Jorge Durand and Nolan J. Malone in their study of recent Mexican immigration, "simply transferred the costs and risks [of hiring the undocumented] to the workers themselves in the form of lower pay."[5]

At the same time, the amnesty, which made all those workers legal residents, and the accompanying guest-worker program, brought a new wave of illegal immigrants, many of them wives, children, and siblings of those who had been amnestied, as well as a new generation of workers attracted by the jobs that their newly legalized predecessors left as they took the better positions now open to them. Partly as a consequence, the two decades after IRCA became law saw the total foreign-born population, legal and illegal (between a third and a half of them visa overstayers from all over the world, not illegal border crossers), increase even faster than before. Between 1990 and 2006, it almost doubled, from 19.8 million to 37.5 million, at the time comprising roughly one of every eight U.S. residents and including 10 percent of all people born in Mexico.

The other major policy change driving increased immigration was the North American Free Trade Agreement (NAFTA), which, after it went into effect in 1994, opened the Mexican and Canadian borders to an increasingly free flow of goods and capital. But unlike the European Union, on which NAFTA was partly modeled, it made no provisions for the movement of labor, despite the fact that it was likely to have a major impact on workers. One of NAFTA's original selling points against warnings from people like Ross Perot, who famously predicted it would produce a "giant sucking sound" as jobs fled to Mexico, was that by creating more economic opportunities south of the border, it would reduce the pressure to emigrate. But the result was almost precisely the opposite. In making it easier for multinationals to import parts from their own suppliers, domestic Mexican manufacturers were eviscerated. And by allowing the import of cheap agricultural products from highly efficient U.S. farms, corn particularly, it drove tens of thousands of Mexicans off their less productive land to join the stream of migrants heading north.[6] Some became part of the million-plus workforce at the maquiladoras, the multinational manufacturing plants along the border—Siemens, Delphi, Ford, General Electric, Hitachi, Sony, among others—crowding the growing border cities and the hovels around them. Many more followed well-worn trails to join relatives and friends in the United States.

• • •

Like their predecessors at the turn of the century, the new generation of immigrants created whole new neighborhoods or revitalized decaying old ones: the Hispanicization of large swaths of California and the Southwest, where, as in South Central Los Angeles, Latinos often replaced blacks; Little Saigon in Orange County and the Japantowns and Koreatowns elsewhere in California; the peripatetic families of Indian Silicon Valley engineers shuttling between Fremont, California, and Bangalore or Mumbai; the Cubanization of Miami. New York's Washington Heights, once the first home of German refugees, became the first home of Dominicans. Mexicans appeared in Astoria and Flushing, Queens; the Hmong in St. Paul. A new wave of Armenians, this time refugees not from the Turks but from Russia, settled in the traditional Armenian enclaves of Fresno and Glendale, California, and Watertown, Massachusetts, whose high school boasted the only Armenian bilingual program in America. In many towns in California, if someone was described as bilingual, it meant that he or she could also speak English. In New York City in the 1990s, if you asked the Haitian cab driver how things were going, he was likely to tell you that it was better before the Pakistanis arrived.

Collectively the post-IRCA and -NAFTA immigrants intensified a new presence—hundreds of native-language newspapers, magazines, radio and TV stations, churches, mosques and temples, restaurants, bodegas, banks, new musical harmonies and rhythms, new dances, new dress and hairstyles, new menus. The nation is dotted with ethnic chambers of commerce and other business associations, sports and social and political clubs as well as immigrant-founded and/or operated billion-dollar enterprises like Google and Yahoo. Americans learned to savor Thai and Cambodian food and to understand that chow mein was no longer offered in self-respecting Chinese restaurants. In Los Angeles, where the idea of the kosher burrito had long been an old joke, you could get kosher Thai food. In the first decade of the twenty-first century, the Univision TV outlets in Los Angeles, Houston, Miami, San Antonio, and New York drew more viewers for the *noticias,* their Spanish-language news programs, than their mainline network competitors. A Chinese-language paper in Los Angeles published two editions, one for readers from Taiwan, the other for readers from the mainland.

By now most Americans have heard Spanish on the radio and on TV—for American soccer fans, the Spanish outlets are indispensable. But in a growing number of places, dial surfers now also run across Hmong, Armenian, Tagalog, Cantonese, Farsi, and countless other languages that not long ago they might not have known existed at all. There are Spanish-language billboards all over the Southwest, and in many towns the school marquees carry the academic calendar and other school events in English on one side and Spanish on the other. Under the Voting Rights Act, five states—Alaska, Arizona, California, New Mexico, and Texas—and many local jurisdictions have to provide multilingual ballots and other election materials. In Los Angeles, election materials are provided in Spanish, Chinese, Japanese, Korean, Tagalog, and Vietnamese. That, too, has produced its backlash, including the common complaint about having "to press one for English, two for Spanish." If you're a citizen, shouldn't you be literate in English? Some of that isn't all that different from the year 1900, when bilingual schooling in German or Polish was common in the cities of the Midwest and when foreign-language papers in every major American city had commanding circulations and, in more than a few cases, eventually morphed into mainstream publications. The *Staats-Zeitung,* which Herman Ridder bought in 1892 and was once the widest-circulating German-language paper in the country, became the base of the Knight Ridder chain, which, until it was bought by the McClatchy Company in 2006, was one of the pillars of the newspaper industry. New Mexico has had printed bilingual ballots ever since it became a state in 1912. The California Constitution of 1849, which was printed in both English and Spanish, provided that "all laws, decrees, regulations, and provisions, which from their nature require publication, shall be published in English and Spanish."[7] But who remembers that?

More and more, in the years beginning in 1990, the letters and later the e-mails to politicians and newspaper editors were full of declarations from people saying they'd be damned if they'd ever pay one additional cent of taxes to educate a bunch of illegals; without them the schools wouldn't be crowded and the other kids wouldn't be held back while teachers focused on immigrants who came to school not even speaking English. In 1993, Representative Anthony Beilenson, a solidly liberal Democrat from Beverly Hills, warned about the growing anger over illegal immigrants and proposed a constitutional amendment that would deny citizenship to the U.S.-born children of illegal immigrants. He also proposed a list of administrative changes—strengthening the Border Patrol, introducing tamper-proof Social Security cards for all legal U.S. residents, and requiring them for employment—to curtail illegal immigration. The Fourteenth Amendment, he said, attracted a "growing number of pregnant women who come here for the precise purpose of having their 'American' babies." That "creates an illogical situation in which the parents of a child who is an American citizen by virtue of birth cannot legally provide for that child because they are prohibited from holding a job here; it is no surprise, therefore, that such children are disproportionately dependent on government welfare programs." It was better, he said, to deal with the issue then, before things became really ugly.[8]

The only thing notable about Beilenson's statements, other than the source, was how prophetic they turned out to be. In 1994, barely a year later, as Los Angeles was issuing reports about the burden immigrants were putting on its public hospital emergency rooms and other medical facilities, the voters of California, at the time just coming out of a recession, enacted Proposition 187, an initiative that would have denied virtually all public services, including schooling and higher education, to illegal immigrants and their children. It would also have required every public employee, teacher, physician, and social worker to report all illegal aliens to the head of his or her agency, to the attorney general, and to immigration authorities. Because the initiative was drawn by Alan Nelson, the former U.S. immigration commissioner, at the time a paid advisor to the Federation for American Immigration Reform (FAIR), it was quickly targeted as part of the racist agenda of the Pioneer Fund, which had given FAIR more than $1 million in the prior decade. In the days following the disclosure of the link, FAIR withdrew its funding and went out of its way to prove that it wasn't a cat's paw of Pioneer and that in any case Pioneer wasn't racist.[9]

Proposition 187 nonetheless passed with 59 percent of the vote. Although it was quickly blocked and later struck down as unconstitutional by the federal courts, relying in part on the *Plyler* decision, the campaign to pass it had long-lasting consequences, particularly for Latino politics and for Governor Pete Wilson and the California Republican Party. In 1986, as a U.S. senator with a big agricultural constituency, Wilson had been a major advocate of a generous guest-worker program. But in 1994, running for a second gubernatorial term, he rested much of his campaign on his support of Proposition 187.

Although he claimed he was only opposing illegal immigration, and was just trying to send a signal to Washington to tighten the border, his campaign sent a different message: the new Supreme Court, with its Ronald Reagan and George H.W. Bush appointees, he suggested at one point, might even overturn the narrow *Plyler* decision. Wilson's TV ads featured a clip taken from grainy Border Patrol infrared film footage showing shadowy figures running across the I-5 freeway in Southern California, with the ominous line: "They keep coming." To many people, especially Latinos, that resonated with broader racist overtones. The film *Border under Siege,* which had been commissioned by the Border Patrol's San Diego District in its campaign to get more manpower and funding, was itself a reaction to the reaction against efforts to toughen border enforcement. After the erection of a fence from the Pacific Ocean to the major entry port of San Ysidro, about five miles inland, groups of illegal crossers made nighttime "banzai runs" around the east end of the fence. Then, in their often successful attempts to outrun the then-undermanned Border Patrol trying to catch them, they dashed across the southbound lanes of the freeway, dodging vehicles and their startled drivers.[10] It was those scenes that appeared in the agency's film.

Wilson, who'd been trailing his opponent Kathleen Brown a few months before the election, easily won a second term. But both his campaign and that for Proposition 187 with which it was linked generated widespread fear even among legal aliens that they might lose public benefits if the measure passed. Although soon overturned by the courts, it generated a powerful reaction among Latinos, many of them legalized by IRCA less than a decade before. By the tens of thousands they took out naturalization papers and, as soon as they became citizens, marched out the door into the welcoming arms of the Democrats, who just as quickly registered them as new voters. In 1990, in his first campaign for governor, Wilson, at the time running as a moderate Republican, won 40 percent of the Latino vote. In 1998, his would-be Republican successor got 22 percent of a now much larger Latino vote. In Texas, where Governor George W. Bush had developed a much friendlier relationship with Latinos and with neighboring Mexico, he got nearly half the Hispanic vote. In California, the GOP never recovered from "they keep coming." With the exception of the extraordinary circumstances leading to the recall of Governor Gray Davis and the election of Arnold Schwarzenegger in 2003, Republicans have won almost no statewide office in California in the years since.[11]

• • •

The fifteen years of enhanced border enforcement that began with the recession of the early 1990s—the major increase in the staffing of the Border Patrol, the new armamentarium of electronic sensors on the border, the occasional use of National Guard troops as backups, the construction of hundreds of miles of new fences decreed by Congress in the first decade of the twenty-first century, and the hit-or-miss operations of the Minutemen and other uninvited volunteers—had almost the opposite effect from the one intended. Paradoxically, while forcing the trail of illegal border crossers—Mexicans, Guatemalans, Salvadorans, Nicaraguans, and others—into the hot and dangerous deserts and mountains of Arizona, the additional border enforcement drove up the illegal resident population.

Where illegal workers had historically shuttled between their home villages in the Mexican interior and the fields and orchards of Texas, California, Arizona, Florida, and Washington, the mounting dangers and expense of the crossing—the deaths in the desert, the extortionate prices, and often the fatal betrayals by the coyotes smuggling people across—sharply reduced seasonal migration. Workers who had once been migrants simply stayed in the United States, in many cases sending for their relatives and becoming permanent, if not altogether committed, residents. Between 1980 and 2006, according to demographer Wayne A. Cornelius, the proportion of illegal immigrants who followed the old pattern of periodically returning home fell by almost 75 percent.[12] In 1990, four years after the passage of IRCA, which legalized 3 million undocumented workers, there were roughly 3.5 million illegal immigrants in the country. By 2005, after greatly enhanced border enforcement—or, more plausibly, because of it—that number had more than tripled to roughly 11.5 million. Of those 11.5 million, 84 percent had arrived since 1990.[13] In late 2006 or early 2007, before the recession of 2008 and federal raids on workplaces and the harsh treatment of families that often accompanied them drove many home, the number was closer to 12.5 million. In California, where the foreign-born made up 26 percent of the general population by the middle of the first decade of the century, nearly half of public school students were children of immigrant fathers; one-fourth were officially identified as English learners. And though not as dramatic as in California, there were similar proportions of foreign-born schoolchildren in Texas, Arizona, New York, and other high-immigrant states. Those children included not only Spanish speakers but speakers of some eighty other languages.

What got forgotten, particularly as post-IRCA Latino and other immigrants fanned north and east where there were more jobs and life was cheaper—to Georgia and the Carolinas, to the Midwest and into towns that had never seen anything but a white face before—was that many of the parents and grandparents of those children weren't illegal immigrants. They included the Dominican and Venezuelan baseball players who became the great stars of the game—no one complained that they were taking jobs from good American boys. There were Mexican contractors and doctors, Filipino nurses, Korean entrepreneurs, musicians and artists of all kinds, Indian and Chinese engineers, and millions of others. At the turn of the century, roughly 30 percent of Silicon Valley tech firms were headed by Asian immigrants.[14] "The definitive smell inside a Silicon Valley start-up," reporter Michael Lewis would observe, "was of curry."[15] As did the black migrants from the South and the European émigrés in the prior three generations, the new immigrants and their children infused yet another enriching strain into American literature and culture—the essays of Richard Rodriguez, and the fiction of Maxine Hong Kingston, Amy Tan, Chitra Banerjee Divakaruni, Bharati Mukherjee, Khaled Hosseini—many of these writers again exploring the interstices and friction between the old and new.

But as brown faces spread into Iowa, Illinois, Oklahoma, Arkansas, the Carolinas, and Wisconsin, where many worked the cold, wet, ugly, and sometimes dangerous jobs in the poultry and meatpacking plants, it was the illegal immigrants who got the attention. As soon as he became president, the younger Bush and his "boy genius" political advisor Karl Rove, hoping to broaden the Republican base and bring in more Latinos, tried to heed the California lesson in forging national policy. Twice they proposed broad-based reform to regularize immigration. In both attempts, the Bush plan, originally a bipartisan bill sponsored by Senators Edward Kennedy of Massachusetts and John McCain of Arizona, to give illegal aliens a chance at legalization, to further tighten border enforcement, and to establish a guest-worker program, too nearly resembled IRCA, leading restrictionists to call it amnesty or, as one radio talker later labeled it, "shamnesty."

The first attempt, never likely to have been approved anyway, was derailed by the 9/11 attacks on the World Trade Center and the Pentagon and the fear of terrorism they generated. The second try, in 2006–7, ran afoul of the intense campaigns of immigration restrictionists—academics like Samuel Huntington, George Borjas, and Victor Davis Hanson, the radio talkers, FAIR, the Center for Immigration Studies, and countless right-wing and sometimes blatantly racist groups. In response, the GOP-dominated Congress, many of whose members continued to carry the exclusionist gene that had animated their party for much of the prior century and a half, and who had been eager to go in a very different direction from Bush even before his election, not only blocked Bush's reform plan, but passed a string of measures to make life for illegal immigrants and those who helped them as miserable as possible.

In 1996, the new Republican majority in Congress, picking up the signs from the California vote on Proposition 187 in 1994, and having already passed a major welfare reform bill that cut food stamp aid and other federal benefits to all immigrants, legal and illegal, had enacted the Illegal Immigration Reform and Immigrant Responsibility Act (IIRIRA), a huge piece of legislation that covered everything from hiring additional Border Patrol agents and installing more sophisticated surveillance equipment at the border to a long list of tougher deportation procedures. IIRIRA also included a rule, which seemed almost gratuitous at the time, prohibiting illegal aliens from getting in-state tuition breaks to state colleges and universities not also granted to legal residents of other states.[16] Also in 1996, California voters passed Proposition 209, a measure prohibiting the use of race preferences in all public education, employment, and contracting, effectively marking the beginning of the end of the era of affirmative action that had begun under Lyndon Johnson some thirty years before. In the succeeding years, Ward Connerly, the black Sacramento businessman who, with his friend Pete Wilson's strong support, had launched the campaign against affirmative action as a regent of the University of California in 1995, succeeded in passing similar measures in Washington State, Michigan, and Nebraska (he failed in several others) and, with the threat of yet another initiative, forced Florida to abandon its race preferences in higher education. Connerly almost certainly believed that he was acting in the name of racial fairness—he would also try, and fail, to get voters to pass a measure to prevent the state of California from counting official statistics by race altogether.

But public support for his Proposition 209 almost certainly also reflected public reaction against the extension of affirmative action preferences to Latinos. African Americans, who had been affirmative action's original beneficiaries, were indisputable victims of three centuries of slavery and Jim Crow. Latinos, on the other hand, had come here voluntarily, were often recent arrivals, and thus had far more dubious claims to the amelioration of the lingering effects of historic discrimination. And since Asians in the prior generations had more often been the victims of ethnic quotas in university admissions than the beneficiaries, and, as highly successful students were now being admitted on merit in huge numbers, they were as likely (though often quietly) to be on Connerly's side as against him.[17]

Two years after the passage of Connerly's Proposition 209, voters in California, later followed by voters in Arizona and Massachusetts, also approved initiatives, all sponsored by a Silicon Valley millionaire named

Ron Unz, that put an end to most bilingual education classes in the public schools. Some of Unz's opponents read all these votes as at least marginally racist and anti-immigrant, a contention that seemed verified by the outcome in Colorado, where the Unz measure failed in large part because its liberal opponents ran ads warning that, if it passed, Latino immigrants would be put in classes with the kids of Americans. In one ad, part of a blitz called "Chaos in the Classroom," featuring dark faces against ominous music, the announcer warned that "children who speak little English, largely Hispanic students, would disrupt the education of 'your children'—presumably the majority white families of Colorado."[18] The defenders of bilingual education won their case by attacking the immigrant kids who presumably were to benefit from it.

As Americans quickly learned, the years after the 9/11 terrorist attacks, years not all that different from those of the Red Scare and the later McCarthy era, brought a near orgy of national security measures. In 2002, Congress enacted a "special registration" law requiring all alien males over sixteen from twenty-four countries, all but one of those countries predominantly Muslim, to be registered, photographed, and fingerprinted; thirteen thousand were ordered into deportation proceedings. In 2005, Congress passed the REAL ID Act, which prohibited states from issuing driver's licenses or other identification documents to people who couldn't prove they were legally in the country. In December of the same year, the House also passed the sweeping Sensenbrenner Bill, HR 4437, the Border Protection, Anti-terrorism, and Illegal Immigration Control Act of 2005, named for Representative James Sensenbrenner, a suburban Milwaukee Republican, sometimes known as the "pit bull" of the House who was then the chairman of the House Judiciary Committee.[19]

The Sensenbrenner Bill was a huge piece of legislation, this time including everything from where to build seven hundred miles of additional border fences to a study on the feasibility of building fences on the Canadian border. A provision making illegal entry a felony was removed before the vote. But there were sections on better ways to stop the entry of terrorists; on immigration and visa fraud; on electronic verification of employees' legal status; a mandate for developing a training manual for local cops on catching illegal immigrants; a requirement that all Border Patrol uniforms be made in the United States, "substantially all from articles, materials, or supplies mined, produced, or manufactured, as the case may be, in the United States"; on deportation procedures; and, what probably got the most attention, a provision that anyone who "harbors, conceals, or shields from detection a person in the United States knowing or in reckless disregard of the fact that such person is an alien who lacks lawful authority to be in the United States" was committing a crime.[20] "I'm not going to have my name on a bill," Sensenbrenner said as Congress was debating immigration reform a few months later, "that ends up being counterproductive like the Simpson-Mazzoli bill [IRCA] was in 1986."[21] "The Republican Party," said Frank Sharry, who had been the longtime director of the National Immigration Forum, which supported legalization, "is in the grip of nativism."[22]

The Sensenbrenner Bill never got through the Senate, although many of its parts later did, among them e-verify, a requirement that employers check the identities of their workers against the Social Security system database, which, as soon became apparent, was notoriously prone to error. And as immigration reform became an increasingly hot issue both inside and outside Washington in 2006–8, and as the 2008 elections approached, congressional Republicans, with some support from swing-district Democrats, sponsored a set of other tough immigration bills, knowing that they had only a slim chance of passing but that they might serve as wedge issues for the election.[23] Although the Democrats who won control of the House in the 2006 election succeeded in bottling most of them up in committee, the congressional immigration battles and the growing federal raids on workplaces with undocumented employees sparked demonstrations in Los Angeles, Chicago, New York, Washington, and other cities similar to those that had greeted Proposition 187 in Los Angeles a decade earlier (though this time few of the protestors waved the Mexican flags that, not surprisingly, had undermined their cause in 1994).

Although the demonstrations, including a workplace boycott to show how badly employers needed immigrant workers, energized Latinos to political activism, they also fanned the anti-immigrant flames of the national bloggers and talkers. Among them was Peter Brimelow at VDare.com, which is devoted to restricting immigration but denies, not altogether persuasively, that it's white nationalist and racist, as well as the more familiar voices of Pat Buchanan, Rush Limbaugh, Bill O'Reilly, Lou Dobbs, Sean Hannity, Ann Coulter, Michael Savage, and Michelle Malkin. The large supporting cast of local and regional radio talk-show hosts also included Roger Hedgecock in San Diego, Armstrong Williams in New York, Terry Anderson in Los Angeles, Melanie Morgan in San Francisco, Martha Zoller in Atlanta, and Dom Giardano in Philadelphia, all helping to deliver the messages of the anti-immigration organizations that fed them. The Latino demonstrations were part of the "hardcore militant agenda" of *reconquista,* said Fox's O'Reilly. "'You stole our land, and now we're going to take it back by massive, massive migration into the Southwest. And we're going to control those places, because you stole it from us,' and that's the agenda underneath."[24] Or in the indignant words of CNN commentator Jack Cafferty:

> Once again, the streets of our country were taken over today by people who don't belong here. . . . In the wake of Congress failing to pass immigration legislation last week, America's cities once again were clogged with protesters today. Taxpayers who have surrendered highways, parks, sidewalks and a lot of television news time on all these cable news networks to mobs of illegal aliens are not happy about it. . . . March through our streets and demand your rights. Excuse me? You have no rights here, and that includes the right to tie up our towns and cities and block our streets. At some point this could all turn very violent as Americans become fed up with the failure of their government to address the most pressing domestic issue of our time.[25]

The administration's second effort to enact comprehensive reform in 2007 made an easy target. It provided for more serious enforcement of employer sanctions and tighter border control. But while it created a costly and cumbersome process for illegal aliens to get on the track to legalization, its increasingly vocal opponents, who wanted nothing but militarization of the border to protect "U.S. sovereignty," could easily portray the legalization provisions as an IRCA-like amnesty program. In April 2007, in concert with FAIR, thirty-four radio talk-show hosts, who had made immigration their prime issue, organized themselves into a quasi-lobby called Hold Their Feet to the Fire and brought their microphones and some of their listeners to Washington, broadcasting to their home audiences, urging anti-immigration e-mails and faxes, and working congressional offices to head off comprehensive immigration reform.[26] Anything that might lead to legalization was "amnesty."

The talkers' assault on immigration reform in the spring of 2007 was probably the noisiest element in the defeat of both the comprehensive bill and the much narrower bipartisan Dream Act later that year, whose sponsors included Democrat Dick Durbin of Illinois and Republicans Richard Lugar of Indiana and Chuck Hagel of Nebraska, and which would have allowed some 365,000 students and other young illegal immigrants who had been brought to this country as young children, and who had gone to school here, to apply for legalization. Although the Dream Act got a majority of Senate votes (52–44), it too was blocked by threat of a filibuster.[27]

The nonpartisan Project for Excellence in Journalism gave Limbaugh et al. a big share of the credit for killing the immigration bill. But an equally powerful force was John Tanton of Petoskey, Michigan, the retired Michigan eye doctor who in the 1970s and 1980s founded or helped launch the cluster of contemporary anti-immigration groups that ginned up the materials, fed the talkers, and ran the intensive campaign of e-mails, phone calls, and faxes that killed reform and energized the anti-immigrant bills in Congress. Tanton, as much as anyone, deserves the title of godfather—one critic called him the "puppeteer"—of the contemporary anti-immigration movement. Tanton, said National Immigration Forum director Frank Sharry, "initiated and turbocharged the populist revolt against the immigration reform package."[28]

Like some of his nativist predecessors sixty years before, Tanton had a long record as an environmentalist and, in many respects, as a social liberal. Well before he got to immigration restriction, he was a member of the Audubon Society, the League of Conservation Voters, the Sierra Club, and a founder of Northern Michigan Planned Parenthood. Influenced by Paul Ehrlich's *The Population Bomb,* he tried to get existing environmental organizations involved in both population control and immigration. In 1977–79, he was president of Zero Population Growth. In 1979, after he couldn't get support from the Sierra Club for immigration control, he started FAIR. In 2004, he was one of the drivers of the campaign to change the Sierra Club's board and get it into the immigration fight. Tanton and his wife, Mary Lou, were also contributors to the political campaign of Colorado Republican Tom Tancredo, who, as the most vehement opponent of both legal and illegal immigration in Congress and as a candidate for the 2008 Republican presidential nomination in the early months of 2007, staked much of his campaign on the issue.

The quirky and publicity-shy Tanton (who in 2004 quietly contributed $1,500 to Ralph Nader's presidential campaign) never became a household name. But as much as anyone, he's the heir of the old conservationist-nativist tradition. In addition to starting FAIR and NumbersUSA, the first with the support of some $1.5 million from the racialist Pioneer Fund that Harry Laughlin cofounded forty-some years before, he also helped launch the Center for Immigration Studies (CIS), U.S. English, U.S. Inc., and Pro-English. And there were other links to the conservationist-nativist legacy as well. In Tanton's journal *The Social Contract,* the blatantly predatory image of Rome that ran through the nativist tracts in the nineteenth century was replaced by more subtly worded (and imaged) but equally inflammatory renditions of the Vatican as the two-faced exploiter of immigration to further its own imperious (and imperial) strategy. "The Church has virtually sacralized immigration," wrote David Simcox in a piece called "The Catholic Church's War on Borders." "The Church's stress on immigration as a moral imperative has practical as well as mystical roots," he said. "Organizational politics, institutional self-interest, and the desire to maximize utility are hard at work. Migration is central to the Church's history of recovery and growth following its losses from the Reformation and the secession of the Church of England. The catholization by Spain, France and Portugal of much of the Western Hemisphere in the 16th and 17th centuries was essentially a work of colonization and migration."[29]

The Tanton-funded NumbersUSA goes out of its way to show that it's not ethnicity but sheer numbers that motivate its restrictionist campaign. In that respect it's a direct heir of Ehrlich and the zero population growth movement. Yet while there's nothing to discredit the assertion of NumbersUSA president Roy Beck that he's never been in the immigrant-bashing businesses—even his critics acknowledge the group's activities are based "on policy rather than race-based arguments or xenophobia"—the million faxes his organization sent in opposition to the immigration reform bill in 2007 were probably all the more effective for it.[30]

Similarly, Tanton's own evolution from environmentalist to immigration restrictionist gives some credence to his similar denials that he's a racist. In the fall of 2008, his organizations ran large ads in the West Coast edition of the *New York Times* headlined "Population, Immigration and the Foreseeable Limits of America's Capacity: A Conundrum . . . for the Progressive Thinker." But his earnest writings nonetheless echo with the nativism of the nineteenth century, as in his 1986 memo to his colleagues in the movement:

> Can homo contraceptivus compete with homo progenitivo if our borders aren't controlled . . . ? Perhaps this is the first instance in which those with their pants up are going to get caught by those with their pants down. As whites see their power and control over their lives declining, will they simply go quietly into the night? Or will there be an explosion. Will the present majority peaceably hand over its political power to a group that is simply more fertile? . . . Will Latin American migrants bring with them the tradition of the *mordida* (bribe), the lack of involvement in public affairs, etc.? What are the implications of [projected demographic] changes for the separation of church and state? The Catholic Church has never been reticent on this point. If they get a majority of the voters, will they pitch out this concept?[31]

When the memo was leaked by the Southern Poverty Law Center, two of the board members of U.S. English—Walter Cronkite, the former CBS news anchor, and Linda Chavez, who had been prominent in the Reagan administration and the president of the organization—quit. And as a candidate for governor of California during the recall election in 2003, Arnold Schwarzenegger, apparently still a board member, quietly walked away from the group.[32] Almost inevitably, Tanton's projects have become associated with racialist groups and individuals—not just with the Pioneer Fund, but, through Wayne Lutton, coauthor of Tanton's self-published book *The Immigration Invasion* and the editor of Tanton's *Social Contract* magazine, with the white supremacist *Citizens Informer,* where Lutton is a member of the editorial board, and through other links with nativist and white nationalist groups.[33] FAIR's western field representative, Joe Turner, founder and head of a group called Save Our State (named after the group sponsoring Proposition 187) and sponsor of a San Bernardino ordinance to prohibit renting to or employing illegal immigrants, said he was not a racist and had no connection with the neo-Nazis and skinheads drawn to the SOS protests against illegal immigrants and day-labor centers in Southern California.[34]

• • •

Even before the defeat of comprehensive federal immigration reform, state and local governments had been rushing to fill the vacuum, producing their own laws and regulations. Some sought to protect illegal aliens to secure their cooperation in reporting crimes and encourage local business. Others imposed fines on or revoked the licenses of businesses hiring undocumented workers and/or forbade landlords from renting to illegal aliens; still others created programs to train local cops to work with what in 2003 became ICE, the U.S. Immigration and Customs Enforcement agency. In 2007, forty-six state legislatures passed 240 new laws on immigration—some 1,560 were introduced, nearly triple the number for the same period in 2006. In the first six months of 2008, another 1,267 bills were considered in forty-five legislatures, and at least 175 laws and resolutions were enacted in thirty-nine.[35]

Cities and counties enacted hundreds more, ranging all over the philosophical and political map. In Hazleton, Pennsylvania, the city council passed an ordinance to prohibit landlords from renting to undocumented aliens. Hazleton's ordinance, which preceded the Senate vote on comprehensive immigration reform in 2007, became a model for similar measures in the Southern California city of Escondido and in the Dallas suburb of Farmers Branch. All three laws quickly faced constitutional challenges—the Escondido council reversed itself in the face of mounting legal costs; the Hazleton and Farmers Branch laws were blocked by federal courts as intrusions on federal turf. But the anxieties and rage that drove those measures weren't dampened by a couple of judges. Lake Havasu, Arizona, like a number of other cities, made an agreement with the federal government under which local police were to be trained to interrogate and detain all illegal immigrants for deportation by federal agents. Green Bay, Wisconsin, voted to yank the licenses of businesses that hired illegals. In Irving, Texas, the once immigrant-friendly mayor, Herbert Gears, came under so much pressure that, in an effort to head off more severe local measures, he began to report illegal-alien jail inmates to federal authorities.[36]

In Virginia, the Prince William County supervisors voted to crack down on illegal aliens through increased police enforcement, the creation of a Criminal Alien Unit, and denial of virtually all services, including (in what, viewed from the perspective of public safety and health, may have been the most self-defeating provision of all) substance-abuse counseling.[37] In Greeley, Colorado, investigators from the district attorney's office, armed with a warrant, seized thousands of client records of a tax preparer in a search for illegal aliens with false Social Security numbers. In Arizona's Maricopa County, which includes Phoenix, Sheriff Joe Arpaio, operating under another state law, has made a national name for himself—a member, said *New York Times* writer Timothy Egan, of the "Lou Dobbs Gasbag Hall of Fame"—with sweeps searching for, and the subsequent jailing and public humiliation, often under harsh conditions, of hundreds of illegal aliens.[38] Early in 2009, Arpaio's deputies marched some 220 immigrant detainees, shackled and in striped prison uniforms, none convicted of any crime, through the streets of Phoenix on their way to the sheriff's tent-city detention center.[39] In the Long Island community of Patchogue, meanwhile, the police casually ignored a series of attacks by a gang of teenage boys on Latinos until one was murdered.

At the state level, the Oklahoma Taxpayer and Citizen Protection Act of 2007 made it a felony to "harbor, transport, conceal or shelter unauthorized immigrants." In Arizona, as in some other states, the legislature passed a law, since provisionally upheld by the federal courts, which denies business licenses to any enterprise employing illegal immigrants.[40] Alabama created a Joint Interim Patriotic Immigration Commission to figure out a comprehensive approach to illegal aliens (a commission that was immediately attacked as being stacked with probusiness and pro-immigrant voices). In October 2007, Governor Matt Blunt of Missouri issued a press release lavishly praising the arrest and delivery to immigration authorities of a vanload of illegal aliens who were stopped on the pretext of following another vehicle too closely. He promised (in Churchillian cadences) to "make every effort, implement every tool and take every step to ensure that the laws against illegal immigration are enforced."[41] In one law bordering on the absurd, Rhode Island approved legislation providing for the issuance of ID cards to all residents over twenty-one certifying that they were old enough to drink, excepting only illegal aliens. In Jackson County, Mississippi, the Department of Health Services took Cirila Baltazar Cruz's baby from her because her inability to speak English made her an unfit mother, placing "her child in danger."[42]

The responses to the federal failure to deal with the larger immigration issue were hardly consistent. In the summer of 2007, the city council of New Haven, Connecticut, created what it called Elm City Residence Cards—ID cards that also serve as small-balance debit cards—to all local residents, legal and illegal. A few months later, San Francisco adopted a virtually identical program—and later was embarrassed when it was discovered shielding some serious illegal alien felons. At the same time, the Illinois legislature prohibited employers from participating in the mandatory federal employee verification system until the feds got their data systems in order. The Department of Homeland Security (DHS) promptly filed suit to overturn the Illinois law. (A few weeks later, U.S. District judge Charles Breyer in San Francisco, citing the high likelihood of error and jeopardy to legal workers, upheld a challenge filed by the ACLU and a coalition of labor and business groups to the implementation of the employee federal "no-match" verification system.)

Some fifty jurisdictions, among them San Francisco, Los Angeles, and Cambridge, Massachusetts, declared themselves sanctuary cities or cities of refuge and/or ordered their employees not to cooperate with the feds in enforcing federal immigration laws. Some, like Stamford, Connecticut, created "no-hassle" zones for day laborers seeking jobs, nearly all of them undocumented. Detroit enacted an antiprofiling ordinance preventing cops and other city employees from questioning people on the basis of a whole range of characteristics including immigration status. Oakland, California, requires all municipal departments to have bilingual employees to deal with its diversity of non-English-speaking residents. In Cleveland, once also an "immigrant gateway" but now suffering from a shrinking population and economic base, some residents looked longingly across Lake Erie to bustling Toronto with its large immigrant community and associated entrepreneurial energy.[43]

To exacerbate the confusion, some jurisdictions changed their minds. Early in 2008, Phoenix, with a large Latino population, which, unlike surrounding Maricopa County, had declared itself a sanctuary city, modified the policy to allow its police officers to question arrestees about their immigration status and to report illegal aliens to federal authorities.[44] Conversely, Riverside, New Jersey, repealed its anti–illegal immigrant ordinance after the resulting exodus (mostly of Brazilians) hit restaurants, beauty parlors, and other local businesses—some were forced to close—and left a growing number of boarded-up downtown storefronts.[45] In Oregon, the legislature passed a law prohibiting businesses from gouging customers during emergencies, including "a crisis of migrants unmanageable by a county." The state also requires notaries public to translate documents for those who don't speak English, even as Kansas and a number of local jurisdictions have made English their official language. In Pahrump, Nevada, it's illegal to fly a foreign flag unless the American flag is flying alongside it.[46]

Meanwhile, a half-dozen states—Georgia, Hawaii, Illinois, Maine, South Carolina, Montana, Idaho, Nevada—among them some of the most conservative in the country, called for the repeal or deferral of the federal Real ID Act of 2005, which, beginning in May 2008, imposed on states a set of stringent verification requirements for issuing driver's licenses and other state identification documents. Some states pledged not to comply. The issue here was not liberal principle but cost and the expected aggravation of motorists (which would obviously be directed at state bureaucrats and politicians, not at Congress) once the rubber met the road at the state DMV.

But the immigration issue that got the most attention and created the loudest uproar was the news in 2007 from then-governor Eliot Spitzer of New York, who, citing public safety considerations, said that he had decided to allow illegal residents to get driver's licenses. Spitzer was quickly forced, both by pressure from Washington and by an upstate political backlash, first to modify the policy and then, as the backlash continued to eat into his own approval numbers and as upstate county clerks, the elected officials who process license applications in most New York counties, threatened to boycott the program, to abandon it altogether. Four years before, one of the hot issues that reinforced the recall of California governor Gray Davis was his decision to sign a bill allowing illegal immigrants to get driver's licenses that he had vetoed twice before.[47] The law was quickly repealed after Arnold Schwarzenegger succeeded him.

Of all the issues concerning illegal immigrants, giving them driver's licenses—as de facto national ID cards (and as the nation's most ubiquitous *rite de passage* for young males)—was far and away the one that generated the fiercest resistance. By 2007, when Spitzer made his abortive decision, even strong backers of driver's licenses for illegal aliens conceded that it had become a losing issue that they didn't want to fight about. At the same time, however, ten states, beginning with California and Texas in 2001, passed laws making illegal immigrants who graduated from their high schools and who had gone to in-state high schools during the prior three years eligible for in-state tuition in their public universities. Those laws save in-state students, legal and illegal, the thousands of extra dollars that out-of-state students, including American citizens, are required to pay. But they appear to violate the 1995 federal statute cited earlier that prohibits illegal aliens from getting tuition breaks that are denied to legal residents from other states.

The states defended the tuition breaks by arguing that they don't discriminate on the basis of residence and that they treat all graduates of their own schools equally. In 2007, a federal court upheld the Kansas law, but a California appellate court in 2008 ordered a challenge by out-of-state students and their parents to come to trial. That was a strong indication that the tuition breaks, all designed to encourage illegal immigrant students, many of whom were brought to this country as young children, to stay in school and to prevent them from joining the already large number of immigrant dropouts, were in serious jeopardy.[48] FAIR, which with its legal affiliate brought the California case, cheered the decision, presumably in the expectation that it would drive illegal students out of the country. ("These illegal immigrant students," said one letter writer to a supporter of tuition breaks, "have already stolen their primary educations. Now you want to reward them with tuition breaks that American citizens don't get. What is your problem?")[49] But it was far more likely to drive more to the streets. In the meantime, Oklahoma, one of those ten states, reversed itself on in-state tuition; Arizona voters (in 2006) passed a ballot measure denying undocumented students in-state tuition; and at least one other state, South Carolina, enacted a statute excluding illegal aliens from its public institutions altogether, even if they paid full tuition.

If there was any sense in this crazy pattern, it was the geography of the immigrant dispersion itself. As hundreds of thousands of immigrants, Latino immigrants particularly, either moved from or bypassed the traditional immigrant states—California, Arizona, Florida, Texas, and New Mexico—and moved into the Midwest and Southeast, the backlash spread with them. In many places, the new immigrants, stretched to pay for housing, occupied what someone called "backhouses"—sheds or garages—or lived three or four to a room, often a total of ten or twelve people or more, with junk cars crowding the driveways, in houses or condos designed for families of four. Sometimes they just camped in the hills. And, of course, those who had children sent them to schools that under *Plyler* had to take them, questions unasked, many of the students speaking little English and requiring additional services and crowding classrooms that had been all white a few years before. Illegal immigration, the Escondido, California, city council determined, echoing officials in many other places, "diminishes our overall quality of life."[50] Illegal immigration in such contexts, of course, almost always means Latinos. At the same time, there are also towns in California's Central Valley, and often in the Midwest, that would die without those immigrants.

"Over time," wrote Daniel Hopkins, a fellow at Yale's Center for the Study of American Politics, in an unpublished paper that perhaps articulated the obvious, "immigration rises in national salience as the size of the immigrant population reaches a critical mass, as immigration's opponents become organized and vocal, and as political elites sense an opportunity."[51] But it's the rapidity of change that may be the most crucial factor. California, where in 2008 the foreign-born made up 26–27 percent of residents and that went through a period of intense anti-immigrant backlash in the early 1990s, appears to have become accustomed to its brown and Asian faces and to the countless accents and languages of its residents—and of course has assimilated their cuisine, music, and art. (Recent data from the census indicate that 70 percent of California's "Mexicans" are U.S. citizens.) The laws seeking to drive out illegal immigrants that Arizona enacted in the first decade of the twenty-first century indicated that even a long history of Latino immigration might not necessarily make a state immune to virulent anti-immigrant politics in the future. But such circumstances do reduce the likelihood. California's population is now majority minority; in another generation, it will have an absolute Hispanic majority—assuming that the state's high rate of ethnic intermarriage will make any such count still possible or pertinent. Many parts of Iowa, South Carolina,

Wisconsin, Oklahoma, Virginia, Georgia, and Missouri are just starting on the route that California has already traveled.

More than anything else, however, the crazy quilt of contradictory local responses—like Washington's failure to enact comprehensive immigration reform—seemed to reflect the nation's own ambivalence and uncertainty about immigration. The same states that granted illegal aliens in-state tuition have denied them driver's licenses. In 2004, California governor Arnold Schwarzenegger lauded the Minutemen, the self-appointed enforcers of a tight border, for doing "a terrific job." He's also consistently vetoed bills passed by the Democratic legislature that would have made undocumented residents eligible for driver's licenses. But in the fall of 2007, he signed a bill that prohibited cities from requiring landlords to check whether tenants are in the country legally. In 2009, stuck in a monstrous $24 billion budget deficit, he pointedly repudiated those who blamed his state's fiscal problems on illegal immigrants. "I'm glad that they can get the (state) services," he said in response to a question at an editorial board meeting of the *Sacramento Bee.* "Everything we eat today is picked and created by undocumented immigrants, to a large extent. Every time we go and move into a building, a lot of those buildings are built by undocumented immigrants' hands."[52]

National polls have confirmed the ambivalence: In 2007, 69 percent of U.S. adults said that the illegal resident population should be reduced; 75 percent said they should not be allowed to get driver's licenses. But 55 percent also said that when illegal aliens who've committed no crime encounter local cops they shouldn't be arrested. By a margin of 58–35, U.S. adults supported "a program giving illegal immigrants now living in the United States the right to live here legally if they pay a fine and meet other requirements." By 66–33, they said they're not bothered when they encounter Spanish speakers. Some 45 percent (in another poll) said immigration is a good thing, 19 percent a bad thing; some 33 percent had no opinion.[53]

But as with issues like gun control, the intensity of an opposition fueled by economic insecurity and fanned by radio and TV talkers tended to overwhelm the immigrant rights groups, the pressure from the ag and business lobbies claiming dependency on cheap labor, and the broader but generally passive and uncertain prolegalization plurality. The anti-immigration activists drove the major Republican presidential candidates who tilted toward tolerance to abandon those positions; the ambivalence caused them to go silent on the issue altogether. John McCain had been among the original Senate sponsors of comprehensive reform; Rudy Giuliani, as New York's mayor a decade before, had been a strong defender—for the sake of public safety and health—of providing services for illegal immigrants; Mike Huckabee, as governor of Arkansas, sponsored tuition breaks for illegal immigrants. By the end of the 2008 presidential primary, they had all embraced Colorado Republican Tom Tancredo's stance—to the point where he said he was no longer needed. Even Democrat Hillary Clinton, also running for president, flopped and waffled after her initial support for Governor Spitzer's plan to allow illegal aliens to get driver's licenses. (That, too, wasn't new. In 1993, during the California recession when Governor Wilson was preparing his "they keep coming" campaign, Senator Barbara Boxer, among the most liberal members of the Senate, wondered whether California could afford to educate the children of illegal immigrants.)[54] In the 2008 general election itself, the issue vanished almost entirely.

Maybe the most unfortunate victim of the 2007 anti-immigration campaign wasn't comprehensive reform, which, in its complexity and its countless facets, was vulnerable on both the right and left on any number of points, but the appealing Dream Act, which would have put undocumented students who were brought here by their parents as young children, who attended and graduated from high school and intended to go to college or serve in the military, on the path to legalization. No one could claim that they were lawbreakers. Most never knew their native countries, many don't speak the language, and few have any interest in going back. More important, at a time when the imminent retirement of millions of baby boomers is predicted to leave major shortages of skilled workers in the U.S. economy and when the nation has already invested billions in their education, deporting them seems as self-defeating as it is cruel. But none of that reduced the intense pressure on a Senate minority—nearly all Republicans—to threaten a filibuster and kill the bill.

• • •

The extended battle over, and ultimate defeat of, comprehensive immigration reform also triggered a sharp turn in government worksite enforcement. Bush and Rove, who, with their Texas background, understood the importance of the growing Latino vote in their hopes of creating a long-term Republican majority—Latinos, though liberal on economic issues, the theory went, were socially conservative and could well fit under the GOP tent—also knew what Governor Wilson had done to the GOP with his immigrant bashing in California. In narrowly focusing on illegal immigrants, many with stolen or forged Social Security cards and other false identification documents, Bush and Rove might reassure as many Latinos, who feared wider discrimination, as they alienated. Even before comprehensive reform failed, the administration, sensing the political drift and hearing the increasing level of noise from FAIR and its brethren and from the blogs, the talkers, and the faxes, had tried to reestablish some credibility with its own right flank on enforcement. It cranked up roundups of illegal immigrants at packing plants and other businesses with a severity that began to resemble the Hoover administration's raids and detentions in the first years of the Depression.

In one sweep in 2006, ICE agents arrested both executives and some 1,100 illegal workers at eight IFCO Systems plants that made crates and pallets for produce shipping in a half-dozen states. In another instance, called Operation Wagon Train—ICE couldn't resist military-sounding labels—the agency raided six Swift meatpacking plants in the West, Southwest, and Midwest and detained nearly 1,300 illegal aliens, many of them alleged to be working with stolen identification documents. Since ID theft is a felony, this not only gave federal authorities more leverage in incarcerating or rapidly deporting the illegals but also linked the arrests to a hot issue that made it, in the words of Homeland Security Secretary Michael Chertoff, a case not only involving immigration but the "violation of the privacy rights and the economic rights of innocent Americans."[55] In California, Border Patrol agents complained that they were given arrest quotas to fill—150 detentions a month and twenty vehicle seizures—which prompted them to sweep bus stations and Home Depot stores and, according to other complaints, to detain American citizens among those caught in the net.[56] Those complaints reflected what appeared to be a distinct shift in focus in Justice Department policy from prosecution of white-collar, weapons, and organized crime to a determined effort to run up the numbers on immigrant crimes. One judge complained that he was sentencing lots of smuggler "foot soldiers" to prison on immigration violations while ignoring crimes like gun smuggling from the United States to Mexico.[57]

But among all the raids on factories and sweeps of public places, it was the raid at the Agriprocessors plant in Postville, Iowa, the nation's largest butcher of kosher meat products, that may have been the most glaring illustration both of the exploitative conditions under which illegal aliens were willing to work and the tactics the feds used to get around the procedural immigrant rights that had been developed in the prior seventy-five years. The Agriprocessors raid, which took place on May 12, 2008, would make a book-length story all by itself. Some four hundred workers, most of them Guatemalans, several of them young boys, were detained and nearly three hundred sentenced to five months in prison followed by immediate deportation.

The sentences came in a five-day star-chamber-like legal process conducted in trailers on the grounds of the National Cattle Congress in Waterloo. Few of the defendants, who were charged not just with illegal entry but with "aggravated identity theft" and marched into the "courtrooms" with shackles on their hands and feet, had a chance to meet with lawyers and learn their rights, which made it easy for prosecutors to coerce them with threats of more severe punishment if they didn't accept the plea deals they were offered. Most of their families, some four hundred women and children, many of them longtime residents and now virtually destitute, took refuge in St. Bridget's Catholic Church, "the safest place they knew," where, with help of the Red Cross and some old-time Postville residents, many of them descendants of Scandinavian immigrants, who brought food, they found sanctuary. The feds called it "the largest criminal enforcement operation ever carried out by immigration authorities at a workplace." The superintendent of schools in Postville, who spent until midnight to make sure all his students had a place to go to, compared the raid to a natural disaster, the only difference being "that it was a man-made disaster, not a natural one."[58]

It wasn't until after the detained had been sentenced that the long story of Agriprocessors's brutal treatment of animals and its multiple labor, health, and safety violations began to emerge—the employment of adolescents as young as fourteen, some of them working fourteen-hour days on dangerous machinery, and the general exploitation and abuse of workers. It would be more than three months after the federal raid before the state attorney general filed child labor law violations against the company and its owners and managers (who said the younger workers had lied about their ages and vowed "to put to rest the insidious notion that it knowingly employed under-age workers").[59] What was notable about the labor charges, however, was not that they were slow in coming—the state investigation had apparently begun before the federal raid—but that they were among the very few labor law violations that had ever been charged against any employer of illegal immigrants by any agency, state or federal. The founder of Agriprocessors, a Russian-born Brooklyn butcher named Aaron Rubashkin, first hired illegal eastern European immigrants and, when he couldn't fill his needs with them, employed Latinos, some of whom were forced to pay exorbitant rents at houses Rubashkin had bought all over Postville.[60]

In 2006, the latest year for which data were available, ICE reported 272,000 "removals," meaning deportations from the United States, two-thirds of them to Mexico. One million more illegal immigrants had voluntarily agreed to leave without a removal order. There's no way to know how many of those removals were ordinary undocumented immigrants caught in sweeps of worksites, and how many were felons or suspected felons and fugitives from prior deportation orders. In addition, the Border Patrol and other federal agencies recorded 1.2 million "apprehensions" at or near the border, a lower number than five years before, which the government attributed to a decline in attempted border crossings resulting from enhanced enforcement efforts.[61]

An estimated 10 percent decline in illegal alien residents from roughly 12.5 million to just over 11 million between the summer of 2007 and May 2008, assuming it actually took place, was also partly attributed to stepped-up federal enforcement (which resulted in some 4,010 "worksite arrests" in 2007 compared to a little under 700 in 2004), as well as to local police actions and to the latter-day state and local laws seeking to prohibit employment and housing for illegal aliens.[62] The enforcement, said Steven A. Camarota, the head researcher of the Center for Immigration Studies, was amplified by the consequent "megaphone effect" of the Spanish-language media in inadvertently frightening illegal immigrants away. But even Camarota, who used Census Population Survey data to make those estimates, conceded that at least part of the exodus was probably the result of economic recession, and particularly the decline of jobs in home construction, which began before the full recession hit. Wayne Cornelius, director of the Center for Comparative Immigration Studies at the University of California at San Diego, among others, put considerably more emphasis on the economic effects.[63] As in past recessions, protests against immigration went up at the same time as immigration declined.[64]

There wasn't much question that the ICE raids affected not only the families of the targeted workers, among them many legal residents, but also the communities in which they lived. In June 2008, the U.S. Conference of Mayors passed a resolution noting that "ICE worksite enforcement activities are often the result of 'anonymous' tips from the competitors of legitimate employers, thereby using ICE raids to disrupt production; and [that] ICE enforcement activities targeting companies that have had no record or suspicion of engagement in exploitative practices will negatively impact local economies and may drive employers to locate manufacturing facilities overseas." The mayors therefore called on the feds "to develop a national policy for its workforce enforcement activities that focuses on employers with a demonstrated history or reasonable suspicion of engaging in exploitative practices, such as violation of wage, hour or occupational safety laws and regulations; and . . . that ICE not prioritize responsible employers for worksite enforcement activities before accurate verification systems are available or comprehensive immigration reform regularizes the status of workers on whom they rely."[65]

What's indisputable was that the failure of immigration reform—not just in regularizing the status of illegal aliens, and developing less-capricious and more-predictable employer sanctions, but, most of all, in creating economic conditions south of the border to ease the pressure to migrate north—left a thousand questions unanswered. If your name was Hernandez, or you had dark skin and spoke little English, could you risk reporting a crime to the local police without being turned over to Immigration and Customs Enforcement? If you had a contagious disease or a drug habit, how willing would you be to seek treatment, and how safe were your neighbors and families because of that fear? And what about those driver's licenses? What would happen when a car driven by an American citizen collided with one driven by an undocumented—and therefore probably uninsured—immigrant?

As the combination of recession and anti-immigrant groups, turned up anti-immigrant anxieties, those unresolved questions, which reinforced legitimate fears, got little airtime. And there were many more: what were the chances of being stopped on the highway by sheriff's deputies empowered to arrest illegal immigrants, or of coworkers reporting you to the feds, or of legal residents being rousted at midnight by warrantless raids? Of the sixteen thousand federal prosecutions in March 2008, presumably not an atypical month, more than half were immigration cases, which Homeland Security Secretary Michael Chertoff lauded as a great success in deterring illegal immigration.[66] But was the spending on what the government called Operation Streamline, and which Chertoff said would increase, really worth the payoff in deterrence and the strain on a legal system already overburdened by other cases?

There were also important questions of social policy crying out for redress. What sort of future would face an eighteen-year-old high school graduate who was brought here by her parents as a young child and who knows no other country but who can't go to college, get a driver's license, or fill a legal job? Conversely, how large a price should local schools have to pay to teach English to the children of illegal immigrants? How much should states have to compensate for the failure of the federal government in the costs of incarcerating illegal-alien felons? A nation struggling with such issues is in dire need of leadership from its central government.

In another few years the nation may look back on the first decade of the twenty-first century, and especially the years after 9/11, as another of those xenophobic eras, like the Red Scare of the 1920s or the McCarthy years of the 1950s, when the nation became unhinged, politicians panicked, and scattershot federal, state, and local assaults led to unfocused and often cruel harassment of non-Anglo foreigners. It may also be seen in retrospect as a period when groups of anxious Americans made desperate rearguard attempts to freeze Anglo-white places and power in a mythic past. But it's equally likely that much of today's policy vacuum stems from our collective uncertainty. A new society with new kinds of people and new voters is rapidly growing under and around us—just as it grew under the old native Anglo-Saxons a century ago. By 2042, according to the Census Bureau, a majority of Americans will be something other than non-Hispanic white. The wild cheers for Sarah Palin at the 2008 Republican National Convention, whose delegates were 93 percent white, 5 percent Latino, and 1.7 percent black, a larger proportion of whites than in 2000 or 2004 (the Democrats were 65 percent white), could easily be interpreted as the cries of a class and race that sensed—as indeed the nativists of yore had predicted—that its days were numbered.[67] The convention scene in St. Paul was eerily reminiscent of what Norman Mailer had written about another Republican convention—that one in Miami—a long forty years before. The attendees, he said, had served "as the sentinel in concert halls and the pews on the aisle in the church, at the desk in schools, had served for culture, served for finance, served for salvation, served for America—and so much of America did not wish them to serve any longer, and so many of them doubted themselves, doubted that the force of their faith could illumine their path in these new modern horror-head times."[68]

Sarah Palin—and John McCain, too—were each in her or his own way a symbol of a glorious past that had come to an end and may, in fact, never have fully existed. Many of us, even those, maybe especially those, whose forebears arrived with the first settlers, are immigrants in this new society and still have no idea how to deal with it. The 2008 election, with its overwhelming Democratic votes from blacks and Latinos, made clear that it's coming fast. There were 7.6 million Latino voters in 2004; there were 9.8 million in 2008, up 28 percent. The Asian electorate had grown by 21 percent, from 2.8 million to 3.4 million.[69] In the context of all the historical comparisons of the Obama election with the coming of the New Deal in 1932, it may be that the coming of this new electorate, like the one represented by the children of the "new immigrants" three generations before, is the epochal event.

CHAPTER 7

A Border without Lines

The history of American attitudes about immigration and immigration policy has long been a spiral of ambivalence and inconsistency, a sort of double helix, with the strands of welcome and rejection wound tightly around one another. Current law allows admission of about 400,000 "new arrivals" a year, with priorities based on family reunification, employer sponsorship for special skills, and humanitarian cases. First preference goes to spouses and minor children of U.S. citizens, though for countries like Mexico, China, and the Philippines the wait can be many years. In addition, hundreds of thousands of others already in the country are granted "adjustment of status" each year, which makes them legal permanent residents—the number in 2007 came to roughly 600,000—of whom a large percentage had at some prior time been illegal immigrants. That meant, in the count of the federal government, a little more than 1.052 million "immigrants"—the number is the total of "adjustments" plus the number of those newly admitted—down from about 1.266 million in 2006.[1] Meanwhile, net growth in the number of illegal immigrants declined sharply, from an average of about 525,000 annually before 2005 to roughly 275,000 since.[2]

But there's been a telling sameness going back almost two centuries in the arguments against the admission of new people, especially those from "races"—themselves subject to endless reclassification and redefinition—different from the "American." Against that long and complex history, with its mutations and uncertainties, the arguments of contemporary opponents to non-European immigration—crime, disease, culture, language, educability, costs over benefits—resonate with the contentions of the past, many of them long refuted, some absurd. Ominous warnings like those about the ongoing, if not already accomplished, Mexican *reconquista* and slogans like "What don't you understand about illegal?" demand more nuanced responses than such a question allows. Similarly, use of the word *illegal* as a noun, something many of us have casually done, resonates uncomfortably with *Mexican.* Illegal and Mexican, said a federal expert on the history of immigration law, have been "conflated."[3]

As historian Mae Ngai and others have also pointed out, the "illegal alien" is a creature of policy. Law and administrative decisions have both made the illegal immigrant and, from time to time, unmade him as well, often with racial overtones. Our first illegal immigrants were Chinese. The Border Patrol was originally created to stop bootlegging and the smuggling of Chinese immigrants—sometimes said to have disguised themselves as Mexicans—across the southern border, and sometimes across the northern border as well. Much more recently the hard-line backers of tougher immigration enforcement have issued similar warnings about Muslim terrorists darkening their faces and disguising themselves as Latino immigrants to cross the Mexican border—or, even more improbably, wearing insignia identifying themselves as Muslim militants. Early in 2006, in testimony that got a lot of attention from the conservative radio talkers and made its way into Tom Tancredo's book on the dangers of immigration, Sheriff Wayne Jernigan of Val Verde County, Texas, told the Senate Judiciary Committee that,

> recently, a jacket with patches was found in Jim Hogg County, Texas, by agents of the U.S. Border Patrol. The patches on the jacket show an Arabic military badge with one depicting an airplane flying over a building and heading towards a tower, and another showing an image of a lion's head with wings and a parachute emanating from the animal (lion). It is believed from an undisclosed document that Department of Homeland Security translators concluded that the patches read "defense center," "minister of defense," or "defense headquarters." The bottom of one patch read "martyr," "way to eternal life" or "way to immortality."[4]

In addition to the military patches, other sheriffs reported finding badges, Iranian currency, and people speaking Spanish with a funny accent—all presumably Muslims—who, in Tancredo's words, "have been streaming into the U.S. across our porous border." The anarchist rats and the Mafiosi swimming off the ships in New York harbor a century ago have become Arab terrorists wading across the Rio Grande or making their way across the deserts of Arizona. Sometimes they're Mexican gangs shuttling their contraband, human and pharmacological, across the border in underground tunnels. "One of our witnesses," said Representative Edward Royce of California, chairman of a House subcommittee on terrorism in 2006, "smuggled radioactive material, enough to make a dirty bomb, through two land ports of entry, one on the northern border, one on the southwestern border."[5] In 2005, the "loathsome" contagious diseases of the old immigration laws comprised, in the estimate of CNN's Lou Dobbs, seven thousand new cases of leprosy in the prior three years, most of them associated with illegal immigrants. The criminal tendencies of the illegal immigrants were substantiated, Dobbs said on another broadcast, by the fact that one-third of all convicts in U.S. prisons were illegal immigrants.[6]

Dobbs, like many of the nation's radio talkers, got a lot of his material from FAIR and the Center for Immigration Studies, whose representatives often appeared both on Dobbs's programs and on the shows of other conservative broadcasters. Some of the material, according to Christine Romans, a CNN reporter on Dobbs's program, also came from the late Madeleine Cosman, who was in her various careers a recognized medieval scholar, a Southern California lawyer, an author, and a medical consultant. Cosman had spent much of the two years before her death in 2006 circulating a film warning about "Mexican predators," "bastards" who rape young girls or boys or nuns, and lecturing about the "horrific diseases common in Third World poverty [that] suddenly are appearing in American emergency rooms and medical offices."[7] The part about the "Mexican predators" Dobbs did not report.

Dobbs's disease and crime statistics were mostly wrong. It was seven thousand new cases of leprosy in the prior *thirty* years, not the past three, and the number of illegal immigrants in U.S. prisons was closer to 2 percent.[8] In June 2008, PPIC, the nonpartisan Public Policy Institute of California, reported that the national incarceration rate was 813 per 100,000 for U.S.-born adults compared to 297 per 100,000 for foreign-born adults, a ratio of more than two to one. "National studies," the report said, "have examined crime rates in jurisdictions with large and/or increasing immigrant populations and have found either no discernible link or a slightly negative one."[9] Dobbs, confronted by Lesley Stahl on CBS's *60 Minutes*, flatly denied that there was a gross error in the leper numbers. "I can tell you this," Dobbs responded. "If we reported it, it's a fact." Dobbs on his own program followed the *60 Minutes* interview the next day with an Alphonse and Gaston conversation with Romans, who (of course) agreed with him wholeheartedly that CNN checked things out thoroughly and rarely made mistakes.[10]

The arguments woven into the thread of exclusion also run through the recent work of academics like Samuel P. Huntington and Victor Davis Hanson, who fervently contend that what they regard as the huge indigestible lump of Spanish-speaking immigrants in the Southwest and increasingly in many other parts of the country puts the newcomers beyond assimilation. The immigrant flood poses a major threat to what Huntington calls the "Anglo-Protestant culture that has been central to American identity for three centuries"—something he sometimes also refers to as "the Creed."[11] Huntington's comments aren't exactly like Harry Laughlin's congressional testimony in 1922 that "the logical conclusion is that the differences in institutional ratios, by races and nativity groups . . . represents real differences in social values, which represent, in turn, real differences in the inborn values of the family stocks from which the particular inmates have sprung. These degeneracies and hereditary handicaps are inherent in the blood."[12] But they're close enough.

Huntington gins up the same kinds of numbers for the educational backwardness of Mexicans that Laughlin assembled in his tables for Italians and Poles: in 2000, Huntington said, 86.6 percent of U.S. "native born adults" had graduated from high school; for Latin Americans, it was 49.6 percent; for Mexicans, 33.8 percent. He made similar comparisons for citizenship, intermarriage, and other characteristics. "Mexican-Americans," he said in an article first published in *Foreign Policy* and later in somewhat different form in his book *Who Are We?* "argue that the Southwest was taken from them by military aggression in the 1840's, and that the time for *la reconquista* has arrived. Demographically, socially and culturally that is well under way."[13] Their low rates of assimilation "could eventually change America into a country of two languages, two cultures and two peoples. . . . There is no Americano dream. There is only the American dream created by an Anglo-Protestant society."[14]

Hanson, in his book *Mexifornia,* projects a similarly grim future—a society segregated by class and ethnicity in which "Spanish, *de facto,* becomes co-equal with English, poverty becomes endemic . . . schools erode; crime soars and there seems to be little cultural opportunity for integration and Americanization"—the very things that Lodge,

Theodore Roosevelt, and countless others warned about at the turn of the twentieth century. "In the bilingualism that emerges," Hanson warns, "a new argot of Spanglish, neither Spanish nor English, is mastered as a language to be read and written with little real facility, while waves of newcomers, whether literate or no, demand or at least expect Spanish-only businesses and social services. Provocateurs in the race industry, government, and academia all rise up to meet the emerging opportunities offered by balkanization, giving ideological and political support to the idea of a true postmodern society without borders."[15]

Hanson writes in the tones of the inherently reasonable man, but his book and his subsequent writing are also laced with nostalgia for the orderly arrangements of his Central Valley childhood:

> The slow progress made in rural California since the 1950s of my youth—in which the county inspected our farm's rural dwellings, eliminated the once-ubiquitous rural outhouse, shut down substandard housing, and fined violators in hopes of providing a uniform humane standard of residence for all rural residents—has been abandoned in just a few years of laissez-faire policy toward illegal aliens. My own neighborhood is reverting to conditions common about 1950, but with the insult of far higher tax rates added to the injury of nonexistent enforcement of once-comprehensive statutes. . . .
>
> Ever since the influx of illegals into our quiet valley became a flood, I have had five drivers leave the road, plow into my vineyard, and abandon their cars, without evidence of either registration or insurance. On each occasion, I have seen them simply walk or run away from the scene of thousands of dollars in damage. Similarly, an intoxicated driver who ran a stop sign hit my car broadside and then fled the scene. Our farmhouse in the Central Valley has been broken into three times. We used to have an open yard; now it is walled, with steel gates on the driveway. Such anecdotes have become common currency in the American Southwest. Ridiculed by elites as evidence of prejudice, these stories, statistical studies now show, reflect hard fact.[16]

Hanson is right that countless immigrant farmworkers, the majority of them illegal, live in what one observer long ago called "backhouses"—barns, toolsheds, garages, and various other outbuildings not really fit for human habitation. But how many of those drivers with no registration or insurance who crashed into his place are illegal? How many would have driver's licenses and auto registrations—and thus insurance—if there were no laws denying them to illegal aliens? How many would be better drivers? In 1940, a decade before the time he longingly remembers (the year after Steinbeck's *Grapes of Wrath* was published), Hanson's Central Valley was also notorious as the place where armed sheriff's deputies confronted and sometimes drove away the Okies who were looking for farm work and who were more than happy to live in substandard housing. (In parts of California's San Joaquin Valley, Latinos now live in shacks once occupied by Okies.) In 1950, getting rid of that ramshackle housing may have been a way to provide a "humane standard of residence for all rural residents," but it was also a means of getting rid of the people many growers housed in them. Fifteen years before that blessed time, some leading citizens of Sacramento, just up the road in the Central Valley, were testifying in Congress and writing letters to newspapers and public officials warning that the place was being overrun by Mexicans. In the early 1930s, those Mexicans had been rounded up by the hundreds of thousands and shipped back to Mexico. Two decades before that another great intellectual, the Progressive-era sociologist Edward Ross, had bitterly complained about the "Caliban type" of immigrant fouling up the cities, bringing filth, illiteracy, crime, disease, and vile morals, "oxlike men [who] belong in skins in wattled huts at the close of the Great Ice Age."[17]

Michael Savage, born Michael Weiner, who may be the most virulent of the radio talkers and whose audience of some eight million puts him behind only Rush Limbaugh and Sean Hannity in listeners, is the son of a father who would have qualified as one of Ross's "oxlike men," a Russian Jewish immigrant in the Bronx who had a little shop on the Lower East Side. Savage, a relentless self-promoter whose own hippie background in San Francisco is too long and bizarre to be recounted here—on his Web site he proclaims himself a "world famous herbal expert"—doesn't seem to hear the ironic "oxlike" echoes in his complaints.

> When you start bringing in masses of immigrants from everywhere on Earth, you don't have a melting pot; they cannot be melted into an American, and that's what's going on in the country today. We're bringing in millions of people from countries that have no compatibility with the values of Europe, not any values whatsoever. And I will argue with you as long as you want on this, if you want. There was no history of the liberation of people in China for example, to choose one nation, there was no Magna Carta, there was no evolution. There's been no Middle Ages for the Muslims coming into America.[18]

Was there a Magna Carta in Russia or Austria? Does Savage, who is often quoted approvingly by white supremacists and anti-Semites, know that a century before now a lot of respectable Americans declared that there was no melting pot for people like his immigrant forebears, no matter how much he now pretends he really isn't one of them?

• • •

No contemporary text—not Huntington's book, or Hanson's sentimentality, or Tom Tancredo's historical myopia—embraces the old Anglo-Saxon nativism more fervently than Richard Herrnstein and Charles Murray's 1995 best-seller, *The Bell Curve*. The book's central (and familiar) argument, similar to that of Berkeley psychologist Arthur Jensen's, among many others, is that group differences in IQ between blacks and whites are primarily genetic and thus not subject to school improvement or other social intervention. What makes *The Bell Curve* different is its sympathetic discussion of "dysgenic pressures" in contemporary America, a thesis not so different from Madison Grant's or Lothrop Stoddard's constructs of seventy or eighty years before.

Herrnstein and Murray relied heavily on the work of fourteen researchers funded, according to one estimate, with $3.5 million in grants from the Pioneer Fund that Harry Laughlin and Wickliffe Draper established back in 1937. Pioneer's directors for many years included the racial theorist Henry E. Garrett of Columbia, who testified in one of the 1950s school desegregation cases that blacks were inferior to whites in intelligence, and John B. Trevor Jr., son of the New York lawyer who helped devise the national origins immigration quota formula in 1924. The Pioneer Fund, wrote Paul A. Lombardo, director of the Program in Law and Medicine at the University of Virginia, who has probably done the most extensive research on the group, "represents a missing link in the history of eugenics that connects the racial radical branch of American eugenics in the first third of the [twentieth] century to eugenics in 1930s Germany, and to hereditarian politics of recent years as exemplified in books like *The Bell Curve*."[19]

In a long afterword to the paperback edition of *The Bell Curve*, published in 1996, Murray went out of his way to respond to charges that the book "rests on data concocted by neo-Nazi eugenicists." The relationship between "the founder of the Pioneer Fund and today's Pioneer Fund," he said, is no more analogous than that "between Henry Ford and today's Ford Foundation."[20] But the Ford Foundation's original charter didn't establish as one of its main purposes research on eugenics and "race betterment," didn't commit itself to helping only children who were descendants of "white persons who settled in the original thirteen colonies," and isn't headed, or was ever headed, by someone like J. Philippe Rushton, the psychology professor at the University of Western Ontario who became Pioneer's president in 2002 and whose work, in the words of one recent critic, "reads like a parody of 19th-century race phobia dressed up as 20th-century science."[21] Rushton, also a source for Murray and Herrnstein, who has authored studies purporting to show a hierarchical order in the development of races—with the Mongoloid (Asians) at the top, the whites in the middle, and the Negroid at the bottom—also contends that there's an inverse correlation between intelligence and the size of genitalia. Similarly, "Black babies mature faster than White babies. Oriental babies mature slower than Whites. The same pattern is true for sexual maturity, out of wedlock births, and even child abuse. Around the world, Blacks have the highest crime rate, Orientals the least, Whites fall in between. The same pattern is true for personality. Blacks are the most outgoing and even have the highest self-esteem. Orientals are the most willing to delay gratification. Whites fall in between. . . . The three-way racial pattern holds up from cradle to grave."[22]

By the time Rushton was writing all this, he had to be well aware of the "Flynn effect," named for James R. Flynn, the New Zealand psychologist who discovered almost by accident that IQs as measured by conventional tests had been rising consistently everywhere. Flynn concluded that a person's IQ was not fixed and that the reason Asians were so successful in the professions was not because of superior intelligence—their tested IQs were in fact similar to those of whites—but because of more determination and ambition, and that the gaps between blacks and whites were also culturally determined. He also pointed out that some of the most widely used intelligence tests, such as the WISC (formally the Wechsler Intelligence Scale for Children), have been frequently recalibrated so that a score of 100 today is the equivalent of a 103 a decade ago and 115 fifty years ago. That the most "culture-free" parts of such tests may often be the most culturally determined should have raised even more questions for both Rushton and the authors of *The Bell Curve*.[23] Herrnstein and Murray, who simply ignore some of the inconvenient history associating early testers like Henry Goddard with eugenics and national origins immigration quotas, also pass lightly by the Flynn effect. (As early as 1912, Goddard warned about the birth of "more feeble-minded children with which to clog the wheels of human progress.")[24] And while Herrnstein and Murray say they don't embrace Rushton's racist theories, they come to the dodgy conclusion that as science, "there is nothing wrong with Rushton's work in principle."[25] Immigration, they conclude, is helping to make the country more stupid: "Putting the case together—higher fertility and a faster generational cycle among the less intelligent and an immigrant population that is probably somewhat below the native-born average—the case is strong that something worth worrying about is happening to the cognitive capital of the country."[26]

To Herrnstein and Murray, that's hardly surprising. Immigration has become too easy, even cushy. A century ago, they write:

> There were no guarantees, no safety nets. One way or another, the immigrant had to make it on his own. Add to that the wrench of tearing himself and his family away from a place where his people might have lived for centuries, the terrors of having to learn a new language and culture, and often the prospect of working at jobs he had never tried before, a dozen other reasons for apprehension, and the United States had a crackerjack self-selection mechanism for attracting immigrants who were brave, hard-working, imaginative, self-starting—and probably smart. Immigration can still select for those qualities, but it does not have to. Someone who comes here because his cousin offers him a job, a free airline ticket, and a place to stay is not necessarily self-selected for those qualities.[27]

That, too, echoes the arguments of a century ago, when steamship crossings became cheaper and when rugged "settlers" cleaving homes and farms out of the forests or the plains, fighting Indians in Deerfield or locust plagues on the prairies of Kansas, were contrasted with the "immigrant hordes" pouring off the ships in New York and Boston. Similarly, Herrnstein and Murray's argument ignores the latter-day immigrants' hardships and risks of crossing the mountains and deserts of Arizona, the betrayals by coyotes (and more recently the extortion and kidnappings by violent drug gangs who have been taking over the smuggling of aliens), and the dirty, hot, and often risky jobs that these immigrants, too, "had never tried before."

• • •

In one major respect, however, Hanson, Huntington, and other hardline immigration restrictionists were right. California and the Southwest are part of a growing, amorphous "border" that is rapidly becoming more region than line in a nation whose population will by midcentury look very much like California's did in the later 1990s. Whites will become a minority as the number of Latinos and Asians continues to grow. And since most Latinos already list their race as white, and since a large percentage of Latinos and Asians intermarry with people of other ethnicities, most of the old categories will become more tenuous by the year, leaving, sadly, only the black-white divide, the oldest and the most intractable of them all. Not long ago, the essayist Richard Rodriguez, the son of Mexican immigrants in California's Central Valley, observed that the children now being born in California don't look like their grandparents. The census category "Hispanic," Rodriguez pointed out, is itself a creature of the Nixon administration. No "Hispanic" ever thought of himself as such before arriving in the United States, and many still don't.

In the same way that Poles, Greeks, and Italians were whitened in the twentieth century, Latinos may also be whitened in the coming decades. At the same time, as Gregory Rodriguez (who is not related to Richard) observed in 2007 in his *Mongrels, Bastards, Orphans and Vagabonds: Mexican Immigration and the Future of Race in America,* a book that deserves more attention than it's gotten, "Mexican Americans are forcing the United States to reinterpret the concept of the melting pot to include racial as well as ethnic mixing." Gregory Rodriguez is no flaming liberal. He looks askance at the way leaders of Latino groups have tried to classify themselves as an oppressed minority in order to hitchhike on affirmative action programs designed for blacks. Those efforts he says, tend to obscure the rise of a Latino middle class, whose success is among the elements "calling into question the validity of the nation's racial category system."[28] For some Americans the accompanying possibility of "mongrelization" may be the biggest threat of all.

More immediately, the border that rhetoric says we've lost control of has become a bicultural place of shared medical resources and energy generation, binational environmental action and water management, joint educational and arts programs, high levels of tourism and transborder manufacturing, and hundreds of joint business and cultural associations. Nearly two thousand Mexican students commute across the border daily to the University of Texas at El Paso; the American managers and technicians at Sony, Delphi Ford, and the other Mexican maquiladoras commute daily in the other direction to their jobs in Juarez, Tijuana, Tecate, and Mexicali; thousands of Americans come from as far away as Minneapolis to see Mexican dentists and doctors and to buy medicines, which are cheaper south of the border; hospitals in Arizona provide assistance to hospitals in the neighboring state of Sonora, in part to enable them to ship Mexican patients south and thus reduce their own costs; shoppers from each side cross the border to get better or cheaper goods, or simply because the shops are more accessible.[29]

More than a dozen border cities have twins on the other side—El Paso and Juarez; Calexico and Mexicali; Laredo and Nuevo Laredo;

Nogales, Arizona, and Nogales, Sonora; Brownsville and Matamoras—where lives and business are deeply intertwined. In places like Calexico, you can look through the border fence and see a place that in virtually every physical respect is indistinguishable from the one you're standing in. Some of those links—the maquiladoras, the flow of students to U.S. universities, the transmission of electric power, and natural gas from Mexico—are relatively new. Some—the cross-border Indian reservations and the ranches—have been there, in the latter case, since before the Mexican War that first produced the line we are now said to have lost control of and, in the case of the Indian tribes, since before the first white man set foot on the continent. In Calexico, school officials hired a photographer to identify the Mexican students crossing the border to attend the overcrowded but presumably better U.S. schools. The issue, they told a reporter, isn't citizenship. It's residency outside the district; they don't get state money for the Mexicali kids. Nobody knows how many other schools on the border have similar problems.[30]

In the lower Rio Grande Valley, as in Santa Ana, California, and countless other cities in the border states, more than three-fourths of the population is Latino, most of whom are American citizens, either native or naturalized. Many live in families with a mix of citizens and legal and illegal residents. In 2005, according to the Pew Hispanic Center, some 14.6 million people lived in a household with at least one illegal immigrant, but those households also included 3.1 million citizen children and millions more who were legal residents.[31] The first generation, and sometimes the second, has strong family ties in Mexico or in El Salvador, Nicaragua, or Guatemala. In the early years of the twenty-first century, immigrants sent some thirty billion dollars annually in remittances to those families or, through hundreds of hometown associations, to public projects—road, school, and church improvements, playgrounds, and small-business investments—in the villages they came from and where at least some hope to retire. In 2007, according to the Bank of Mexico, remittances to that country totaled twenty-four billion dollars. The recession that began that year drove the total down sharply, by some 18 percent between April 2008 and April 2009, but remittances still topped twenty billion dollars, the second-largest source of foreign revenue for Mexico after oil (and with the drop in oil prices in 2008, probably the largest).[32] In that respect, Latino immigrants aren't all that different from the Italian "birds of passage" that Lodge complained about before the turn of the twentieth century. By the third generation, however, the links to countries of origin wash out.

There are similar transpacific links, especially among the families of Indian and Chinese Silicon Valley engineers and technicians, many of whom are also investors in the schools and high-tech businesses (and often part-time residents as well) of Mumbai, Bangalore, and Taipei. In their shuttles from coast to coast they seem to be people who, as Stanford University sociologist Aneesh Aneesh described them a few years ago, want to be there when they're here and here when they're there. "In either country they miss the other. They want to be in both countries at once," members of an emerging "transnational elite." They don't represent a "brain drain," said Aneesh, as much as a form of "brain circulation."[33] These were the kinds of people—Indians, ex-pat Americans, and Indo-Americans—who were the targets of the Pakistani terrorists in the Mumbai hotels and watering places in 2008. Many professionals—Indian, Mexican, Filipino—hold dual citizenship, something that drives nationalists crazy no matter what nation they belong to. In India, as in China or Mexico, and often in the United States, those transnationals have far more in common with their overseas colleagues and class, regardless of where they are, than they do with people of other classes in their own countries. This, too, is an element of the global economy and culture that American political attitudes and institutions have yet to catch up with. It is also, incidentally, the continuation of a cosmopolitanism that goes back at least to the nation's founders, the transnational elite—Jefferson, Franklin, Jay, John Adams—that was as much at home in Paris or London as it was in Boston or Philadelphia. In the age of Obama, when hundreds, if not thousands, of the children of immigrants sit in state and federal legislatures, mayors' offices, and city councils, that historical universalism and its present diversity give the nation a far better opportunity to adapt to, and connect with, the global world growing around it.

Assimilation is often more visible with hindsight than it is as it's taking place. We tend to see the new arrivals more starkly than those who came a generation ago. As with previous generations of immigrants, many, perhaps most, adult grandchildren, and sometimes children, of immigrants (unfortunately) don't speak their native languages. Many have spouses of other ethnicities. In the West and Southwest, it's the rare campus where a majority of students won't tell you they have close friends of some other racial or ethnic group. Scholars like Alejandro Portes of Princeton and Rubén Rumbaut of the University of California at Irvine worry, as they put it, that "the lot of today's Mexican immigrant children may be even worse than those of their predecessors because of persistent external discrimination, the disappearance of industrial job ladders, and the increasing educational requirements of a technology-driven economy."[34] Portes and Rumbaut see similar handicaps and threats of downward assimilation among Nicaraguans, Haitians, West Indians, and other contemporary immigrant groups where the second generation loses the drive, ambition, and discipline of the immigrant parents.

Yet the rate of assimilation and upward mobility of prior immigrant groups has often been as diverse and, in some cases, as tentative as that of more recent immigrants. Nor has upward progress been any slower than it was for many prior immigrant groups. In the mid–twentieth century, second-generation Italians were incessantly compared unfavorably with their Jewish peers, as Latinos are now sometimes compared with Asians. To this day, Notre Dame and other American Catholic colleges can't totally get over George Bernard Shaw's snippy remark that a Catholic university is a contradiction in terms. Latinos own millions of businesses—six hundred thousand in California alone—ranging from little garden maintenance services, taquerias, and supermercados to sprawling for-profit medical operations like Molina Health Care and billion-dollar corporations like Los Angeles Angels owner Arte Moreno's outdoor advertising business. At last count there were some thirty thousand Latino-owned businesses in the United States netting over a million dollars each annually. There are wineries in the Napa Valley that are owned by families—the Cejas, the Renterias, the Robledos—who began as bracero farmhands pruning the vines they now own.

In light of questions like Huntington's and Hanson's about the ability of Latinos in particular to assimilate, as have prior generations of European immigrants, study results by Rand economist James P. Smith are illuminating:

> These fears are unwarranted: 2nd- and 3rd-generation Hispanic men have made great strides in closing their economic gaps with native whites. The reason is simple: each successive generation has been able to close the schooling gaps with native whites which then have been translated into generational progress in incomes. Each new Latino generation not only has had higher incomes than their forefathers, but their economic status converged toward the white men with whom they competed. The methodological problems that have marred interpretation of immigrants' generational progress in schooling and earnings would apply equally to health, where it is alleged that the descendants of immigrants lose their initial health advantage.[35]

Smith, in another study, draws similar conclusions about education, finding that the grandchildren of Latino immigrants (those born in the

1920s and who came with an average of 5.9 years of schooling) have nearly closed the educational gap with their non-Hispanic white contemporaries. Here again, Smith says, "the conventional view regarding Hispanic immigrants' ability to secure a better life for their kids and grand kids was pessimistic. They were seen as not sharing in the successful European experience, perhaps due to a reluctance to assimilate into American culture. These fears are unwarranted. Second and third generation Hispanic men have made great strides in closing their education gaps with native whites."[36]

Like other scholars, Smith also points to the gaps among immigrant groups, showing that while most Latinos come with low education and skill levels, European and Asian immigrants arrive with higher average education levels than native-born Americans, although here also there are differences within groups. But for Latinos, as well as for earlier Europeans, the gains from generation to generation are significant, not only from the first to the second generation but, properly calculated, from the second to the third.[37] And not surprisingly, in the words of a voluminous National Research Council report to which Smith was a major contributor, "after adjusting for the levels of human capital (e.g., schooling and English language proficiency), Hispanics do almost as well as whites with respect to both employment and labor market earnings. This fact is all the more notable, given that such adjustments for differences in these observable measures of human capital do not end up accounting for much of the gaps in labor market outcomes between blacks and whites. . . . Taken together, this evidence clearly suggests that comparably skilled Hispanics are treated no differently from whites in the U.S. labor market."[38] Like earlier immigrants, and contra Hanson, the second generation of Latinos—those born in this country—is almost always fluent in English. By the third generation, when 97 percent speak English well or very well, just half still know their grandparents' native language.[39] By then, most have stopped watching or listening to Spanish-language media. For better or worse, they get their *telenovelas* in English.

Although Latinos are, like African Americans, still proportionately underrepresented in American colleges and universities, as were Poles and Italians a half century ago, their numbers are increasing. In California and the Southwest, their presence in college professorships and deanships, in law firms, in corporate board rooms, in medical practices and hospitals, and in high political office has long been beyond remarking. In California in 2008, a state that in the early 1990s was the epicenter of the nativist tremors against illegal immigrants, barely over 40 percent of the population are now non-Hispanic white; 36 percent are Latinos and over 12 percent are Asian, double the percentage of African Americans. According to demographer Dowell Myers of the University of Southern California, in 2005, the latest year for which data were available, the five most common names of California home buyers were Garcia, Hernandez, Rodriguez, Lopez, and Martinez. Similarly, in the nation as a whole, four of the ten most common home buyers' names were Hispanic.[40] By the same token, it's likely that Latinos were high on the list of those caught in the subprime housing crash that began in 2008.

The relative costs and benefits associated with illegal immigration will forever be subject to debate. Harvard economist George J. Borjas, supported by a fair amount of anecdotal material, maintained (in 2003) that by "increasing the supply of labor between 1980 and 2000, immigration reduced the average annual earnings of native-born men by an estimated $1700 or roughly 4 percent." Among natives without a high school education, meaning primarily African Americans, "the estimated impact was even larger, reducing their wages by 7.4 percent."[41] That complaint has been echoed by black leaders like T. Willard Fair, who headed the Miami Urban League (and was a board member of the Center for Immigration Studies), who told a House subcommittee in 2007 that the immigrants "flooding the job market and overwhelming the public schools and other government services undermine all our efforts. The interests of black Americans are clear: No amnesty, no guest workers; enforce the immigration law."[42]

But Smith and others, in the same National Research Council study, throw doubt on Borjas's findings. "The evidence points to the conclusion," said the report, "that there is only a small adverse impact of immigration on the wage and employment opportunities of competing native groups. . . . The one group that appears to suffer substantially from new waves of immigrants are immigrants from earlier waves, for whom the recent immigrants are close substitutes in the labor market." The wage problems of low-skilled blacks, the study concluded, derived from factors other than competition from immigrants. In general, the report found, immigrants benefit the economy more than they diminish it.[43]

Immigrants and their children almost certainly put a strain on local public services in many communities—sometimes on law enforcement, hospital emergency rooms, and other health facilities, more often on schools. Yet the alarms sounded by immigration restrictionists may not come any closer to the real costs of immigration, much less the offsetting benefits, than the dubious accuracy of the Lou Dobbs reports about the seven thousand lepers and the alien criminals overcrowding U.S. prisons. Undereducated low-wage illegal immigrants who collectively pay FICA taxes for Social Security benefits most will never collect—a net gain to the Social Security Trust Fund of seven billion dollars a year—have been a substantial boon to the federal treasury.[44] In 2007, the Congressional Budget Office, reviewing some twenty-nine studies of the net costs of providing local and state services to illegal immigrants, concluded that while the resulting revenues offset only a portion of the costs incurred by those jurisdictions for providing services related to education, health care, and law enforcement, the overall "amount that state and local governments spend on services for unauthorized immigrants represents a small percentage of the total amount spent by those governments to provide such services to residents in their jurisdictions."[45]

The experience of the different states varies; the data are themselves subject to a great range of uncertainty and to external circumstances. But in the long run, as the skills and experience of illegal immigrants increase, they appear to pay their share, and perhaps more than their share, of the costs of the services they receive—and would pay still more if they could take better jobs as legal residents.[46] In Texas, according to the state comptroller, illegal immigrants, nearly all of them low skilled, cost local governments and school districts far more than they pay in taxes. But at the state level, they contribute some $400 million a year more in revenues than they cost the state in services. In addition, the comptroller said, the illegal immigrants add roughly $17.7 billion a year to the state's economy. There have been similar findings in Arizona, Florida, Nevada, and New York.[47] And despite the common complaint that emergency rooms and clinics are crowded with aliens, the best data indicate that noncitizens and their children consume less than half the health care per capita that citizens do.[48] Far and away the largest proportion of immigrants, moreover, are adults who were educated somewhere else and who thus, notwithstanding the low levels of schooling many arrive with, represent a net gain in human capital against very little American investment.

• • •

What seems almost certain is that trying to solve the nation's immigration problems through enforcement at the border alone is a Sisyphean enterprise. Since between a third and half of illegal immigrants, a lot of them Asian or European, are visa overstayers who arrived legally, building walls through the border regions as the United States had been doing—walls between towns (and sometimes, as in the Canadian border town of Derby Line, Vermont, between adjacent neighbors), through parks and wildlife preserves, across college campuses, and through the millions of families composed of both legal and illegal residents—verges between the self-defeating and the impossible. "Show me a 50-foot wall," said former Arizona governor Janet Napolitano before she became Obama's secretary of Homeland Security in 2009, "and I'll show you a 51-foot ladder."[49] As noted in chapter 6, every major study of the effects of the increasingly tough border controls shows that, in increasing the cost and dangers of illegal border crossings, the fences, electronics, and expanded Border Patrol presence during the past two decades, rather than reducing the illegal alien population, have greatly increased it. Workers who once migrated back to Latin America—the latter-day "birds of passage"-cum-"homers"—now simply stay and send for their families, becoming permanent residents.[50] Recent data, incidentally, indicate that a large number of visa overstayers have not been Mexicans but East Indians. Some came as Silicon Valley engineers or technicians; when they lost their jobs in one or another industry downturn, and their H1-B visas with them, they simply stayed. Others arrived on tourist visas to visit relatives and never went back.[51]

The altogether new though perhaps predictable feature of the twenty-first-century border landscape was the blowback of Mexican drug violence that spilled into Tucson, Atlanta, and other American cities beginning in late 2008, taking over the headlines and seizing the attention of border-state law enforcement officials, Congress, and the Obama administration. What made it predictable was Mexican president Felipe Calderón's attempt to please his American neighbors by cracking down on the drug cartels, a crackdown that jeopardized established supply routes and the cozy arrangements with Mexican drug cops and public officials that in effect had stabilized the trade. As a consequence, the gangs, which were also seizing a growing segment of the migrant smuggling business, were at war not just with Mexico's federal cops, the army, and the shrinking number of honest prosecutors and judges who tried to confront them but with one another for shares of that now-destabilized market. In 2008, some six thousand Mexicans, including judges, cops, and government officials, were murdered—some of them in hideously brutal fashion—and countless others kidnapped.[52]

The cross-border drug violence was ironic on three or four different levels. It was Americans' addiction that fed the largest part of the marijuana, cocaine, and methamphetamine market that made up the lion's share of the cartels' business. Ironic also because some 90 percent of the guns used by the drug gangs, including a growing number of military-type assault weapons and explosives, were supplied by American gun dealers, most in the border states. Ironic because it was American politicians who were always the loudest in demanding crackdowns by Mexican officials. And ironic again because, as noted in chapter 4, the federal prohibition of marijuana had been enacted (in 1937) after a media-driven campaign fanning hysteria about "reefer madness" based in large measure on the drug's association with Mexicans. If possession of small amounts of marijuana were legal—and if drugs in general were treated as a medical rather than a criminal issue as they are in much of Europe—a good part of the drug gangs' market might vanish.

Predictably, however, Washington's reaction to the encroaching drug violence was to walk away from serious confrontation with even obvious things like renewal of the federal assault-weapons ban, which had expired in 2004, much less with addressing the increasingly apparent failures in U.S. drug policy and the costly "war on drugs." For Senator Jeff Sessions of Alabama, a senior Republican on the Senate Judiciary Committee, Representative Edward Royce of California, and many of their fellow Second Amendment hard-liners, guns weren't the problem. The prime culprit was illegal immigration and the government's failure to close the border; the solution was a demand that President Obama send National Guard troops to do so. Obama promised more agents to check for southbound weapons and more intense searches for northflowing drugs but said nothing about the fundamental policy issues. A few weeks later, when he met with President Calderón, he promised help but pointedly declined to promise any effort on reinstating the assault-weapons ban.[53]

The contemporary warnings against America's "Mexifornias" aren't all that different from turn-of-the-twentieth-century narratives of the burdens imposed on charitable institutions and the ugliness of life in the slums of New York, Boston, Chicago, and other eastern cities; or from Harry Laughlin's congressional testimony in the 1920s about immigrant crime and racial inferiority; or from Madison Grant's *Passing of the Great Race;* or from the race-suicide predictions of Progressive-era sociologists like Edward Ross and American heroes like Theodore Roosevelt; or from the intelligence test reports of the Robert Yerkeses, Carl Brighams, and Henry Goddards; or from Henry James's admonition to the unwary never to visit Ellis Island or from his grim conclusion that there "was no escape from the ubiquitous alien" except into the past. But we survived it all and thrived on most of it. All those unassimilable aliens, the inferior races from eastern and southern Europe, were whitened and became Americans and in many cases first certified their Americanness by directing the ethnic prejudices and language of their predecessors at those who came after them. Tom Tancredo, who before his retirement from the House in 2008 was the leader of its anti-immigration caucus, had proudly proclaimed himself the grandson of someone who was a "legal" Italian immigrant but failed to acknowledge (and may not have known) that his grandfather came at a time when there was no such thing as an "illegal" immigrant. Nor did he seem to think it ironic that his immigrant grandfather belonged to a "race" (of southern Italians and Sicilians) who in their time were widely regarded and often officially listed as among the most inferior in morals and intelligence of any group entering the United States. (Recently, one of Tancredo's fellow immigration restrictionists, raging against illegal-immigrant "thugs" even recalled "those Sicilian immigrants at the turn of the 20th century [who] did a great job bringing the Mafia to America.")[54] And like his Know-Nothing antecedents, Tancredo, once a Catholic, now an evangelical Protestant, declared that the Pope's pro-immigration comments during his U.S. visit in 2008 "may have less to do with spreading the gospel than they do about recruiting new members of the Church. . . . This isn't preaching; it is 'faith based' marketing."[55] He didn't explain how the Pope's "faith-based" marketing related to his belief (as per Huntington) that "we are in a clash of civilizations."[56] And like the Know-Nothings and other immigration restrictionists in the nineteenth century, Tancredo also believed, as he told an interviewer in 2007, that "Democrats look on massive immigration as a source of votes."[57]

No, to paraphrase the restrictionist version of our immigration history, now is not like any other "then." We live in a different country in a different world with a different economy. Much of the great assimilation of the half century between 1930 and 1970 occurred in an era of record low immigration. Even in the Depression—and in part because of the two world wars and Korea—that hiatus offered an opportunity for Americanizing and, despite the ongoing racism and anti-Semitism of the 1930s and 1940s, provided those newly eligible for whitening a chance to accomplish it or have it done for them. Almost certainly, the hiatus in immigration also provided a much larger opening for the development of New Deal and Great Society social programs that might have met much more resistance had they been perceived as benefiting thousands of newly arriving aliens. Arguably, today's economy and society are less able to absorb unskilled workers. Illegal immigrants with low skills—maybe all low-wage immigrants—tend to drive wages down (though apparently not by much, and then mainly the wages of prior immigrants) and compete for jobs (again not very much) with descendants of the African slaves to whom the nation owes much more.

Mark Krikorian, head of the restrictionist Center for Immigration Studies, whose predecessors had to go to court to prove that as Armenians they were "white" and thus entitled to naturalization, argues that, as in the past, if the supply of cheap illegal labor dried up, there'd be better-paying jobs for legal residents. And, as in industrial America after World War I, he argues, it would also drive corporations and farmers to increase mechanization and automation, which in turn would create still more high-level jobs.[58] The large commercial growers in California and elsewhere in the Southwest, who, with the support of a bipartisan group of senators, claim that much of their farm labor consists of illegal immigrants—an odd claim for employers theoretically at risk of heavy fines—counter that higher wages would both raise prices of produce and drive a lot more production out of the country.[59]

Unfortunately for the immigration debate, most of the defenders of amnesty and other regularization of illegal aliens offer little in the way of comprehensive ideas for immigration controls that won't repeat the mistakes of the Immigration Reform and Control Act of 1986. If you ask them, nearly all will argue that they don't favor open borders but that we should control them more humanely—not (for example) forcing desperate people into devilish deserts where hundreds die of heat and dehydration—but they rarely offer a politically persuasive alternative. Most immigration policy doves (many of whom tend to be political liberals) also neglect the growing body of research indicating that the more ethnic diversity there is in a society the less likely it is to support generous public programs. When, as in California, that diversity consists in large part of immigrants, and when voters are still overwhelmingly middle-class whites, the resistance is all the greater.[60] Voters are always more likely to support social programs when the beneficiaries could be people like themselves or their families. In that respect, at least, the politics of the liberal agenda on immigration conflicts squarely with the liberal agenda for generous social programs and, in many cases, for better-funded schools. Whenever someone begins to ask tough questions about immigration controls, said Berkeley historian David Hollinger "everybody leaves the room."[61]

Yet, despite the fact that this is a different era with a different economy, it's still the economy that continues to bring immigrants here (or that drives them back to the old country), an economy that despite its high-tech modernity still provides the same kinds of exploitative, underpaid jobs it has always offered unskilled immigrants. In that respect the United States today is not so different from much of western Europe, where the boom of the 1990s through the early years of the twenty-first century, combined with low birthrates and ongoing labor shortages, drew millions of immigrants from eastern Europe and the third world, whose presence in turn has fueled a nationalist backlash (and brought both domestic riots and sometimes real terrorism).[62] As in the years before the strikes and the radicalism of the first decades of the twentieth century, there's still a fundamental division in this country between (on the one hand) the alliance of liberal pro-immigrant groups (like the National Council of La Raza, the Mexican American Legal Defense and Education Fund, the ACLU, and the Immigration Policy Center) and the employers who want cheap labor and (on the other) the combination of blue-collar workers, earnest nationalists, nativists, demagogic political opportunists, and the liberals and environmentalists who worry about jobs and the economy and resent what they regard as the elitism of the other side.

In a world in which broad trade pacts like the North American Free Trade Agreement foster the easy flow of goods and capital, it's unimaginable that labor and jobs wouldn't flow as well. Ross Perot's "great sucking sound" hasn't been that of jobs moving to Mexico as much as it's been produced by outsourcing to India, China, Korea, and Ireland. Even some of the maquiladoras' production has fled Mexico for China. And, as with the reported sharp decline in illegal immigrants in 2007–9, it seems that declines in the U.S. economy, as much as any enforcement program, are what drive illegal immigrants home. Meanwhile, enforcement and the longer waiting times at ports of entry, again combined with recession, have sharply reduced legal border crossings and ordinary cross-border business, tourism, and social contacts. While there were still thousands of daily border crossings, they were down 21 percent at San Ysidro (San Diego) between 2005 and 2008, with similar declines elsewhere. That hurts. In San Ysidro, according to the director of that city's chamber of commerce, 85 percent of retail business customers are shoppers crossing from Mexico.[63]

• • •

Sometime around 2006 or 2007, Lou Dobbs, Pat Buchanan, Sean Hannity, Phyllis Schlafly, the right-wing hatchet man Jerome R. Corsi, and other immigration absolutists discovered what Dobbs later described as the "unbelievable" scheme of the "hell-bent" Bush administration and "the elites of corporate America, academia, and of course our political elites as well," all indifferent "to the needs and desires of the American people," to create a North American Union of the United States, Canada, and Mexico. That union, as Dobbs had it, would threaten national security and "weaken U.S. laws and regulations and diminish American sovereignty," all of which was denied by the "snarky little darlings" of the left wing.[64] The basis of the rumor, which reverberated around the blogosphere, was a report by the Council on Foreign Relations and a book, articles, and Senate testimony by Robert Pastor, codirector of the Center for North American Studies at American University, a former diplomat, former national security advisor on Latin America, and consultant to the State and Defense departments and the CIA, arguing that the only effective way to confront common regional crime, drug, labor, and trade problems was to establish a North American Community.

Such an entity, controlled by representatives of the United States, Canada, and Mexico, Pastor proposed, would have a common customs union, a continental barrier and other common security measures against terrorists, and collaborative law-enforcement and drug-control policies. It would also facilitate travel and commerce among the three countries and, perhaps most important, would help develop the Mexican economy by upgrading both its physical infrastructure and its human capital. That, he argued, would gradually reduce, if not altogether eliminate, illegal immigration. Most of those ideas were also part of the Council on Foreign Relations report *Building a North American Community*, issued in 2005, to which Pastor was a contributor.[65] Although ultimately the North American Community might also create a common currency, currently as unthinkable as it was in Europe one or two generations ago, Pastor said that event was a long way off. With NAFTA, the region already constituted the largest free-trade area in the world. It had enormous energy reserves that, in Mexico especially, begged for development and efficient management. NAFTA, Pastor argued, was just a beginning.

Although he never proposed anything exactly like the European Union, Pastor pointed out that with the inclusion of Spain and Portugal in the EU, many immigrants from those countries in France and Germany returned home. In any case, he said in his 2005 testimony at the Senate Foreign Relations Committee, "Instead of trying to fashion a North American approach to continental problems, we continue to pursue problems on a dual-bilateral basis, taking one issue at a time. But incremental steps will no longer solve the security problem, or allow us to grasp economic opportunities. What we need to do now is forge a North American Community, based on the premise that each member benefits from its neighbor's success and is diminished by its problems."[66]

Pastor wasn't alone. Similar arguments have been advanced by others, perhaps most notably by Richard Alba of the State University of New York at Albany, who has likewise pointed to the futility of unilateral efforts to control immigration and the corresponding obsolescence of old American attitudes in the age of NAFTA. Again the comparisons were with western Europe, whose nations once regarded the free movement of workers—from, say, Italy to Germany—with as much suspicion as Americans regard Mexican immigrants. And, as in western Europe, tight immigration restrictions can only exacerbate a rapidly growing shortage of young workers as the U.S. population grows rapidly older. Once NAFTA was created, Alba said, "the U.S. legal frame for immigration was utterly inadequate to handle the movements of Mexican workers unleashed by growing economic integration." Those movements can only be managed through collaborative efforts with Mexico by reforming a legal system of entry "that stingily assigns Mexico the same quota of green cards that are allotted to any other country—Jamaica say—despite its large size and immediate proximity to us" and by encouraging temporary migrants to return to Mexico by reforming banking regulations to make it easier for them to invest at home. As to fears of Hispanics becoming the Hanson-Huntington indigestible lump, descendants of southern Italian immigrants of a century ago, people who also brought very low levels of human capital, are now nearly at parity with all other Americans today.[67]

It seems to have been Corsi, coauthor of *Unfit for Command: Swift Boat Veterans Speak Out against John Kerry* and, more recently, author of the 2008 campaign smear book *The Obama Nation,* who turned Pastor's ideas and the Council on Foreign Relations report into a sinister plot to establish a New World Order that echoed nothing so much as the manufactured paranoia about the Trilateral Commission of a generation before, or the old canards about the Illuminati. In May 2006, Corsi published a piece in the ultraconservative *Human Events* claiming that "President Bush intends to abrogate U.S. sovereignty to the North American Union, a new economic and political entity which the President is quietly forming, much as the European Union has formed."[68]

As the rumors circulated they were adorned with additional details: The U.S. Mint was already working on prototypes of the Amero, which was to be the common currency of the North American Union, a name first proposed by a Canadian economist on the model of the euro. One blogger claimed he'd even been slipped an Amero by someone at the Treasury (which, it turned out, had been privately produced by a medallion designer named Daniel Carr as a way to increase public awareness of the idea). In Canada, there were denunciations of the North American Union as a plot by American business to further dominate the Canadian economy. There was also talk about plans for a hemispheric superhighway disgorging Mexican trucks driven by Mexican drivers into the U.S. heartland. A year after Corsi's *Human Events* piece, the *Phyllis Schlafly Report* warned that "more than 20 working groups are already quietly operating [on plans for the North American Union] in the NAFTA office in the U.S. Department of Commerce, which refuses to reveal the groups' members because, in the words of spokesperson Geri Word, the Bush Administration does not want them 'distracted by calls from the public.'" *The New American,* the ironically titled magazine of the all-but-forgotten ultraright John Birch Society, would follow in 2007 with a couple of articles, one headed "Invasion," about the alleged scheme to merge the three countries and destroy American sovereignty.[69]

Nearly all of this frenzy was hyperventilation by conservative broadcasters and bloggers, but it got enough exposure to produce a House resolution early in 2007 cosponsored by fifty-two members "that the United States should not engage in the construction of a North American Free Trade Agreement (NAFTA) Superhighway System or enter into a North American Union with Mexico and Canada."[70] More important, the North American Union exaggerations, coming just when Congress was working on its comprehensive immigration legislation, almost certainly reinforced suspicions about the sponsors' real intentions. Paradoxically, they also reinforced fears on the left that NAFTA was draining the nation of jobs—the old sucking sound again—and damaging the environment both north and south of the border.

In an angry piece attacking both Dobbs et al. and the 2008 presidential candidates in *Foreign Affairs* in the summer of 2008 (and which Corsi twisted into a surrender on the North American Union), Pastor pointed out that "these two sets of fears came together in a perfect storm that was pushed forward by a surplus of hot air from talk-show hosts on radio and television. In the face of this criticism, the Bush administration was silent, and the Democratic candidates competed for votes in the rust-belt states." What the attacks ultimately amounted to, Pastor suggested, were isolationist head-in-the-sand denials of the realities of the North American economy and of the ever-deeper integration of the region. It wasn't China that was the United States' most important trading partner; it was Canada and Mexico. It wasn't Saudi Arabia and Venezuela that were the nation's biggest sources of energy; again, it was Canada and Mexico. NAFTA, Pastor said,

> has become a diversion, a piñata for pandering pundits and politicians—even though it succeeded in what it was designed to do. . . . The new U.S. administration needs to replace a bad neighbor policy with a genuine dialogue with Canada and Mexico aimed at creating a sense of community and a common approach to continental problems. The new president must address the full gamut of North American issues not covered by NAFTA, as well as the governance issues arising from the successful enlargement of the market. North America's leaders should deepen economic integration by negotiating a customs union. They should establish a North American investment fund to narrow the income gap between Mexico and its northern neighbors. This would have a greater effect on undocumented immigration to the United States than so-called comprehensive immigration reform.[71]

Given the dismal state of the American economy in the first years of the Obama administration, the chances that Pastor's ambitious proposals would see enactment were close to nil. The kind of frustration, self-involvement, and isolationism that often accompany economic crises make a self-destructive America First xenophobia at least equally probable. Worse, the pervasive corruption of Mexican cops and other law-enforcement institutions, and the growing drug-related gang violence along the border—in some cases the total breakdown of civic order—make any multinational development program even more complicated. For conservatives like Representatives Edward Royce and Brian Bilbray of California and a dozen other Republicans, the violence provided yet additional reasons for militarizing the border.[72] At the same time, since both the demand for the marijuana, cocaine, and methamphetamines that fuels the drug trade is overwhelmingly American and an estimated 90 percent of the drug cartels' weapons come from American dealers, there's hardly a question that here, too, only a multinational approach to changing the situation has any chance of success.[73] The encouraging element was that in the early months of 2009, American officialdom at least began to recognize U.S. responsibility for the Mexican violence.

Pastor's picture of the economic integration of the three nations and of globalism generally is altogether consistent with the realities of the demographic and social integration of the emerging border region. It is American political institutions and cultural attitudes that remain stuck somewhere between the recent and the very distant past. In 2008, ProjectUSA, one of the more virulent anti-immigration groups, responding to Census Bureau projections, warned darkly that "whites in America are going to be disempowered (assuming we remain a democracy) through a radical and rapid transformation of the nation's demography on a scale unprecedented in world history." Whites who remained calm or indifferent to that threat were "a bunch of panglossian ninnies."[74]

It's crucial that American voters have confidence that immigration is under control, especially in times of economic crisis, not only to dampen ethnic tensions, but, as in the 1930s, to reduce voter resistance to progressive social and educational programs that are particularly essential in recessionary periods. But Pastor is right that, with the possible exception of their ability to reduce cross-border violence, more fences and other tougher border controls are likely to be as counterproductive as they've been for most of the past two decades, both in locking more unauthorized aliens into this country and in deterring the productive flow of commerce, energy, and labor on which the United States increasingly depends. Economic downturns, also as in the past, will be a major deterrent to immigration, legal and illegal. So would tougher penalties for employers who hire illegal immigrants and, more generally, tougher administration of wage and hour laws.

Mark Krikorian may be right that wages for low-skilled workers would rise and productivity increase through increased mechanization if illegal low-wage workers weren't so readily available. But the reverse is just as likely: if the states and especially the federal government raised the minimum wage; did more to enforce wage, hour, and workplace safety laws; cracked down on, rather than ignoring, illegal employer interference with workers' right to organize; created a reliable national ID system; and shut down chronic, flagrant labor law violators like Agriprocessors, not just by rounding up and jailing workers with stolen IDs, but by jailing the exploiter-owners, then wages and working conditions would almost certainly improve and American citizens and legal residents might be more likely to take the jobs that have been going to illegal immigrants. That applies especially to violators like the

Rubashkins, who had been cited for their proclivity to skirt labor and worker-safety laws long before the Agriprocessors debacle.[75]

The decline of the illegal immigrant population in the recession that began in 2007 indicates that the economic cycles in the United States and Latin America will, as always, be among the principal forces driving immigration. As might have been expected, as fewer people sought to come north, detentions at the border declined as well, and more immigrants returned home.[76] That pattern, too, replicated earlier flows of immigrants, particularly the return flows of Italians at the turn of the twentieth century. Along the way, that decline, combined with noisy federal raids and the growing power of the Latino vote, also lowered the political heat under illegal immigration, which in 2007 had promised to be a hot wedge issue. With the exception of Obama's sotto voce promises that he would address comprehensive reform if elected, both presidential candidates avoided immigration as an issue. (Ultimately, despite his statement that he would take up immigration in his first year as president, Obama, probably wisely, deferred it until 2010. To do otherwise would almost surely have killed his chances on both a health-care program, the hot issue in 2009, and immigration reform.) Nor did immigration seem to have much effect in the congressional races. In 2008, before the great fiscal meltdown triggered by the collapse of the U.S. subprime housing market became a general recession, it also appeared that the strengthening economies in Brazil, Chile, Colombia, and Peru might "have compelled" more people in the region to stay home or to move to places where the language and culture were more familiar—and the jobs more plentiful—than in the United States.[77]

For the long term, moreover, as demographer Dowell Myers argues, most of the millions of American boomers who will retire in the first two decades of the twenty-first century will have to be replaced in the workforce in large part by recent immigrants and their children and grandchildren. There simply aren't enough other Americans to fill all the jobs, which means that better education and training for that new generation become absolutely essential. By 2039, the nation's working-age population will be 50 percent minority, many of them now in school or college. It's not merely the general economy that will depend on them but the home values and the pensions of the retiring boomers. For everyone's sake, that means the nation had better invest in their education. At the same time, Mexico's fertility rate is down from 6.8 births per woman in 1970 to 2.4 births in 2000, which is just above the replacement level, making it likely that in another decade or two there will be fewer young adults to migrate north and a stronger labor market in Mexico.[78]

On a related issue—and reinforcing Myers's larger point—a 2008 report from the Council on Hemispheric Affairs (COHA) complained about what it regarded as America's excessively tight quota of H-1B visas, visas issued to skilled engineers and other high-tech workers who, at least in theory, were in short supply and badly needed by U.S. industry. While other modern nations—Canada, Australia, Great Britain—were benefiting from their liberal immigration policies and filling high-skill jobs, COHA said, American companies, Microsoft among them, were hamstrung by outdated immigration policies and moving more operations offshore.[79] A few months later, even as Congress was writing yet more protectionist provisions into the economic stimulus package, the overstretched Pentagon disclosed plans to recruit military personnel by offering a quick road to citizenship to holders of temporary visas who have education, experience, and training in languages, medical work, and other skills that the military desperately needs.[80] That need makes enactment of the Dream Act an all-the-more self-evident step in the nation's interest.

COHA, Myers, and the military all substantiate Pastor's thesis. The United States is trying to approach twenty-first-century issues—security, the economy, labor, the environment, law enforcement, drug-harm reduction, natural resources, health—with obsolete attitudes and institutions. The comprehensive immigration reform legislation that died in Congress in 2007 and that, in any case, was so larded with restrictive hurdles to legalization that it lost as many votes on the left as it gained on the right, was, as Pastor contended, barely a start on addressing the more fundamental issues. The debate, in fact, was mostly irrelevant, indicating how far we still are from a rational immigration policy. The arguments of the past decade against immigration, legal and illegal, virtually replay what was heard for more than a century; they're the same arguments that each generation used against the next—some of them blatantly racist, some defensibly economic, some true in their time, many, judging by subsequent history, dreadfully false. But all are mostly irrelevant to the emerging world.

The 670-plus miles of border fences, walls, bollards, and spikes that Congress decreed in 2006, now almost completed, are likely to cost four billion dollars, plus hundreds of millions more for maintenance. The Border Patrol, which was increased from nine thousand agents in 2001 to some twenty thousand in 2009, costs an estimated four billion dollars annually. The electronics, surveillance aircraft, training of local cops and deputies; the detention, incarceration, and deportation of illegal aliens; and the countless other items for border security—including the long list of things required to mitigate the delays of ordinary cross-border commerce imposed by the new security systems—run to a few billion more.[81] The cost in missed commercial opportunities, in inefficiency, and in ill will on both sides of both borders is incalculable.

Pastor envisaged a two-hundred-billion-dollar ten-year program of combined investment by Canada, the United States, and Mexico—twenty billion a year—to upgrade the Mexican infrastructure and economy. To make it work would require both a major attack on official corruption and the upgrading of Mexico's law-enforcement and legal systems, something that Calderón appeared to be attempting in 2009, but an enormous challenge especially at a time when the drug trade was corrupting ever more officials. But Mexicans managed to break their long-standing one-party rule; the combination of promises of investment and pressure from the north might do much to make Mexico take the next step. How much of what the United States now spends on border control could more effectively be spent on that?

Given the estimated four hundred million annual land crossings by shoppers, workers, tourists, and students; the scores of millions of travelers arriving by plane and the cargo arriving by ship; the one-third-plus of illegal residents, visa overstayers who arrived in the country legally; and the contraband, including northbound drugs and southbound guns crossing the Mexican border, no determined terrorist is likely to be deterred by more fences, walls, and Border Patrol agents. Each of the 9/11 terrorists entered the country legally. As one cynic said, if terrorists wanted to smuggle a bomb across the southern border, all they'd have to do is disguise it as cocaine. (On that point, more investment in treatment of hard-drug addicts and legalization and taxation of drugs like marijuana might also help reduce the drug wars and the accompanying violence at the border. So might tougher gun control laws and enforcement on the U.S. side, where the bulk of the drug gangs' weapons come from. That violence, including torture and extrajudicial executions, is inflicted not only by warring drug gangs but by police officers, the military, and other government forces in Mexico.)[82]

What's almost certain is that the new economy, new technologies, new demographics, and the great range of cross-border issues have made the old "border" and the narrow territorially defined parameters of the national interest that symbolized them look more like a thing of threads and patches than the foundation for effective national policy. As the global economy grows, it may become nearly as hard to control the flow of people at the borders as it is to control the flow of capital and goods, or the outsourcing of jobs. Conversely, as in the past, the nation's economic strength, its cultural resources, and its international credibility will depend on the talents and energy of immigrants: Europeans once, Africans more recently, Asians and Latinos now. Effective checks on the exploitation of cheap immigrant workers will almost necessarily have to come through enforcement in the labor market, not at the border.

At the same time, and notwithstanding the urgent need to educate the children of immigrants, the left can't logically demand legalization for newly arrived undocumented aliens and support ethnicity-based preferences in higher education and employment through policies and programs that were designed to compensate for historical injustices inflicted on an entirely different group of people. Early in June 2007, as the comprehensive immigration bill was still being debated, Ward Connerly, the godfather of state campaigns against affirmative action, sent a letter to Congress demanding that "any legislation addressing immigration should make explicit that while immigrants and their descendants should be afforded the right to compete fairly and freely in every aspect of American life, they should receive no special benefit on the basis of race, ethnicity or national origin."[83] But in the meantime, as the *New York Times* said in an editorial, "a nation of immigrants is holding another nation of immigrants in bondage, exploiting its labor while ignoring its suffering, condemning its lawlessness while sealing off a path to living lawfully."[84] In the process, that nation is also depriving itself of the urgently needed high-grade skills that decent educational opportunities for immigrants could provide.

Latinos are already the nation's largest ethnic minority; in another generation, according to the Census Bureau's current definitions, they will be a majority or near majority in California, Texas, and a number of other states. By 2042, non-Hispanic whites, whose absolute numbers are projected to decline after 2030, will no longer be a majority in the United States as a whole—like California and Texas now, the United States will be a majority-minority nation. In the meantime, the Latino population will nearly triple, reaching 30 percent by 2050.[85]

Because of ethnic intermarriage, moreover, ethnic categories will become increasingly shaky. In the words of a Population Reference

Bureau report, "the majority of inter-Hispanic children are reported as Hispanic, [and] Hispanic intermarriage may have been a factor in the phenomenal growth of the U.S. Hispanic population in recent years, [which] has important implications for future growth and characteristics of the Hispanic population. In particular," the report continues, "if Hispanic intermarriage rates increase, more and more people who identify as Hispanic may be part Hispanic and part non-Hispanic."[86] Obama's election—the election of a mixed-blood son of an immigrant—was itself a milestone on that road. It's more than likely that the next generation of Latinos will be whitened just as Poles, Italians, and the other "inferior" immigrants were whitened a century before. Most already define themselves as racially white. At the same time the increasing rates of ethnic intermarriage, following the pattern of the "mongrel" Latinos, may finally make all the old racial and ethnic categories only puzzling matters of a nearly forgotten history.

Epilogue

The United States is hardly the only destination in the great migrations of the modern era or the only developed nation confronting the problems or evaluating the opportunities that its third-world immigrants bring. Nor is it the only nation trying to deal with the backlash newcomers generate. Every day's headlines bring reminders of the conflicts: Pakistanis in Great Britain, Turks in Germany, Algerians in France, Indonesians and other Muslims in Holland, Tunisians in Italy, Guatemalans and other Central Americans in Mexico, Koreans in Japan. And we are far from being the only country on earth with a streak of nativism and xenophobia, much less Middle East– or African-style tribalism. Nor despite warnings like Huntington's are we likely to divide ourselves by language or religion as the Canadians, the Belgians, and the Irish have.

But we are the only nation founded on the principles of equality and opportunity and on the expectation, indeed the imperative, that our growth would require immigrants from other places. We began both with an appeal to the opinions of mankind and, implicitly, with an invitation. Partly that invitation grew from humanitarian idealism, partly from an economic premise that soon became an essential element of continental expansion glorified as Manifest Destiny and later stretched into imperial ambition. Who else was going to fell the trees, clear the land, build the canals and the railroads, work the fields, factories, and mines? How else could we verify the promise Americans had made both to themselves and to the world? It's those expansionist ambitions and the need for workers to pursue them that, mixed with the founders' egalitarian principles, have been the greatest checks on American racism and nativism. The debate, sometimes the struggle, between them is what has so often given the American story its particular texture and drama.

If this book tells anything about that three-hundred-year narrative, it's that almost everything that's being said in the arguments for closing the border and shutting down immigration has been said before, often in literally the same terms and tones. The basic drama has been reenacted again and again. Replace Irish or Italian or Slav or Jew with Mexican or Muslim, and what comes from immigration restrictionists now could have come from the opponents of immigration a century or more ago; again and again history proved them mostly wrong. At the same time, that history also tells us that the greatest social and economic progress of the last century—and probably of any period in our history—took place in the forty years when the nation's immigration was the lowest it had ever been and, most likely, would ever be again. It was the period when new and old Americans forged the powerful industrial unions that helped produce the great middle class, sent their children to common schools, fought together at St. Lo and Anzio, on Guadalcanal and at Bastogne, often against their cousins and uncles from the old country, went to college together on the GI Bill, and became neighbors in the same developments. It was the half century of the New Deal and the Great Society and the period when the millions of immigrants from southern and eastern Europe, the once-unmeltable ethnics of the prior two generations, were "whitened" and became Americans.

Sociologists Alejandro Portes and Rubén Rumbaut coined the acronym PULLAM to describe the immigrants and their children and grandchildren who, having succeeded in America, want, like Tom Tancredo, to "pull the ladder after me." They cite previous generations of immigrants to show "how successful the process of assimilation has been in turning descendants of recent immigrants into ardent American patriots." The process, Portes and Rumbaut say, has always depended not on pressure (as in forced enrollment into English-immersion classes and elimination of bilingual education) but on immigrants' gradual, voluntary use of "religious and ethnic institutions" to "carve niches for themselves, preserving their values, language and customs and using them as platforms to find their way into their new social environment," a "creative combination of the old and new."[1] But they nonetheless worry about, and seem uncomfortably troubled by, downward assimilation—the break from the strong moral and personal values of the immigrant parents to a less stable, socially negative set of street-corner peer-group values. Equally important, as noted elsewhere in this book, the rhetoric of ardent American patriotism-cum-nativism is often adopted as proof of real assimilation. We proved we were real Americans by calling somebody else a wop or a spick. For most Americans, the impulse seemed to pass after a generation or two; the hope is that it will again.

There are multiple ironies here. The inferior "races" of the seventy years after the Civil War proved they were neither inferior nor unassimilable. They joined the descendants of the older immigrants in becoming the essential Americans of the next generation—the entrepreneurs, labor leaders, scientists, writers, artists, entertainers, and political leaders who forged the nation's modern economy, shaped its culture, and waved its flag. The great nation that our current nativists are trying to protect is the nation made in large measure by men and women whose grandmothers and grandfathers weren't wanted a hundred years ago. Yet, paradoxically, their chances of becoming what they and their children have become were almost certainly improved both by the immigration restrictions imposed on the next generation and on the intense desire of most, notwithstanding the "birds of passage," to Americanize and succeed. Here, too, the strands of immigration and the effects of anti-immigrant nativism are tightly woven around one another.

By the same token, that history, not to mention the laws of economics and of nature—energy, environmental, psychological—imposes an equal burden on the advocates of unchecked immigrant demands. There are limits to the numbers the nation can absorb—limits especially on the rate at which it can absorb them. More important, the affirmative action demands of militant immigrant rights advocates are logically inconsistent both with their demand for equal rights and with their pursuit of liberalized immigration policies and legalization of the undocumented. You can't come in and immediately claim to be a historically victimized group demanding to be put at the head of the line. Yes, German and Polish were widely taught in the schools of the Midwest before World War I. Yes, we still have countless German *turnvereins*, French schools, and Italian American cultural societies; the Hibernians still parade every St. Patrick's Day (and quarrel about who can march with them); many Jewish children still go to Hebrew school. But the activists' politicized demands for public support for the maintenance of distinct ethnic identities, and, as historian David Hollinger says, to look on the state as a source of entitlements, inevitably raise fears even among liberals about the future of a common culture and the integrity of the national community. We can have too much pluribus, as Arthur Schlesinger said, and too little unum. And, most of all, the multiculturalists' demands play inexorably into the hands of the nativist opponents of immigration.

The ultimate irony—so far only a possibility—is that the contemporary wave of Latino immigrants, the feared "mongrels" of the last century, instead of being whitened will end America's obsession with race and ethnicity altogether. Within a generation or two, most Americans, like most Californians today, will see brown as an American color that's as normal as whiteness was a generation or two back. Even today, as the essayist Richard Rodriguez has said, growing numbers of California children don't look like their grandparents. Combined with the rapidly increasing levels of racial intermarriage, will the growing number of Latino and Asian voters—and the election of Obama—at last take the nation beyond its age-old racialized categories to what Hollinger calls "Postethnic America"?[2] It was therefore more than a little odd to see a group of UCLA students from Middle Eastern countries—Lebanese, Iranian, Egyptian, Jordanian—demanding that the university add a Middle Eastern category to its application forms. The omission, one claimed, made them invisible. Worse, without a category of their own they were denied the aid given to other minority groups.[3]

For the better part of a half century, as we've come to understand that "race" is less a science or a condition that genes impose on us than a cultural and legal construct into which we lock ourselves or that we impose on others, the nation's immigration laws have moved beyond the eugenics and the racial and ethnic stereotypes on which the national origins quota acts of the 1920s were based. The complicated (and frequently revised) provisions of current immigration law give preferences to skilled workers and to close relatives of citizens. But the law still includes a formula that in effect sets a limit of approximately twenty thousand for each country—not including spouses and children of citizens—which leaves waits of many years for applicants in nations like Mexico, China, the Philippines, and India from which millions want to emigrate.[4] Given the relative economic and geographic positions of the United States and Mexico, and by extension, much of the rest of Central America, it should hardly be surprising, therefore, that unrealistic legal limits will produce large numbers of illegal immigrants. It's not a stretch to say, as historian Mae Ngai has, that we have created the illegal immigrant. Although the flow of immigrants has always been driven by the economy, albeit slowly and imperfectly, the only real checks on illegal immigration are (1) in the U.S. labor market, and especially through the labor laws and their enforcement, and (2) in the civic and economic health of other societies. For the United States, that means Mexico especially.

If there is any single lesson of the several that can be drawn from the interplay of immigration and American anti-immigration movements through the last three centuries, it's that their intricate and complex connections caution against simplistic bumper-sticker policies. To be sure, nativism, xenophobia, and the pressure for protectionism almost inevitably increase in hard times, as they have again in the recession that began in 2007. But especially in a globalized age, attempts to revive some tortured modern version of seventeenth-century mercantilism are as irrelevant as belief in the flat earth. Given the world's integrated economy, and the rapidly changing nature of, and constraints on, the nation-state—think terrorism, or the flow of illegal drugs, or multinational corporations, or the Internet—our history of failed tariffs and America First isolationism should also teach us that no unilateral action will by itself be sufficient to stabilize or normalize the flow of immigrants. Our oceans can no longer protect us against the world as the Atlantic and the British Navy once did.

That doesn't mean creating borders without controls or jettisoning all vestiges of sovereignty. It does mean harnessing contemporary realities into multinational arrangements that address and manage the panoply of economic, political, and cultural forces—the push and the pull—that drive the immigrant flow. As the Obama administration settled into office in the spring of 2009, the president, reflecting increasing pressure both from activists and employers and from the widely acknowledged dysfunctionality of existing immigration policy, announced his intention to "start the debate" on some new version of comprehensive reform. The first small step in that new direction, announced soon after by Janet Napolitano, Obama's secretary of Homeland Security, was a declared shift, responding to mounting complaints about the unfairness and brutality of Bush administration worksite immigration law enforcement practices, from crackdowns on illegal workers to their employers. Employers, according to the announcement, would be targeted before—or maybe instead of—workers.[5]

As it turned out, the new administration retained much more of the enforcement policies of its predecessor than it abandoned. In response to lawsuits and intense criticism from activists, it closed down one notorious detention center, but its promised shift to "a truly civil detention system" remained and, lacking formal rules, was probably unenforceable. It expanded the flawed Bush-era e-verify worker identification program and increased coordination between federal immigration authorities and local law-enforcement agencies.[6] And it deferred the promised start of action on a comprehensive immigration reform bill until at least 2010, a not surprising decision given the rest of Obama's agenda, health-care reform particularly. To have tried to push both at the same time would almost certainly have destroyed the chances of achieving either. Predictably, however, as soon as Obama made his first announcement, there began the corresponding push-back by a variety of groups warning that immigrants were taking American jobs, jeopardizing recovery from the recession, bringing disease, destroying the nation's Anglo-Protestant culture, and describing all illegal aliens as lawbreakers who must be punished.

Maybe it was equally predictable that despite the Obama election and the new political majorities that made it possible, the Republican Party remained so unwilling to reach out to those new voters. Instead it seemed to become even more withdrawn and, in its most defensive and reactionary precincts, to blame its loss not on its aloofness from those voters and their issues but on its failure to be even more strident in its nativism. Republicans lost, said Marcus Epstein, a member of a group of right-wingers who call themselves the American Cause, because, following Bush and Karl Rove, they chose to "pander to pro-amnesty Hispanics and swing voters."[7] Other American Cause members included many of the characters who've appeared before in this book: Pat Buchanan and his sister Bay, Tom Tancredo, Phyllis Schlafly, Tony Blankley, the former spokesman for Newt Gingrich, and Peter Brimelow, who runs a Web site called VDare that seems unembarrassed by its nativist and racialist excesses. Even beyond that hard core, the GOP now more nearly resembles a besieged cult that cannibalizes its members who stray from the true faith on taxes, immigration, and gay rights than a traditional political party. As a group the GOP seems to sense that, ethnically and socially, the world in which they grew up and once felt comfortable is shrinking rapidly and time is running out.

Maybe Hollinger is right when he says that the immigration debates of 2007 confirm that "the United States positively demands an underclass of workers and finds it convenient to obtain most of them from Mexico."[8] Yet if he is right, our immigrants, Italian, Polish, Irish, never remained a permanent underclass, and there is no iron law that it will be different for Mexicans. Certainly, the elements of our immigration policy failures have to be familiar: the eleven or twelve million illegal aliens living in the shadows of American society; their hundreds of thousands of children who were brought here at a young age, went to school here, or are going to school now, but under current law have no real future; a long-term economic prospect that, notwithstanding any recession, will require millions of new skilled workers that we are denying ourselves; the ongoing social and economic dangers, not to say the hypocrisy of keeping millions as legal *Untermenschen* in a nation that professes equality and equal opportunity. We have our violent Mexican drug gangs, just as we had our violent (mostly Italian and Jewish) gangs of bootleggers, but significantly, unlike Britain, Spain, or Germany, we haven't yet experienced any acts of homegrown terrorism, nor, as far as we know, have any terrorist acts elsewhere been launched by American-grown bombers. (The one exception, the 1995 bombing of the Alfred P. Murrah Federal Building in Oklahoma City, was the work of three all-American fanatics who were neither immigrants nor Latinos nor Muslims.) Nor, unlike France, have immigrant mobs rioted in the streets. But the continued existence of those *Untermenschen* is a declaration of no confidence in our own professed ideals and an act of economic self-deprivation, if not of immediate social endangerment.

Political reality, if nothing else, requires that amnesty, by whatever name, be accompanied by a high degree of certainty that a new round of immigration reform not generate a new wave of illegal aliens, as the Immigration Reform and Control Act did two decades ago. That, in turn, may involve both a tightening of family reunification standards and the creation of a reliable and secure electronic identification system for all residents—not the threadbare error-riddled Social Security database that the federal government has been trying to employ and that thousands of entities, public and private, have misappropriated for their own use. Creation of such a system can't be so technically difficult: every bank and credit-card company seems to manage it, often with more at stake than access to a decent job, a driver's license, or Medicaid. Nor should creating such a system be politically insurmountable. For better or worse, Americans have been made to sacrifice a piece of their privacy in a thousand ways—and have happily volunteered it on Facebook and scores of other Web sites.

America, to come full circle, is famously a nation of immigrants. What's Anglo-European about it are the institutions and ideals of equal rights, constitutionally guaranteed due process, and democratic government. But today all of us are also immigrants in the new cosmopolitan and multiethnic—perhaps postethnic—society that's grown around us, whether we're Mayflower descendants, Sons of the Golden West, or the most recent arrival from Kenya or El Salvador. The diverse nation that past immigrants and their children and grandchildren made—contra all the warnings from the Know-Nothings, the eugenicists, the Klan, the Pioneer Fund, and our latter-day radio and TV talkers—refutes not only the restrictionists' dire predictions but the very premises on which they are based. The society whose immigration policy now begs to be reformed and the history that made it are not the society and history that most of us, much less our parents, imagined a generation or two ago. The more the nation and its policy makers excavate that history from the myths of their imaginations, the more rational, humane, and productive the immigration debate will be, and the better will be the uniquely American future that grows from it.

Notes

INTRODUCTION

1. The quote about innocence and exceptionalism is from Geoffrey S. Smith, "Nativism," in *Encyclopedia of American Foreign Policy,* vol. 2, 2nd ed., ed. Alexander DeConde, Richard Dean Burns et al. (New York: Scribner, 2002), 512. Definitions of nativism vary widely, but the impulse was generally linked to American efforts at self-definition through disdain of alien people or influences.

2. Samuel Johnson's statement was apparently made in 1769, quoted in James Boswell, *The Life of Samuel Johnson,* vol. 1 (London: H. Frowde), 560; Benjamin Franklin, *Observations Concerning the Increase of Mankind, Peopling of Countries, etc.* (1751), in *The Papers of Benjamin Franklin,* vol. 4, ed. Leonard W. Labaree (New Haven, Conn.: Yale University Press, 1959), 234. Here, as in most other quotes, I've tried to retain the original spelling and syntax

3. Thomas Jefferson, *Notes on the State of Virginia,* Query VIII, 1782, pp. 211–12, Electronic Text Center, University of Virginia Library, http://xroads.virginia.edu/~HYPER/JEFFERSON/ch08.html (accessed Sept. 2008).

4. Tom Tancredo at the GOP debate at Saint Anselm College, June 3, 2007, www.ontheissues.org/Archive/2007_GOP St Anselm_Immigration.htm (accessed Sept. 2008).

5. The "official" declaration of the closing of the frontier, which came after the census of 1890, was the trigger for Frederick Jackson Turner's frontier hypothesis about the roots of American democracy, first enunciated in a lecture, "The Significance of the Frontier in American History," delivered at the meeting of the American Historical Association in Chicago in 1893. The best discussion is still Henry Nash Smith, *Virgin Land: The American West as Symbol and Myth* (Cambridge, Mass.: Harvard University Press, 1950).

6. Richard Hofstadter, *The Age of Reform: From Bryan to F.D.R.* (New York: Knopf, 1956), 180.

7. Alexander Graham Bell, "Is Race Suicide Possible?" *Journal of Heredity,* vol. 11, no. 8 (Nov.–Dec. 1920): 341.

8. See, for example, James P. Lubinskas, "A Warning from the Past," *American Renaissance,* vol. 11, no. 1 (Jan. 2000), www.amren.com/ar/2000/01 (accessed Oct. 2008).

9. Testimony of Parker Friselle in House Committee on Immigration and Naturalization, *Hearings on Seasonal Agricultural Laborers from Mexico,* 69th Congress, 1st session (Washington, D.C.: Government Printing Office, 1926).

10. Steven Taylor, "Progressive Nativism: The Know-Nothing Party in Massachusetts," paper presented at the annual meeting of the American Political Science Association, Boston, Aug. 28, 2002, www.allacademic.com/meta/p65998_index.html (accessed Aug. 2008).

11. John Higham, *Strangers in the Land: Patterns of American Nativism, 1860–1925* (New York: Atheneum, 1965), 6.

12. "Race Betterment," *Pacific Medical Journal,* vol. 58 (Oct. 1915): 603–5; *Official Proceedings of the Second National Conference on Race Betterment, August 4, 5, 6, 7 and 8, 1915* (Battle Creek, Mich.: Race Betterment Foundation, 1915), 147. The foundation's methods ranged from outdoor exercise and abstinence from drugs and alcohol to "Sterilization or Isolation of Defectives" (160). There is also a very useful description of the whole conference by Elizabeth Nicole Arruda, titled "The Mother of Tomorrow: American Eugenics and the Pacific-Panama International Exposition 1915," http://www.elisabetharruda.com/Elisabeth_Arruda_thesis.pdf (accessed Aug. 2009).

13. Testimony of V.S. McClatchy on Japanese immigration legislation, before Senate Committee on Immigration, 68th Congress, 1st session, Mar. 11–15, 1924.

14. *Reports of the Immigration Commission: Immigration Legislation,* vol. 39, 61st Congress, 3rd session (Washington, D.C.: Government Printing Office, 1911), 533. "Dillingham Commission Reports," Stanford University Libraries, http://site.ebrary.com/lib/stanfordimmigrationdillingham/EDF?id=10006566&jsenabled=yes&useNSAPI=0 (accessed Sept. 2008).

15. Henry H. Goddard, "Mental Tests and the Immigrant," *Journal of Delinquency,* vol. 2, no. 5 (Sept. 1917): 249, quoted in Edwin Black, *War against the Weak: Eugenics and America's Campaign to Create a Master Race* (New York: Thunder's Mouth Press, 2003), 78.

16. Carl C. Brigham, *A Study of American Intelligence* (Princeton, N.J.: Princeton University Press, 1923), 192.

17. The case was *Dorothy Davis et al. v. County School Board of Prince Edward County, VA, et al.,* 103 F. Supp. 337 (1952).

18. Harry H. Laughlin, *Report of the Committee to Study and to Report on the Best Practical Means to Cut Off the Defective Germ-Plasm in the American Population,* Eugenics Record Office Bulletin no. 10a (Cold Spring Harbor, N.Y., Feb. 1914). On Laughlin's background, see Laughlin biography and obituary, Box 2–5:13, Harry H. Laughlin Papers, Pickler Memorial Library, Truman State University, Kirksville, Mo., http://library.truman.edu/manuscripts/laughlinbio

.htm (accessed Sept. 2008); also, Daniel Kevles, *In the Name of Eugenics: Genetics and the Uses of Human Heredity* (New York: Knopf, 1985), 102.

19. Quoted in Nancy Ordover, *American Eugenics: Race, Queer Anatomy and the Science of Nationalism* (Minneapolis: University of Minnesota Press, 2003), 48; see also Grace Lichtenstein, "Fund Backs Controversial Study of 'Race Betterment,'" *New York Times*, Dec. 11, 1977.

20. Margaret Sanger, "A Plan for Peace," *Birth Control Review* (Apr. 1932): 107–8. The link from eugenics through Sanger to Planned Parenthood is also one that opponents of choice in abortion try not to let the world forget.

21. Lichtenstein, "Fund Backs Controversial Study of 'Racial Betterment.'"

22. Ibid.; Richard J. Herrnstein and Charles Murray, *The Bell Curve: Intelligence and Class Structure in American Life* (New York: Free Press, 1994), 348ff.

23. Edward A. Ross, *The Old World in the New* (New York: The Century Co., 1914), 219.

24. Mexicans, said historian Mae Ngai, "emerge as iconic illegal aliens." Mae M. Ngai, "The Strange Career of the Illegal Alien: Immigration Restriction and Deportation Policy in the United States, 1921–1965," *Law and History Review*, vol. 21, no. 1 (Spring 2003), www.historycooperative.org/journals/lhr/21.1/ngai.html (accessed Aug. 2008).

25. "American History in Terms of Human Migration," testimony of Harry H. Laughlin before House Committee on Immigration and Naturalization, 70th Congress, 1st session, Mar. 7, 1928, 10–11.

26. Michael Gerson, "Division Politics: The GOP's Ruinous Immigration Stance," *Washington Post*, Sept. 19, 2007.

27. Alexis de Tocqueville, *Democracy in America*, vol. 1 (New York: Vintage, 1957), 299–300n. Tocqueville, however, viewed Catholics as a whole entirely compatible with American ideals of equality and democracy.

28. Herrnstein and Murray, *Bell Curve*, 361. Tancredo echoes the argument in his book *In Mortal Danger: The Battle for America's Border and Security* (Nashville, Tenn.: WND Books, 2006), 22–23.

29. Hector St. Jean de Crèvecoeur, *Letters from an American Farmer* (1782) (Philadelphia: Matthew Carey, 1793), 47–48.

CHAPTER 1

1. John Winthrop, "A Model of Christian Charity," in Robert C. Winthrop, *Life and Letters of John Winthrop* (Boston: Ticknor and Fields, 1867), 18; "The Examination of Mrs. Ann Hutchinson at the Court of Newtown, November 1637," in Lawrence Shaw Mayo, ed., *The History of the Colony and Province of Massachusetts-Bay* (Cambridge: Harvard University Press, 1936), 391; Vernon L. Parrington, *Main Currents in American Thought*, vol. 1, *The Colonial Mind* (New York: Harcourt Brace, 1927), 24; Eve LaPlante, *American Jezebel: The Uncommon Life of Anne Hutchinson* (New York: Harper Collins, 2005), 211; Peter G. Gomes, "Anne Hutchinson, Brief Life of Harvard's 'Midwife,' 1595–1643," *Harvard Magazine*, Nov.–Dec. 2002, 32. What's most striking in the transcript of the trial was Hutchinson's theological understanding and her impressive rhetorical and forensic skills.

2. David D. Hall, *The Antinomian Controversy, 1636–1638: A Documentary History* (Durham, N.C.: Duke University Press, 1990), 312–48. See also *The Trial of Anne Hutchinson,* excerpts from the examination of Anne Hutchinson in the General Court of the Massachusetts Bay Colony, http://history.missouristate.edu/FTMiller/Docs/hutchinsontrial.htm (accessed Nov. 2008).

3. Robert Frost, "The Gift Outright," in *Collected Poems* (New York: Henry Holt, 1949), 467.

4. Horace Bushnell, "The True Wealth or Weal of Nations," Phi Beta Kappa address delivered before the Alpha of Connecticut, Yale College, Aug. 15, 1837, in Clark Sutherland Northup, William Coolidge Lane, and John Christopher Schwab, *Representative Phi Beta Kappa Orations* (New York: Houghton Mifflin, 1915), 2.

5. Klaus J. Hansen, "The Millennium, the West, and Race in the Antebellum Mind," *Western Historical Quarterly,* vol. 3, no. 4 (Oct. 1972): 374. For additional background on this belief, see Leland H. Gentry, "Adam-ondi-Ahman: A Brief Historical Survey," *B.Y.U. Studies,* vol. 13, no. 4 (Summer 1973): 553–76.

6. Karl Frederick Geiser, "Redemptioners and Indentured Servants in the Colony and Commonwealth of Pennsylvania," *Yale Review,* vol. 10, no. 2 (Aug. 1901): 31–32. See also Sanford H. Cobb, "The Palatine, or, German Immigration to New York and Pennsylvania," paper read before the Wyoming Historical and Geological Society, Wilkes-Barre, Pa., n.d., printed for the society in 1897, http://pds.lib.harvard.edu/pds/view/4859935?n=5&s=4 (accessed Aug. 2008).

7. Geiser, "Redemptioners and Indentured Servants," 32.

8. Benjamin Franklin, "The Support of the Poor," letter to Peter Collinson, May 9, 1753, in *The Writings of Benjamin Franklin,* Volume II: *Philadelphia, 1726—1757,* letter available at www.historycarper.com/resources/twobf2/letter18.htm (accessed Aug. 2008).

9. Thomas Jefferson, *Notes on the State of Virginia,* Query VIII, 1782, pp. 211–12, Electronic Text Center, University of Virginia Library, http://xroads.virginia.edu/~HYPER/JEFFERSON/ch08.html (accessed Sept. 2008).

10. Ray Allen Billington, *The Protestant Crusade, 1800–1860* (New York: Macmillan, 1938), 1.

11. Constitution of the State of New York, Apr. 20, 1777, text from the Avalon Project at Yale Law School, www.yale.edu/lawweb/avalon/states/ny01.htm#14 (accessed June 2008); James J. Kirschke, *Gouverneur Morris: Author, Statesman, Man of the World* (New York: Macmillan, 2005), 61; Arnold Whitridge, "A Representative of America," *American Heritage,* vol. 27, no. 4 (June 1976): 33–37, 89–93.

12. Marian L. Smith, "Race, Nationality and Reality: INS Administration of Racial Provisions in U.S. Immigration and Nationality Law Since 1898, Part I," *Prologue,* vol. 34, no. 2 (Summer 2002), 91–104, www.archives.gov/publications/prologue/2002/summer/immigration-law-1.html (accessed Dec. 2008).

13. Richard D. Brown, "The Founding Fathers of 1776 and 1787: A Collective View," *William and Mary Quarterly,* 3rd series, vol. 33, no. 3 (July 1976): 474–76.

14. The Alien Act, which allowed the president to deport individuals regarded as dangerous aliens—dangerous, that is, to the Federalists—expired in 1800. It was never used.

15. Smith, "Race, Nationality and Reality."

16. Ian Haney Lopez, *White by Law: The Legal Construction of Race* (New York: New York University Press, 1996).

17. Gregory Rodriguez, *Mongrels, Bastards, Orphans and Vagabonds: Mexican Immigration and the Future of Race in America* (New York: Pantheon, 2007), xiv.

18. William V. Shannon, *The American Irish: A Political and Social Portrait* (New York: Macmillan, 1963), 28.

19. Ibid., 39.

20. Henry Duhring, "Immigration: Remarks on the United States of America, with regard to the Actual State of Europe," *North American Review,* vol. 40, no. 87 (Apr. 1835): 476.

21. Shannon, *American Irish,* 39.

22. Ibid.

23. "The Convent," *Boston Evening Transcript,* Aug. 12, 1834; Ray Allen Billington, "The Burning of the Charlestown Convent," *New England Quarterly,* vol. 10, no. 1 (Mar. 1937): 4–24; Billington, *Protestant Crusade,* 68–76.

24. O.R. Butler, "'The Uncle Tom's Cabin of Nativism': Anti-Catholic Novels, Politics and Violence in the Antebellum United States," in "Literary Fads and Fashion," special issue, *Working with English: Medieval and Modern Language, Literature and Drama,* vol. 2.1 (2006): 14–15, www.nottingham.ac.uk/english/working_with_english (accessed Sept. 2008).

25. Maria Monk, *The Awful Disclosures of Maria Monk . . .* (New York: Howe and Bates, 1836), 36. It was rumored that Howe and Bates was a dummy imprint that Harper Brothers created in an effort to reap the likely profits from the book without bearing the onus for its scurrilous and inflammatory story.

26. Billington, *Protestant Crusade,* 122–26.

27. *Address of the Board of Managers of the American Protestant Association* (Philadelphia, 1843), 7. See also David Montgomery, "The Shuttle and the Cross: Weavers and Artisans in the Kensington Riots of 1844," *Journal of Social History,* vol. 5, no. 4 (Summer 1972): 427, 431–33; Jacob Rader Marcus, *United States Jewry, 1776–1985* (Detroit: Wayne State University Press, 1989), 283; *The Full Particulars of the Late Riots with a View of the Burning of the Catholic Churches St. Michaels and St. Augustines* (Philadelphia, 1844), Villanova University Digital Library, http://digital.library.villanova.edu/Catholica%20Collection/Catholica-00004.xml (accessed June 2008); "Killed and Wounded," *Pennsylvania Freeman,* July 18, 1844; John B. Perry, *A Full and Complete Account of the Late Awful Riots in Philadelphia* (Philadelphia, 1844).

28. *Full Particulars of the Late Riots,* 8.

29. On the "worst class of mankind," see the affidavit of George S. Roberts quoted in "The Southwark Riots," *Philadelphia Public Ledger,* July 23, 1844. For more general accounts of the riots and rioters, see "Additional Evidence in Relation to the Riot," *Philadelphia Public Ledger,* July 24, 1844; and Vincent P. Lannie and Bernard C. Diethorn, "For the Honor and Glory of God: The Philadelphia Bible Riots of 1840," *History of Education Quarterly,* vol. 8, no. 1 (Spring 1968): 104.

30. Shannon, *American Irish,* 46.

31. Lyman Beecher, *A Plea for the West* (Cincinnati: Truman and Smith, 1835), 51–52. The book was based in large part on one of Beecher's sermons just before the burning of the Ursuline convent, though it's not clear to what extent Beecher inadvertently helped incite that riot.

32. M.W. Cluskey, *The Political Text Book or Encyclopedia* (Philadelphia: James B. Smith and Co., 1857), 57.

33. See, for example, Tyler Anbinder, *Nativism and Slavery: The Northern Know-Nothings and the Politics of the 1850s* (New York: Oxford, 1992).

34. *Platform of the American Party of Massachusetts* (ca. 1855), "An American Time Capsule: Three Centuries of Broadsides and Other Printed Ephemera," Library of Congress, http://memory.loc.gov/ammem/rbpehtml (accessed Oct. 2008).

35. "Rome and America Eternal Opposites," *The True American's Almanac and Politician's Manual for 1857*, ed. Tisdale (New York, 1857), Gilder Lehrman Center for the Study of Slavery, Resistance and Abolition at Yale University, www.yale.edu/glc/archive/973.htm (accessed Oct. 2008).

36. "The Know-Nothing Platform," Duke University Special Collections Library, http://scriptorium.lib.duke.edu/americavotes/know-nothing.html (accessed June 2008).

37. Steven Taylor, "Progressive Nativism: The Know-Nothing Party in Massachusetts," paper presented at the annual meeting of the American Political Science Association, Boston, Aug. 28, 2002. Another version of this paper is at *Historical Journal of Massachusetts* (Summer 2000), 167–85, http://findarticles.com/p/articles/mi_qa3837/is_200007/ai_n8908750 (accessed Oct. 2008).

38. "Native Americanism," *New York Tribune*, vol. 4, no. 186 (Nov. 11, 1844). The "statesman" was Henry Clay, who was defeated by Democrat James K. Polk. Greeley was then a faithful Whig.

39. Billington, *Protestant Crusade*, 412–16.

40. Abraham Lincoln letter to Joshua F. Speed, Aug. 24, 1855, in *Collected Works of Abraham Lincoln*, vol. 2 (New Brunswick, N.J.: Rutgers University Press, 1953), 323.

41. Constitution of the State of California, 1849, California State Archives, www.sos.ca.gov/archives/level3const1849txt.html (accessed Sept. 2008).

42. J. Ross Browne, *Report of the Debates in the Convention of California on the Formation of the State Constitution, October and November, 1849* (Washington, D.C.: John T. Towers, 1850), 48.

43. H.W. Brands, *The Age of Gold: The California Gold Rush and the New American Dream* (New York: Random House, 2002), 330.

44. Kerry Abrams, "Polygamy, Prostitution and the Federalization of American Immigration Law," *Columbia Law Review*, vol. 105, no. 3 (Apr. 2005): 642–48.

45. Mark Kanazawa, "Immigration, Exclusion and Taxation: Anti-Chinese Legislation in Gold Rush California," *Journal of Economic History*, vol. 65, no. 3 (Sept. 2005): 779–805.

46. "Governor's Special Message," *Daily Alta California*, Apr. 25, 1852. See also Charles J. McClain Jr., "The Chinese Struggle for Civil Rights in Nineteenth Century America: The First Phase, 1850–1870," *California Law Review*, vol. 72, no. 4 (July 1984): 529–68.

47. *People v. Hall,* Supreme Court of California, October term, 1854. Hugh Murray, a Know-Nothing judge named to the bench at the age of twenty-five in frontier California, appeared to have been a drunk, a brawler, and (in the words of a comprehensive history of California Supreme Court justices)"not much of a lawyer." He died at the age of thirty-two of tuberculosis brought on by "overwork and heavy drinking." Edward Johnson, *History of the Supreme Court Justices of California,* vol. 1 (San Francisco: Bender-Moss, 1963), 43.

48. Iris Chang, *The Chinese in America* (New York: Viking, 2003), 44.

49. Ibid.

50. Quoted in Susan Lee Johnson, *Roaring Camp: The Social World of the California Gold Rush* (New York: Norton, 2000), 248, excerpted as "Season of Dashed Hopes," *Humanities,* vol. 27, no. 5 (Sept.–Oct. 2006): 22–25, www.neh.gov/news/humanities/2006–09/SeasonOfDashedHopes.html (accessed Sept. 2008).

51. Norman Assing, "To His Excellency Gov. Bigler," *Daily Alta California* (San Francisco), May 5, 1852. See also McClain, "Chinese Struggle for Civil Rights," 550.

52. See "Negro Exclusion Bill," 1858, LP:1223, California State Archives, Sacramento, www.learncalifornia.org/doc.asp?id=1916 (accessed Oct. 2008). For a fuller discussion of the Negro exclusion issue in 1850s California, see Eugene H. Berwanger, *The Frontier Against Slavery: Western Anti-Negro Prejudice and the Slavery Extension Controversy* (Urbana: University of Illinois Press, 1967), 63–95.

53. "A Bill to Prevent Negroes or Mulattoes from Coming to, or Residing in Oregon," Oregon Provisional and Territorial Government Records no. 6075, Oregon State Archives, Salem; "Crafting the Oregon Constitution," an online exhibit of the Office of the Oregon Secretary of State, http://arcweb.sos.state.or.us/exhibits/1857/index.htm (accessed Aug. 2008); Elizabeth McLagan, *A Peculiar Paradise: A History of Blacks in Oregon, 1788–1940* (Portland: Georgian Press, 1980), chapter 2, http://gesswhoto.com/paradise-chapter2.html (accessed Oct. 2008).

54. *Journal of the Constitutional Convention of the State of Oregon Held at Salem, Commencing August 17, 1857, together with the Constitution Adopted by the People, November 9, 1857* (Salem: W.H. Byars, State Printer, 1882), 104–5.

55. *Alta California,* Jan. 13, 1859. The law was "An Act to Prevent the Further Immigration of Chinese or Mongolians to This State," chapter 313, *Statutes of California* (1858), 295–96.

56. "Shall Negroes and Chinamen Vote in California? . . . An Address by the Democratic State Central Committee to the Voters of California," *San Francisco Daily Examiner,* Aug. 1869, Online Archive of California, http://content.cdlib.org/ark:/13030/hb8779n968/?&brand=oac (accessed Oct. 2008).

57. Najia Aarim-Heriot, *Chinese Immigrants, African Americans, and Racial Anxiety in the United States 1848–82* (Urbana: University of Illinois Press, 2003).

58. "The Anglo-Saxon Race," *American Whig Review,* vol. 7, no. 1 (Jan. 1848): 43.

CHAPTER 2

1. For various reasons—the lower number of immigrants who settled in the South, Southern distrust of foreigners—far and away the largest part of the Confederate Army was native-born. There were some immigrant units—the New Orleans Jaegers was one—but the immigrant record on behalf of the Confederacy seems to have been far less distinguished than was the bravery and devotion of the Germans, the Irish, and other immigrants in the Union Army. See, for example, Sean Michael O'Brien, *Irish-Americans in the Confederate Army* (Johnson, N.C.: McFarland, 2007).

2. William V. Shannon, *The American Irish: A Political and Social Portrait* (New York: Macmillan, 1963), 59.

3. "General Orders No. 11. Hdqrs. 13th A.C. Department of the Tennessee, Holly Springs, Dec. 17, 1862," in *Official Records of the War of the Rebellion,* series 1, vol. 17, part 2, p. 424. See also John Higham, *Strangers in the Land: Patterns of American Nativism, 1860–1925* (New York: Atheneum, 1965), 12–14.

4. Stephen Birmingham, *Our Crowd: The Great Jewish Families of New York* (New York: Dell, 1968), 102.

5. James Anthony Feoude, "Romanism and the Irish Race in the United States," *North American Review,* vol. 129, no. 277 (Dec. 1879): 531ff.

6. Quoted in Pam Epstein, "The American Protective Association," http://projects.vassar.edu/1896/apa.html (accessed Aug. 2009).

7. "Chapter III: The End of State Legislation," in *Reports of the Immigration Commission: Immigration Legislation,* 61st Congress, 3rd session (Washington, D.C.: Government Printing Office, 1911), 19. "Dillingham Commission Reports," Stanford University Libraries, http://site.ebrary.com/lib/stanfordimmigrationdillingham/EDF?id=10006566&jsenabled=yes&useNSAPI=0 (accessed Sept. 2008).

8. Ibid., 21–22.

9. Ibid., 19.

10. Henry Nash Smith, *Virgin Land: The American West as Symbol and Myth* (Cambridge, Mass.: Harvard University Press, 1950), 165–73.

11. "An Act to Establish a Bureau of Immigration and Appoint Agents Therefore," Kansas State Laws, 1864, chapter 75, p. 143, in *Reports of the Immigration Commission: Immigration Legislation,* vol. 39, 649. Occasionally, the European agents appear to have tried to persuade Europeans preparing to immigrate to a competing state that conditions there were inferior to what their state offered. Iowa, some Norwegians were told, was much too hot in the summer. Minnesota was preferable. "Official Encouragement of Immigration to Iowa," *Iowa Journal of History and Politics,* vol. 19, no. 2 (Apr. 1921): 159–95.

12. Missouri, acts of 1864–65, in *Reports of the Immigration Commission: Immigration Legislation,* vol. 39, 721, http://site.ebrary.com/lib/stanfordimmigrationdillingham/Doc?id=10006566&ppg697 (accessed Aug. 2008).

13. John Higham, "Origins of Immigration Restriction, 1882–1897: A Social Analysis," *Mississippi Valley Historical Review,* vol. 39, no. 1 (June 1952): 77.

14. *Reports of the Immigration Commission: Immigration Legislation,* 519.

15. Long before the publication of his seminal book on nativism, Higham argued that immigration restrictionism in the 1880s and 1890s was driven more by a dislike of all foreigners than by hatred of any particular group, and, more generally, by the "crisis in the whole American social order." Higham, "Origins of Immigration Restriction, 1882–1897," 77–88. But the anti-immigrant mood was certainly fed by fears of anarchist violence, labor strife, and Catholic power, all of which were associated with specific groups.

16. W.H. Poole, *Anglo-Israel, or The British Nation the Lost-Tribes of Israel* (Toronto: Bengough Bros., 1879).

17. Josiah Strong, *Our Country: Its Present Crisis and Its Possible Future* (New York: Baker and Taylor, for the American Home Missionary Society, 1885), 165ff.

18. Ibid., 40.

19. Francis Amasa Walker, "Restriction on Immigration," *Atlantic Monthly,* vol. 77, no. 464 (June 1896): 824; Francis Amasa Walker, *Discussions in Economics and Statistics,* vol. 2 (New York: Henry Holt, 1899), 122–24, 418–26, 439.

20. Francis Amasa Walker, "Immigration and Degradation," *The Forum,* vol. 11 (1891): 642.

21. Henry David, *The Haymarket Affair: A Study in the American Social-Revolutionary and Labor Movements* (New York: Farrar and Rinehart, 1936).

22. "Pardon for the Anarchists," *New York Times,* June 27, 1893.

23. "Anarchy's Red Hand . . . " *New York Times,* May 6, 1886.

24. Quoted in Higham, *Strangers in the Land,*. 55.

25. Henry Cabot Lodge, "The Restriction of Immigration," *North American Review,* vol. 152, no. 410 (Jan. 1891): 34; Henry Cabot Lodge, "Lynch Law and Unrestricted Immigration," *North American Review,* vol. 152, no. 414 (May 1891): 602–12. There were demurrers, among them one from the U.S. Immigration Commission, who contended that Italians were certainly fit for farm work in the South and on the West Coast., J.H. Senner, "Immigration from Italy," *North American Review,* vol. 162, no. 475 (June 1896): 657.

26. Lodge, "Lynch Law," 609.

27. Henry Cabot Lodge, "The Restriction of Immigration," in *The Speeches and Addresses, 1884–1909* (Boston: Houghton Mifflin, 1909), 245–66. The speech has the same title as one of his *North American Review* articles nearly two decades earlier (see note 25).

28. Lodge, "Lynch Law," 602ff.

29. Ibid., 604–5.

30. Lodge, "Restriction of Immigration," *North American Review,* 31.

31. Lodge, "Lynch Law," 610–11. "Birds of passage" was a common description of immigrants who intended to return home.

32. "Evil Effects," cited in Richard T. Ely, *Scrapbook: American Economic Association, 1885–1906* (Madison: Wisconsin State Historical Society, n.d.), 27.

33. *Extracts from the Report of the Commissioner-General of Immigration, for the Year Ending June 30, 1903,* in "An American Time Capsule: Three Centuries of Broadsides and Other Printed Ephemera," Library of Congress,

http://memory.loc.gov/cgi-bin/query/h?ammem/rbpebib:@field(NUMBER+@band(rbpe+07902100) (accessed Sept. 2008).

34. Mark Krikorian, *The New Case Against Immigration—Both Legal and Illegal* (New York: Sentinel Books, 2008), 1.

35. Frederick Jackson Turner, "The Significance of the Frontier in American History," in *The Frontier in American History* (New York: Henry Holt and Co., 1921), 1–39.

36. Henry George, *Social Problems* (New York: Henry George, 1886), 48.

37. Lodge, "Restriction of Immigration," *North American Review,* 34.

38. Henry James, *The American Scene* (Boston: Harper Brothers, 1907), 84–86. The book was based on the magazine articles about his American tour and lectures delivered in the course of it in 1904–5.

39. Ibid., 95. James "seems like a kind of fascinated, horror-stricken, cultural (and literal) germ-o-phobe who resents the very fastidiousness that separates him from the material he wants to probe." Author e-mail communication with Mitzi Schrag, professor of English, Clark College, Sept. 2008.

40. John B. Weber and Charles Stewart Smith, "Our National Dumping Ground—A Study of Immigration," *North American Review,* vol. 154, no. 425 (Apr. 1892): 424ff.

41. Senner, "Immigration from Italy," 657.

42. Kate Holladay Claghorn, "Our Immigrants and Ourselves," *Atlantic Monthly,* vol. 86, no. 516 (Oct. 1900): 547.

43. *Scrapbook, Immigration Restriction League, 1896–98,* MS Am 2245, Houghton Library, Harvard University, http://pds.lib.harvard.edu/pds/view/5400295?n=4&imagesize=1200&jp2Res=.25 (accessed Aug. 2008).

44. Higham, *Strangers in the Land*, 164.

45. What no one ever addressed, then or now, is who these immigrants, roughly two-thirds of whom were men, ultimately married. Even subtracting the many who went back to Italy or Poland leaves a lot of marriageable immigrant men for whom there were no foreign-born women. Did they marry native Americans? Was that one of the major steps to assimilation?

46. "A Sensation at Saratoga—New Rules for the Grand Union—No Jews to Be Admitted," *New York Times,* June 19, 1877. See also Birmingham, *Our Crowd,* 169ff.

47. Birmingham, *Our Crowd,* 177.

48. "Mr. Seligman Blackballed—Union League Declares Itself against Hebrews," *New York Times,* Apr. 15, 1893; Birmingham, *Our Crowd,* 283.

49. Henry Adams, *The Education of Henry Adams* (New York: Modern Library, 1931), 266.

50. Thomas Nast, "The American River Ganges," *Harper's Weekly,* May 8, 1876.

51. *The Wasp,* Oct. 12, 1889; *Buffalo Evening News,* Feb. 1, 1904.

52. William Allen White, *The Old Order Changeth: A View of American Democracy* (New York: Macmillan, 1910), 130.

53. Richard Hofstadter, *The Age of Reform: From Bryan to F.D.R.* (New York: Knopf, 1956), 180.

54. John Koren, *Boston, 1822–1922: The Story of Its Government and Principal Activities* (Boston: City of Boston Printing Department, 1922), 14.

55. James J. Connolly, "Reconstituting Ethnic Politics, 1909–1925," *Social Science History*, vol. 19, no. 4 (Winter 1995): 480.

56. In 1965, when I counted the names in the directory of the Boston school system, among the 3,700 people listed there were 68 Sullivans, 61 Murphys, 21 Lynches, 18 Kelleys, 14 Kellys, 25 Walshes, 30 O'Briens, 40 McCarthys, 22 Dohertys, 21 McLaughlins, and countless other Irish names. Peter Schrag, *Village School Downtown: Boston Schools, Boston Politics* (Boston: Beacon Press, 1966), 51.

57. E. C. Leffingwell, "San Francisco's Mayor Wants Exclusion Act to Bar the Japs," Newspaper Enterprise Association, Apr. 1, 1905, in "An American Time Capsule: Three Centuries of Broadsides and Other Printed Ephemera," Library of Congress, http://memory.loc.gov/rbc/rbpe/rbpe00/rbpe002/0020220a/001dr.jpg (accessed Oct. 2008).

58. Richard Coke Lower, *A Bloc of One: The Political Career of Hiram W. Johnson* (Stanford, Calif.: Stanford University Press, 1993), 38–40. Wilson, who had just won election over Roosevelt, then running as a Bull Mooser with Hiram Johnson, didn't have much credit with the California governor. In the campaign, Wilson's Democrats had themselves tried to exploit anti-Japanese animus against Roosevelt. After he narrowly took California, Wilson dispatched Secretary of State William Jennings Bryan to plead with Governor Johnson to derail the bill. Johnson, it was reported, took "malicious pleasure" in turning the tables on the president.

59. John R. Commons, *Races and Immigrants in America* (New York: Macmillan, 1907), 238.

60. Ibid., 198ff.

61. Edward A. Ross, "The Causes of Race Superiority," *Annals of the American Academy of Political and Social Science*, no. 18 (July 1901): 85, 87.

62. Albert J. Beveridge, U.S. Senate speech, Jan. 9, 1900, in Henry Steele Commager, *Living Ideas in America* (New York: Harper and Row, 1964), 673.

63. Ross, "Causes of Race Superiority," 67–89.

64. Edward A. Ross, *The Old World in the New* (New York: The Century Co., 1914), 299–304.

65. Walker, "Restriction on Immigration," 822–29.

66. Prescott F. Hall, *Immigration and Its Effects Upon the United States* (New York: Henry Holt, 1906), 180.

67. Ross, *Old World in the New*, 101.

68. Ibid., 127, 129, 150.

69. Hall, *Immigration and Its Effects*, 187.

70. Ibid.

71. Ibid., 321.

72. "The Anglo-Saxon Race," *American Whig Review*, vol. 7 (Jan. 1848): 43.

73. Hall, *Immigration and Its Effects*, 321–22.

74. Ibid., 101–2.

75. Theodore Roosevelt, "On American Motherhood," speech before the National Congress of Mothers, Washington, D.C., Mar. 13, 1905, www.nationalcenter.org/TRooseveltMotherhood.html (accessed Aug. 2009).

76. Higham, *Strangers in the Land*, 161–62.

77. *Chy Lung v. Freeman*, 92 U.S. 275 (1875).

78. Iris Chang, *The Chinese in America: A Narrative History* (New York: Viking, 2003), 131ff. Chang offers a vivid summary of the brutal attacks in western states. In some instances, the federal troops sent in to control the mobs appeared themselves to be cheering on the people they were sent to stop.

79. *Brief Statement of the Immigration Commission with Conclusions and Recommendations and Views of the Minority*, vol. 1 of *Reports of the Immigration Commission: Immigration Legislation*, http://site.ebrary.com/lib/stanfordimmigrationdillingham/Doc?id=10006604&ppg=47 (accessed Sept. 2008).

80. *Children of Immigrants in Schools*, vol. 29 of *Reports of the Immigration Commission: Immigration Legislation*, 31, http://library.stanford.edu/depts/dlp/ebrary/dillingham/body.shtml (accessed Sept. 2008).

81. *Brief Statement of the Immigration Commission*, vol. 1 of *Reports of the Immigration Commission*, 46–48.

82. Marian L. Smith, "INS-U.S. Immigration and Naturalization Service History" (Washington, D.C.: U.S. Citizenship and Immigration Services, n.d.), www.uscitizenship.info/ins-usimmigration-insoverview.html (accessed Aug. 2009).

83. Act of March 3, 1903: An Act to Regulate the Immigration of Aliens into the United States, in *Immigration Laws and Regulations, August 1903* (Washington, D.C.: Government Printing Office, 1904), 23ff.

84. Higham, *Strangers in the Land*, 203.

85. Ross, "Causes of Race Superiority," 89. On Grant and conservation generally, see Jonathan Spiro, *Defending the Master Race: Conservation, Eugenics and the Legacy of Madison Grant* (Burlington: University of Vermont Press, 2008).

86. Theodore Roosevelt to president of the American Defense Society, Jan. 3, 1919, in Albert Bushnell Hart, ed., *Theodore Roosevelt Cyclopedia* (New York: Roosevelt Memorial Association, 1941), 243. The letter was written shortly before Roosevelt's death.

87. "Madison Grant, 71, Zoologist, Is Dead," *New York Times*, May 31, 1937. The obituary was highly respectful in tone, emphasizing Grant's good deeds in New York and his conservationism and making little mention of his racism or the forced eugenic sterilizations that he encouraged.

88. Madison Grant, *The Passing of the Great Race* (New York: Scribner's, 1916), 14.

89. Ibid., 66, 200.

90. Madison Grant, "Discussion of Article on Democracy and Heredity," *Journal of Heredity*, vol. 10, no. 4 (1919): 165.

91. Grant, *Passing of the Great Race*, 8.

92. Ibid., 80.

93. Ibid., 81–82.

94. Ibid., 228.

95. Ibid., 46–47.

96. The Hitler letter to Grant is quoted widely, most reliably in Stefan Kuhl, *The Nazi Connection: Eugenics, American Racism, and German National Socialism* (New York: Oxford, 1994), and in Edwin Black, *War against the Weak* (New York: Thunder's Mouth Press, 2003), 259. But all authors rely on the unpublished autobiography of eugenicist Leon F. Whitney, who reported that Grant showed him the Hitler letter. No date or other details were provided. "Autobiography of Leon F. Whitney," unpublished ms., pp. 204–5, American Philosophical Society Manuscript Collection, Philadelphia.

97. Adolf Hitler, *Mein Kampf* (1923), vol. 2, trans. James Murphy (London: Hurst and Blackett Ltd., 1939), 154. Murphy's introduction leaves no question that he was himself a great sympathizer. This translation can still be found at a number of contemporary Nazi sites.

CHAPTER 3

1. *Children of Immigrants in Schools*, vol. 29 of *Reports of the Immigration Commission: Immigration Legislation*, 61st Congress, 3rd session (Washington, D.C.: Government Printing Office, 1911), 31. "Dillingham Commission Reports," Stanford University Libraries, http://library.stanford.edu/depts/dlp/ebrary/dillingham/body.shtml (accessed Sept. 2008).

2. Stephen Jay Gould, *The Mismeasure of Man* (New York: Norton, 1981), 162.

3. Theodore Roosevelt letter to Charles B. Davenport, Jan. 3, 1913, B D27 in American Philosophical Society Digital Collections, Eugenics Archive, www.amphilsoc.org/library/digcoll (accessed Aug. 2008).

4. "Race Betterment," *California State Journal of Medicine* (Nov. 1915): 453.

5. Ibid.

6. Henry Fairfield Osborn, "Address of Welcome," in *Eugenics, Genetics and the Family*, vol. 1 (Baltimore: Williams and Wilkins, 1923), 1, quoted in Edwin Black, *War against the Weak* (New York: Thunder's Mouth Press, 2003), 237.

7. Henry H. Goddard, *The Kallikak Family: A Study in the Heredity of Feeble-Mindedness* (New York: Macmillan, 1912); Gould, *Mismeasure of Man*, 168.

8. "Two Immigrants Out of Five Feebleminded," *The Survey*, vol. 38 (Sept. 15, 1917): 528–29.

9. Henry H. Goddard, "Mental Tests and the Immigrant," *Journal of Delinquency*, vol. 2, no. 5 (Sept. 1917): 243–77.

10. Ibid., 277. It was also during this prewar period that a commissioner of immigration at the port of New York, first appointed by President Roosevelt and then reappointed by President William Howard Taft, was cleaning the place of corrupt officials who had been notoriously lenient in the enforcement of immigration laws.

11. Robert M. Yerkes, ed., *Psychological Examining in the United States Army*, vol. 15 (Washington, D.C.: Memoirs of the National Academy of Sciences, 1921).

12. Carl C. Brigham, *A Study of American Intelligence* (Princeton, N.J.: Princeton University Press, 1923); Nicholas Lemann, *The Big Test: The Secret History of the American Meritocracy* (New York: Farrar, Straus and Giroux, 1999), 29–35.

13. Brigham, *Study of American Intelligence,* 54–56.

14. Lewis M. Terman, *The Measurement of Intelligence* (Boston: Houghton Mifflin, 1916), 11.

15. Brigham, *Study of American Intelligence,* 178.

16. There's an extensive critique of the test in Gould's *Mismeasure of Man,* 195ff, in which he concluded, among many other things, that Brigham "had virtually proved the environmentalist claim that the army tests measured familiarity with American language and customs; but again he devised an innatist fudge" (228).

17. Brigham, *Study of American Intelligence,* 94. Their data did show that in the prior decade the number of immigrants going back to their countries of origin was close to one-third of those arriving. For Italians, it was over half.

18. Ibid., 192.

19. Ibid., 190.

20. Ibid., 210.

21. Ibid., vii–viii.

22. Robert M. Yerkes, "Testing the Human Mind," *Atlantic Monthly* (Mar. 1923): 358.

23. Walter Lippmann, "The Mental Age of Americans," *New Republic,* Oct. 25, 1922, 213. This was one of a series of articles whose immediate targets were both Yerkes's army studies and, later, a book by Lothrop Stoddard. Stoddard's subsequent book, *The Rising Tide of Color against White World-Supremacy* (1920) became something of a sensation and continues to be cited by the intellectual wing of American nativism.

24. Kimball Young, "Review of *A Study of American Intelligence,*" *Science,* new series, vol. 57, no. 1484 (June 8, 1923): 670.

25. Edwin G. Boring letter to Carl C. Brigham, quoted in Dale Stout and Sue Stuart, "E. G. Boring's Review of Brigham's *A Study of American Intelligence:* A Case Study in the Politics of Reviews," *Social Studies of Science,* vol. 21, no. 1 (Feb. 1991): 136.

26. Edwin G. Boring, "Facts and Fancies of Immigration," *New Republic,* Apr. 23, 1923, 245–46.

27. See, for example, A. J. Snow, "Review of *A Study of American Intelligence,*" *American Journal of Psychology*, vol. 34, no. 2 (Apr. 1923): 306.

28. Lewis M. Terman, "The Conservation of Talent," *School and Society,* vol. 19 (Mar. 29, 1924): 359–64.

29. William L. Harding, "No German in Iowa," letter to the *New York Times,* June 18, 1918. See also Carol L. Schmid, *The Politics of Language: Conflict, Identity and Cultural Pluralism in Comparative Perspective* (New York: Oxford, 2001), 36; and Rosemary G. Feal, "Scaring (Up) 'Foreign' Language Speakers: One Hundred Years of Multitude," *MLA Newsletter,* vol. 36, no. 4 (Winter 2004): 4.

30. In Russia, Berkman and Goldman soon became disillusioned by the Bolsheviks. Goldman subsequently went to England and became a prolific writer and lecturer—a vehement anti-Communist and antifascist. She went to help the loyalists during the Spanish Civil War and ultimately died in 1940 in Canada. She was buried in Chicago not far from the scene of the Haymarket Riot that first radicalized her in 1886.

31. Frederick Lewis Allen, *Only Yesterday* (New York: Harper, 1931), 47.

32. Lothrop Stoddard, *The Rising Tide of Color against White World-Supremacy* (New York: Scribner's, 1920), 165.

33. Lothrop Stoddard, *The Revolt against Civilization: The Menace of the Under Man* (New York: Scribner's, 1922), 30. Translated as *der Untermensch,* the "under man"—a term Stoddard seems to have coined, maybe in contrast with Nietzsche's superman—would soon become a stock item in the Nazi vocabulary.

34. F. Scott Fitzgerald, *The Great Gatsby* (New York: Scribner's, 1925), 17.

35. Kansas Bureau of Child Research, *Fitter Families for Future Firesides: A Report of the Eugenics Department of the Kansas Free Fair* (Eugenics Committee of the United States of America, ca. 1924), 4.

36. Clifford Kirkpatrick, "Selective Immigration: The New Mercantilism," *Journal of Social Forces,* vol. 3, no. 3 (Mar. 1925), 497–503.

37. Madison Grant, "Failures of the Melting Pot," *New York Times,* Nov. 12, 1922.

38. George William Hunter, *A Civic Biology Presented in Problems* (New York: American Book Company, 1914), 262–63.

39. H.L. Mencken, "In Memoriam: W.J.B.," first published in the *Baltimore Sun,* July 27, 1925, revised by Mencken for the *American Mercury* (Oct. 1925), where Bryan became "a charlatan, a mountebank, a zany without sense or dignity," and reprinted in Alistair Cooke, ed., *The Vintage Mencken* (New York: Vintage, 1956), 164.

40. Stephen Jay Gould, "William Jennings Bryan's Last Campaign," in *Bully for Brontosaurus: Reflections on Natural History* (New York: Norton, 1991), 428. The piece originally appeared in *Natural History,* vol. 96, no. 11 (1987): 416–30, and in somewhat different form in Stephen Jay Gould, *Rocks of Ages: Science and Religion in the Fullness of Life* (New York: Ballantine, 1999), 150–70.

41. The normal school is now Truman State University, in Kirksville, Missouri, whose Pickler Memorial Library houses the Harry H. Laughlin Papers and a vast collection of other documents from the Eugenics Record Office and from which much of this information comes. The Laughlin papers are indexed at http://library.truman.edu/manuscripts/laughlinindex.htm (accessed Sept. 2008).

42. Mary Harriman was also the mother of Averell Harriman, one-term governor of New York, Franklin Roosevelt's ambassador to the Soviet Union and to Great Britain, and a prominent diplomat on countless other crucial fronts.

43. Copies of these studies and articles are filed with the Harry H. Laughlin Papers in the Pickler Memorial Library at Truman State University, www.eugenicsarchive.org/html/eugenics/static/archives/hla.html (accessed Sept. 2009) and

in the Eugenics Archive at the American Philosophical Society, which holds most of the materials from the Eugenics Record Office, www.amphilsoc.org/library/digcoll (accessed Sept. 2008).

44. Charles B. Davenport, *Heredity in Relation to Eugenics* (New York: Henry Holt, 1911), 211.

45. Harry H. Laughlin, *Report of the Committee to Study and to Report on the Best Practical Means to Cut Off the Defective Germ-Plasm in the American Population,* Eugenics Record Office Bulletin no. 10a (Cold Spring Harbor, N.Y., Feb. 1914), 7, 45–56, 58.

46. Higham, *Strangers in the Land,* 323; *Eugenical News: Current Record of Race Hygiene,* vol. 8 (1923): 53.

47. *Buck v. Bell,* 274 U.S. 200, 47 S. Ct. 584 (1927). There are countless legal analyses of the eugenic sterilization cases. One of the most succinct is Walter Berns, "*Buck v. Bell:* Due Process of Law?" *Western Political Quarterly,* vol. 6, no. 4 (Dec. 1953): 762–75. The *Buck v. Bell* decision, incidentally, was cited by lawyers for some of the Nazi defendants at the Nuremberg war crime trials.

48. Paul A. Lombardo, "Eugenic Sterilization Laws," Eugenics Archive, www.eugenicsarchive.org/html/eugenics/essay8text.html (accessed Sept. 2008).

49. Margaret Sanger, *The Pivot of Civilization* (New York: Brentano's, 1922), 45.

50. Margaret Sanger, "A Plan for Peace," *Birth Control Review* (Apr. 1932): 106.

51. Black, *War against the Weak,* 125ff.

52. There's a thoughtful discussion of Sanger's legacy in Esther Katz, "The Editor as Public Authority: Interpreting Margaret Sanger," *Public Historian,* vol. 17, no. 1 (Winter 1995): 41–50. Katz, who edited Sanger's papers, argues that while Sanger reflected the social biases of her time, her calls to eliminate the unfit were never based on race, only on personal characteristics. Still, Katz acknowledges her "dilemma."

53. "Eugenical Sterilization in Germany," *Eugenical News,* vol. 18, no. 5 (Sept.–Oct. 1933): 89–93.

54. Harry Laughlin letter to Carl Schneider, dean of the Faculty of Medicine, University of Heidelberg, May 28, 1936, image no. 1221, Harry H. Laughlin Papers, Pickler Memorial Library, Truman State University, Kirksville, Mo. Laughlin was one of forty-three foreigners honored at the ceremony, among them the Finnish composer Jean Sibelius, four other Americans, and one Canadian geologist who was on the Harvard faculty.

55. House Committee on Immigration and Naturalization, *Biological Aspects of Immigration: Hearings,* 66th Congress, 2nd session, Apr. 16–17, 1920, 3.

56. "Analysis of America's Modern Melting Pot," testimony of Harry H. Laughlin in *Hearings of the Committee on Immigration and Naturalization, House of Representatives,* 67th Congress, 3rd session, Nov. 21, 1922 (Washington, D.C.: Government Printing Office, 1923), 733.

57. Ibid., 740

58. Ibid., 737.

59. Ibid., 738.

60. Paul Popenoe, "In the Melting Pot," *Journal of Heredity,* vol. 14, no. 5 (Aug. 1923): 223.

61. "Europe as an Emigrant-Exporting Continent and America as an Immigrant-Receiving Nation," testimony of Harry H. Laughlin before House Committee on Immigration and Naturalization, 68th Congress, 1st session, Mar. 8, 1924, graph facing p. 1278.

62. "Analysis of America's Modern Melting Pot," testimony of Laughlin, 737; "Estimate of Comparative Natural Intelligence of the Total White and Foreign-Born Population of the United States," Lantern Slides, Black Case, Section 7,1730, Harry H. Laughlin Papers, Pickler Memorial Library, Truman State University, Kirksville, Mo.

63. Joseph M. Gillman, "Statistics and the Immigration Problem," *American Journal of Sociology,* vol. 30, no. 1 (July 1924): 38.

64. "Analysis of America's Modern Melting Pot," testimony of Laughlin, 748.

65. Gillman, "Statistics and the Immigration Problem," 48.

66. Ibid., 752.

67. "Europe as an Emigrant-Exporting Continent and America as an Immigrant-Receiving Nation," testimony of Laughlin, 1305

68. Ibid., 1278.

69. Ibid., 1277. Laughlin's proposal for examination and investigation of the hereditary qualifications of applicants for immigration visas was endorsed by Madison Grant and the other members of the Subcommittee on Selective Immigration of the Eugenics Committee of America. Madison Grant et al., "Third Report of the Sub-Committee on Selective Immigration of the Eugenics Committee of America," *Journal of Heredity,* vol. 16 (1925): 293–98.

70. Terman, "Conservation of Talent," 363. This article was based on a speech Terman gave to the National Education Association the previous year, in 1923.

71. Karl Pearson, Galton's friend, colleague, and biographer, quoted in Daniel J. Kevles, *In the Name of Eugenics: Genetics and the Uses of Human Heredity* (New York: Knopf, 1985), 48.

72. David Heron, "Mendelism and the Problem of Mental Defect: A Criticism of Recent American Work," *Questions of the Day and of the Fray* (London), no. 7 (1913): 12, quoted in Hamish G. Spencer and Diane B. Paul, "The Failure of a Scientific Technique: David Heron, Karl Pearson and Mendelian Eugenics," *British Journal of the History of Science,* vol. 31 (1998): 443.

73. David Heron, "English Expert Attacks American Eugenic Work," *New York Times,* Nov. 9, 1913.

74. Nicole Hahn Rafter, *Creating Born Criminals: Biological Theories of Crime and Eugenics* (Urbana: University of Illinois Press, 1997), 161.

75. Charles B. Davenport, "American Work Strongly Defended," *New York Times,* Nov. 9, 1913.

76. Henry H. Goddard, "Feeblemindedness: A Question of Definition," *Journal of Psycho-Asthenics,* vol. 33 (1928): 224.

77. See, for example, Steven A. Gelb, "Spilled Religion: The Tragedy of Henry H. Goddard," *Mental Retardation* (June 1999): 240–41.

78. The SAT, as many educators know, is also under increasing attack. A growing number of colleges, regarding its value as a predictor of college success with growing skepticism (and perhaps increasingly unable to separate it from its legacy in IQ testing), have ceased requiring it.

79. Carl C. Brigham, "Intelligence Tests of Immigrant Groups," *Psychological Review,* vol. 37 (Mar. 1930): 164, 165.

80. Gould, *Mismeasure of Man,* 191.

81. Lewis M. Terman and Maud A. Merrill, *Measuring Intelligence: A Guide to the Administration of the New Revised Stanford-Binet Tests of Intelligence* (Boston: Houghton Mifflin, 1937), 30.

82. "Tax on Childless Urged for Nation," *New York Times,* June 6, 1937.

83. "Relaxing Quotas for Exiles Fought," *New York Times*, May 4, 1934.

84. Higham, *Strangers in the Land,* 327.

85. "Relaxing Quotas for Exiles Fought," *New York Times,* May 4, 1934; "Immigration Curb Is Urged in Survey," *New York Times,* June 8, 1939; Harry H. Laughlin, *Immigration and Conquest* (New York: Special Committee on Immigration and Naturalization of the Chamber of Commerce of the State of New York, 1939).

86. R. Hart Phillips, "907 Refugees Quit Cuba on Liner; Ship Reported Hovering Off Coast," *New York Times,* June 3, 1939. Some refugees were subsequently granted asylum by Britain, Belgium, and France; all but those in England would be caught by the Nazis in 1940 after the German invasion. Most would be sent to the gas chambers.

87. Box C 4–3:1, Henry H. Laughlin Papers, Pickler Memorial Library, Truman State University, Kirksville, Mo.

88. Quoted in "Immigration Curb."

89. "Aliens Defended in 'Race' Dispute," *New York Times,* July 23, 1939.

90. James D. Watson, *DNA: The Secret of Life* (New York: Knopf, 2003), 31–32.

91. Robin Shulman, "Scientist Retires after Race Remark," *Washington Post,* Oct. 26, 2007.

92. Robert Yerkes letter to Princeton University Press, quoted in David R. Hubin, "The Scholastic Aptitude Test: Its Development and Introduction, 1900–1948" (PhD dissertation, University of Oregon, 1988), 18; Brigham quoted in "Congress to Tighten Immigration Curb," *New York Times,* Jan. 27, 1927.

93. Gould, *Rocks of Ages,* 163ff.

94. Ibid., 164–70.

95. For some concise background on the test-prep industry, see, for example, Lemann, *Big Test,* 110–14, 227–29.

CHAPTER 4

1. "Europe as an Emigrant-Exporting Continent and America as an Immigrant-Receiving Nation," testimony of Harry H. Laughlin before House Committee on Immigration and Naturalization, 68th Congress, 1st session, Mar. 8, 1924, 1293.

2. *Immigration Act of Feb. 20, 1907, to Regulate the Immigration of Aliens into the United States, U.S. Statutes at Large* 34 (1905–7): 898.

3. Ibid.

4. "Europe as an Emigrant-Exporting Continent," testimony of Laughlin, 1248.

5. *U.S. Statutes at Large* 16 (1870): 256.

6. Marian L. Smith, "Race, Nationality and Reality: INS Administration of Racial Provisions in U.S. Immigration and Nationality Law Since 1898, Part I," *Prologue,* vol. 34, no. 2 (Summer 2002): 91–104, www.archives.gov/publications/prologue/2002/summer/immigration-law-1.html (accessed Aug. 2009); "The Racial Prerequisite Cases," in Ian Haney-López, *White by Law: The Legal Construction of Race* (New York: New York University Press, 1996), 163ff.

7. "Racial Prerequisite Cases," 163ff.

8. *Rollins v. State,* 18 Ala. App. 354, and 92 So. 35 (1922). The accused couple were both elderly; moreover, it appeared that a deputy extorted Jim Rollins's "confession" at gunpoint.

9. Quoted in David Katzman, *Before the Ghetto: Black Detroit in the Nineteenth Century* (Urbana: University of Illinois Press, 1973), 166.

10. John Tehranian, "Performing Whiteness: Naturalization Litigation and the Construction of Racial Identity in America," *Yale Law Journal,* vol. 109, no. 4 (Jan. 2000): 819.

11. Ibid., 821.

12. Kenneth Prewitt, "Beyond Census 2000: As a Nation, We Are the World," *Carnegie Reporter,* vol. 1, no. 3 (Fall 2001), www.carnegie.org/reporter/03/census/index.html (accessed Aug. 2009).

13. Mae M. Ngai, "The Strange Career of the Illegal Alien: Immigration Restriction and Deportation Policy in the United States, 1921–1965," *Law and History Review,* vol. 21, no. 1 (Spring 2003), www.historycooperative.org/journals/lhr/21.1/ngai.html (accessed Aug. 2008).

14. "Ellis Island Jam Halts Immigration," *New York Times,* Sept. 24, 1920.

15. "New Plea to Wilson," *New York Times,* Feb. 14, 1921.

16. Albert Johnson, report to accompany HR 14461, "Temporary Suspension of Immigration," 66th Congress, 3rd session, Dec. 6, 1920 (Washington, D.C.: Government Printing Office, 1920), 9–10.

17. In recent years, the racial theorist J. Philippe Rushton (about whom more in chapter 7) argued vehemently that Harry Laughlin and the intelligence testers had no impact on the national origins immigration quotas, and he castigated Stephen Jay Gould particularly for contending otherwise. J. Philippe Rushton, "The Mismeasure of Gould," *National Review,* Sept. 15, 1997, 30–34.

18. Pursuant to the ratification of the Seventeenth Amendment in 1913, all members of the Senate had been elected by popular vote, but its elitist House of Lords legacy remained (and often still remains) very much in evidence.

19. "Immigration Bill in the Senate Today," *New York Times,* Feb. 11, 1921; "Senate Limits Immigration to 355,461 a Year," *New York Times,* Feb. 20, 1921.

20. "Relief Is Promised for Ellis Island," *New York Times,* Mar. 24, 1921.

21. "Notified Too Late, Cunard Line Says . . . ," *New York Times,* Dec. 20, 1921; "Blame Ellis Island for Liners' Delays," *New York Times,* May 26, 1921; "Ships Await August to Land Immigrants," *New York Times,* July 28, 1921; "130 Americans Held on Ship off Coast," *New York Times,* July 30, 1921.

22. John B. Trevor, *An Analysis of the American Immigration Act of 1924* (New York: Carnegie Endowment for International Peace, 1924), 21–24. The full Trevor *Analysis* is also attached to Laughlin's "Europe as an Emigrant-Exporting Continent," testimony before the House Committee on Immigration and Naturalization, p. 1412.

23. Henry Fairfield Osborn, "Lo, the Poor Nordic," letter to the *New York Times,* Apr. 8, 1922.

24. Joseph W. Bendersky, *The Jewish Threat: Anti-Semitic Politics in the U.S. Army* (New York: Basic Books, 2000), 65–67.

25. "Europe as an Emigrant-Exporting Continent," testimony of Laughlin, 1277.

26. "U.S. Steel Growth a Billion in Value," *New York Times,* Apr. 17, 1923; "Harding Convinced of Labor Shortage," *New York Times,* Apr. 18, 1923.

27. "Harding Convinced."

28. John Higham, "American Immigration Policy in Historical Perspective," *Law and Contemporary Problems,* vol. 21, no. 2 (Spring 1956): 230.

29. Trevor, *Analysis,* 54–63.

30. "Analysis of America's Modern Melting Pot," testimony of Harry H. Laughlin in *Hearings of the Committee on Immigration and Naturalization, House of Representatives,* 67th Congress, 3rd session, Nov. 21, 1922 (Washington, D.C.: Government Printing Office, 1923), 757.

31. V.S. McClatchy, *Japanese Immigration and Colonization,* brief addressed to the secretary of state, July 18, 1921 (Washington, D.C.: Government Printing Office, 1921), 11–12.

32. The full text of the Japanese protest, accompanied by the response of Secretary of State Charles Evans Hughes, is in Trevor, *Analysis,* 65ff.

33. Quoted in Trevor, *Analysis,* 68.

34. Herbert Hoover, "Proclamation 1872, Limiting the Immigration of Aliens in the United States on the Basis of National Origin, March 22nd, 1929,"American Presidency Project, www.presidency.ucsb.edu/ws/index.php?pid=21838 (accessed Aug. 2009).

35. David A. Reed, "America of the Melting Pot Comes to End . . . ," *New York Times,* Apr. 27, 1924.

36. Ibid.

37. John B. Trevor, "Immigration Quotas: An Explanation of Their Methods and Their Practical Effects," *New York Times,* Aug. 14, 1925.

38. Trevor, *Analysis,* 7, 19.

39. Report of the secretary of labor for the year ending June 30, 1923, in "Europe as an Emigrant-Exporting Continent," testimony of Laughlin, 1377–79.

40. U.S. Department of Homeland Security, "Border Patrol History," July 15, 2003, www.cbp.gov/xp/cgov/border_security/border_patrol/border_patrol_ohs/history.xml (accessed Aug. 2008).

41. Arif Dirlik and Malcolm Yeung, *Chinese on the American Frontier* (Lanham, Md.: Rowan and Littlefield, 2003), 177.

42. "American History in Terms of Human Migration," testimony of Harry H. Laughlin before House Committee on Immigration and Naturalization, 70th Congress, 1st session, Mar. 7, 1928, 10–11.

43. Ibid., 13, 17.

44. Ibid., 16.

45. Higham, "American Immigration Policy in Historical Perspective," 230.

46. Ngai, "Strange Career of the Illegal Alien," 28.

47. National Commission on Law Observance and Enforcement (the Wickersham Commission), *Administration of Deportation Law* (Washington, D.C.: Government Printing Office, 1931), 137. Reuben Oppenheimer, a Baltimore lawyer, wrote most of the report, which was signed by nine of the commission's eleven members. Two thought it was too harsh on the government. In addition to Chairman Wickersham, the commission's members included Roscoe Pound, the dean of the Harvard law school; former secretary of war Newton D. Baker; Ada L. Comstock, the president of Radcliffe College; three federal judges; the former chief justice of the State of Washington; and several others. In its voluminous documents, the commission reported on every aspect of the crime problem, but its prime purpose was to struggle with the impossible task of enforcing Prohibition, which led to considerable public speculation about which members were closet wets. In the end, the commission seemed to conclude that Prohibition was impossible to police but that, with some fiddles to the Eighteenth Amendment, it should be retained. "Hoover's Message on the Wickersham Report," *New York Times*, Jan. 20, 1931.

48. Wickersham Commission, *Deportation*, 55.

49. Ibid., 69, 85.

50. Ibid., 137.

51. Ibid., 177.

52. National Commission on Law Observance and Enforcement (the Wickersham Commission), *Report on Crime and the Foreign Born* (Washington, D.C.: Government Printing Office, 1931), 400.

53. Wickersham Commission, *Crime*, 61.

54. "Dark Age Cruelty Charged in System for Deportations," *New York Times*, Aug. 8, 1931.

55. "Attacks as Biased Report on Aliens," *New York Times*, Aug. 10, 1931.

56. Ngai, "Strange Career of the Illegal Alien," 28.

57. Quoted from *Grizzly Bear* (Dec. 1927) in Emily K. Abel, "Only the Best Class of Immigration," *American Journal of Public Health*, vol. 94, no. 6 (June 2004): 932.

58. Edythe Tate-Thompson, "Introduction," in California Bureau of Tuberculosis, *A Statistical Study of Sickness among the Mexicans in the Los Angeles County Hospital, from July 1, 1922 to June 30, 1924* (Sacramento: California State Printing Office, 1925). See also Abel, "Only the Best Class of Immigration."

59. Charles M. Goethe, "To the Press," Mar. 21, 1935, copy of handout, document C-4–6, Harry H. Laughlin Papers, Pickler Memorial Library, Truman

State University, Kirksville, Mo., www.eugenicsarchive.org/html/eugenics/static/images/1049.html (accessed Sept. 2008); Charles M. Goethe letter to the *New York Times,* Sept. 15, 1935.

60. Kenneth Roberts, "The Docile Mexican," *Saturday Evening Post,* Mar. 10, 1928, 40.

61. Charles M. Goethe, "The Influx of Mexican Amerinds," *Eugenics,* vol. 2, no. 1 (1929): 6–9. There is a great deal of authoritative research on Goethe in Tony Platt's paper "What's in a Name? Charles M. Goethe, American Eugenics and Sacramento State University," www.csus.edu/cshpe/eugenics/docs/goethe_report.pdf (accessed Sept. 2008).

62. Charles M. Goethe, copy of unaddressed letter, Jan. 12, 1935, document D-2–4, Harry H. Laughlin Papers, Pickler Memorial Library, Truman State University, Kirksville, Mo., www.eugenicsarchive.org/eugenics/view_image.pl?id=1038 (accessed Aug. 2008).

63. Charles M. Goethe, "Filipino Immigration Viewed as a Peril," *Current History,* Jan. 1934, 354.

64. The marijuana ban in Utah, among the first states to outlaw the drug, appears to have been prompted by Mormons who, after having moved to Mexico when the state began to enforce the federal ban on polygamy, later moved back, bringing marijuana with them. In response, church leaders pressed the state to ban it. Charles Whitebread, "History of the Non-Medical Use of Drugs in the United States," speech to the California Judges Association, 1995, www.druglibrary.org/schaffer/History/whiteb1.htm (accessed Aug. 2008). In California, which in banning cannabis in 1913 was among the first states to do so, the impetus may not have come from the Mexican connection but simply from "the emergence of a new class of professional public policy bureaucrats with the authority and will to regulate drugs in California." Dale H. Gieringer, "The Forgotten Origins of Cannabis Prohibition in California," *Contemporary Drug Problems,* vol. 26, no. 2 (Summer 1999): 237–88, www.canorml.org/background/caloriginsmjproh.pdf (accessed Sept. 2008).

65. There has also been a long-running belief among critics of the marijuana laws that, as a large producer of paper pulp, Hearst didn't want competition from paper made of cheap hemp. But Hearst was as much a consumer of paper as he was a producer, so that contention remains dubious.

66. Anslinger's statement was allegedly made in congressional testimony in 1937, along with other inflammatory remarks, but the record doesn't show it. He did, however, add to the record a number of documents, all of which associate marijuana with Mexicans and describe marijuana, in the words of the New Orleans district attorney, "as a developer of criminals." Among those documents was a letter to Anslinger's agency from a newspaper editor in Colorado saying that the writer wished "I could show you what a small marihuana cigaret can do to one of our degenerate Spanish-speaking residents." Additional statements submitted by H. J. Anslinger in House Committee on Ways and Means, *Hearings on HR 6385, the Marijuana Tax Act,* 75th Congress, 1st session, Apr. 27–30 and May 4, 1937. See also David F. Musto, "The 1937 Marijuana Tax Act," *Archives of General Psychiatry,* vol. 26 (Feb. 1972): 419–40.

67. *Gary Post-Tribune,* Feb. 24, 1932, quoted in Neil Betten and Raymond A. Mohl, "From Discrimination to Repatriation: Mexican Life in Gary, Indiana, during the Great Depression," *Pacific Historical Review,* vol. 42, no. 3 (Aug. 1973): 374.

68. *Gary Post-Tribune,* Jan. 14, 1932, quoted in Betten and Mohl, "From Discrimination to Repatriation," 379.

69. Wendy Koch, "U.S. Urged to Apologize for 1930s Deportations," *USA Today,* Apr. 5, 2006.

70. Exceptions to this blind spot are Paul Taylor, *Mexican Labor in the United States* (Berkeley: University of California Press, 1928–34) and, recently, Francisco E. Balderrama and Raymond Rodriguez, *Decade of Betrayal* (Albuquerque: University of New Mexico Press, 2003).

71. And the warning Smoot-Hawley should still represent for those tempted to flirt with protectionism in our own times.

CHAPTER 5

1. Matthew Frye Jacobson, *Whiteness of a Different Color: European Immigrants and the Alchemy of Race* (Cambridge, Mass.: Harvard University Press, 1998), 12.

2. "Ford and Sapiro Settle Libel Suit," *New York Times,* July 17, 1927. The suit was filed by Aaron Sapiro, leader of an agricultural cooperative movement who had been accused by Ford's paper of defrauding farmers.

3. "Disraeli of America—a Jew of Super Power," *Dearborn Independent,* Nov. 27, 1920.

4. Henry Ford, "How the 'Jewish Question' Touches the Farm," reprinted from the *Dearborn Independent* in *The International Jew—The World's Foremost Problem,* www.churchoftrueisrael.com/Ford/original/ijtoc.html (accessed Aug. 2009).

5. "Does a Definite Jewish World Program Exist?" *Dearborn Independent,* July 10, 1920.

6. "An Address to 'Gentiles' on the Jewish Problem," *Dearborn Independent,* Jan. 14, 1922.

7. "Berlin Heard Ford Is Backing Hitler," *New York Times,* Dec. 20, 1922.

8. The new Klan was in part inspired by the lynching in 1915 of Leo Frank, the Jewish manager of an Atlanta pencil factory, who, in an infamous trial, was convicted in the killing of Mary Phagan, a worker in his factory. When his death sentence was commuted to life imprisonment, a mob that included some of the leading citizens of Marietta, Georgia, stormed the state prison and hanged Franks. Later that year, a group calling itself the Knights of Mary Phagan burned a cross on a nearby hilltop and became the core of the new secret Klan. No one has ever been charged with the Frank lynching.

9. Glen Jeansonne, *Gerald L.K. Smith, Minister of Hate* (Baton Rouge: Louisiana State University Press, 2007), 188–206. Smith's "Sacred Projects" have helped make Eureka Springs a major tourist attraction. The new "Great Passion Play" with "new dialogue" and "hundreds of actors and live animals" continues

to be performed in a 4,100-seat amphitheater five nights a week from May to late October. There's also a Holy Land Tour, a Sacred Art Center, and, of course, Smith's Christ of the Ozarks statue. Eureka Springs Advertising and Promotions Commission Web site, www.eurekasprings.org/things-to-do (accessed Sept. 2008).

10. Coughlin radio address, Dec. 11, 1938, audio in the Internet Archive, http://ia341217.us.archive.org/1/items/Father_Coughlin/FatherCoughlin_1938-12-11_JewsSupportCommunism.mp3 (accessed Aug. 2009). See also *Father Coughlin, His "Facts" and Arguments* (New York: American Jewish Committee, American Jewish Congress, and B'nai Brith, 1939), 11ff.

11. Charles Coughlin, "The National Union for Social Justice," radio address, Nov. 11, 1934, www.ssa.gov/history/fcspeech.html (accessed Aug. 2009).

12. Charles Coughlin, "A Reply to General Hugh Johnson," radio address, Mar. 11, 1935, www.ssa.gov/history/fcspeech.html (accessed Aug. 2009).

13. But no one called Townsend's plan a "stimulus package," a phrase that hadn't yet been coined.

14. Charles Coughlin, "Persecution—Jewish and Gentile," radio broadcast, Nov. 20, 1938, transcript and audio published on David Duke's Web site, www.stormfront.org/forum/showthread.php/father-charles-e-coughlin-1938-518742.html (accessed Sept. 2008).

15. Charles Coughlin, untitled radio address, Jan. 8, 1939, audio at the Internet Archive, www.archive.org/details/Father_Coughlin; also quoted at www.fathercoughlin.org/father-coughlin-quotes html and elsewhere (both accessed Aug. 2009). Coughlin was wrong on this point: since Jews had been declared stateless by Hitler, they weren't citizens of Germany either.

16. Charles A. Lindbergh, "Geography, Aviation and Race," *Reader's Digest* (Nov. 1939): 64–67. The article is still posted on various neo-Nazi Web sites.

17. Wayne Coffey, "The Queen and Her Court," *New York Daily News,* Aug. 26, 2007.

18. Bosley Crowther, "'Gentleman's Agreement,' Study of Anti-Semitism, Is Feature at Mayfair—Gregory Peck Plays Writer Acting as Jew," *New York Times,* Nov. 12, 1947; William Du Bois, "Schuyler Green's Metamorphosis," *New York Times Book Review,* Mar. 2, 1947.

19. George F. Custen, "Over 50 Years, a Landmark Loses Some of its Luster," *New York Times,* Nov. 16, 1997. Ironically, Representative Thomas, who was himself later convicted of taking kickbacks from friends he'd put on his congressional payroll, would serve in the same federal prison where some of the Hollywood Ten were incarcerated.

20. David R. Roediger, *Working toward Whiteness* (New York: Basic Books, 2005), 13.

21. "If we had refused admission to the 16,500,000 foreign-born who are living in this country today, we would have no unemployment problem to distress and harass us." Martin Dies, "America for Americans," radio address, May 6, 1935, transcript in *Congressional Record,* vol. 79, 74th Congress, 1st session, May 10, 1935, 10.

22. It probably does not need saying that a lot of other nations—Switzerland, among others, and Britain, in severely restricting immigration to Palestine—behaved no more honorably in opening their doors to refugees from the Nazis and, in some instances, behaved much worse.

23. Rafael Medoff, "The Day the Rabbis Marched," the David S. Wyman Institute for Holocaust Studies, www.wymaninstitute.org/special/rabbimarch/pg02.php (accessed Sept. 2008).

24. "Text of Truman's Statement on the Refugee Bill," *New York Times,* June 26, 1948. Truman also said that if Congress hadn't delayed the bill until just before adjournment, he would have vetoed it. This was the famous Eightieth "Do Nothing" Congress that Truman relentlessly attacked in his reelection campaign that fall.

25. "Table 2, Region of Birth of the Foreign-Born Population: 1850 to 1930 and 1960 to 1990," in Campbell J. Gibson and Emily Lennon, "Historical Census Statistics on the Foreign-Born Population of the United States: 1850–1990," Population Division Working Paper No. 29, U.S. Bureau of the Census, Feb. 1999, www.census.gov/population/www/documentation/twps0029/twps0029.html (accessed Sept. 2008).

26. Anthony Leviero, "Presses for Rights; President Acts Despite Split in His Party Over the Chief Issue," *New York Times,* July 27, 1948. On the same day, Truman also ordered creation of a fair-employment policy in the rest of the federal government. That fall, Senator Strom Thurmond of South Carolina, who had joined other segregationist southern Democrats in walking out of the Democratic National Convention, would run against Truman. Although he finished third, it would be the first big break in what had long been regarded as the safely Solid South.

27. Warren would later, of course, become chief justice of the United States on the Court that declared racial segregation unconstitutional and whose decisions made the "Warren Court" a synonym for expansive, liberal interpretations of the Constitution.

28. It was never certain to what extent the Zoot Suit riots of 1943 were provoked by the *pachucos* in their pegged pants, who had wandered out of the Latino neighborhoods and thus into foreign territory, and to what extent the real provocation came from the servicemen. What was clear was that the cops and the newspapers blamed the Latinos. Gene Sherman, "Youth Gangs Leading Cause of Delinquencies," *Los Angeles Times,* June 2, 1943; "Not a Race Issue, Mayor Says," *New York Times,* June 10, 1943; "Zoot Suit War," *Time,* June 21, 1943, www.time.com/time/magazine/article/0,9171,766730,00.html (accessed Aug. 2008).

29. Jennifer L. Hochschild, *Facing Up to the American Dream: Race, Class and the Soul of the Nation* (Princeton, N.J.: Princeton University Press, 1995), 243.

30. Roediger, *Working toward Whiteness,* 148–49.

31. Michael Novak, *Unmeltable Ethnics: Politics and Culture in American Life* (Edison, N.J.: Transaction Books, 1995), lvii. This is a revised paperback edition of the book that was originally published in 1972 as *The Rise of the Unmeltable Ethnics.*

32. Roediger, *Working toward Whiteness,* 149.

33. Mae M. Ngai, "The Strange Career of the Illegal Alien: Immigration Restriction and Deportation Policy in the United States, 1921–1965," *Law and History Review,* vol. 21, no. 1 (Spring 2003), www.historycooperative.org/journals/lhr/21.1/ngai.html (accessed Aug. 2008).

34. "Repeal of the Chinese Exclusion Act, 1943," U.S. State Department, www.state.gov/r/pa/ho/time/wwii/86552.htm (accessed Sept. 2008).

35. Cited in Mae M. Ngai, "Braceros, 'Wetbacks' and the Boundaries of Class," in Marc S. Rodriguez, *Repositioning North American Migration History* (Rochester, N.Y.: University of Rochester Press, 2004), 241.

36. Interview with Ed Idar, from *Justice for My People: The Dr. Hector P. Garcia Story,* produced by Jeff Felts for WEDT-TV, Corpus Christi, Tex., 2007, www.justiceformypeople.org/interview_idar.html.

37. "Wetbacks: Can the States Act to Curb Illegal Entry?" *Stanford Law Review,* vol. 6, no. 2 (Mar. 1954): 287.

38. Summary of the Immigration and Nationality Act of 1952 (McCarran-Walter Act), U.S. Department of State, www.state.gov/r/pa/ho/time/cwr/87719.htm# (accessed Sept. 2008).

39. For a full biography of a man who, as a native of the Silver State, began as a follower of populist William Jennings Bryan, gained fame in Mary Pickford's sensational (in 1920) suit for divorce so she could marry Douglas Fairbanks Jr., and ended as a red-baiting bigot, see Michael J. Ybarra, *Washington Gone Crazy: Senator Pat McCarran and the Great American Communist Hunt* (Hanover, N.H.: Steerforth Press, 2004).

40. "Celler Criticizes Policy on Refuges," *New York Times,* Apr. 5, 1943.

41. *The Immigration and Nationality Act of 1952 (McCarran-Walter Act),* www.state.gov/r/pa/ho/time/cwr/87719.htm# (accessed Sept. 2008).

42. *McCarran-Walter Act of 1952,* Public Law 82–414, 82nd Congress, 2nd session, *U.S. Statutes at Large* 66 (1952), 163–282; *Internal Security Act of 1950,* Public Law 81–831, 81st Congress, 2nd session, *U.S. Statutes at Large* 64 (1950), 998.

43. "Texts of President Truman's Speeches at Cleveland and Buffalo," *New York Times,* Oct. 10, 1952.

44. Charles Mohr, "President Asks for Ending of Quotas for Immigrants," *New York Times,* Jan. 14, 1965.

45. Richard Alba and Victor Nee, *Remaking the American Mainstream: Assimilation and Contemporary Immigration* (Cambridge, Mass.: Harvard University Press, 2003), 285–86.

46. Nathan Glazer and Daniel Patrick Moynihan, *Beyond the Melting Pot* (Cambridge, Mass.: MIT Press, 1963), v.

47. Will Herberg, *Protestant, Catholic, Jew: An Essay in American Religious Sociology* (Chicago: University of Chicago Press, 1983), 187–90.

CHAPTER 6

1. *Plyler v. Doe,* 457 U.S. 202 (1982).

2. Howard Jarvis, "Illegal Aliens Take Free Ride on Gravy Train," *Sacramento Bee,* Sept. 17, 1978. (In the interest of full disclosure, I was the editor of the paper's editorial pages at the time.)

3. "Chance of Amnesty Extension Appears Dead," *New York Times,* Apr. 29, 1988.

4. Roberto Suro, "Migrants' False Claims: Fraud on a Huge Scale," *New York Times,* Nov. 12, 1989.

5. Douglas S. Massey, Jorge Durand, and Nolan J. Malone, *Beyond Smoke and Mirrors* (New York: Russell Sage Foundation, 2002), 120.

6. See, for example, Elisabeth Malkin, "Nafta's Promise Unfulfilled," *New York Times,* Mar. 24, 2009. NAFTA, of course, also tied Mexico far more closely to the economic cycles in the United States.

7. California Constitution (1849), Article XI, Section 21, California State Archives, www.sos.ca.gov/archives/level3_const1849txt.html (accessed Aug. 2009).

8. Peter Schrag, "The Issue in Waiting," *Sacramento Bee,* Apr. 21, 1993.

9. Pamela Burdman, "White Supremacist Link Trips Prop. 187," *San Francisco Chronicle,* Oct. 13, 1994; "Radio Ad Opposes Proposition 187," *Sacramento Bee,* Oct. 12, 1994; Brad Hayward, "Immigration Measure Foes Level Charge," *Sacramento Bee,* Sept. 10, 1994.

10. Peter Schrag, *California: America's High Stakes Experiment* (Berkeley: University of California Press, 2006), 83; Peter Andreas, *Border Games: Policing the U.S.-Mexico Divide* (Ithaca, N.Y.: Cornell University Press, 2000), 87.

11. Democrats have also dominated the state legislature and the state's large congressional delegation. The Democratic caucuses in both the legislature and the California congressional contingent have sizable proportions of women and Latinos. The Republicans have almost none of either.

12. Wayne A. Cornelius, Scott Borger, Adam Sawyer, David Keyes, Clare Appleby, Kristen Parks, Gabriel Lozada, and Jonathan Hicken, *Controlling Unauthorized Immigration from Mexico: The Failure of "Prevention Through Deterrence" and the Need for Comprehensive Reform* (Washington, D.C.: Immigration Policy Center, June 10, 2008), www.immigrationpolicy.org/images/file/misc/CCISbriefing061008.pdf (accessed Oct. 2, 2008). Cornelius and his colleagues found that tighter border enforcement was not much of a deterrent, despite the increased dangers. "The end result of a border buildup," agreed Massey and his colleagues in another study, "is typically longer trip durations, lower probabilities of return migration and a shift toward permanent settlement. Geographic diffusion combined with a shift toward permanence guarantees that the effects of Mexican immigration—positive or negative—on the United States are maximized." Massey, Durand, and Malone, *Beyond Smoke and Mirrors,* 129.

13. Jeffrey S. Passel, *The Size and Characteristics of the Unauthorized Migrant Population in the U.S.* (Washington, D.C.: Pew Hispanic Center, Mar. 7, 2006), 2.

14. AnnaLee Saxenian, "Silicon Valley's New Immigrant Entrepreneurs," Working Paper No. 15, University of California Center for Comparative

Immigration Studies, San Diego, May 2000, www.ccis-ucsd.org/publications/wrkg15.pdf (accessed Aug. 2008).

15. Michael Lewis, "The Search Engine," *New York Times Magazine,* Oct. 10, 1999.

16. *Illegal Immigration Reform and Immigrant Responsibility Act of 1996,* Public Law 104–208, 104th Congress, 2nd session, *U.S. Statutes at Large* 110 (1996), Title V, Section 505.

17. One early reviewer of this manuscript has argued, correctly, that *Latinos* in the affirmative action context is a homogenizing term. But it's this term or synonyms like *Hispanics* that are used as catchall categories for assigning affirmative action preferences. It's true, as he says, that Mexican Americans or their forebears were often victims of discrimination (as were Jews, Catholics, the Chinese, and others), but there was no legally enforced Mexican slavery or slave trade. Now it's often the Jews and Chinese who are disadvantaged by affirmative action. In any case, the "broad brush" to which he objects is the same broad brush that opponents of race preferences object to in their distrust of all policies based on ethnic-group classifications.

18. Nancy Mitchell, "Colorado Hands English Immersion Backer His First Loss," *Rocky Mountain News,* Nov. 6, 2002. See also Eric Hubler, "Amendment 31: Bilingual Ed Backers Found Ally in Parents," *Denver Post,* Nov. 7, 2002.

19. Mark Leibovich, "'Pit Bull' of the House Latches on to Immigration," *New York Times,* July 11, 2006.

20. *Border Protection, Antiterrorism, and Illegal Immigration Control Act of 2005,* HR 4437, 109th Congress, 2nd session, Section 274(a)(1)(E), http://74.125.155.132/search?q=cache:uPhdIPmaTfcJ:thomas.loc.gov/cgi-bin/cpquery/%3F%26sid%3Dcp109ose4T%26refer%3D%26r_n%3Dhr345p1.109%26db_id%3D109%26item%3D%26sel%3DTOC_436004%26+%22+shields+from+detection%22,+%22alien+who+lacks+lawful+authority%22&cd=2&hl=en&ct=clnk&gl=us&client=firefox-a (accessed Aug. 2009).

21. Sensenbrenner interview on *Lou Dobbs Tonight,* CNN, Apr. 1, 2006, http://transcripts.cnn.com/TRANSCRIPTS/0604/01/ldt.01.html (accessed Sept. 2008).

22. Call-in press conference conducted by the National Immigration Forum, Washington, D.C., Feb. 7, 2008.

23. Probably the most contentious was HR 4088, the Secure America through Verification and Enforcement Act of 2007 (SAVE), sponsored by Colorado Republican Tom Tancredo, California Republican Brian Bilbray, and North Carolina Democrat Heath Shuler, who was elected from a swing district in the Democrats' near landslide in 2006. Among other provisions, the bill would have resulted in the detention in many more children of illegal aliens.

24. Bill O'Reilly, in his syndicated radio broadcast, May 1, 2006, transcribed by Media Matters, http://mediamatters.org/items/200605030009 (accessed Sept. 2008).

25. *The Situation Room,* CNN, April 10, 2006, http://transcripts.cnn.com/transcripts/0604/10/sitroom.03.html (accessed Sept. 2008).

26. Eunice Moscoso, "Radio Hosts Converge on D.C. to Fight 'Amnesty,'" Cox News Service, Apr. 25, 2007; "Hold Their Feet to the Fire: A National

Drive for Immigration Reform," FAIR handout, Apr. 2007, www.fairus.org/site/PageServer?pagename=feettothefire07 (accessed June 2008).

27. Nicole Gaouette, "Senators Reject Legal Status for Children of Immigrants," *Los Angeles Times*, Oct. 24, 2007.

28. Robert Pear, "Little-Known Group Claims Win on Immigration," *New York Times*, July 15, 2007.

29. David Simcox, "The Catholic Church's War on Borders," *Social Contract*, vol. 5, no. 3 (Spring 1995), www.thesocialcontract.com/artman2/publish/tsc0503/article_451.shtml (accessed Aug. 2009).

30. Pear, "Little-Known Group."

31. "Memo from John Tanton to WITAN IV Attendees," Oct. 10, 1986, reported in *Southern Poverty Law Center Intelligence Report*, www.splcenter.org/intel/intelreport/article.jsp?sid=125 (accessed May 2008). On the publicity-shy Tanton generally, see Christopher Hayes, "Keeping America Empty," *In These Times*, Apr. 24, 2006, www.inthesetimes.com/article/2608/keeping_america_empty (accessed Aug. 2009).

32. Terry M. Neal, "Schwarzenegger Is No One-Dimensional Character," *Washington Post*, Aug. 13, 2003.

33. Wayne Lutton and John Tanton, *The Immigration Invasion* (Petoskey, Mich.: Social Contract Press, 1994).

34. Charlotte Hsu, "Union Rescinds Support: Turner Snubbed over Immigration Stance," *San Bernardino Sun*, Oct. 24, 2006.

35. Immigrant Policy Project, *2007 Enacted State Legislation Related to Immigrants and Immigration* (Washington, D.C.: National Conference of State Legislatures, Jan. 31, 2008), www.ncsl.org/print/immig/2007Immigrationfinal.pdf (accessed Sept. 2008); *State Laws Related to Immigrants and Immigration January 1–June 30, 2008* (Washington, D.C.: National Conference of State Legislatures, July 24, 2008), www.ncsl.org/print/immig/immigreportjuly2008.pdf (accessed Sept. 2008).

36. The Gears story is in Randy Kennedy, "Texas Mayor Caught in Deportation Furor," *New York Times*, Apr. 5, 2009. The others are in Immigration Policy Project.

37. Peter Schrag, "Divided States," *The Nation*, Jan. 7, 2008, 16–20.

38. Randal C. Archibold, "Arizona County Uses New Law to Look for Illegal Immigrants," *New York Times*, May 10, 2006. In October 2008, without notifying city officials, Arpaio sent sixty "heavily armed" deputies on night raids to the Mesa, Arizona, city hall and a local public library to arrest three or four janitors that law enforcement regarded as illegal aliens. The raid was part of Arpaio's policy to stop drivers, raid workplaces, and pursue other actions in his search for illegal immigrants. Paul Giblin, "Arizona Sheriff Conducts Raid at City Hall, Angering Officials," *New York Times*, Oct. 17, 2008. See also Timothy Egan, "Disorder at the Border," *New York Times*, Mar. 29, 2008.

39. "Arpaio's America," *New York Times*, Feb. 5, 2009; "Enforcement without Oversight: Marching Immigrants through the Public Square as Criminals Run Free," National Immigration Forum press release, Feb. 4, 2009.

40. *Chicanos por La Causa, Inc. v. Napolitano*, 544 F.3d 976 (9th Cir. 2008).

41. Carey Gillam, "States Turning Up Heat on Illegal Immigrants," Reuters, Nov. 1, 2007.

42. Tom Padgett and Dolly Mascareñas, "Can a Mother Lose Her Child Because She Doesn't Speak English?" *Time*, Aug. 27, 2009, www.time.com/time/nation/article/0,8599,1918941,00.html (accessed Aug. 2009).

43. Rose A. Zitiello and Richard T. Herman, "Reclaiming Cleveland's Immigrant Entrepreneurs," *Cool Cleveland*, May 5, 2004, www.coolcleveland.com/index.php/Main/ReclaimingClevelandImmigrantEntrepreneurs (accessed Aug. 2009); Neal Pierce, "Cities Scramble for Immigrants," *Nation's Cities Weekly*, May 17, 2004.

44. Randal C. Archibold, "Phoenix Police to Check Arrestees for Immigrant Status," *New York Times*, Feb. 16, 2008.

45. Riverside also got hit by a couple of costly lawsuits that helped change its mind. Ken Belson and Jill P. Capuzzo, "Towns Rethink Laws against Illegal Immigrants," *New York Times*, Sept. 26, 2007.

46. William M. Welch, "Nevada Town to Fine for Foreign Flags," *USA Today*, Nov. 11, 2006. Not long after the town passed the ordinance, the county sheriff announced that he wouldn't enforce it.

47. The recall campaign was already under way when Governor Davis, in an effort to increase Latino support for retaining him in office, signed the bill. But, especially with the conservative radio talkers, the signature was one more major reason to attack him.

48. The California case is *Martinez v. Regents*, Third District Court of Appeals, C054124 (Sept. 15, 2008). The Kansas case is *Day v. Bond*, U.S. Circuit Court of Appeals for the Tenth Circuit, No. 05–3309 (Aug. 30, 2007).

49. This letter, from a man in rural Northern California, was one of many similar ones, some of them much less polite, sent or forwarded to me in 2007 and 2008.

50. Anna Gorman, "Escondido Tries to Rid Itself of Undocumented Immigrants," *Los Angeles Times*, July 13, 2008.

51. Daniel Hopkins, "Threatening Changes: Explaining Where and When Immigrants Provoke Local Opposition," unpublished paper, Center for the Study of American Politics, Yale University, May 16, 2008, http://people.iq.harvard.edu/~dhopkins/immpap75tot.pdf (accessed Sept. 2008).

52. "Schwarzenegger: Don't Blame State Budget Deficit on Illegal Immigrants," *Sacramento Bee*, June 6, 2009.

53. Tarrance Group poll for the Manhattan Institute and National Immigration Forum, Apr. 2007, www.manhattan-institute.org/pdf/Key_Findings_Summary_04–2007TJ.pdf (accessed Sept. 2008). Various polls done in 2007, 2008, and 2009 for the *Washington Post*, CBS, and ABC show similar acceptance of immigrants already in the United States. See www.pollingreport.com/immigration.htm.

54. "The Yes, No and Maybe on Driver's Licenses," debate text, *New York Times*, Nov. 1, 2007; Laura Kellams, "Huckabee Plan Would Give Aid to Illegal Aliens," *Arkansas Democrat-Gazette*, Jan. 12, 2005; Foon Rhee, "Huckabee, Romney Fight over Illegal Immigration," Political Intelligence blog, *Boston Globe*, Nov. 14, 2007, www.boston.com/news/politics/politicalintelligence/2007/11/

huckabee_romney.html (accessed Sept. 2008). Evangelist Huckabee defended his support for tuition by saying that the sins of the fathers shouldn't be visited on their innocent children, but he nonetheless proposed an immigration plan that would require all illegal aliens to leave the country before they had a chance to become legal residents. On Boxer and schooling, see Peter Schrag, "Other People's Children," *Sacramento Bee,* Aug. 25, 1993.

55. Donna Leinwand, "Immigration Raid Linked to ID Theft, Says Chertoff," *USA Today,* Dec. 13, 2006.

56. David Kelly, "Fired Border Patrol Agent Alleges Quota Pressure in Inland Empire," *Los Angeles Times,* Feb. 8, 2009.

57. Solomon Moore, "Push on Immigration Crimes Said to Shift Focus," *New York Times,* Jan. 12, 2009.

58. Julia Preston, "270 Illegal Immigrants Sent to Prison in Federal Push," *New York Times,* May 24, 2008; Samuel G. Freedman, "Immigrants Find Solace after Storm of Arrests," *New York Times,* July 12, 2008; Mary Ann Zehr, "Iowa School District Left Coping with Immigration Raid's Impact," *Education Week,* May 21, 2008.

59. Julia Preston, "Meatpacker Faces Charges of Violating Child Laws," *New York Times,* Sept. 8, 2008.

60. Joey Kurtzman, "How to Avert Future Jewish Catastrophes in One Easy Step!" *Jewry: What Matters Now,* Aug. 10, 2008, www.jewcy.com/tags/kosher (accessed Sept. 2008). Not surprisingly, the disclosures of the Agriprocessors conditions were no surprise to some Orthodox Jews. Kurtzman talks about how the Orthodox Union had certified a "splendidly profitable but ethically abominable slaughterhouse run by Orthodox Jews." In a 1995 case, the National Labor Relations Board (NLRB) found that Cherry Hill Enterprises, a New Jersey textile dyeing and finishing firm owned by Rubashkin and his son Moshe, had "a proclivity for labor law violations." In this instance, they failed to remit to the union dues they'd deducted from employee wages. But the NLRB found it wasn't the company's first offense. *Cherry Hill Textiles, Inc. and United Production Workers Union, Local 17–18,* Case No. 29-CA 17848, in *Decisions of the National Labor Relations Board,* vol. 318, no. 40, 400.

61. *Annual Report: Immigration Enforcement Actions, 2006* (Washington, D.C.: Office of Immigration Statistics, Department of Homeland Security, May 2008), www.dhs.gov/ximgtn/statistics/publications (accessed Sept. 2008).

62. The numbers are themselves in dispute. The nonpartisan Migration Policy Institute concurs that the number of illegal immigrants, which had been climbing, leveled off in 2008, but raises doubts whether that's due to departures or to a drop in new arrivals. Demetrios G. Papademetriou and Aaron Terrazas, *Immigrants and the Current Economic Crisis: Research Evidence, Policy Implication and Challenges* (Washington, D.C.: Migration Policy Institute, Jan. 2009).

63. Michael Chertoff, "Myth vs. Fact: Worksite Enforcement," *Department of Homeland Security Leadership Journal* (July 9, 2008), www.dhs.gov/journal/leadership/2008/07/myth-vs-fact-worksite-enforcement.html (accessed Oct. 2008); Steven A. Camarota and Karen Jensenius, *Homeward Bound: Recent Immigration Enforcement and the Decline in the Illegal Alien Population*

(Washington, D.C.: Center for Immigration Studies, July 2008); author telephone interview with Steven Camarota, Aug. 9, 2008. See also Peter Schrag, "What's Driving Illegal Immigrants Home?" *Sacramento Bee,* Aug. 12, 2008; and Cornelius et al., *Controlling Unauthorized Immigration from Mexico.* At the same time that thousands of workers were moving back to their home countries, a growing number of Mexican professionals, especially those fearing the increasing drug violence along the border, were scrabbling to move north. "Immigrants or Refugees," *FNS News,* June 25, 2008, www.nmsu.edu/~frontera (accessed June 2008). This is the invaluable Web site of Frontera Norte Sur, a center at New Mexico State University that compiles, summarizes, and distributes major border-related stories from the Mexican media.

64. See, for example, John Higham, "Origins of Immigration Restriction, 1882–1897: A Social Analysis," *Mississippi Valley Historical Review,* vol. 39, no. 1 (June 1952): 82. American xenophobia in the last decades of the nineteenth century, Higham argues, was generated more by the larger crisis in the American social order—the emergence of the trusts and growing industrial unrest—than by racism or religion. That may be partly true of the anger directed at illegal immigrants in the first decade of the twenty-first century as well.

65. "Adopted Resolutions," 76th U.S. Conference of Mayors, June 20–24, 2008, www.usmayors.org/resolutions/76th_conference/csj_15.asp (accessed Nov. 2008).

66. Nicole Gaouette, "Federal Prosecution of Illegal Immigrants Soars," *Los Angeles Times,* June 18, 2008.

67. Patrick Healy, "Two Conventions with No Shortage of Contrasts," *New York Times,* Sept. 4, 2008. The percentage of blacks in St. Paul was the lowest at any GOP convention since 1964. *Blacks and the 2008 Republican National Convention* (Washington, D.C.: Joint Center for Political and Economic Studies, Aug. 2008), 17.

68. Norman Mailer, "Miami Beach and Chicago," *Harper's,* Nov. 1968, 41ff, later published in somewhat expanded form as *Miami and the Siege of Chicago* (New York: New American Library, 1968) and republished in 2008 in a new edition by the *New York Review of Books.*

69. By contrast, the white vote increased by less than 500,000. "Latino and Asian Clout in the Voting Booth," Immigration Policy Center, Aug. 13, 2009.

CHAPTER 7

1. Data from Kelly Jefferys and Randall Monger, *U.S. Legal Permanent Residents: 2007,* Annual Flow Report (Washington, D.C.: Office of Immigration Statistics, Department of Homeland Security, Mar. 2008), table 2, www.dhs.gov/xlibrary/assets/statistics/publications/LPR_FR_2007.pdf (accessed Sept. 2008). The best study of the number of illegal residents securing a change of status to legalization, mainly through family or employer sponsorship, estimates that over 40 percent of legalized immigrants in 2003 had been in this country either as illegal border crossers or visa overstayers. In California, it's over 50 percent. Laura Hill and Joseph Hayes, *Immigrant Pathways to Legal Permanent Residence: Now and Under a Merit-Based System* (San Francisco: Public Policy

Institute of California, June 2008), 8. But because, for a variety of reasons, the federal government classifies many of those newly legalized people as new arrivals, the percentages in this study can't be applied to the total number of changes of status reported by the federal government. The official statistical scheme also suggests that of the four hundred thousand legal admissions in 2006, some had been in the country illegally, then had returned home and reentered the United States with their legal documents. Nonetheless, even many Homeland Security officials appeared surprised at the large percentage of formerly illegal immigrants who became legal admits that Hill and Hayes reported in their study. Author telephone interview with Laura Hill, Oct. 29, 2008.

2. Jefferys and Monger, *U.S. Permanent Legal Residents: 2007,* 1–2; Jeffrey S. Passel and D'Vera Cohn, *Trends in Unauthorized Immigration: Undocumented Inflow Now Trails Legal Inflow* (Washington, D.C.: Pew Hispanic Center, Oct. 2, 2008), 2.

3. The statement comes from an interview with an immigration scholar in a federal agency who does not wish to be identified.

4. "Federal Strategies to End Border Violence," testimony of Sheriff Wayne Jernigan before Senate Judiciary Committee, 109th Congress, 2nd session, Mar. 1, 2006, www.sheriffs.org/userfiles/file/Congressional%20Testimony/Jernigan_Senate_Testimony_on_Border_Violence.pdf (accessed Sept. 2008).

5. Tom Tancredo, *In Mortal Danger: The Battle for America's Border and Security* (Nashville: WND Books, 2007), 86–87; Kevin Mooney, "Texas Sheriffs Say Terrorists Entering US from Mexico," CNS (Cybercast News Service), Aug. 21, 2006. The CNS story was picked up by many right-wing blogs and Web sites as well as by Tancredo for his book. See, for example, American Renaissance News, www.amren.com/mtnews/archives/2006/08/texas_sheriffs.php (accessed Aug. 2008). See also, Edward Royce, quoted in "Backgrounder: The Weaponization of Immigration" (Washington, D.C.: Center for Immigration Studies, Feb. 2008), 8. The author of the Center for Immigration Studies report is identified as an unnamed "former Senior Counsel" of the Justice Department, writing as "Cato," who warns, despite his acknowledgment that most of the 9/11 bombers were in the country legally, that "illegal immigration is the strategy and the tactic by which America has been attacked and without greater safeguards will be attacked."

6. *Lou Dobbs Tonight,* CNN, Apr. 14, 2005, http://edition.cnn.com/TRANSCRIPTS/0504/14/ldt.01.html (accessed Sept. 2008). See also the Mar. 17, 2005 broadcast of *Lou Dobbs Tonight* on YouTube, www.youtube.com/watch?v=AJipzBL4Lns (accessed Aug. 2009).

7. The film is *Illegal Aliens and America's Medicine.* It can be found at www.youtube.com/watch?v=Dmnt5ZhWTmw (accessed June 2008). "Most of these bastards," Cosman says on the tape, "rape [and] molest girls under twelve, though some specialize in boys and others in nuns." See also Jack Williams, "Madeleine Cosman, 68; Medical Lawyer, Author," obituary, *San Diego Union-Tribune,* Mar. 11, 2006.

8. In 2007, according to the Pew Research Center, the Pew Hispanic Center, the Pew Center on the States, and data from the Justice Department, one-third of all inmates in *federal* prisons were Latinos, nearly half of them sentenced for

immigration violations. But since federal prisons account for only about one in twelve of all inmates in U.S. prisons and jails—local, state, and federal—and since the Latino prison population is itself in large part the result of the concerted effort by the Justice Department in the last years of the Bush administration to crack down on illegal aliens, and since all those convicted of immigration law felonies are sent to federal prisons, Dobbs's statement that one-third of inmates in U.S. prisons are illegal immigrants is wildly misleading. See, for example, Pew Center on the States, *One in 100: Behind Bars in America 2008* (Washington, D.C.: Pew Charitable Trusts, Feb. 2008), www.pewcenteronthestates.org/uploadedFiles/One%20in%20100.pdf?sid=ST2008022803016 (accessed Oct. 2008); and Mark Hugo Lopez and Michael T. Light, *A Rising Share: Hispanics and Federal Crime* (Washington, D.C.: Pew Hispanic Center, Feb. 18, 2009), http://pewresearch.org/pubs/1124/hispanic-immigrant-crime-report (accessed Oct. 2008). See also Solomon Moore, "Hispanics Are Largest Ethnic Group in Federal Prisons, Study Shows," *New York Times,* Feb. 19, 2009.

9. *Just the Facts: Immigrants and Crime* (San Francisco: Public Policy Institute of California, June 2008). The institute reported very similar data for crime in California. See Kristin F. Butcher and Anne Morrison Piehl, *Crime, Corrections and California* (San Francisco: Public Policy Institute of California, Feb. 2008).

10. "Lou Dobbs: 'Advocacy Journalist?'" CBS *60 Minutes,* May 6, 2007. A CNN transcript of the exchange with Romans is at http://transcripts.cnn.com/transcripts/0705/07/ldt.01.html (accessed Sept. 2008). For a fuller report, see David Leonhardt, "Truth, Fiction and Lou Dobbs," *New York Times,* May 30, 2007. Dobbs, said Leonhardt, an economics columnist for the *Times* business section, "has a somewhat flexible relationship with reality."

11. Samuel P. Huntington, "The Hispanic Challenge," *Foreign Policy* (Mar.–Apr. 2004): 37; Samuel P. Huntington, *Who Are We? The Challenges to America's National Identity* (New York: Simon and Schuster, 2004), 176.

12. "Analysis of America's Modern Melting Pot," testimony of Harry H. Laughlin in *Hearings of the Committee on Immigration and Naturalization, House of Representatives,* 67th Congress, 3rd session, Nov. 21, 1922 (Washington, D.C.: Government Printing Office, 1923), 752, 755.

13. Huntington, "Hispanic Challenge," 37.

14. Huntington, *Who Are We?* 256. "If we flipped this omelet," said the Mexican writer Carlos Fuentes, "we'd find that the most widely spoken Western language is English. Does Huntington believe that this fact bespeaks a silent North American invasion of the entire world?" Carlos Fuentes, "Looking for Enemies in the Wrong Places," *Miami Herald,* Mar. 21, 2004.

15. Victor Davis Hanson, *Mexifornia: A State of Becoming* (San Francisco: Encounter Books, 2002), 148.

16. Victor Davis Hanson, "Mexifornia: Five Years Later," *City Magazine* (Winter 2007), http://www.city-journal.org/html/17_1_mexifornia.html (accessed Sept. 2008).

17. Edward A. Ross, *The Old World in the New* (New York: The Century Co., 1914), 285–86.

18. *Savage Nation* radio broadcast of Oct. 13, 2006. Many similar statements by Savage are quoted, presumably with his approval, on the white supremacist

Web site Stormfront.org. For an extensive profile on Savage/Weiner's career, see David Gilson, "Michael Savage's Long, Strange Trip," *Salon,* Mar. 5, 2003, http://dir.salon.com/story/news/feature/2003/03/05/savage (accessed Oct. 2008).

19. Richard J. Herrnstein and Charles Murray, *The Bell Curve: Intelligence and Class Structure in American Life* (New York: Free Press, 1994), 348ff; Paul A. Lombardo, "The American Breed: Nazi Eugenics and the Origins of the Pioneer Fund," *Albany Law Review,* vol. 65, no. 3 (2002): 747; Grace Lichtenstein, "Fund Backs Controversial Study of 'Racial Betterment,'" *New York Times,* Dec. 11, 1977. Among the Pioneer Fund's other postwar grantees were Arthur Jensen of Berkeley; J. Philippe Rushton of the University of Western Ontario, who now heads the fund; Linda Gottfredson of the University of Maryland; Richard Lynn of the University of Ulster; and Garret Hardin of the University of California at Santa Barbara. A longer list can be found at www.pioneerfund .org. Henry E. Garrett was also an advisor to Wickliffe Draper.

20. Herrnstein and Murray, *Bell Curve*, 564.

21. Stephen Metcalf, "Moral Courage: Is Defending *The Bell Curve* an Example of Intellectual Honesty?" *Slate,* Oct. 17, 2005, www.slate.com/id/ 2128199 (accessed Oct. 2008).

22. J. Philippe Rushton, *Race, Evolution and Behavior,* 2nd special abridged ed. (Port Huron, Mich.: Charles Darwin Research Institute, 2000), 17, 19. In one article Rushton was quoted as saying, "It's a trade-off, more brains or more penis. You can't have everything." Adam Miller, "Professors of Hate: Academia's Dirty Secret," *Rolling Stone,* Oct. 20, 1994, 110. Although he later said he was misquoted, his book says pretty much the same thing: more sex, less brains. Rushton subdivides Asians between Japanese, Chinese, and Koreans, who are smart, and South Asians (Indians), who aren't.

23. James R. Flynn, *What Is Intelligence: Beyond the Flynn Effect* (Cambridge: Cambridge University Press, 2007), 1–47. In their brief discussion of Flynn's findings, Herrnstein and Murray suggest that the generational increases in test scores may result either from improvements "in the general environment" or from "increased test sophistication," and they accurately point out, as Flynn himself acknowledged, that it's absurd to project those IQ changes indefinitely either into the future or to overlay them on the past. Herrnstein and Murray, *Bell Curve,* 348. But that hardly changes the conclusion that *g*, which the testers have posited as the fundamental intelligence factor, is not an immutable quantity. Analyzing the IQ debate in full is beyond the scope of this book. But a great deal of recent research, and not just Flynn's, raises so many additional questions on top of a century of uncertainty that touching on it is unavoidable. For a very accessible and well-written discussion of the Flynn effect, see Malcolm Gladwell, "None of the Above," *New Yorker,* Dec. 17, 2007. As any Google search will show, the literature—psychological, psychometric, political, polemical—about *The Bell Curve* is extensive. For a slightly more detailed critique of the book's historical slights, see, for example, Franz Samuelson, "On the Uses of History: The Case of *The Bell Curve,*" *Journal of the History of the Behavioral Sciences,* vol. 33, no. 2 (Spring 1997): 129–33.

24. Henry H. Goddard, *The Kallikak Family: A Study in the Heredity of Feeble-Mindedness* (New York: Macmillan, 1912), 78. Goddard's preference

was for segregation in "colonies" rather than forced sterilization of the feebleminded; he objected to a New Jersey law that sought to sterilize criminals because it was punitive rather than medical (105–7). But *The Bell Curve* never deals with his eugenic conclusions at all. See Samuelson, "On the Uses of History."

25. Herrnstein and Murray, *Bell Curve,* 667.

26. Ibid., 364.

27. Ibid., 361.

28. Gregory Rodriguez, *Mongrels, Bastards, Orphans and Vagabonds: Mexican Immigration and the Future of Race in America* (New York: Pantheon, 2007), 259.

29. Tyche Hendricks, "On the Border," *San Francisco Chronicle,* Dec. 1, 2005. This article is part of Hendricks's outstanding series on the border that ran in the *Chronicle* in 2005–6 and that will become the core of a forthcoming book from the University of California Press. Some of this material on the border is also based on my own writing, some of which appeared in my *California: America's High-Stakes Experiment* (Berkeley: University of California Press, 2006), 22–88.

30. Elliott Sagai, "Border-Crossing Photos Tag Students," *San Francisco Chronicle,* Jan. 2, 2008.

31. Jeffrey S. Passel, *The Size and Characteristics of the Unauthorized Migrant Population in the U.S.* (Washington, D.C.: Pew Hispanic Center, Mar. 7, 2006), 7.

32. "U.S. Slowdown Hits Mexico as Remittances Drop," *Wall Street Journal,* July 30, 2008.

33. Author telephone interview with Aneesh Aneesh, Apr. 20, 2004; Aneesh Aneesh, remarks at the Conference on Diaspora and Homeland Development, Berkeley Center for Globalization and Information Technology, Apr. 13, 2004.

34. Alejandro Portes and Rubén Rumbaut, "The Forging of a New America: Lessons for Theory and Policy," in *Ethnicities: Children of Immigrants in America* (Berkeley: University of California Press, 2001), 304.

35. James P. Smith, "Latino Assimilation across the Generations," *American Economic Review,* vol. 93, no. 2 (May 2003): 318–19.

36. James P. Smith, "Immigrants and Their Schooling," Working Paper No. 108, Center for Comparative Immigration Studies, University of California at San Diego, 2005, p. 25. See also James P. Smith, "Immigrants and the Labor Market," *Journal of Labor Economics,* vol. 24, no. 2 (2006): 226–29. Smith finds that the third generation of Latinos has gained as much ground as other third generations. The reason they appear behind is that in most studies the "third" generation is in fact all generations after the second; since most Europeans in the "three-plus generation" have been in the United States much longer than most Latinos, they appear to have gained more in schooling.

37. Smith also points out that most conventional measures of educational progress compare the educational attainment of today's third generation with that of today's new arrivals, which leads to a false comparison. The accurate comparison is between today's third generation and the generation of their grandfathers, whose educational levels were lower than even the relatively low attainment of contemporary immigrants.

38. Brian Duncan, V. Joseph Hotz, and Stephen J. Trejo, "Hispanics in the U.S. Labor Market," in *Hispanics and the Future of America,* ed. Marta Tienda and Faith Mitchell (Washington, D.C: National Academies Press, 2006), 268–69.

39. Shirin Hakimzadeh and D'Vera Cohn, *English Usage among Hispanics in the United States* (Washington, D.C.: Pew Hispanic Center, Nov. 29, 2007), http://pewhispanic.org/files/reports/82.pdf (accessed Oct. 2008).

40. Dowell Myers, *Immigrants and Boomers: Forging a New Social Contract for the Future of America* (New York: Russell Sage Foundation, 2007), 116–18, 240–42; author interview with Dowell Myers, Feb. 14, 2007. See also Peter Schrag, "Guess Who Will Have to Help with Your Retirement?" *Sacramento Bee,* Feb. 21, 2007.

41. George J. Borjas, "Backgrounder: Increasing the Supply of Labor through Immigration; Measuring the Impact on Native-born Workers"(Washington, D.C.: Center for Immigration Studies, May 2004), www.cis.org/articles/2004/back504.pdf (accessed Sept. 2008). This is Borjas's nontechnical summary of his "The Labor Demand Curve Is Downward Sloping: Reexamining the Impact of Immigration on the Labor Market," *Quarterly Journal of Economics* (Nov. 2003): 1335–74.

42. "Mass Immigration vs. Black America," testimony of T. Willard Fair, president and CEO, Urban League of Greater Miami, before House Judiciary Committee, Subcommittee on Immigration, Citizenship, Refugees, Border Security, and International Law, 110th Congress, 1st session, May 9, 2007, http://judiciary.house.gov/hearings/May2007/Fair070509.pdf (accessed Oct. 2008).

43. James P. Smith and Barry Edmonston, eds., *The New Americans: Economic, Demographic, and Fiscal Effects of Immigration* (Washington, D.C.: National Academies Press, 1997), 4–6, 236. Though old, this is still the most comprehensive study of this issue.

44. Eduardo Porter, "Illegal Immigrants Are Bolstering Social Security with Billions," *New York Times,* Apr. 5, 2005.

45. *The Impact of Unauthorized Immigrants on State and Local Budgets* (Washington, D.C.: Congressional Budget Office, Dec. 2007), 1.

46. Smith and Edmonston, *New Americans,* 347–48.

47. *Special Report: Undocumented Immigrants in Texas; A Financial Analysis of the Impact on the State Budget and Economy* (Austin: Office of the Texas State Comptroller, Dec. 2006), 1, 2, 22, www.cpa.state.tx.us/specialrpt/undocumented/undocumented.pdf (accessed Oct. 2008). The Arizona study is Judith Gans, *Immigrants in Arizona: Fiscal and Economic Impacts* (Tucson: Udall Center for Studies in Public Policy, University of Arizona, 2007). The Florida study is Emily Eisenhauer, Alex Angee, Cynthiz Hernandez, and Yue Zhang, *Immigrants in Florida: Characteristics and Contributions* (Miami: Research Institute for Social and Economic Study, Florida International University, May 2007).

48. Peter Cunningham, "What Accounts for Differences in the Use of Hospital Emergency Departments across U.S. Communities?" *Health Affairs,* July 18, 2006; Leighton Ku, Shawn Fremstad, and Matthew Broaddus, *Noncitizens' Use of Public Benefits Has Declined Since 1996* (Washington, D.C.: Center on Budget and Policy Priorities, Apr. 2003).

49. The data on visa overstayers are from *Modes of Entry for the Unauthorized Migrant Population,* fact sheet (Washington, D.C.: Pew Hispanic Center, May 22, 2006), http://pewhispanic.org/files/factsheets/19.pdf (accessed Oct. 2008). The story of the split of the Vermont town is in Keith B. Richburg, "Homeland Security Comes to Vermont—Changes in Border Town Unsettle Some Residents," *Washington Post,* Aug. 8, 2008. One of the wildlife preserves, which would be totally cut off from the United States and probably forced to close, is the Sabal Palm Audubon Center in Brownsville, Texas. The Napolitano quote is in Timothy Egan, "Disorder on the Border," *New York Times,* Mar. 29, 2008. After his election in 2008, Obama named Napolitano to head the Department of Homeland Security, which had been charged with the construction of the border fence.

50. See, for example, Belinda I. Reyes, Hans P. Johnson, and Richard Van Swearingen, *Holding the Line? The Effect of Recent Border Build-Up on Unauthorized Immigration* (San Francisco: Public Policy Institute of California, 2002). See also Wayne A. Cornelius, Scott Borger, Adam Sawyer, David Keyes, Clare Appleby, Kristen Parks, Gabriel Lozada, and Jonathan Hicken, *Controlling Unauthorized Immigration from Mexico: The Failure of "Prevention Through Deterrence" and the Need for Comprehensive Reform* (Washington, D.C.: Immigration Policy Center, June 10, 2008), 1, www.immigrationpolicy.org/images/file/misc/CCISbriefing061008.pdf (accessed Oct. 2, 2008).

51. Mike Swift, "Illegal Émigrés Defy the Image," *San Jose Mercury News,* Feb. 18, 2008, www.mercurynews.com/valley/ci_8293975 (accessed Dec. 2008).

52. Marc Lacey, "In an Escalating Drug War, Mexico Fights the Cartels, and Itself," *New York Times,* Mar. 30, 2009; John Meyer, "Drug Cartels Raise the Stakes on Human Smuggling," *Los Angeles Times,* Mar. 23, 2009; Randal C. Archibold, "Drug Cartel Violence Spills Over from Mexico, Alarming U.S.," *New York Times,* Mar. 23, 2008. The growing realization that the warring gangs were supplied and financed from north of the border brought, for the first time, an intensified effort to check traffic moving south. But it did not prompt any reexamination of the American "war on drugs"; on the contrary, Attorney General Eric Holder said he was "exploring ways to lower the minimum amount of marijuana required to allow for federal prosecution of possession cases." Ginger Thompson, "Mexican and U.S. Attorneys General Confer to Strengthen Cooperation on Drug Violence," *New York Times,* Apr. 3, 2009.

53. Senate Judiciary Committee, Subcommittee on Crime and Drugs, hearings on Law Enforcement Responses to Mexican Drug Cartels, 111th Congress, 1st session, Mar. 17, 2009; Ginger Thompson, "Obama Says He Will Review Request for Guard on Border," *New York Times,* Mar. 14, 2009; Peter Schrag, "Blowback at the Border," *The Nation,* May 4, 2009, 16–20. At the hearings, Senator Richard Durbin, the Illinois Democrat, angrily shot back that American guns were indeed a problem and that it was irresponsible to claim that they weren't. Peter Nicholas and Tracy Wilkinson, "Obama Pledges Help in Mexico's War on Drug Lords, with an Exception," *Los Angeles Times,* Apr. 17, 2009.

54. Unsolicited e-mail to author from West Springfield, Virginia, Feb. 16, 2008. This e-mail was not unusual in its anti-immigrant passion, but given Tancredo's background as the grandson of a Sicilian immigrant, its reference to Sicilians and the Mafia seemed particularly ironic.

55. "Tancredo Criticizes Pope's Comments on Immigration," Tom Tancredo press release, Apr. 17, 2008.

56. Tom Tancredo on *Hannity and Colmes,* Fox News broadcast, June 26, 2006.

57. "Tom Tancredo on His Bid for the Presidency," NPR interview, July 20, 2007, http://www.npr.org/templates/story/story.php?storyId=12125327 (accessed Dec. 2008).

58. Author interview with Mark Krikorian, Sept. 9, 2004.

59. Dianne Feinstein press release, Jan. 10, 2007, on introducing S 237, the AgJOBS bill, which would have legalized agricultural workers already here and created a guest-worker program.

60. Alberto Alesina, Reza Baqir, and William Easterly, "Public Goods and Ethnic Division," *Quarterly Journal of Economics,* vol. 114, no. 4 (Nov. 1999): 1243; Peter H. Lindert, *Growing Public: Social Spending and Economic Growth Since the Eighteenth Century* (Cambridge: Cambridge University Press, 2004), 29, 187; Erzo F.P. Luttmer, "Group Loyalty and the Taste for Redistribution," *Journal of Political Economy,* vol. 109, no. 3 (June 2001): 500–528.

61. Author interview with David Hollinger, Feb. 1, 2005.

62. Unlike the United States, European nations don't guarantee citizenship to the son or daughter of any immigrant born there, which creates a deeper level of immigrant alienation and resentment that the United States is largely immune to.

63. Leslie Berestein, "Decline in Border Crossings Crimps Economy," *San Diego Union-Tribune,* Mar. 11, 2008.

64. *Lou Dobbs Tonight,* CNN, June 21, 2007, http://transcripts.cnn.com/transcripts/0706/21/ldt.01.html (accessed Oct. 3, 2008).

65. *Building a North American Community* (New York: Council on Foreign Relations, 2005).

66. "A North American Community Approach to Security," testimony of Robert A. Pastor before Senate Foreign Relations Committee, Subcommittee on the Western Hemisphere, 109th Congress, 1st session, June 9, 2005.

67. Richard Alba, "Looking Beyond the Moment: American Immigration Seen from Historically and Internationally Comparative Perspectives," in *Border Battles: The U.S. Immigration Debates (online essays),* Social Science Research Council, July 28, 2006, http://borderbattles.ssrc.org/Alba (accessed Aug. 2008).

68. Jerome R. Corsi, "North American Union to Replace USA?" *Human Events,* May 19, 2006, www.humanevents.com/search.php (accessed Aug. 2009); Jerome R. Corsi, "Bush Administration Advances on Path of Creating North American Union," *Human Events,* Sept. 21, 2006, www.humanevents.com/search.php (accessed Aug. 2009).

69. "Pursuing the 'North American' Agenda," *Phyllis Schlafly Report,* vol. 40, no. 2 (Sept. 2006), www.eagleforum.org/psr/2006/sept06/psrsept06.html (accessed Aug. 2009). The name *Amero* came from an article by Herbert G. Grubel, an international economist at Simon Fraser University in Vancouver, British Columbia: "The Case for the Amero: The Economics and Politics of a North American Monetary Union," *Critical Issues* (1999), http://oldfraser.lexi.net/publications/critical_issues/1999/amero (accessed Oct. 4, 2008). See also

Kelly Taylor, "Express Route to Poverty," *The New American,* Oct. 15, 2007, www.thenewamerican.com/index.php/usnews/politics/682-express-route-to-poverty (accessed Aug. 2009).

70. HR Res. 40, Jan. 22. 2007, Library of Congress THOMAS database, http://thomas.loc.gov/cgi-bin/bdquery/z?d110:h.con.res.00040: (accessed Sept. 2008).

71. Robert Pastor, "The Future of North America: Replacing a Bad Neighbor Policy," *Foreign Affairs,* vol. 87, no. 4 (July–Aug. 2008): 84–99.

72. Letter from Edward Royce and others to President Obama asking for deployment of the National Guard on the border. "Royce Calls on President Obama to Resume Operation Jump-Start," press release from Royce's office, Mar. 11, 2009.

73. By 2009, border violence—the killings, kidnappings, and torture of public officials as well as members of competing gangs—approached a level such that it began to overshadow immigrant smuggling as a source of border concern. See, for example, Senate Judiciary Committee, Subcommittee on Crime and Drugs, hearings on Law Enforcement Responses to Mexican Drug Cartels, 111th Congress, 1st session, Mar. 17, 2009; and Carolyn Lochhead, "Mexico's Drug War Stirs Fear in U.S.," *San Francisco Chronicle,* Mar. 12, 2009.

74. "The White Minority," ProjectUSA e-mail, Aug. 19, 2008, http://projectusa.org/2008/08/19/the-white-minority (accessed Oct. 2008).

75. One of the Rubashkins was belatedly prosecuted. The "proclivity" was cited in a 1995 National Labor Relations Board case, *Cherry Hill Textiles, Inc. and United Production Workers Union, Local 17–18,* Case No. 29-CA-17848, in *Decisions of the National Labor Relations Board,* vol. 318, no. 40.

76. Richard Marosi, "Border Arrests Drop to 1970s Levels," *Los Angeles Times,* Mar. 8, 2009.

77. Augusto de la Torre, chief economist at the World Bank, quoted in Ginger Thompson, "Illegal Immigration Down, Following Economy," *New York Times,* Oct. 2, 2008.

78. Myers, *Immigrants and Boomers,* 254. In Missouri, in 2006, Republicans on a legislative panel produced a report linking illegal immigration to abortions in the United States, saying that the latter was causing a shortage of American workers. Davis A. Lieb, "Mo. Panel: Immigration, Abortion Linked," *Boston Globe,* Nov. 13, 2006, www.boston.com/news/nation/articles/2006/11/13/mo_panel_immigration_abortion_linked (accessed Oct. 2008).

79. Jamie Heine, *Skilled Labor: Outdated Immigration Policy Threatens U.S. Economic Well-Being* (Washington, D.C.: Council on Hemispheric Affairs, July 18, 2008). The H-1B visas have long been a controversial issue, particularly with underemployed American engineers and technicians. These workers often contend that employers use foreign labor to undercut the wages of American workers, some of whom have been put out of jobs—this was well before the recession that began in 2007—to make room for Indians, Taiwanese, and others willing to work for less. Employers counter that the people they lay off don't (or can't) learn new skills and thus, in effect, have become obsolete in rapidly changing technological industries. What's probably closest to the truth is that

hiring a new person who already knows new technologies or software codes is probably cheaper than retraining an old one.

80. Julia Preston, "U.S. Military Will Offer Path to Citizenship," *New York Times*, Feb. 14, 2009.

81. FY 2009 budget for Department of Homeland Security, Office of Management and Budget, www.whitehouse.gov/omb/budget/fy2009/homeland.html (accessed Oct. 2009).

82. Early in 2009, a group of Mexican human rights organizations issued a formal report complaining to the United Nations that "torture continues, extrajudicial executions and forced disappearances occur . . . and practically none of the cultural and economic rights is guaranteed or protected." Summary of Mexican press reports from Frontera Norte Sur, Center for Latin American and Border Studies, New Mexico State University, Feb. 9, 2009.

83. Ward Connerly, "Open Letter to Congress," American Civil Rights Institute press release, June 7, 2007.

84. "The Great Immigration Panic," *New York Times* editorial, June 3, 2008.

85. Robert Bernstein and Tom Edwards, "An Older and More Diverse Nation by Midcentury," *U.S. Census Bureau News*, Aug. 14, 2008, www.census.gov/Press-Release/www/releases/archives/population/012496.html (accessed Aug. 2008).

86. Sharon M. Lee and Barry Edmonston, "New Marriages, New Families: U.S. Racial and Hispanic Intermarriage," *Population Bulletin*, vol. 60, no. 2 (June 2005): 26–27.

EPILOGUE

1. Alejandro Portes and Rubén Rumbaut, *Immigrant American: A Portrait* (Berkeley: University of California Press, 2006), 371, 372.

2. David A. Hollinger, *Postethnic America* (New York: Basic Books, 1995).

3. Raja Abdulrahim, "Students Push UC to Expand Terms of Ethnic Identification," *Los Angles Times*, Mar. 31, 2009.

4. I'm grateful to Marshall Fitz of the Immigration Lawyers Association for explaining the complicated provisions of the Immigration and Nationality Act and the web of current policy that implements it.

5. Ginger Thompson, "Immigration Agents to Turn Their Focus on Employers," *New York Times*, Apr. 30, 2009; Julia Preston, "Obama to Push Immigration Bill as One Priority," *New York Times*, Apr. 9, 2009.

6. Nina Bernstein, "U.S. to Overhaul Detention Policy for Immigrants," *New York Times*, Aug. 4, 2009; Julia Preston, "Staying Tough in Crackdown on Immigrants," *New York Times*, Aug. 4, 2009.

7. Marcus Epstein, "An Analysis of All House Losses," the American Cause, Feb. 2009, www.theamericancause.org/index.php?page=reports (accessed June 2009).

8. David Hollinger, "Obama, the Instability of Color Lines, and the Promise of a Postethnic Future," *Callaloo*, vol. 31, no. 4, (Fall 2008): 1036.

Index

Text:	10/13 Sabon
Display:	Sabon
Compositor:	BookComp, Inc.
Indexer:	Barbara Roos
Printer and binder:	Sheridan Books, Inc.